THE
NIGHT OFFICES

Sing psalms and hymns and inspired songs among yourselves,
singing and chanting to the Lord in your hearts, always and everywhere giving
thanks to God who is our Father in the name of the Lord Jesus Christ.

Ephesians 5:19, 20 NJB

THE
NIGHT OFFICES

PRAYERS FOR THE HOURS
FROM SUNSET TO SUNRISE

Compiled and with an Introduction by

Phyllis Tickle

Author of The Divine Hours™

OXFORD
UNIVERSITY PRESS

2006

OXFORD
UNIVERSITY PRESS

Oxford University Press, Inc., publishes works that
further Oxford University's objective of excellence
in research, scholarship, and education.

Oxford New York
Auckland Cape Town Dar es Salaam Hong Kong Karachi
Kuala Lumpur Madrid Melbourne Mexico City Nairobi
New Delhi Shanghai Taipei Toronto

With offices in
Argentina Austria Brazil Chile Czech Republic France Greece
Guatemala Hungary Italy Japan Poland Portugal Singapore
South Korea Switzerland Thailand Turkey Ukraine Vietnam

Published by Oxford University Press, Inc.
198 Madison Avenue, New York, NY 10016
www.oup.com

Oxford is a registered trademark of Oxford University Press
The Divine Hours™ Tickle, Inc.

Library of Congress Cataloging-in-Publication Data
The night offices : prayers for the hours from sunset to sunrise / compiled and
with an introduction by Phyllis A. Tickle.
p. cm. Includes index.
ISBN-13: 978-0-19-530671-2
ISBN-10: 0-19-530671-6
1. Divine office—Texts.
2. Catholic Church. Liturgy of the hours.
I. Tickle, Phyllis.
BV199.D3N54 2006
264'.15—dc22
2006008428

1 3 5 7 9 8 6 4 2
Printed in the United States of America
on acid-free paper

Contents

An Introduction to
This Manual

A Brief History of Fixed-Hour Prayer and the Offices

Fixed-hour prayer has many names, the very abundance of them bearing witness to its long history and widely broadcast presence in the Church universal. Like the observance of a Sabbath or the exercise of tithing, like fasting or the sharing of a sacred meal, like the measuring of time by the seasons of the liturgical year or the making of holy pilgrimage, fixed-hour prayer is a spiritual discipline or practice that came into Christianity by inheritance rather than by intention. Together, those seven practices were and are the temporal architecture for faithful observance in Judaism, an architecture so fundamental to their own spiritual formation and conduct that our progenitors in the faith—the disciples and apostles and early Church Fathers—could not envision an obedient life structured and maintained in any other way; nor, for that matter, have all the ages and variations of Christendom managed to do so in the centuries since.

Whether one speaks of "fixed-hour prayer" or instead uses other terms like "the Liturgy of the Hours" or "the Daily Offices," "the keeping the Liturgical Hours" or "observing the Divine Hours" makes little or no difference, for all of those terms refer to the same historic exercise. They refer to the holy and regimented interruption of diurnal time for the purposes of prayer and praise before the throne of God.

While we do not know exactly when or where fixed-hour prayer entered Judaism, we do know that by the time of King David, the psalmist was singing, "Seven times a day do I praise you." (Ps. 119:164) And though we do not know exactly when the seven times were positioned within the ancient Jewish day, we do know also that the setting of the number of offices at seven per day has been a fairly consistent part of fixed-hour prayer. From time to time in earlier Christian history, the number has been increased to eight daily offices in order to divide or mark the day evenly into three-hour blocks. More commonly, the number has been reduced to three or four offices. And sometimes, as is the case with *The Divine Hours*™ manuals, seven offices are provided for the observant in order that such hours as may be kept will be readily available.

Historically, the daily offices are clustered into: The Night (or Nocturnal) Offices of Vespers, Matins, and Lauds; the Day (or Little) Offices of Terce, Sext, and None; and the Morning and Evening Offices of Prime and Compline, which list, the reader will immediately notice, adds up to eight, rather than seven. It speaks, as well, to the issue of names and definitions.

The Little or Day Offices, sometimes called "the dear Offices," are the familiar treasures of millions of Christians who gather each day every day at 9:00 a.m. (Terce, or Third Hour of a day commonly reckoned as commencing for most of us at 6:00 a.m.) in their respective time zones; and again at high noon (12:00 or Sext or the Sixth Hour of a day which begins at 6:00 a.m.); and again at 3:00 p.m. (None, or the day's ninth hour) in their respective time zones. "Gathering" for those observant Christians may mean actually ceasing the moment's secular activities in order to physically join with other observant Christians in an office or domestic setting for the purposes of celebrating the appropriate office and appointed prayer. We know that such was the usual practice for the disciples. Thus we are told that the first healing miracle after the Ascension of Our Lord took place on the steps of the Temple when, the book of Acts tells us, Saints Peter and John were on their way to three o'clock or ninth-hour prayers. Likewise, the coming of the Spirit upon those gathered in the Upper Room on Pentecost came, we are told, at 9:00 a.m., or the third hour, as they were gathered for prayer.

Sometimes, we know as well, however, that the observant early Christians were forced by circumstances to keep the Offices alone. Such was certainly the case for Saint Peter who saw the vision of the descending sheet while he was alone on the rooftop of Simon the Tanner's house in Joppa; for, as the book of Acts again tells us, he was there for noon or sixth (Sext) hour prayers. Most western Christians today are like Peter, finding themselves more often than not in the Joppa situation of praying an office in physical seclusion, if not exactly alone.

Saint Paul refers to "a constant cascade of prayer before the throne of God," which is what fixed-hour prayer is. Thus, as Christians in one time zone (a contemporary and arbitrary invention unknown, of course, to Paul) begin their prayers at the hours fixed for each office, they enter the presence of God, bearing the words of praise and the hymns that their fellow Christians in the prior time zone have just offered. As an office ends, the observant are equally aware that the prayers and hymns they have just offered before that Divine Throne will be picked up soon by their fellow Christians in the next time zone, for the words of fixed-hours prayer are as fixed as is the timing of their offering.

Gathering, in such a holy construct as fixed-hour prayer, is not just a matter of shared physical presence, however. Rather, it is the acute awareness that prayer is itself a place, a place that lacks dimensions and meridians but that is the natural habitat of the soul. To go there at the same moment as, and in the company of, thousands and thousands of one's fellow Christians is to understand the communion of the saints as it accrues simultaneously in both spiritual and real time.

The Offices of Morning and Evening Prayer were traditionally known as Prime and Compline respectively. Prime, a variant of the Latin word *primus*, is observed, as one would expect, at 6:00 a.m., or the first hour of the day. Compline, richly enjoyed by many Christians today as the one office most easily observed in a group and sometimes even in a formal, church setting, is the only one of the offices that is not fixed per se. That is, marking as it does, the "completion" of the day, it is the office prayed as each Christian or group of Christians come to the end of their respective day and approach the night's rest. That leads us to the Night Offices.

Notes for the Use of This Manual

The Divine Hours™ manuals were compiled and published in the order I have discussed them here. That is, the first manuals were for use only with the Little Offices and Compline. The release of this present manual completes the work the earlier volumes began; for, as its title indicates, this manual contains the Night or Nocturnal Offices and thus brings to completion the entirety of the full seven daily offices.

As was the case in the manuals for the Day Offices, *The Night Offices* volume uses English, rather than Latinate terms. Thus the Christian will find here: the Office of Midnight, the Office of the Night Watch, and the Office of Dawn. In addition and as was true in the Little Offices manual, the offices are somewhat abbreviated, and the fixing of the time of their observation is allowed to vary but only insofar as they are offered on the hour or half-hour. Such a restricted accommodation to the vicissitudes and realities of contemporary living assures that each individual supplicant or pray-er is indeed held within the communion of the saints, albeit sometimes by those in a different time zone and/or midway of Christians leaving an office and those about to enter it.

The Nocturnal Offices are, in several ways, more "set" or their content more prescribed than is the case with the other offices. While a somewhat shortened rendering of the offices does not allow for the inclusion of every possibility, the pray-er will none the less notice, and quickly become dependent upon, the presence of some of the characteristic or customary parts of the offices. Thus, the Office of Midnight is defined here by the presence of a Canticle. The Church recognizes at least a dozen such treasures that have come down to us from the very beginning—the Songs of Moses, the Songs of Isaiah, the Song of the Three Young Men, the Benedictus, and so forth. The offering up of the Canticles in that time of no time when one day is going and another coming and neither yet is . . . the offering up of those ancient chants causes both Heaven and earth to resound with surety and constancy and gratitude for the soul's life beyond dimensions. Originally most often called by the name of Matins, the Office of Midnight is often the one most fondly observed by Christians, even by those who have to briefly rouse themselves from sleep in order to pray it.

The Office of the Night Watch, as its name suggests, comes into human reckoning during those hours when sleep is upon almost all of us. For those who are restless or sleepless, however, the office is often a personal balm and an easing, as well as an act of worship. For others, its beauty alone is sufficient to justify setting a clock for its keeping. For those who travel across time zones and shift diurnal patterns abruptly, the Office of the Night Watch is often a portable sanctuary, a way of entering into the company of believers wherever one is and on however skewed a schedule. The glory of this middle one of the Nocturnal Offices is its emphasis upon the writings of the Church Fathers. At no other point in the day does the observant Christian enjoy such focused and deliberated acquaintance with the writings of the ancients who bred and shaped and then passed on our faith to us. The Office also always contains a litany, that revered tool for raising prayers to God for all of Christendom and of His divine creation.

The Office of Dawn, as it is presented in *The Night Offices*, combines elements of both Lauds and Prime. Always it welcomes the coming day with a hymn of praise and allegiance; it offers the Gloria in rejoicing for the return of light and work; and it leans heavily upon those psalms that reverberate with praise, particularly Psalms 148, 149, and 150, the last three of the Psalter. There is also one additional, but more general, matter that needs mentioning here.

For many Christians who come from Reformation communions of confessing or professing faith, the hindrance to, or hesitancy about, assuming the discipline of fixed-hour prayer has to do with the fact that the words employed are indeed "fixed." They are the same—or are variations upon the same—words that are being used at the same time by thousands of other Christians, most of them not visible or present to the pray-er. Such hesitancy usually dissipates as soon as the would-be observer perceives three things: The first is that fixed-hour prayer has informed the Church and the faithful from the beginning, and it is firmly rooted not only in Church practice but also in scripture itself. Second is the realization that reading the words of a hymn or a psalm or a section of Holy Writ is precisely what every Christian always does in worship, whether that worship be corporate on the Sabbath or corporate through the communion of the saints in the offices.

An understanding of the third point is perhaps even more important, however; namely that fixed-hour prayer is *not* private prayer, nor is it ever to be the sum total of any believer's prayer life. Fixed-hour prayer is worship—corporate worship in the presence of the ages and of all those gathered around each pray-er in the offering up of the words and in the lifting up of the sacrifice of praise and thanksgiving. Private prayer—prayer of petition or intercession or lament or the like—is always and everywhere to be offered. Fixed-hour prayer, on the other hand, is specific worship. The two things must never be confused, just as neither should ever take precedence over, or be pursued to the exclusion of, the other.

The Symbols and Conventions Used in This Manual

Those already familiar with *The Divine Hours*™ manuals for the Day Offices will discover a few changes or differences here. Most obvious is the fact that this manual, while still organized by the physical rather than the liturgical calendar, is closer to the treatment of Compline employed in the earlier volumes than to that used with the Little Offices in those books. That is, while the segmenting of material is still by months, the weeks within each month are segmented simply by the day of the week, there being only one Office of Midnight for each Monday in January, only one Office of the Night Watch for each Monday in that month, and so on. In addition, the scripture selections employed here are taken from the *Revised Standard Version* of the Bible, rather than from the *New Jerusalem Bible* as was done in the manuals for the Day Offices. The one exception to this is that the Psalms, the Canticles, and the Litanies all are taken and/or adapted, with few exceptions, from the *Book of Common Prayer*. Such exceptions as there may be are clearly marked.

In general, and as is the case in all *The Divine Hours*™ manuals, the language used is not gender inclusive. If the pray-er wishes to effect that change, he or she may easily do so simply by changing a pronoun to the desired form. Likewise, the prayers are rendered here in the singular pronominal forms of "I," "me," and "my" because most pray-ers will indeed be without prayer partners physically present. These pronouns can also readily be changed to incorporate the circumstances of two or more present together to offer the appointed prayers. The user will discover as well that the process of modernizing and adapting some of the hymns has already effected some such changes.

The poetry of the Psalms is, in origin, Hebrew poetry and works on a system of poetics very different from than of English poetry. It is, in fact, best "heard" or incorporated by the native English speaker if it is chanted, though clearly such is neither requisite nor even necessary, unless it adds depth to the offering. To accommodate those who wish to chant the psalms, however, we have followed here the *BCP*'s practice of "pointing" the psalms. That is, an asterisk (*) marks the place in each line where poetic breaks appear in the original Hebrew. In general, psalms are sung or chanted on one single tone chosen by the observant as pleasing or comfortable to maintain. The asterisk, indicating the break in the Hebrew line, indicates as well the place just before which the chanter is to raise the tone by one note. At the end of the second half of any given line (that is, of the portion after the asterisk) the singer lowers by one full note the last accented syllable. Pronouns like "me, he, thee" are never raised or lowered. A little experience will also reveal the fact that many English words have three syllables and that the accent is frequently on the first of the three. In that case, when the trisyllabic word is just before the asterisk or immediately before the end of a line, the first unaccented syllable goes up (or down, as the case may be) a full or a half note, and the second unaccented syllable goes up (or down) another full or half note.

As one progresses in the use of chant, the singer will also discover that there are numerous books and workshops and tapes for teaching chant. If, however, as is the case with many of us, chanting a psalm seems distracting or alien, there is comfort in knowing that one is probably in the majority of office-keepers. Whether singing or speaking, however, such is good company to be in and rejoices the soul as surely as it nourishes the Church universal.

And last but hardly least, in speaking of the Offices, Saint Benedict always reminded his monks, and has reminded all of us since, that *Orare laborare et laborare orare est.* To pray is to work, and to work is to pray. Those words, too, are good company for the soul and nourishment for the Body of Christ on earth. *Amen.*

THE
NIGHT OFFICES

The Gloria

Glory be to God the Father, God the Son, and God the Holy Spirit. As it was in the beginning, so it is now and so it shall ever be, world without end. Alleluia. *Amen.*

The Lord's Prayer

Our Father, who art in heaven, hallowed be your Name.
May your kingdom come, and your will be done, on earth as in heaven.
Give us today our daily bread.
Forgive us our sins as we forgive those who sin against us.
Lead us not into temptation, but deliver us from evil;
for yours are the kingdom and the power and the glory
forever and ever. *Amen.*

The following major holy days occur in January:
The Holy Name of Our Lord Jesus Christ and/or
The Feast of the Circumcision of Our Lord and/or
The Feast of Mary, Mother of God: *January 1*
The Epiphany of Our Lord Jesus Christ: *January 6*
The Confession of St. Peter, the Apostle: *January 18*
The Confession of St. Paul, the Apostle: *January 25*

Prayer for use in the observation of a holy day:
Almighty God, by your Holy Spirit you have made us one with your saints in heaven and on earth: Grant that in my earthly pilgrimage, I may always be supported by this fellowship of love and prayer, and know myself to be surrounded by their witness to your power and mercy. I ask this for the sake of Jesus Christ, in whom all my intercessions are acceptable through the Spirit, and who lives and reigns forever and ever. *Amen.*

✤ The Office of Midnight is always taken from the prayers for the day nearest to the hour of actual observation. Thus, if the office is to be observed at 10:30 p.m. on Sunday, the prayers will be taken from the Monday offices, and so forth.

JANUARY

Sunday, Month of January

The Office of Midnight   **Observed on the Hour or Half-Hour**
                                     Between 10:30 p.m.✠ and 1:30 a.m.

The Call to Prayer

Behold now, bless the LORD, all you servants of the LORD,* you that stand by night
  in the house of the LORD.
Lift up your hands in the holy place and bless the LORD;* the LORD who made
  heaven and earth bless you out of Zion.

Psalm 134

The Request for Presence

O LORD, let my prayer be set forth in your sight as incense,* the lifting up of my
  hands as the evening sacrifice.

Psalm 141:2, adapted

The Greeting

Our Father, Who art in Heaven, hallowed be Your name forever.

The Canticle   *The Song of Moses*
                                              Cantemus Domino

I will sing to the Lord, for he is lofty and uplifted;*
  the horse and its rider has he hurled into the sea.
The Lord is my strength and my refuge;*
  the Lord has become my Savior.
This is my God and I will praise him,*
  the God of my people and I will exalt him.
The Lord is a mighty warrior;*
  Yahweh is his Name.
Who can be compared with you, O Lord, among the gods?*
  who is like you, glorious in holiness, awesome in renown, and worker of wonders?
With your constant love you led the people you redeemed;*
  with your might you brought them in safety to your holy dwelling.
You will bring them in and plant them*
  on the mount of your possession,
The resting-place you have made for yourself, O Lord,*
  the sanctuary, O Lord, that your hand has established.
The Lord shall reign*
  for ever and for ever.

Exodus: 15:1–6, 11–13, 17–18

The Psalm   *I Have a Goodly Heritage*

O LORD, you are my portion and my cup;* it is you who uphold my lot.
My boundaries enclose a pleasant land;* indeed, I have a goodly heritage.

I will bless the LORD who gives me counsel;* my heart teaches me, night after night.
I have set the LORD always before me;* because he is at my right hand I shall not fall.
My heart, therefore, is glad, and my spirit rejoices;* my body also shall rest in hope.
For you will not abandon me to the grave,* nor let your holy one see the Pit.
You will show me the path of life;* in your presence there is fullness of joy, and in
  your right hand are pleasures for evermore.

Psalm 16:5–11

The Gloria

The Small Verse
Then was our mouth filled with laughter,* and our tongue with shouts of joy.

Psalm 125:2

The Final Thanksgiving
I will greatly rejoice in the LORD, my soul shall exult in my God; for he has
  clothed me with the garments of salvation, he has covered me with the robe of
  righteousness, as a bridegroom decks himself with a garland, and as a bride
  adorns herself with her jewels.

Isaiah 61:10

The Petition
May the Lord GOD, father of grace and mercy, grant all who dwell here a peaceful
  night and a perfect end. *Amen.*

The Office of the Night Watch   Observed on the Hour or Half-Hour
                                        Between 1:30 and 4:30 a.m.

The Call to Prayer
Behold now, bless the LORD, all you servants of the LORD,* you that stand by night
  in the house of the LORD.
Lift up your hands in the holy place and bless the LORD;* the LORD who made
  heaven and earth bless you out of Zion.

Psalm 134

The Request for Presence
O God, come to my assistance.
O Lord, make haste to help me.

The Greeting
For you are my hope, O Lord GOD,* my confidence since I was young.
I have been sustained by you ever since I was born; from my mother's womb you
  have been my strength;* my praise shall be always of you.

Psalm 71:5–6

The Refrain for the Night Watch

Happy are they who have not walked in the counsel of the wicked,* nor lingered
    in the way of sinners, nor sat in the seats of the scornful!
Their delight is in the law of the LORD,* and they meditate on his law day and night.

Psalm 1:1–2

The Psalm   My Soul Waits for the LORD

If you, LORD, were to note what is done amiss,* O Lord, who could stand?
For there is forgiveness with you;* therefore you shall be feared.
I wait for the LORD; my soul waits for him;* in his word is my hope.

Psalm 130:2–4

The Refrain

Happy are they who have not walked in the counsel of the wicked,* nor lingered
    in the way of sinners, nor sat in the seats of the scornful!
Their delight is in the law of the LORD,* and they meditate on his law day and night.

A Reading

Soul of Christ, be my sanctification
Body of Christ, be my salvation
Blood of Christ, fill all my veins
Water of Christ's side, wash out my stains
Passion of Christ, my comfort be
O good Jesu, listen to me
In your wounds, I fain would hide
Never to be parted from your side.

Anima Christi (14th c.), translated by John Henry Newman, adapted

The Refrain

Happy are they who have not walked in the counsel of the wicked,* nor lingered
    in the way of sinners, nor sat in the seats of the scornful!
Their delight is in the law of the LORD,* and they meditate on his law day and night.

The Litany

For the peace from above, for the loving-kindness of God, and for the salvation of
    my soul, I pray to the Lord.
      Lord, have mercy.
For the peace of the world, for the welfare of the Holy Church of God, and for the
    unity of all peoples, I pray to the Lord.
      Lord, have mercy.
For the leaders of the nations and for all in authority, I pray to the Lord.
      Lord, have mercy.
For the aged and infirm, for the widowed and orphans, and for the sick and the
    suffering, I pray to the Lord.
      Lord, have mercy.

For the poor and the oppressed, for the unemployed and the destitute, for prisoners
and captives, and for all who remember and care for them, I pray to the Lord.
Lord, have mercy.
For all who have died in the hope of the resurrection, and for all the departed, I
pray to the Lord.
Lord, have mercy.

The Thanksgiving

Lord, you now have set your servant free to go in peace as you have promised; for
these eyes of mine have seen the Savior whom you have prepared for all the
world to see: A Light to enlighten the nations, and the glory of your people
Israel. *Amen.*

Nunc Dimittis

The Final Petition

Now guide me waking, O Lord, and guard me sleeping; that awake I may watch
with Christ, and asleep, I may rest in peace. *Amen.*

The Office of Dawn   Observed on the Hour or Half-Hour
Between 4:30 and 7:30 a.m.

The Call to Prayer

Let everything that has breath* praise the Lord. Hallelujah!

Psalm 150:6

The Request for Presence

My soul waits for the Lord, more than watchmen for the morning,* more than
watchmen for the morning.

Psalm 130:5

The Greeting

Glory be to the Father, and the Son, and the Holy Spirit.
As it was in the beginning, it is now
And ever shall be, world without end. *Amen.*

Gloria Patri

The Hymn

Praise to the Lord, the Almighty, the King of creation.
O my soul, praise him, for he is your health and salvation!
All you who hear, now to his temple draw near;
join me in glad adoration!

Praise to the Lord, who prospers your work and defends you;
surely his goodness and mercy here daily attend you.

5

Ponder anew what the Almighty can do,
who with his love befriends you.

Praise to the Lord! O let all that is in me adore him!
All that has life and breath, come now with praises before him!
Let the amen sound from his people again;
and gladly forever adore him.

Joachim Neander

The Psalm   Praise Him in the Heights

Praise the Lord from the heavens;* praise him in the heights.
Praise him, all you angels of his;* praise him, all his host.
Praise him, sun and moon;* praise him, all you shining stars.
Praise him, heaven of heavens,* and you waters above the heavens.
Let them praise the Name of the Lord;* for he commanded, and they were created.
He made them stand fast for ever and ever;* he gave them a law which shall not
    pass away.

Psalm 148: 1b–6

The Gloria in Excelsis

Glory to God in the highest, and on earth peace to people of good will.
    We praise you.
    We bless you.
    We adore you.
    We glorify you.
We give thanks to you for your great glory.

The Small Verse

Guard your steps when you go to the house of God; to draw near to listen is better
    than to offer the sacrifice of fools.

Ecclesiastes 5: 1

The Lord's Prayer

The Final Blessing

May the Lord bless us and keep us and cause His face to shine upon us from this
    day forth and forever more. *Amen.*

Monday, Month of January

The Office of Midnight

**Observed on the Hour or Half-Hour
Between 10:30 p.m.✢ and 1:30 a.m.**

The Call to Prayer

Ascribe to the LORD the honor due his Name;* bring offerings and come into his
    courts.

Psalm 96:8

The Request for Presence

O LORD, let my prayer be set forth in your sight as incense,* the lifting up of my
    hands as the evening sacrifice.

Psalm 141:2, adapted

The Greeting

Our Father, may Your kingdom come on earth as in Heaven.

The Canticle

A Song of Creation—Part One
Benedicite, omnia opera Domini

Glorify the Lord, all you works of the Lord,*
    praise him and highly exalt him for ever.
In the firmament of his power, glorify the Lord,*
    praise him and highly exalt him for ever.
Glorify the Lord, you angels and all powers of the Lord,*
    O heavens and all waters above the heavens.
Sun and moon and stars of the sky, glorify the Lord,*
    praise him and highly exalt him for ever.
Glorify the Lord, every shower of rain and fall of dew,*
    all winds and fire and heat.
Winter and summer, glorify the Lord,*
    praise him and highly exalt him for ever.
Glorify the Lord, O chill and cold,*
    drops of dew and flakes of snow.
Frost and cold, ice and sleet, glorify the Lord,*
    praise him and highly exalt him for ever.
Glorify the Lord, O nights and days,*
    O shining light and enfolding dark.
Storm clouds and thunderbolts, glorify the Lord,*
    praise him and highly exalt him for ever.

Song of the Three Young Men, 35–51

The Psalm   *He Gives His Beloved Sleep*

Unless the LORD builds the house,* their labor is in vain who build it.
Unless the LORD watches over the city,* in vain the watchman keeps his vigil.
It is vain that you rise so early and go to bed so late;* vain, too, to eat the bread of
   toil, for he gives his beloved sleep.

Psalm 127:1–3

The Gloria

The Small Verse

I charge you to keep the commandment unstained and free from reproach until the
   appearing of our Lord Jesus Christ.

I Timothy 6:14

The Final Thanksgiving

I will greatly rejoice in the LORD, my soul shall exult in my God; for he has
   clothed me with the garments of salvation, he has covered me with the robe of
   righteousness, as a bridegroom decks himself with a garland, and as a bride
   adorns herself with her jewels.

Isaiah 61:10

The Petition

May the Lord GOD, father of grace and mercy, grant all who dwell here a peaceful
   night and a perfect end. *Amen.*

The Office of the Night Watch   Observed on the Hour or Half-Hour
                                         Between 1:30 and 4:30 a.m.

The Call to Prayer

Behold now, bless the LORD, all you servants of the LORD,* you that stand by night
   in the house of the LORD.
Lift up your hands in the holy place and bless the LORD;* the LORD who made
   heaven and earth bless you out of Zion.

Psalm 134

The Request for Presence

O God, come to my assistance.
O Lord, make haste to help me.

The Greeting

Who is like you, LORD God of hosts?* O mighty LORD, your faithfulness is all
   around you.

Psalm 89:8

8

The Refrain for the Night Watch

The heavens declare the glory of God,* and the firmament shows his handiwork.
One day tells its tale to another,* and one night imparts knowledge to another.

Psalm 19:1–2

The Psalm   The Idols of the Heathen Are the Work of Human Hands

The idols of the heathen are silver and gold,* the work of human hands.
They have mouths, but they cannot speak;* eyes have they, but they cannot see.
They have ears, but they cannot hear;* neither is there any breath in their mouth.
Those who make them are like them,* and so are all who put their trust in them.

Psalm 135:15–18

The Refrain

The heavens declare the glory of God,* and the firmament shows his handiwork.
One day tells its tale to another,* and one night imparts knowledge to another.

A Reading

But if it be true that "all things were made by Him," [as John teaches], then it is
    established that both every age, and time, and all space, and that "when" in
    which the "was not" is, is error when it says of Him that He at some time was not.

Alexander, Bishop of Alexandria (d. 312), Epistles on the Arian Heresy

The Refrain

The heavens declare the glory of God,* and the firmament shows his handiwork.
One day tells its tale to another,* and one night imparts knowledge to another.

The Litany

Father, I pray for your holy catholic Church;
    That we all may be one.
Grant that every member of the Church may truly and humbly serve you;
    That your Name may be glorified by all people.
I pray for all who govern and hold authority in the nations of the world;
    That there may be justice and peace on the earth.
Have compassion on those who suffer from any grief or trouble;
    That they may be delivered from their distress.
Give to the departed eternal rest.
    Let light perpetual shine upon them.
I praise you for your saints who have entered into joy;
    May I also come to share in your heavenly kingdom.

The Thanksgiving

Lord, you now have set your servant free to go in peace as you have promised; for
    these eyes of mine have seen the Savior whom you have prepared for all the

world to see: A Light to enlighten the nations, and the glory of your people
Israel. *Amen.*

Nunc Dimittis

The Final Petition

Now guide me waking, O Lord, and guard me sleeping; that awake I may watch
with Christ, and asleep, I may rest in peace. *Amen.*

The Office of Dawn · Observed on the Hour or Half-Hour Between 4:30 and 7:30 a.m.

The Call to Prayer

Hallelujah! Sing to the Lord a new song;* sing his praise in the congregation of
the faithful.

Psalm 149:1

The Request for Presence

My soul waits for the Lord, more than watchmen for the morning,* more than
watchmen for the morning.

Psalm 130:5

The Greeting

Glory be to the Father, and the Son, and the Holy Spirit.
As it was in the beginning, it is now
And ever shall be, world without end. *Amen.*

Gloria Patri

The Hymn

Open my eyes, that I may see
glimpses of truth You have for me;
place in my hands the wonderful key
that shall unclasp and set me free.
Silently now I wait for Thee,
ready, my God, Your will to see.
Open my eyes, illumine me, Spirit Divine!

Open my ears, that I may hear
voices of truth You send me clear;
and while the wave notes fall on my ear,
everything false will disappear.
Silently now I wait for Thee,
ready, my God, Your will to see.
Open my ears, illumine me, Spirit Divine!

Open my mouth, and let me bear
gladly the warm truth everywhere;
open my heart and let me prepare
love with Your children thus to share.
Silently now I wait for Thee,
ready, my God, Your will to see.
Open my heart, illumine me, Spirit Divine.

Clara H. Scott

The Psalm   *Happy Are They Whose Hope Is in the LORD*

Happy are they who have the God of Jacob for their help!* whose hope is in the
    LORD their God;

Who made heaven and earth, the seas, and all that is in them;* who keeps his
    promise for ever;

Who gives justice to those who are oppressed,* and food to those who hunger.

The LORD loves the righteous; the LORD cares for the stranger;* he sustains the
    orphan and widow, but frustrates the way of the wicked.

The LORD shall reign for ever,* your God, O Zion, throughout all generations.
    Hallelujah!

Psalm 146:4–6, 8–9

The Gloria in Excelsis

Glory to God in the highest, and on earth peace to people of good will.
    We praise you.
    We bless you.
    We adore you.
    We glorify you.
We give thanks to you for your great glory.

The Small Verse

The Apostle Paul wrote, saying: I do not cease to give thanks for you,
    remembering you in my prayers, that the God of our Lord Jesus Christ, the
    Father of glory, may give you a spirit of wisdom and of revelation in the
    knowledge of him, having the eyes of your heart enlightened that you may
    know what is the hope to which he has called you.

Ephesians 1:16–18a

The Lord's Prayer

The Final Blessing

May the LORD bless us and keep us and cause His face to shine upon us from this
    day forth and forever more. *Amen.*

11

Tuesday, Month of January

The Office of Midnight   **Observed on the Hour or Half-Hour
Between 10:30 p.m.✢ and 1:30 a.m.**

The Call to Prayer
Tell it out among the nations: "The LORD is King!* he has made the world so firm
that it cannot be moved; he will judge the peoples with equity."

Psalm 96:10

The Request for Presence
O LORD, let my prayer be set forth in your sight as incense,* the lifting up of my
hands as the evening sacrifice.

Psalm 141:2

The Greeting
Our Father, may Your will be done, on earth as in Heaven.

The Canticle   *The First Song of Isaiah*
Ecce, Deus

Surely, it is God who saves me;*
    I will trust in him and not be afraid.
For the Lord is my stronghold and my sure defense,*
    and he will be my Savior.
Therefore you shall draw water with rejoicing*
    from the springs of salvation.
And on that day you shall say,*
    Give thanks to the Lord and call upon his Name;
Make his deeds known among the peoples;*
    see that they remember that his Name is exalted.
Sing praises of the Lord, for he has done great things,*
    and this is known in all the world.
Cry aloud, inhabitants of Zion, ring out your joy,*
    for the great one in the midst of you is the Holy One of Israel.

Isaiah 12:2–6

The Psalm   *The LORD Is the Strength of My Life*
The LORD is my light and my salvation; whom then shall I fear?* the LORD is the
    strength of my life; of whom then shall I be afraid?
When evildoers came upon me to eat up my flesh,* it was they, my foes and my
    adversaries, who stumbled and fell.
Though an army should encamp against me,* yet my heart shall not be afraid;
And though war should rise up against me,* yet will I put my trust in him.

12

One thing have I asked of the LORD; one thing I seek;* that I may dwell in the house of the LORD all the days of my life;

To behold the fair beauty of the LORD* and to seek him in his temple.

For in the day of trouble he shall keep me safe in his shelter;* he shall hide me in the secrecy of his dwelling and set me high upon a rock.

Even now he lifts up my head* above my enemies round about me.

Therefore I will offer in his dwelling an oblation with sounds of great gladness;* I will sing and make music to the LORD.

Psalm 27:1–9

The Gloria

The Small Verse
Never flag in zeal, be aglow with the Spirit, serve the Lord.

Romans 12:11

The Final Thanksgiving
I will greatly rejoice in the LORD, my soul shall exult in my God; for he has clothed me with the garments of salvation, he has covered me with the robe of righteousness, as a bridegroom decks himself with a garland, and as a bride adorns herself with her jewels.

Isaiah 61:10

The Petition
May the Lord GOD, father of grace and mercy, grant all who dwell here a peaceful night and a perfect end. *Amen.*

The Office of the Night Watch   Observed on the Hour or Half-Hour Between 1:30 and 4:30 a.m.

The Call to Prayer
Behold now, bless the LORD, all you servants of the LORD,* you that stand by night in the house of the LORD.

Lift up your hands in the holy place and bless the LORD;* the LORD who made heaven and earth bless you out of Zion.

Psalm 134

The Request for Presence
O God, come to my assistance.

O Lord, make haste to help me.

13

The Greeting

Exalt yourself above the heavens, O God,* and your glory over all the earth.
So that those who are dear to you may be delivered,* save with your right hand
    and answer me.

Psalm 108:5–6

The Refrain for the Night Watch

The LORD grants his loving-kindness in the daytime;* in the night season his song
    is with me, a prayer to the God of my life.

Psalm 42:10

The Psalm   *The LORD Sustains Me*

How many there are who say of me,* "There is no help for him in his God."
But you, O LORD, are a shield about me;* you are my glory, the one who lifts up
    my head.
I call aloud upon the LORD,* and he answers me from his holy hill;
I lie down and go to sleep;* I wake again, because the LORD sustains me.

Psalm 3:2–5

The Refrain

The LORD grants his loving-kindness in the daytime;* in the night season his song
    is with me, a prayer to the God of my life.

A Reading

Therefore, in your concord and harmonious love, Jesus Christ is sung. And so do
    you then, person by person, become a choir, in order that being harmonious in
    love, and taking up the song of God in unison, you may with one voice sing to
    the Father through Jesus Christ; so thus He may both hear you, and perceive by
    your works that you are indeed members of His Son.

Ignatius (ca. 30–107 CE), Epistles of Ignatius, V:50–52

The Refrain

The LORD grants his loving-kindness in the daytime;* in the night season his song
    is with me, a prayer to the God of my life.

The Litany

Grant, Almighty God, that all who confess your Name may be united in your truth,
    live together in your love, and reveal your glory in the world.
    Lord, in your mercy, hear my prayer.
Guide the people of this land, and of all the nations, in the ways of justice and
    peace; that we may honor one another and serve the common good.
    Lord, in your mercy, hear my prayer.
Give us all a reverence for the earth as your own creation, that we may use its
    resources rightly in the service of others and to your honor and glory.
    Lord, in your mercy, hear my prayer.

Bless all whose lives are closely linked with mine, and grant that I may serve
Christ in them, and love even as he loves me.
Lord, in your mercy, hear my prayer.
Comfort and heal all those who suffer in body, mind, or spirit; give them courage
and hope in their troubles, and bring them the joy of your salvation.
Lord, in your mercy, hear my prayer.
I commend to your mercy all who have died, that your will for them may be
fulfilled; and I pray that I may share with all your saints in your eternal
kingdom.
Lord, in your mercy, hear my prayer.

The Thanksgiving
Lord, you now have set your servant free to go in peace as you have promised; for
these eyes of mine have seen the Savior whom you have prepared for all the
world to see: A Light to enlighten the nations, and the glory of your people
Israel. *Amen.*

Nunc Dimittis

The Final Petition
Now guide me waking, O Lord, and guard me sleeping; that awake I may watch
with Christ, and asleep, I may rest in peace. *Amen.*

The Office of Dawn   Observed on the Hour or Half-Hour
Between 4:30 and 7:30 a.m.

The Call to Prayer
Hallelujah! Praise the LORD, O my soul!* I will praise the LORD as long as I live; I
will sing praises to my God while I have my being.

Psalm 146:1

The Request for Presence
My soul waits for the LORD, more than watchmen for the morning,* more than
watchmen for the morning.

Psalm 130:5

The Greeting
Glory be to the Father, and the Son, and the Holy Spirit.
As it was in the beginning, it is now
And ever shall be, world without end. *Amen.*

The Hymn
Come, and let us sweetly join,
to praise our Christ in hymns divine;

15

give we all with one accord
glory to our risen Lord.

Hands and hearts and voices raise,
sing as in the ancient days;
antedate the joys above,
and celebrate His saving love.

Sanctify us, Lord, and bless,
breathe Your Spirit, give Your peace;
may You within us move,
make from our praise a feast of love.

Charles Wesley, adapted

The Psalm   *He Gives Snow Like Wool*

The LORD sends out his command to the earth,* and his word runs very swiftly.
He gives snow like wool;* he scatters hoarfrost like ashes.
He scatters his hail like bread crumbs;* who can stand against his cold?
He sends forth his word and melts them;* he blows with his wind, and the waters
    flow.

Psalm 147:16–19

The Gloria in Excelsis

Glory to God in the highest, and on earth peace to people of good will.
    We praise you.
    We bless you.
    We adore you.
    We glorify you.
We give thanks to you for your great glory.

The Small Verse

So speak and so act as those who are to be judged under the law of liberty. For
    judgment is without mercy to one who has shown no mercy; yet mercy
    triumphs over judgment.

James 2:12–13

The Lord's Prayer

The Final Blessing

May the LORD bless us and keep us and cause His face to shine upon us from this
    day forth and forever more. *Amen.*

Wednesday, Month of January

The Office of Midnight　　　　　**Observed on the Hour or Half-Hour Between 10:30 p.m.✣ and 1:30 a.m.**

The Call to Prayer
Sing to the LORD a new song,* for he has done marvelous things.
With his right hand and his holy arm* has he won for himself the victory.

Psalm 98:1–2

The Request for Presence
O LORD, let my prayer be set forth in your sight as incense,* the lifting up of my hands as the evening sacrifice.

Psalm 141:2, adapted

The Greeting
Our Father, give us this day our daily bread.

The Canticle　　　　　　　　　*A Song of Creation—Part Two*
Benedicite, omnia opera Domini

Glorify the Lord, all you works of the Lord,*
　praise him and highly exalt him for ever.
In the firmament of his power, glorify the Lord,*
　praise him and highly exalt him for ever.
Let the earth glorify the Lord,*
　praise him and highly exalt him for ever.
Glorify the Lord, O mountains and hills, and all that grows upon the earth,*
　praise him and highly exalt him for ever.
Glorify the Lord, O springs of water, seas, and streams,*
　O whales and all that move in the waters.
All birds of the air, glorify the Lord,*
　Praise him and highly exalt him for ever.
Glorify the Lord, O beasts of the wild,*
　and all you flocks and herds.
O men and women everywhere, glorify the Lord,*
　praise him and highly exalt him for ever.

Song of the Three Young Men, 52–61

The Psalm　　　　　　*That the Generations To Come Might Know*
That which we have heard and known, and what our forefathers have told us,* we
　will not hide from their children.
We will recount to generations to come the praiseworthy deeds and the power of
　the LORD,* and the wonderful works he has done.

17

He gave his decrees to Jacob and established a law for Israel,* which he
   commanded them to teach their children;
That the generations to come might know, and the children yet unborn;* that they
   in their turn might tell it to their children;
So that they might put their trust in God,* and not forget the deeds of God, but
   keep his commandments;
And not be like their forefathers, a stubborn and rebellious generation,* a
   generation whose heart was not steadfast, and whose spirit was not faithful to
   God.

Psalm 78:3– 8

The Gloria

The Small Verse

Now may the God of peace who brought again from the dead our Lord Jesus, the
   great shepherd of the sheep, by the blood of the eternal covenant, equip you
   with everything good that you may do his will.

Hebrews 13 20–21a

The Final Thanksgiving

I will greatly rejoice in the LORD, my soul shall exult in my God; for he has
   clothed me with the garments of salvation, he has covered me with the robe of
   righteousness, as a bridegroom decks himself with a garland, and as a bride
   adorns herself with her jewels.

Isaiah 61:10

The Petition

May the Lord GOD, father of grace and mercy, grant all who dwell here a peaceful
   night and a perfect end. *Amen.*

The Office of the Night Watch   Observed on the Hour or Half-Hour
Between 1:30 and 4:30 a.m.

The Call to Prayer

Behold now, bless the LORD, all you servants of the LORD,* you that stand by night
   in the house of the LORD.
Lift up your hands in the holy place and bless the LORD;* the LORD who made
   heaven and earth bless you out of Zion.

Psalm 134

The Request for Presence

O God, come to my assistance.
O Lord, make haste to help me.

The Greeting

But I put my trust in your mercy;* my heart is joyful because of your saving help.
I will sing to the LORD, for he has dealt with me richly;* I will praise the Name of
the Lord Most High.

Psalm 13:5–6

The Refrain for the Night Watch

Yours is the day, yours also the night;* you established the moon and the sun.

Psalm 74:15

The Psalm   *The LORD Is My Shepherd*

The LORD is my shepherd;* I shall not be in want.
He makes me lie down in green pastures* and leads me beside still waters.
He revives my soul* and guides me along right pathways for his Name's sake.
Though I walk through the valley of the shadow of death, I shall fear no evil;* for
you are with me; your rod and your staff, they comfort me.
You spread a table before me in the presence of those who trouble me;* you have
anointed my head with oil, and my cup is running over.
Surely your goodness and mercy shall follow me all the days of my life,* and I
will dwell in the house of the LORD for ever.

Psalm 23

The Refrain

Yours is the day, yours also the night;* you established the moon and the sun.

A Reading

The Lord revealed to me that I would sin. When I realized this, I felt a sort of
gentle fear, and the Lord answered this fear: "I protect you. I'll keep you safe."
God said this to me with more love and assurance than I can possibly tell you.
Julian of Norwich, Revelations of Divine Love, translated by Carmen Acevedo Butcher

The Refrain

Yours is the day, yours also the night;* you established the moon and the sun.

The Litany

For the holy Church of God, that it may be filled with truth and love, and be found
without fault at the day of your coming, I pray to you, O Lord.
> *Lord, in your mercy, hear my prayer*

For all who fear God and believe in you, Lord Christ, that our divisions may cease,
and that all may be one as you and the Father are one, I pray to you, O Lord.
> *Lord, in your mercy, hear my prayer.*

For those who do not yet believe, and for those who have lost their faith, that they
may receive the light of the Gospel, I pray to you, O Lord.
> *Lord, in your mercy, hear my prayer.*

For my enemies and those who wish me harm, and for all whom I have injured or offended, I pray to you, O Lord.
Lord, in your mercy, hear my prayer.
For all who have commended themselves to my prayers; for my family, friends, and neighbors; that being freed from anxiety, they may live in joy, peace, and health, I pray to you, O Lord.
Lord, in your mercy, hear my prayer.
For myself; for the forgiveness of my sins, and for the grace of the Holy Spirit to amend my life, I pray to you, O Lord.
Lord, in your mercy, hear my prayer

The Thanksgiving
Lord, you now have set your servant free to go in peace as you have promised; for these eyes of mine have seen the Savior whom you have prepared for all the world to see: A Light to enlighten the nations, and the glory of your people Israel. *Amen.*

Nunc Dimittis

The Final Petition
Now guide me waking, O Lord, and guard me sleeping; that awake I may watch with Christ, and asleep, I may rest in peace. *Amen.*

The Office of Dawn   Observed on the Hour or Half-Hour
Between 4:30 and 7:30 a.m.

The Call to Prayer
Hallelujah! How good it is to sing praises to our God!* how pleasant it is to honor him with praise!

Psalm 147:1

The Request for Presence
My soul waits for the LORD, more than watchmen for the morning,* more than watchmen for the morning.

Psalm 130:5

The Greeting
Glory be to the Father, and the Son, and the Holy Spirit.
As it was in the beginning, it is now
And ever shall be, world without end. *Amen.*

Gloria Patri

The Hymn
We've a story to tell to the nations,
that shall turn their hearts to the right,
a story of truth and mercy,
a story of peace and light.

20

We've a song to be sung to the nations,
that shall lift their hearts to the Lord,
a song that shall conquer evil
and shatter the spear and sword,
and shatter the spear and sword.

We've a message to give to the nations,
that the Lord who reigns above
has sent us His Son to save us
and show us that God is love,
and show us that God is love.

For the darkness shall turn to the dawning,
and the dawning to noonday bright;
and Christ's great kingdom shall come on earth,
the kingdom of love and light.

H. Ernest Nichol

The Psalm   *Praise Him with Lyre and Harp*
Praise him for his mighty acts;* praise him for his excellent greatness.
Praise him with the blast of the ram's-horn;* praise him with lyre and harp.
Praise him with timbrel and dance;* praise him with strings and pipe.
Praise him with resounding cymbals;* praise him with loud-clanging cymbals.
Let everything that has breath* praise the LORD. Hallelujah!

Psalm 150:2–6

The Gloria in Excelsis
Glory to God in the highest, and on earth peace to people of good will.
> We praise you.
> We bless you.
> We adore you.
> We glorify you.
We give thanks to you for your great glory.

The Small Verse
I, Jesus, have sent my angel to you with this testimony for the churches. I am the
root and the offspring of David, the bright morning star. The Spirit and the
Bride say, "Come." And let him who hears, say, "Come." And let him who is
thirsty come, let him who desires take the waters of life without price.

Revelation 22:16–17

The Lord's Prayer

The Final Blessing

May the LORD bless us and keep us and cause His face to shine upon us from this day forth and forever more. *Amen.*

చా

Thursday, Month of January

The Office of Midnight

Observed on the Hour or Half-Hour Between 10:30 p.m.✢ and 1:30 a.m.

The Call to Prayer

Know this: The LORD himself is God;* he himself has made us, and we are his; we are his people and the sheep of his pasture.

Psalm 100:2

The Request for Presence

O LORD, let my prayer be set forth in your sight as incense, the lifting up of my hands as the evening sacrifice.

Psalm 141:2, adapted

The Greeting

Our Father, forgive us our sins as we forgive those who have sinned against us.

The Canticle

A Song of Penitence
Kyrie Pantokrator

And now, O Lord, I bend the knee of my heart,*
    and make my appeal, sure of your gracious goodness.
I have sinned, O Lord, I have sinned,*
    and I know my wickedness only too well.
Therefore I make this prayer to you:*
    Forgive me, Lord, forgive me.
Do not let me perish in my sin,*
    nor condemn me to the depths of the earth.
For you, O Lord, are the God of those who repent,*
    and in me you will show forth your goodness.
Unworthy as I am, you will save me, in accordance with your great mercy,*
    and I will praise you without ceasing all the days of my life.
For all the powers of heaven sing your praises,*
    and yours is the glory to ages of ages. Amen.

Prayer of Manasseh 11–15

22

The Psalm   ***God Takes His Stand in the Council of Heaven***

God takes his stand in the council of heaven;* he gives judgment in the midst of
     the gods:

"How long will you judge unjustly,* and show favor to the wicked?

Save the weak and the orphan;* defend the humble and needy;

Rescue the weak and the poor;* deliver them from the power of the wicked.

They do not know, neither do they understand; they go about in darkness;* all the
     foundations of the earth are shaken.

Now I say to you, "You are gods,* and all of you children of the Most High;

Nevertheless, you shall die like mortals,* and fall like any prince."

Psalm 82:1–7

The Gloria

The Small Verse

Heaven and earth will pass away, but my words will not pass away.

Mark 13:31

The Final Thanksgiving

I will greatly rejoice in the LORD, my soul shall exult in my God; for he has
     clothed me with the garments of salvation, he has covered me with the robe of
     righteousness, as a bridegroom decks himself with a garland, and as a bride
     adorns herself with her jewels.

Isaiah 61:10

The Petition

May the Lord GOD, father of grace and mercy, grant all who dwell here a peaceful
     night and a perfect end. *Amen.*

The Office of the Night Watch   **Observed on the Hour or Half-Hour
Between 1:30 and 4:30 a.m.**

The Call to Prayer

Behold now, bless the LORD, all you servants of the LORD,* you that stand by night
     in the house of the LORD.

Lift up your hands in the holy place and bless the LORD;* the LORD who made
     heaven and earth bless you out of Zion.

Psalm 134

The Request for Presence

O God, come to my assistance.

O Lord, make haste to help me.

23

The Greeting

I am bound by the vow I made to you, O God;* I will present to you
    thank-offerings;
For you have rescued my soul from death and my feet from stumbling,* that I may
    walk before God in the light of the living.

Psalm 56:11–12

The Refrain for the Night Watch

I commune with my heart in the night;* I ponder and search my mind.

Psalm 77:6

The Psalm   *He Shall Give His Angels Charge over You*

Because you have made the LORD your refuge,* and the Most High your
    habitation,
There shall no evil happen to you,* neither shall any plague come near your
    dwelling.
For he shall give his angels charge over you,* to keep you in all your ways.
They shall bear you in their hands,* lest you dash your foot against a stone.

Psalm 91:9–12

The Refrain

I commune with my heart in the night;* I ponder and search my mind.

A Reading

Fear and patience, then, are helpers of our faith; and long-suffering and continence
    are things which fight on our side. So long as these remain pure in what
    respects the Lord, then Wisdom, Understanding, Science, and Knowledge
    rejoice along with them.

Epistle of Barnabas, chap. 2 (ca. 100 CE)

The Refrain

I commune with my heart in the night;* I ponder and search my mind.

The Litany

For the peace of the world, that a spirit of respect and forbearance may grow
    among nations and peoples, I pray to you, O Lord.
>   *Lord, hear my prayer.*
For those in positions of public trust, that they may serve justice, and promote the
    dignity and freedom of every person, I pray to you, O Lord.
>   *Lord, hear my prayer.*
For the poor, the persecuted, the sick, and all who suffer; for refugees, prisoners,
    and all who are in danger; that they may be relieved and protected, I pray to
    you, O Lord.
>   *Lord, hear my prayer.*

For the forgiveness of my sins, and for the grace of the Holy Spirit to amend my
life, I pray to you, O Lord.
Lord, hear my prayer.
For all who have died in the communion of your Church, and those whose faith is
known to you alone, that, with all the saints, they may have rest in that place
where there is no pain or grief, but life eternal, I pray to you, O Lord.
Lord, hear my prayer
Rejoicing in the fellowship of the ever-blessed Virgin Mary and all the saints, I
commend my self and all your faithful to Christ our God.
To you, O Lord our God.

The Thanksgiving

Lord, you now have set your servant free to go in peace as you have promised; for
these eyes of mine have seen the Savior whom you have prepared for all the world
to see: A Light to enlighten the nations, and the glory of your people Israel. *Amen.*

Nunc Dimittis

The Final Petition

Now guide me waking, O Lord, and guard me sleeping; that awake I may watch
with Christ, and asleep, I may rest in peace. *Amen.*

The Office of Dawn   Observed on the Hour or Half-Hour
Between 4:30 and 7:30 a.m.

The Call to Prayer

Worship the LORD, O Jerusalem;* praise your God, O Zion;
For he has strengthened the bars of your gates.

Psalm 147: 13–14a

The Request for Presence

My soul waits for the LORD, more than watchmen for the morning,* more than
watchmen for the morning.

Psalm 130:5

The Greeting

Glory be to the Father, and the Son, and the Holy Spirit.
As it was in the beginning, it is now
And ever shall be, world without end. *Amen.*

The Hymn

Guide me, O thou great Jehovah,
pilgrim through this barren land.
I am weak, but You are mighty;
hold me with Your powerful hand.

25

Bread of heaven, bread of Heaven,
feed me til I want no more;
feed me til I want no more.

Open now that crystal fountain,
from which the healing stream can flow;
let the fire and cloudy pillar
lead me all my journey through.
Strong deliverer, strong deliverer,
be now my strength and shield.
Be now my strength and shield.

William Williams

The Psalm   *He Covers the Heavens with Clouds*

He covers the heavens with clouds* and prepares rain for the earth;
He makes grass to grow upon the mountains* and green plants to serve mankind.
He provides food for flocks and herds* and for the young ravens when they cry.
He is not impressed by the might of a horse;* he has no pleasure in the strength of
a man;
But the LORD has pleasure in those who fear him,* in those who await his gracious
favor.

Psalm 147:8–12

The Gloria in Excelsis
Glory to God in the highest, and on earth peace to people of good will.
> We praise you.
> We bless you.
> We adore you.
> We glorify you.
We give thanks to you for your great glory.

The Small Verse
A new heart I will give you, and a new spirit I will put within you; and I will take
out of your flesh the heart of stone and give you a heart of flesh. And I will put
my spirit within you, and cause you to walk in my statutes and be careful to
observe my ordinances.

Ezekiel 36:26–27

The Lord's Prayer

The Final Blessing
May the LORD bless us and keep us and cause His face to shine upon us from this
day forth and forever more. *Amen.*

Friday, Month of January

The Office of Midnight   **Observed on the Hour or Half-Hour**
Between 10:30 p.m.✢ and 1:30 a.m.

The Call to Prayer
Open my lips, O Lord,* and my mouth shall proclaim your praise.

Psalm 51:16

The Request for Presence
O LORD, let my prayer be set forth in your sight as incense,* the lifting up of my
    hands as the evening sacrifice.

Psalm 141:2, adapted

The Greeting
Our Father, lead us not into temptation, but deliver us from evil.

The Canticle   *A Song of Penitence*
                        Kyrie Pantokrator

O Lord and Ruler of the hosts of heaven,*
    God of Abraham, Isaac, and Jacob, and of all their righteous offspring:
You made the heavens and the earth,*
    with all their vast array.
All things quake with fear at your presence;*
    they tremble because of your power.
But your merciful promise is beyond all measure;*
    it surpasses all that our minds can fathom.
O Lord, you are full of compassion,*
    long-suffering, and abounding in mercy.
You hold back your hand;*
    you do not punish as we deserve.
In your great goodness, Lord, you have promised forgiveness to sinners,*
    that they may repent of their sin and be saved.

Prayer of Manasseh 1–2, 4, 6–7

The Psalm   *Out of Zion, Perfect in Its Beauty*
The LORD, the God of gods, has spoken;* he has called the earth from the rising of
    the sun to its setting.
Out of Zion, perfect in its beauty,* God reveals himself in glory.
Our God will come and will not keep silence;* before him there is a consuming
    flame, and round about him a raging storm.
He calls the heavens and the earth from above* to witness the judgment of his
    people.

27

"Gather before me my loyal followers,* those who have made a covenant with me
   and sealed it with sacrifice."
Let the heavens declare the rightness of his cause;* for God himself is judge.

Psalm 50:1–6

The Gloria

The Small Verse
And it shall come to pass afterward, that I shall pour out my spirit on all flesh;
   your sons and your daughters shall prophesy, your old men shall dream
   dreams, and your young men shall see visions. Even upon the menservants and
   the maidservants in those days, I will pour out my spirit.

Joel 2:28–29

The Final Thanksgiving
I will greatly rejoice in the LORD, my soul shall exult in my God; for he has
   clothed me with the garments of salvation, he has covered me with the robe of
   righteousness, as a bridegroom decks himself with a garland, and as a bride
   adorns herself with her jewels.

Isaiah 61:10

The Petition
May the Lord GOD, father of grace and mercy, grant all who dwell here a peaceful
   night and a perfect end. *Amen.*

The Office of the Night Watch   **Observed on the Hour or Half-Hour
                                        Between 1:30 and 4:30 a.m.**

The Call to Prayer
Behold now, bless the LORD, all you servants of the LORD,* you that stand by night
   in the house of the LORD.
Lift up your hands in the holy place and bless the LORD;* the LORD who made
   heaven and earth bless you out of Zion.

Psalm 134

The Request for Presence
O God, come to my assistance.
O Lord, make haste to help me.

The Greeting
Let not those who hope in you be put to shame through me, Lord GOD of hosts;*
   let not those who seek you be disgraced because of me, O God of Israel.

Psalm 69:7

28

The Refrain for the Night Watch

You shall not be afraid of any terror by night,* nor of the arrow that flies by day;

Psalm 91:5

The Psalm   The LORD Will Not Forsake His Own

The LORD knows our human thoughts;* how like a puff of wind they are.
Happy are they whom you instruct, O Lord!* whom you teach out of your law;
To give them rest in evil days,* until a pit is dug for the wicked.
For the LORD will not abandon his people,* nor will he forsake his own.

Psalm 94:11–14

The Refrain

You shall not be afraid of any terror by night,* nor of the arrow that flies by day;

A Reading

In me there is darkness, but in you there is light; I am lonely, but you do not leave
me; I am feeble in heart, but with you there is help; I am restless, but with you
there is peace. In me there is bitterness, but with you there is patience; I do not
understand your ways, but you know the way for me.

Dietrich Bonhoffer, Prayer from a Nazi Concentration Camp

The Refrain

You shall not be afraid of any terror by night,* nor of the arrow that flies by day;

The Litany

For all people in their daily life and work;
*For my family, friends, and neighbors, and for those who are alone, I pray
to you, Lord God.*
For this community, the nation, and the world;
For all who work for justice, freedom, and peace, I pray to you, Lord God.
For the just and proper use of your creation;
*For the victims of hunger, fear, injustice, and oppression, I pray to you,
Lord God.*
For all who are in danger, sorrow, or any kind of trouble;
*For those who minister to the sick, the friendless, and the needy, I pray to
you, Lord God.*
For the peace and unity of the Church of God;
*For all who proclaim the Gospel, and all who seek the Truth, I pray to you,
Lord God.*
Hear me, Lord;
For your mercy is great.

The Thanksgiving

Lord, you now have set your servant free to go in peace as you have promised; for
these eyes of mine have seen the Savior whom you have prepared for all the

world to see: A Light to enlighten the nations, and the glory of your people Israel. *Amen.*

Nunc Dimittis

The Final Petition

Now guide me waking, O Lord, and guard me sleeping; that awake I may watch with Christ, and asleep, I may rest in peace. *Amen.*

The Office of Dawn   Observed on the Hour or Half-Hour
Between 4:30 and 7:30 a.m.

The Call to Prayer

Sing to the LORD with thanksgiving;* make music to our God upon the harp.

Psalm 147:7

The Request for Presence

My soul waits for the LORD, more than watchmen for the morning,* more than watchmen for the morning.

Psalm 130:5

The Greeting

Glory be to the Father, and the Son, and the Holy Spirit.
As it was in the beginning, it is now
And ever shall be, world without end. *Amen.*

The Hymn

Praise, my soul, the King of heaven,
to His throne your tribute bring;
ransomed, healed, restored, forgiven,
evermore God's praises sing.
Alleluia! Alleluia!
Praise the everlasting King.

Fatherlike, He tends and spares us;
well our feeble frame He knows;
motherlike, God gently bears us,
rescues us from all our foes.
Alleluia! Alleluia!
Widely yet, God's mercy flows.

Angels in the heights adoring,
you behold the Godhead face to face;
saints triumphant, now adoring,

30

gathered in from every race.
Alleluia! Alleluia!
Praise with us the God of grace.

Henry F. Lyte, adapted

The Psalm   Praise the LORD from the Earth
Praise the LORD from the earth,* you sea-monsters and all deeps;
Fire and hail, snow and fog,* tempestuous wind, doing his will;
Mountains and all hills,* fruit trees and all cedars;
Wild beasts and all cattle,* creeping things and winged birds;
Kings of the earth and all peoples,* princes and all rulers of the world;
Young men and maidens,* old and young together.
Let them praise the Name of the LORD,

Psalm 148:7–13a

The Gloria in Excelsis
Glory to God in the highest, and on earth peace to people of good will.
    We praise you.
    We bless you.
    We adore you.
    We glorify you.
We give thanks to you for your great glory.

The Small Verse
He is the image of the invisible God, the first-born of all creation; for in him all
    things were created, in heaven and on earth, visible and invisible, whether
    thrones or dominions or principalities or authorities–all things were created
    through him and for him.

Colossians 1:15–16

The Lord's Prayer

The Final Blessing
May the LORD bless us and keep us and cause His face to shine upon us from this
    day forth and forever more. *Amen.*

Saturday, Month of January

The Office of Midnight   **Observed on the Hour or Half-Hour
Between 10:30 p.m.✛ and 1:30 a.m.**

The Call to Prayer
Worship the LORD in the beauty of holiness;* let the whole earth tremble before
   him.

Psalm 96: 9

The Request for Presence
O LORD, let my prayer be set forth in your sight as incense,* the lifting up of my
   hands as the evening sacrifice.

Psalm 141:2

The Greeting
Our Father, Yours are the kingdom, the power, and the glory forever.

The Canticle   ***The Song of Zechariah***
                                      Benedictus Dominus Deus

Blessed be the Lord, the God of Israel;*
   he has come to his people and set them free.
He has raised up for us a mighty savior,*
   born of the house of his servant David
You, my child, shall be called the prophet of the Most High,*
   for you will go before the Lord to prepare his way,
To give his people knowledge of salvation*
   by the forgiveness of their sins.
In the tender compassion of our God*
   the dawn from on high shall break upon us,
To shine on those who dwell in darkness and the shadow of death,*
   and to guide our feet into the way of peace.
Glory to the Father, and to the Son, and to the Holy Spirit:*
   as it was in the beginning, is now, and will be for ever. *Amen.*

Luke 1:68–69, 76–79

The Psalm   ***God Sits upon His Holy Throne***
Clap your hands, all you peoples;* shout to God with a cry of joy.
God has gone up with a shout,* the LORD with the sound of the ram's-horn.
Sing praises to God, sing praises;* sing praises to our King, sing praises.
For God is King of all the earth;* sing praises with all your skill.
God reigns over the nations;* God sits upon his holy throne.

The nobles of the peoples have gathered together* with the people of the God of
    Abraham.
The rulers of the earth belong to God,* and he is highly exalted.

Psalm 47:1, 5–10

The Gloria

The Small Verse
So faith, hope, love abide, these three; but the greatest of these is love.

1 Corinthians 13:13

The Final Thanksgiving
I will greatly rejoice in the LORD, my soul shall exult in my God; for he has
    clothed me with the garments of salvation, he has covered me with the robe of
    righteousness, as a bridegroom decks himself with a garland, and as a bride
    adorns herself with her jewels.

Isaiah 61:10

The Petition
May the Lord GOD, father of grace and mercy, grant all who dwell here a peaceful
    night and a perfect end. *Amen.*

The Office of the Night Watch   **Observed on the Hour or Half-Hour
Between 1:30 and 4:30 a.m.**

The Call to Prayer
Behold now, bless the LORD, all you servants of the LORD,* you that stand by night
    in the house of the LORD.
Lift up your hands in the holy place and bless the LORD;* the LORD who made
    heaven and earth bless you out of Zion.

Psalm 134

The Request for Presence
O God, come to my assistance.
O Lord, make haste to help me.

The Greeting
"You are my God, and I will thank you;* you are my God, and I will exalt you."

Psalm 118:28

The Refrain for the Night Watch
It is a good thing to give thanks to the LORD,* and to sing praises to your Name,
    O Most High;

To tell of your loving-kindness early in the morning* and of your faithfulness in
the night season.

Psalm 92:1–2

The Psalm   *Lᴏʀᴅ, I Am Your Servant*

Lᴏʀᴅ, I am your servant;* I am your servant and the child of your handmaid; you
have freed me from my bonds.
I will offer you the sacrifice of thanksgiving* and call upon the Name of the Lᴏʀᴅ.
I will fulfill my vows to the Lᴏʀᴅ* in the presence of all his people,
In the courts of the Lᴏʀᴅ's house,* in the midst of you, O Jerusalem. Hallelujah!

Psalm 116:14–17

The Refrain

It is a good thing to give thanks to the Lᴏʀᴅ,* and to sing praises to your Name,
O Most High;
To tell of your loving-kindness early in the morning* and of your faithfulness in
the night season.

A Reading

Let your children be partakers of true Christian training; let them learn of how
great avail humility is with God—how much the spirit of pure affection can
prevail with Him—how excellent and great His fear is, and how it saves all
those who walk in it with a pure mind. For He is a Searcher of the thoughts and
desires [of the heart]: His breath is in us; and when He pleases, He will take it
away.

Clement of Rome (ca. 57 CE), 1st Epistle of Clement to the Corinthians, 21, 94–95

The Refrain

It is a good thing to give thanks to the Lᴏʀᴅ,* and to sing praises to your Name,
O Most High;
To tell of your loving-kindness early in the morning* and of your faithfulness in
the night season.

The Litany

For the peace from above, for the loving-kindness of God, and for the salvation of
my soul, I pray to the Lord.
 Lord, have mercy.
For the peace of the world, for the welfare of the Holy Church of God, and for the
unity of all peoples, I pray to the Lord.
 Lord, have mercy.
For my city [town, village], for every city and community, and for those who live
in them, I pray to the Lord.
 Lord, have mercy.

For seasonable weather, and for an abundance of the fruits of the earth, I pray to the Lord.

> *Lord, have mercy.*

For the good earth which God has given us, and for the wisdom and will to conserve it, I pray to the Lord.

> *Lord, have mercy.*

For deliverance from all danger, violence, oppression, and degradation, I pray to the Lord.

> *Lord, have mercy.*

For the absolution and remission of my sins and offenses, I pray to the Lord.

> *Lord, have mercy.*

Defend me, deliver me, and in your compassion protect me, O Lord, by your grace.

> *Lord, have mercy.*

The Thanksgiving

Lord, you now have set your servant free to go in peace as you have promised; for these eyes of mine have seen the Savior whom you have prepared for all the world to see: A Light to enlighten the nations, and the glory of your people Israel. *Amen.*

Nunc Dimittis

The Final Petition

Now guide me waking, O Lord, and guard me sleeping; that awake I may watch with Christ, and asleep, I may rest in peace. *Amen.*

The Office of Dawn · Observed on the Hour or Half-Hour Between 4:30 and 7:30 a.m.

The Call to Prayer

Worship the LORD, O Jerusalem;* praise your God, O Zion;
For he has strengthened the bars of your gates.

Psalm 147:13–14a

The Request for Presence

My soul waits for the LORD, more than watchmen for the morning,* more than watchmen for the morning.

Psalm 130:5

The Greeting

Glory be to the Father, and the Son, and the Holy Spirit.
As it was in the beginning, it is now
And ever shall be, world without end. *Amen.*

The Hymn

O love, how deep, how broad, how high,
it fills the heart with ecstasy,
that God, the Son of God, should take
our mortal form for mortals' sake!

For us he prayed; for us he taught;
for us his daily works he wrought;
by words and signs and actions thus
still seeking not himself, but us.

All glory to our Lord and God
for love so deep, so high, so broad;
the Trinity whom we adore,
forever and forevermore.

15th c. Latin, translated by Benjamin Webb

The Psalm   ***The LORD Takes Pleasure in His People***

Let Israel rejoice in his Maker;* let the children of Zion be joyful in their King.
Let them praise his Name in the dance;* let them sing praise to him with timbrel
     and harp.
For the LORD takes pleasure in his people* and adorns the poor with victory.
Let the faithful rejoice in triumph;* let them be joyful on their beds.

Psalm 149:2–5

The Gloria in Excelsis

Glory to God in the highest, and on earth peace to people of good will.
     We praise you.
     We bless you.
     We adore you.
     We glorify you.
We give thanks to you for your great glory.

The Small Verse

Jesus taught us, saying: If you love me, you will keep my commandants. And I
     will pray the Father, and he will give you another Counselor, to be with you
     forever, even the Spirit of truth, whom the world cannot receive, because it
     neither sees him nor knows him; you know him, for he dwells with you, and
     will be in you.

John 14:15–16

The Lord's Prayer

The Final Blessing

May the LORD bless us and keep us and cause His face to shine upon us from this
     day forth and forever more. *Amen.*

The Gloria
Glory be to God the Father, God the Son, and God the Holy Spirit. As it was in the beginning, so it is now and so it shall ever be, world without end. Alleluia. *Amen.* ✤

The Lord's Prayer
Our Father, who art in heaven, hallowed be your Name.
May your kingdom come, and your will be done, on earth as in heaven.
Give us today our daily bread.
Forgive us our sins as we forgive those who sin against us.
Lead us not into temptation, but deliver us from evil;
for yours are the kingdom and the power and the glory
forever and ever. *Amen.*

The following major holy days occur in February:
The Feast of the Presentation of Our Lord Jesus Christ in the Temple and/or
The Feast of the Purification of the Blessed Virgin Mary: *February 2*
The Feast of St. Mathias, the Apostle: *February 24*

Prayer for use in the observation of a holy day:
Almighty God, by your Holy Spirit you have made us one with your saints in heaven and on earth: Grant that in my earthly pilgrimage, I may always be supported by this fellowship of love and prayer, and know myself to be surrounded by their witness to your power and mercy. I ask this for the sake of Jesus Christ, in whom all my intercessions are acceptable through the Spirit, and who lives and reigns forever and ever. *Amen.*

✤ *Alleluia* (or *Hallelujah)* is always omitted during Lent.
Likewise, the *Gloria* is omitted during Lent by many Christian communities.

✤ The Office of Midnight is always taken from the prayers for the day nearest to the hour of actual observation. Thus, if the office is to be observed at 10:30 p.m. on Sunday, the prayers will be taken from the Monday offices, and so forth.

FEBRUARY

Sunday, Month of February

The Office of Midnight   Observed on the Hour or Half-Hour
Between 10:30 p.m.✛ and 1:30 a.m.

The Call to Prayer
Come, let us sing to the LORD;* let us shout for joy to the Rock of our salvation.
For the LORD is a great God,* and a great King above all gods.

Psalm 95:1, 3

The Request for Presence
O LORD, let my prayer be set forth in your sight as incense,* the lifting up of my
hands as the evening sacrifice.

Psalm 141:2, adapted

The Greeting
Our Father Who art in Heaven, hallowed be Your name.

The Canticle   *You Are God*
Te Deum laudamus

You are God: we praise you;
You are the Lord; we acclaim you;
You are the eternal Father:
All creation worships you.
To you all angels, all the powers of heaven,
Cherubim and Seraphim, sing in endless praise:
    Holy, holy, holy Lord, God of power and might,
    heaven and earth are full of your glory.
The glorious company of apostles praise you.
The noble fellowship of prophets praise you.
The white-robed army of martyrs praise you.
Throughout the world the holy Church acclaims you;
    Father, of majesty unbounded,
    your true and only Son, worthy of all worship,
    and the Holy Spirit, advocate and guide.
You, Christ, are the king of glory,
the eternal Son of the Father.
When you became man to set us free
you did not shun the Virgin's womb.
You overcame the sting of death
and opened the kingdom of heaven to all believers.
You are seated at God's right hand in glory.

We believe that you will come and be our judge.
   Come then, Lord, and help your people,
   bought with the price of your own blood,
   and bring us with your saints
   to glory everlasting.

The Psalm   The Sparrow Has Found a House

How dear to me is your dwelling, O Lord of hosts!* My soul has a desire and longing
   for the courts of the Lord; my heart and my flesh rejoice in the living God.
The sparrow has found her a house and the swallow a nest where she may lay her
   young;* by the side of your altars, O Lord of hosts, my King and my God.
Happy are they who dwell in your house!* they will always be praising you.
Happy are the people whose strength is in you!* whose hearts are set on the
   pilgrims' way.
Those who go through the desolate valley will find it a place of springs,* for the
   early rains have covered it with pools of water.
They will climb from height to height,* and the God of gods will reveal himself in
   Zion.

Psalm 84:1–6

The Gloria

The Small Verse

And a voice came out of the cloud, saying, "This is my Son, my Chosen; listen to
   him!" And when the voice had spoken, Jesus was alone.

Luke 9:35–36a

The Final Thanksgiving

I will greatly rejoice in the Lord, my soul shall exult in my God; for he has
   clothed me with the garments of salvation, he has covered me with the robe of
   righteousness, as a bridegroom decks himself with a garland, and as a bride
   adorns herself with her jewels.

Isaiah 61:10

The Petition

May the Lord God, father of all mercy, grant us who dwell here a peaceful night
   and a perfect end. *Amen.*

The Office of the Night Watch   Observed on the Hour or Half-Hour
                                          Between 1:30 and 4:30 a.m.

The Call to Prayer

Behold now, bless the Lord, all you servants of the Lord,* you that stand by night
   in the house of the Lord.

41

Lift up your hands in the holy place and bless the LORD;* the LORD who made heaven and earth bless you out of Zion.

Psalm 134

The Request for Presence
O God, come to my assistance.
O Lord, make haste to help me.

The Greeting
As the deer longs for the water-brooks,* so longs my soul for you, O God.
My soul is athirst for God, athirst for the living God;* when shall I come to appear before the presence of God?

Psalm 42:1–2

The Refrain for the Night Watch
Behold now, bless the LORD, all you servants of the LORD,* you that stand by night in the house of the LORD.

Psalm 134:1

The Psalm   *I Will Bow Down toward Your Holy Temple in Awe*
For you are not a God who takes pleasure in wickedness,* and evil cannot dwell with you.
Braggarts cannot stand in your sight;* you hate all those who work wickedness.
You destroy those who speak lies;* the bloodthirsty and deceitful, O LORD, you abhor.
But as for me, through the greatness of your mercy I will go into your house;* I will bow down toward your holy temple in awe of you.

Psalm 5:4–7

The Refrain
Behold now, bless the LORD, all you servants of the LORD,* you that stand by night in the house of the LORD.

A Reading
Nothing is more useful than speaking out freely. Open your heart; we heal our woes by not hugging them. We learn simplicity and yieldedness, for people are only reserved about things which they do not mean to give. Finally, we humble ourselves, for nothing is more humbling than to open one's heart and lay bare all one's weaknesses, yet nothing draws down a greater blessing.

Fenelon, On Openness and Candor

The Refrain
Behold now, bless the LORD, all you servants of the LORD,* you that stand by night in the house of the LORD.

The Litany

O God the Father, Creator of heaven and earth,
>   *Have mercy upon me.*

O God the Son, Redeemer of the world,
>   *Have mercy upon me.*

O God the Holy Spirit, Sanctifier of the faithful,
>   *Have mercy upon me.*

O holy, blessed, and glorious Trinity, one God,
>   *Have mercy upon me.*

Remember not, Lord Christ, my offenses, nor the offenses of my forefathers; neither reward me according to my sins. Spare me, good Lord, spare your people, whom you have redeemed with your most precious blood, and by your mercy preserve us, for ever.
>   *Spare us, good Lord.*

The Thanksgiving

Lord, you now have set your servant free to go in peace as you have promised; for these eyes of mine have seen the Savior whom you have prepared for all the world to see: A Light to enlighten the nations, and the glory of your people Israel. *Amen.*

Nunc Dimittis

The Final Petition

Now guide me waking, O Lord, and guard me sleeping; that awake I may watch with Christ, and asleep, I may rest in peace. *Amen.*

The Office of Dawn   Observed on the Hour or Half-Hour
                                        Between 4:30 and 7:30 a.m.

The Call to Prayer

Let everything that has breath* praise the LORD. Hallelujah!

Psalm 150:6

The Request for Presence

My soul waits for the LORD, more than watchmen for the morning,* more than watchmen for the morning.

Psalm 130:5

The Greeting

Glory be to the Father, and the Son, and the Holy Spirit.
As it was in the beginning, it is now
And ever shall be, world without end. *Amen.*

Gloria Patri

43

The Hymn

O for a thousand tongues to sing
my dear Redeemer's praise,
the glories of my God and King,
the triumphs of his grace!

Jesus! The Name that charms our fears
and bids our sorrows cease;
'tis music to the sinner's ears,
'tis life and health and peace.

Hear him, you deaf; his praise, you dumb,
your loosened tongues employ;
you blind, behold, your Savior comes;
and leap, you lame, for joy!

Glory to God and praise and love
be now and ever given
by saints below and saints above
the Church in earth and heaven.

Charles Wesley

The Psalm   *Let Everything That Has Breath Praise the Lord*

Praise him for his mighty acts;* praise him for his excellent greatness.
Praise him with the blast of the ram's-horn;* praise him with lyre and harp.
Praise him with timbrel and dance;* praise him with strings and pipe.
Praise him with resounding cymbals;* praise him with loud-clanging cymbals.
Let everything that has breath* praise the Lord. Hallelujah!

Psalm 150:2–6

The Gloria in Excelsis

Glory to God in the highest, and on earth peace to people of good will.
    We praise you.
    We bless you.
    We adore you.
    We glorify you.
We give thanks to you for your great glory.

The Small Verse

Jesus taught us, saying: Ask, and it shall be given you; seek, and you will find;
    knock, and it will be opened to you. For everyone who asks, receives, and he
    who seeks, finds, and to him who knocks it will be opened.

Matthew 7:7–8

The Lord's Prayer

The Final Blessing

May the LORD bless us and keep us and cause His face to shine upon us from this day forth and forever more. *Amen.*

࿔

Monday, Month of February

The Office of Midnight

Observed on the Hour or Half-Hour Between 10:30 p.m.✠ and 1:30 a.m.

The Call to Prayer

Let the Name of the LORD be blessed,* from this time forth for evermore.
From the rising of the sun to its going down* let the Name of the LORD be praised.

Psalm 113:2–3

The Request for Presence

O LORD, let my prayer be set forth in your sight as incense,* the lifting up of my hands as the evening sacrifice.

Psalm 141:2, adapted

The Greeting

Our Father, may Your kingdom come on earth as in Heaven.

The Canticle

A Song of Creation—Part Two
Benedicite, omnia opera

Glorify the Lord, all you works of the Lord,*
    praise him and highly exalt him for ever.
In the firmament of his power, glorify the Lord,*
    praise him and highly exalt him for ever.
Let the earth glorify the Lord,*
    praise him and highly exalt him for ever.
Glorify the Lord, O mountains and hills, and all that grows upon the earth,*
    praise him and highly exalt him for ever.
Glorify the Lord, O springs of water, seas, and streams,*
    O whales and all that move in the waters.
All birds of the air, glorify the Lord,*
    praise him and highly exalt him for ever.
Glorify the Lord, O beasts of the wild,*
    and all you flocks and herds.
O men and women everywhere, glorify the Lord,*
    praise him and highly exalt him for ever.

Song of the Three Young Men, 52–61

The Psalm   ***The Lord Comes in Holiness from Sinai***

The Lord gave the word;* great was the company of women who bore the tidings:
"Kings with their armies are fleeing away;* the women at home are dividing the
  spoils."
Though you lingered among the sheepfolds,* you shall be like a dove whose
  wings are covered with silver, whose feathers are like green gold.
When the Almighty scattered kings,* it was like snow falling in Zalmon.
O mighty mountain, O hill of Bashan!* O rugged mountain, O hill of Bashan!
Why do you look with envy, O rugged mountain, at the hill which God chose for
  his resting place?* truly, the LORD will dwell there for ever.
The chariots of God are twenty thousand, even thousands of thousands;* the Lord
  comes in holiness from Sinai.

Psalm 68:11–17

The Gloria

The Small Verse
"Hear and understand: not what goes into the mouth defiles a man, but what
  comes out of the mouth, this defiles a man."

Matthew 15:10b–11

The Final Thanksgiving
I will greatly rejoice in the LORD, my soul shall exult in my God; for he has
  clothed me with the garments of salvation, he has covered me with the robe of
  righteousness, as a bridegroom decks himself with a garland, and as a bride
  adorns herself with her jewels.

Isaiah 61:10

The Petition
May the Lord GOD, father of all mercy, grant us who dwell here a peaceful night
  and a perfect end. *Amen*

The Office of the Night Watch   Observed on the Hour or Half-Hour
                                         Between 1:30 and 4:30 a.m.

The Call to Prayer
Behold now, bless the LORD, all you servants of the LORD,* you that stand by night
  in the house of the LORD.
Lift up your hands in the holy place and bless the LORD;* the LORD who made
  heaven and earth bless you out of Zion.

Psalm 134

The Request for Presence
O God, come to my assistance.
O Lord, make haste to help me.

The Greeting

As the deer longs for the water-brooks,* so longs my soul for you, O God.

My soul is athirst for God, athirst for the living God;* when shall I come to appear before the presence of God?

Psalm 42:1–2

The Refrain for the Night Watch

The LORD has pleasure in those who fear him,* in those who await his gracious favor.

Psalm 147:12

The Psalm   In Truth God Has Heard Me

Come and listen, all you who fear God,* and I will tell you what he has done for me.

I called out to him with my mouth,* and his praise was on my tongue.

If I had found evil in my heart,* the Lord would not have heard me;

But in truth God has heard me;* he has attended to the voice of my prayer.

Blessed be God, who has not rejected my prayer,* nor withheld his love from me.

Psalm 66:14–18

The Refrain

But the LORD has pleasure in those who fear him,* in those who await his gracious favor.

A Reading

Since, then, our life is one which comes to us by faith in the Holy Trinity . . . we are baptized as we were commanded, and we believe as we are baptized, and we hold as we believe, so that with one accord our baptism, our faith, and our ascription of praise are to the Father, and to the Son, and to the Holy Spirit.

St. Gregory, Bishop of Nyssa (ca. 380 CE), Letter to the City of Sebasteia

The Litany

From all evil and wickedness; from sin; from the crafts and assaults of the devil; and from everlasting damnation,

Good Lord, deliver me.

From all blindness of heart; from pride, vainglory, and hypocrisy; from envy, hatred, and malice; and from all want of charity,

Good Lord, deliver me.

From all inordinate and sinful affections; and from all the deceits of the world, the flesh, and the devil,

Good Lord, deliver me.

From all false doctrine, heresy, and schism; from hardness of heart, and contempt of your Word and commandment,

Good Lord, deliver me.

By the mystery of your holy Incarnation; by your holy Nativity and submission to
the Law; by your Baptism, Fasting, and Temptation,
> Good Lord, deliver me.

In all time of tribulation; in all time of prosperity; in the hour of death, and in the
day of judgment,
> Good Lord, deliver me.

The Thanksgiving

Lord, you now have set your servant free to go in peace as you have promised; for
these eyes of mine have seen the Savior whom you have prepared for all the
world to see: A Light to enlighten the nations, and the glory of your people
Israel. *Amen.*

Nunc Dimittis

The Final Petition

Now guide me waking, O Lord, and guard me sleeping; that awake I may watch
with Christ, and asleep, I may rest in peace. *Amen.*

The Office of Dawn   Observed on the Hour or Half-Hour
Between 4:30 and 7:30 a.m.

The Call to Prayer

Hallelujah! How good it is to sing praises to our God!* how pleasant it is to honor
him with praise!

Psalm 147:1

The Request for Presence

My soul waits for the LORD, more than watchmen for the morning,* more than
watchmen for the morning.

Psalm 130:5

The Greeting

Glory be to the Father, and the Son, and the Holy Spirit.
As it was in the beginning, it is now
And ever shall be, world without end. *Amen.*

Gloria Patri

The Hymn

Christ is made the sure foundation,
Christ, the head and cornerstone;
chosen of the Lord and precious,
binding all the church in one;
holy Zion's help forever,
and her confidence alone.

Here vouchsafe to all your saints
what they ask of you to gain;
what they gain from you forever
with the blessed to remain,
and hereafter in your glory
evermore with you to reign.

Laud and honor to the Father,
laud and honor to the Son,
laud and honor to the Spirit,
ever three and ever one;
one in might and one in glory,
while unending ages run.

7th c. Latin, translated by John Mason Neale

The Psalm   *He Gives Snow like Wool*
The LORD sends out his command to the earth,* and his word runs very swiftly.
He gives snow like wool;* he scatters hoarfrost like ashes.
He scatters his hail like bread crumbs;* who can stand against his cold?
He sends forth his word and melts them;* he blows with his wind, and the waters flow.

Psalm 147:16–19

The Gloria in Excelsis
Glory to God in the highest, and on earth peace to people of good will.
   We praise you.
   We bless you.
   We adore you.
   We glorify you.
We give thanks to you for your great glory.

The Small Verse
"What no eye has seen, nor ear heard, nor the heart of man conceived, what God
   has prepared for those who love him" God has revealed to us through the
   Spirit. For the Spirit searches everything, even the depths of God.

1 Corinthians 2:9–10

The Lord's Prayer

The Final Blessing
May the LORD bless us and keep us and cause His face to shine upon us from this
   day forth and forever more. *Amen.*

Tuesday, Month of February

The Office of Midnight   **Observed on the Hour or Half-Hour Between 10:30 p.m.✢ and 1:30 a.m.**

The Call to Prayer
Love the LORD, all you who worship him;* the LORD protects the faithful, but
repays to the full those who act haughtily.

Psalm 31:24

The Request for Presence
O LORD, let my prayer be set forth in your sight as incense,* the lifting up of my
hands as the evening sacrifice.

Psalm 141:2, adapted

The Greeting
Our Father, may Your will be done, on earth as in Heaven.

The Canticle   *The Second Song of Isaiah*
Quaerite Dominum

Seek the Lord while he wills to be found;*
    call upon him when he draws near.
Let the wicked forsake their ways*
    and the evil ones their thoughts;
And let them turn to the Lord, and he will have compassion,*
    and to our God, for he will richly pardon.
For my thoughts are not your thoughts,*
    nor your ways my ways, says the Lord.
For as the heavens are higher than the earth,*
    so are my ways higher than your ways, and my thoughts than your thoughts.
For as rain and snow fall from the heavens*
    and return not again, but water the earth,
Bringing forth life and giving growth,*
    seed for sowing and bread for eating,
So is my word that goes forth from my mouth;*
    it will not return to me empty;
But it will accomplish that which I have purposed,*
    and prosper in that for which I sent it.

Isaiah 55:6–11

The Psalm   *I Will Make Him My Firstborn*
You spoke once in a vision and said to your faithful people:* "I have set the crown
upon a warrior and have exalted one chosen out of the people.

50

I have found David my servant;* with my holy oil have I anointed him.
My hand will hold him fast* and my arm will make him strong.
No enemy shall deceive him,* nor any wicked man bring him down.
I will crush his foes before him* and strike down those who hate him.
My faithfulness and love shall be with him,* and he shall be victorious through
    my Name.
I shall make his dominion extend* from the Great Sea to the River.
He will say to me, 'You are my Father,* my God, and the rock of my salvation.'
I will make him my firstborn* and higher than the kings of the earth.
I will keep my love for him for ever,* and my covenant will stand firm for him.
I will establish his line for ever* and his throne as the days of heaven."

Psalm 89:19–29

The Gloria

The Small Verse

I will sing to my God a new song: O LORD, thou art great and glorious, wonderful
    in strength, invincible. Let all thy creatures serve thee, for thou didst speak,
    and they were made. Thou didst send forth thy Spirit, and it formed them.

Judith 16:13–14a

The Final Thanksgiving

I will greatly rejoice in the LORD, my soul shall exult in my God; for he has
    clothed me with the garments of salvation, he has covered me with the robe of
    righteousness, as a bridegroom decks himself with a garland, and as a bride
    adorns herself with her jewels.

Isaiah 61:10

The Petition

May the Lord GOD, father of all mercy, grant us who dwell here a peaceful night
    and a perfect end. *Amen.*

The Office of the Night Watch   Observed on the Hour or Half-Hour
Between 1:30 and 4:30 a.m.

The Call to Prayer

Behold now, bless the LORD, all you servants of the LORD,* you that stand by night
    in the house of the LORD.
Lift up your hands in the holy place and bless the LORD;* the LORD who made
    heaven and earth bless you out of Zion.

Psalm 134

The Request for Presence

O God, come to my assistance.
O Lord, make haste to help me.

51

The Greeting

Blessed is the LORD!* for he has heard the voice of my prayer.

Psalm 28:7

The Refrain for the Night Watch

Happy are they who have not walked in the counsel of the wicked,* nor lingered
    in the way of sinners, nor sat in the seats of the scornful!
Their delight is in the law of the LORD,* and they meditate on his law day and
    night.

Psalm 1:1–2

The Psalm   *Wait Patiently for the LORD*

Hearken to my voice, O LORD, when I call;* have mercy on me and answer me.
You speak in my heart and say, "Seek my face."* Your face, LORD, will I seek.
Hide not your face from me,* nor turn away your servant in displeasure.
What if I had not believed that I should see the goodness of the LORD* in the land
    of the living!
O tarry and await the LORD's pleasure; be strong, and he shall comfort your heart;*
    wait patiently for the LORD.

Psalm 27:10–12ff

The Refrain

Happy are they who have not walked in the counsel of the wicked,* nor lingered
    in the way of sinners, nor sat in the seats of the scornful!
Their delight is in the law of the LORD,* and they meditate on his law day and
    night.

A Reading

We must know before we can love. In order to know God, we must often think of
    him. When we finally love him, we shall automatically think of him all the
    time, because our heart will be with our treasure.

Brother Lawrence (ca. 1605–91 CE), The Practice of the Presence of God

The Refrain

Happy are they who have not walked in the counsel of the wicked,* nor lingered
    in the way of sinners, nor sat in the seats of the scornful!
Their delight is in the law of the LORD,* and they meditate on his law day and
    night.

The Litany

That it may please you to bless and keep all your people,
    I beseech you to hear me, good Lord.
That it may please you to send laborers into your harvest and to draw all
    humankind into your kingdom,
    I beseech you to hear me, good Lord.

That it may please you to give to all people increase of grace to hear and receive your Word, and to bring forth the fruits of the Spirit,
> *I beseech you to hear me, good Lord.*

That it may please you to bring into the way of truth all such as have erred, and are deceived,
> *I beseech you to hear me, good Lord.*

That it may please you to give me a heart to love and fear you, and diligently to live after your commandments,
> *I beseech you to hear me, good Lord.*

The Thanksgiving

Lord, you now have set your servant free to go in peace as you have promised; for these eyes of mine have seen the Savior whom you have prepared for all the world to see: A Light to enlighten the nations, and the glory of your people Israel. *Amen.*

Nunc Dimittis

The Final Petition

Now guide me waking, O Lord, and guard me sleeping; that awake I may watch with Christ, and asleep, I may rest in peace. *Amen.*

The Office of Dawn   Observed on the Hour or Half-Hour Between 4:30 and 7:30 a.m.

The Call to Prayer

Hallelujah! Sing to the LORD a new song;* sing his praise in the congregation of the faithful.

Psalm 149:1

The Request for Presence

My soul waits for the LORD, more than watchmen for the morning,* more than watchmen for the morning.

Psalm 130:5

The Greeting

Glory be to the Father, and the Son, and the Holy Spirit.
As it was in the beginning, it is now
And ever shall be, world without end. *Amen.*

Gloria Patri

The Hymn

O Master, let me walk with thee
in lowly paths of service free;
tell me your secret, help me bear

53

the strain of toil, the fret of care.
Teach me your patience; still with thee
in closer, dearer company,
in work that keeps faith sweet and strong,
in trust that triumphs over wrong.
In hope that sends a shining ray
far down the future's broadening way.
In peace that only you can give,
with thee, O Master, let me live.

Washington Gladden

The Psalm　　　*Happy Are They Who Have the God of Jacob for Their Help*

Happy are they who have the God of Jacob for their help!* Whose hope is in the
　　Lord their God;
Who made heaven and earth, the seas, and all that is in them;* who keeps his
　　promise for ever;
Who gives justice to those who are oppressed,* and food to those who hunger.
The Lord loves the righteous; the Lord cares for the stranger;* he sustains the
　　orphan and widow, but frustrates the way of the wicked.
The Lord shall reign for ever,* your God, O Zion, throughout all generations.
　　Hallelujah!

Psalm 146:4–6, 8–9

The Gloria in Excelsis

Glory to God in the highest, and on earth peace to people of good will.
　　We praise you.
　　We bless you.
　　We adore you.
　　We glorify you.
We give thanks to you for your great glory.

The Small Verse

To another he said, "Follow me." But he said, "Lord, let me first go and bury my
　　father." But he said to him, "Leave the dead to bury their own dead; but as for
　　you, go and proclaim the kingdom of God."

Luke 9:59–60

The Lord's Prayer

The Final Blessing

May the Lord bless us and keep us and cause His face to shine upon us from this
　　day forth and forever more. *Amen.*

Wednesday, Month of February

The Office of Midnight
Observed on the Hour or Half-Hour Between 10:30 p.m.✠ and 1:30 a.m.

The Call to Prayer
Sing to the LORD and bless his Name;* proclaim the good news of his salvation
   from day to day.
Declare his glory among the nations* and his wonders among all peoples.
For great is the LORD and greatly to be praised;* he is more to be feared than all gods
Psalm 96:2–4

The Request for Presence
O LORD, let my prayer be set forth in your sight as incense,* the lifting up of my
   hands as the evening sacrifice.
Psalm 141:2, adapted

The Greeting
Our Father, give us this day our daily bread.

The Canticle
The Song of the Redeemed
Magna et mirabilia

O ruler of the universe, Lord God, great deeds are they that you have done,*
   surpassing human understanding.
Your ways are ways of righteousness and truth,*
   O King of all the ages.
Who can fail to do you homage, Lord, and sing the praises of your Name?*
   for you only are the Holy One.
All nations will draw near and fall down before you,*
   because your just and holy works have been revealed.
Glory to the Father, and to the Son, and to the Holy Spirit:*
   as it was in the beginning, is now, and will be for ever. *Amen.*
Revelation 15:3–4

The Psalm
You Led Your People Like a Flock

The waters saw you, O God; the waters saw you and trembled;* the very depths
   were shaken.
The clouds poured out water; the skies thundered;* your arrows flashed to and fro;
The sound of your thunder was in the whirlwind; your lightnings lit up the world;*
   the earth trembled and shook.
Your way was in the sea, and your paths in the great waters,* yet your footsteps
   were not seen.
You led your people like a flock* by the hand of Moses and Aaron.
Psalm 77:16–20

The Gloria

The Small Verse
He that shows mercy will lend to his neighbor, and he that strengthens him with
his hand keeps the commandments.

Sirach 29:1

The Final Thanksgiving
I will greatly rejoice in the LORD, my soul shall exult in my God; for he has
clothed me with the garments of salvation, he has covered me with the robe of
righteousness, as a bridegroom decks himself with a garland, and as a bride
adorns herself with her jewels.

Isaiah 61:10

The Petition
May the Lord GOD, father of all mercy, grant us who dwell here a peaceful night
and a perfect end. *Amen.*

The Office of the Night Watch   Observed on the Hour or Half-Hour
Between 1:30 and 4:30 a.m.

The Call to Prayer
Behold now, bless the LORD, all you servants of the LORD,* you that stand by night
in the house of the LORD.
Lift up your hands in the holy place and bless the LORD;* the LORD who made
heaven and earth bless you out of Zion.

Psalm 134

The Request for Presence
O God, come to my assistance.
O Lord, make haste to help me.

The Greeting
You are to be praised, O God, in Zion. . . . To you that hear prayer shall all flesh
come,* because of their transgressions.

Psalm 65:1–2

The Refrain for the Night Watch
Happy are they who have not walked in the counsel of the wicked,* nor lingered
in the way of sinners, nor sat in the seats of the scornful!
Their delight is in the law of the LORD,* and they meditate on his law day and
night.

Psalm 1:1–2

The Psalm
You Are the LORD

In sacrifice and offering you take no pleasure* (you have given me ears to hear you);

Burnt-offering and sin-offering you have not required,* and so I said, "Behold, I come.

In the roll of the book it is written concerning me:* 'I love to do your will, O my God; your law is deep in my heart.'"

I proclaimed righteousness in the great congregation;* behold, I did not restrain my lips; and that, O LORD, you know.

Your righteousness have I not hidden in my heart; I have spoken of your faithfulness and your deliverance;* I have not concealed your love and faithfulness from the great congregation.

You are the LORD; do not withhold your compassion from me;* let your love and your faithfulness keep me safe for ever,

Psalm 40:7–12

The Refrain

Happy are they who have not walked in the counsel of the wicked,* nor lingered in the way of sinners, nor sat in the seats of the scornful!

Their delight is in the law of the LORD,* and they meditate on his law day and night.

A Reading

The law, if you use it aright, sends you to Christ. For since the law's aim is to justify humanity, and since it fails to effect this, it remits us to Him who can do so. Another way, again, of using the law lawfully is when we keep it, but as a thing superfluous. And how is a thing superfluous? As the bridle is properly used, not by the prancing horse that chomps it, but by the horse that wears it only for the sake of appearance; so he uses the law lawfully who governs himself, though not as constrained by the letter of it.

St. John Chrysostom, Bishop of Constantinople (ca. 347–407 CE),
Homily on the Epistle of St. Paul to Timothy

The Refrain

Happy are they who have not walked in the counsel of the wicked,* nor lingered in the way of sinners, nor sat in the seats of the scornful!

Their delight is in the law of the LORD,* and they meditate on his law day and night.

The Litany

O God the Father, Creator of heaven and earth,
Have mercy upon me.

O God the Son, Redeemer of the world,
Have mercy upon me.

57

O God the Holy Spirit, Sanctifier of the faithful,
> *Have mercy upon me.*

O holy, blessed, and glorious Trinity, one God,
> *Have mercy upon me.*

Remember not, Lord Christ, my offenses, nor the offenses of my forefathers; neither reward me according to my sins. Spare me, good Lord, spare your people, whom you have redeemed with your most precious blood, and by your mercy preserve us, for ever.
> *Spare us, good Lord.*

The Thanksgiving

Lord, you now have set your servant free to go in peace as you have promised; for these eyes of mine have seen the Savior whom you have prepared for all the world to see: A Light to enlighten the nations, and the glory of your people Israel. *Amen.*

> *Nunc Dimittis*

The Final Petition

Now guide me waking, O Lord, and guard me sleeping; that awake I may watch with Christ, and asleep, I may rest in peace. *Amen.*

The Office of Dawn   Observed on the Hour or Half-Hour Between 4:30 and 7:30 a.m.

The Call to Prayer

Hallelujah! Praise the LORD, O my soul!* I will praise the LORD as long as I live; I will sing praises to my God while I have my being.

> *Psalm 146:1*

The Request for Presence

My soul waits for the LORD, more than watchmen for the morning,* more than watchmen for the morning.

> *Psalm 130:5*

The Greeting

Glory be to the Father, and the Son, and the Holy Spirit.
As it was in the beginning, it is now
And ever shall be, world without end. *Amen.*

> *Gloria Patri*

The Hymn

Sing them over again to me,
wonderful words of life;
let me more of their beauty see,
wonderful words of life;
words of life and beauty

58

teach me faith and duty.
Beautiful words, wonderful words,
wonderful words of life.
Christ, the blessed one, gives to all
wonderful words of life;
sinner, hear his loving call,
wonderful words of life;
all so freely given,
wooing us to heaven.
Beautiful words, wonderful words,
wonderful words of life.

Philip P. Bliss

The Psalm   *Praise Him, Sun and Moon*

Praise the LORD from the heavens;* praise him in the heights.
Praise him, all you angels of his;* praise him, all his host.
Praise him, sun and moon;* praise him, all you shining stars.
Praise him, heaven of heavens,*and you waters above the heavens.
Let them praise the Name of the LORD;* for he commanded, and they were created.
He made them stand fast for ever and ever;* he gave them a law which shall not
  pass away.

Psalm 148:1b–6

The Gloria in Excelsis

Glory to God in the highest, and on earth peace to people of good will.
 We praise you.
 We bless you.
 We adore you.
 We glorify you.
We give thanks to you for your great glory.

The Small Verse

There is therefore now no condemnation for those who are in Christ Jesus. For the law
 of the Spirit of life in Christ Jesus has set me free from the law of sin and death.

Romans 8:1–2

The Lord's Prayer

The Final Blessing

May the LORD bless us and keep us and cause His face to shine upon us from this
 day forth and forever more. *Amen.*

59

Thursday, Month of February

The Office of Midnight   **Observed on the Hour or Half-Hour**
Between 10:30 p.m.✢ and 1:30 a.m.

The Call to Prayer
Praise the LORD, all you nations;* laud him, all you peoples.
For his loving-kindness toward us is great,* and the faithfulness of the LORD
    endures forever. Hallelujah!

Psalm 117

The Request for Presence
O LORD, let my prayer be set forth in your sight as incense,* the lifting up of my
    hands as the evening sacrifice.

Psalm 141:2, adapted

The Greeting
Our Father, forgive us our sins as we forgive those who have sinned against us.

The Canticle   *Song of Praise*
Benedictus es, Domine

Glory to you, Lord God of our fathers;*
    you are worthy of praise; glory to you.
Glory to you for the radiance of you holy Name;*
    we will praise you and highly exalt you for ever.
Glory to you in the splendor of you temple;*
    on the throne of your majesty, glory to you.
Glory to you, seated between the Cherubim;*
    we will praise you and highly exalt you for ever.
Glory to you, beholding the depths;*
    in the high vault of heaven, glory to you.
Glory to you, Father, Son, and Holy Spirit;*
    we will praise you and highly exalt you for ever.

Song of the Three Young Men, 29–34

The Psalm   *Serve the LORD with Gladness*
Be joyful in the LORD all you lands;* serve the LORD with gladness and come
    before his presence with a song.
Know this: The LORD himself is God;* he himself has made us, and we are his; we
    are his people and the sheep of his pasture.
Enter his gates with thanksgiving; go into his courts with praise;* give thanks to
    him and call upon his Name.
For the LORD is good; his mercy is everlasting;* and his faithfulness endures from
    age to age

Psalm 100:1–4

The Gloria

The Small Verse

For David says concerning him, "I saw the Lord always before me, for he is at my right hand that I may not be shaken; therefore my heart was glad, and my tongue rejoiced; moreover my flesh will dwell in hope."

Acts 2:25–26

The Final Thanksgiving

I will greatly rejoice in the LORD, my soul shall exult in my God; for he has clothed me with the garments of salvation, he has covered me with the robe of righteousness, as a bridegroom decks himself with a garland, and as a bride adorns herself with her jewels.

Isaiah 61:10

The Petition

May the Lord GOD, father of all mercy, grant us who dwell here a peaceful night and a perfect end. *Amen.*

The Office of the Night Watch   Observed on the Hour or Half-Hour Between 1:30 and 4:30 a.m.

The Call to Prayer

Behold now, bless the LORD, all you servants of the LORD,* you that stand by night in the house of the LORD.

Lift up your hands in the holy place and bless the LORD;* the LORD who made heaven and earth bless you out of Zion.

Psalm 134

The Request for Presence

O God, come to my assistance.

O Lord, make haste to help me.

The Greeting

I will offer you the sacrifice of thanksgiving* and call upon the Name of the LORD.

Psalm 116:15

The Refrain for the Night Watch

The heavens declare the glory of God,* and the firmament shows his handiwork.

One day tells its tale to another,* and one night imparts knowledge to another.

Psalm 19:1–2

The Psalm   *You Brought Us Out into a Place of Refreshment*

You brought us into the snare;* you laid heavy burdens upon our backs.

You let enemies ride over our heads; we went through fire and water;* but you brought us out into a place of refreshment.

61

I will enter your house with burnt-offerings and will pay you my vows,* which I
   promised with my lips and spoke with my mouth when I was in trouble.
                                                                    Psalm 66:10–12

The Refrain
The heavens declare the glory of God,* and the firmament shows his handiwork.
One day tells its tale to another,* and one night imparts knowledge to another.

A Reading
The great saints and ancient prophets frequently experienced the alternation of up
   and down, joy and sorrow. . . . If the great saints are exposed to such variations,
   we who are poor and weak should not be discouraged if our spiritual life fails
   to be uniformly ecstatic. The Holy Spirit gives and takes according to his own
   divine purpose. I have never met anyone so religious and devout that he has not
   felt occasionally some withdrawing of grace.
                          Thomas à Kempis (ca. 1421 CE), The Imitation of Christ

The Refrain
The heavens declare the glory of God,* and the firmament shows his handiwork.
One day tells its tale to another,* and one night imparts knowledge to another.

The Litany
For the peace from above, for the loving-kindness of God, and for the salvation of
   my soul, I pray to the Lord.
      Lord, have mercy.
For the peace of the world, for the welfare of the Holy Church of God, and for the
   unity of all peoples, I pray to the Lord.
      Lord, have mercy.
For the leaders of the nations and for all in authority, I pray to the Lord.
      Lord, have mercy.
For the aged and infirm, for the widowed and orphans, and for the sick and the
   suffering, I pray to the Lord.
      Lord, have mercy.
For the poor and the oppressed, for the unemployed and the destitute, for prisoners
   and captives, and for all who remember and care for them, I pray to the Lord.
      Lord, have mercy.
For all who have died in the hope of the resurrection, and for all the departed, I
   pray to the Lord.
      Lord, have mercy.

The Thanksgiving
Lord, you now have set your servant free to go in peace as you have promised; for
   these eyes of mine have seen the Savior whom you have prepared for all the

world to see: A Light to enlighten the nations, and the glory of your people
Israel. *Amen.*

Nunc Dimittis

The Final Petition
Now guide me waking, O Lord, and guard me sleeping; that awake I may watch
with Christ, and asleep, I may rest in peace. *Amen.*

The Office of Dawn   **Observed on the Hour or Half-Hour
Between 4:30 and 7:30 a.m.**

The Call to Prayer
Hallelujah! How good it is to sing praises to our God!* how pleasant it is to honor
him with praise!

Psalm 147:1

The Request for Presence
My soul waits for the LORD, more than watchmen for the morning,* more than
watchmen for the morning.

Psalm 130:5

The Greeting
Glory be to the Father, and the Son, and the Holy Spirit.
As it was in the beginning, it is now
And ever shall be, world without end. *Amen.*

Gloria Patri

The Hymn
Immortal, invisible, God only wise,
in light inaccessible hid from our eyes,
most blessed, most glorious, Ancient of Days,
almighty, victorious, your great name we praise.
Unresting, unhasting, and silent as light,
not wanting, not wasting, you rule us in might;
your justice like mountains high soaring above
your clouds which are fountains of goodness and love.
To all, our life you have given, both great and small;
in all life you are living, the true life of all;
we blossom and flourish as leaves on the tree,
and wither and perish, but naught changes thee.

Walter Chalmers Smith

The Psalm   ***He Covers the Heavens with Clouds***

He covers the heavens with clouds* and prepares rain for the earth;

He makes grass to grow upon the mountains* and green plants to serve mankind.

He provides food for flocks and herds* and for the young ravens when they cry.

He is not impressed by the might of a horse;* he has no pleasure in the strength of
a man;

But the LORD has pleasure in those who fear him,* in those who await his gracious
favor.

Psalm 147:8–12

The Gloria in Excelsis

Glory to God in the highest, and on earth peace to people of good will.

> We praise you.
> We bless you.
> We adore you.
> We glorify you.

We give thanks to you for your great glory.

The Small Verse

Thus says the LORD: "Heaven is my throne and the earth is my footstool . . . All
these things my hand has made, and so all these things are mine," says the LORD.
But this is the man to whom I will look, he that is humble and contrite in spirit
and trembles at my word."

Isaiah 66:1–2

The Lord's Prayer

The Final Blessing

May the Lord bless us and keep us and cause His face to shine upon us from this
day forth and forever more. *Amen.*

᪥

Friday, Month of February

The Office of Midnight   **Observed on the Hour or Half-Hour**
Between 10:30 p.m.✝ and 1:30 a.m.

The Call to Prayer

We give you thanks, O God, we give you thanks,* calling upon your Name and
declaring all your wonderful deeds.

Psalm 75:1

The Request for Presence

O LORD, let my prayer be set forth in your sight as incense,* the lifting up of my
hands as the evening sacrifice.

Psalm 141:2, adapted

The Greeting

Our Father, lead us not into temptation, but deliver us from evil.

The Canticle
A Song of Penitence
Kyrie Pantokrator

O Lord and Ruler of the hosts of heaven,*
God of Abraham, Isaac, and Jacob, and of all their righteous offspring:
You made the heavens and the earth,*
with all their vast array.
All things quake with fear at your presence;*
they tremble because of your power.
But your merciful promise is beyond all measure;*
it surpasses all that our minds can fathom.
O Lord, you are full of compassion,*
long-suffering, and abounding in mercy.
You hold back your hand;*
you do not punish as we deserve.
In your great goodness, Lord, you have promised forgiveness to sinners,*
that they may repent of their sin and be saved.

Prayer of Manasseh 1–2, 4, 6–7

The Psalm
Bless the LORD, O My Soul

Bless the LORD, O my soul,* and all that is within me, bless his holy Name.
Bless the LORD, O my soul,* and forget not all his benefits.
He forgives all your sins* and heals all your infirmities;
He redeems your life from the grave* and crowns you with mercy and loving-
kindness;
He satisfies you with good things,* and your youth is renewed like an eagle's.
The LORD executes righteousness* and judgment for all who are oppressed.
He made his ways known to Moses* and his works to the children of Israel.
The LORD is full of compassion and mercy,* slow to anger and of great kindness.
He will not always accuse us,* nor will he keep his anger for ever.
He has not dealt with us according to our sins,* nor rewarded us according to our
wickedness.
For as the heavens are high above the earth,* so is his mercy great upon those who
fear him.
As far as the east is from the west,* so far has he removed our sins from us.

Psalm 103:1–12

The Gloria

65

The Small Verse
The word is near you, on your lips and in your heart (that is, the word of faith
which we preach).

Romans 10:8

The Final Thanksgiving
I will greatly rejoice in the LORD, my soul shall exult in my God; for he has
clothed me with the garments of salvation, he has covered me with the robe of
righteousness, as a bridegroom decks himself with a garland, and as a bride
adorns herself with her jewels.

Isaiah 61:10

The Petition
May the Lord GOD, father of all mercy, grant us who dwell here a peaceful night
and a perfect end. *Amen*

The Office of the Night Watch   Observed on the Hour or Half-Hour
Between 1:30 and 4:30 a.m.

The Call to Prayer
Behold now, bless the LORD, all you servants of the LORD,* you that stand by night
in the house of the LORD.
Lift up your hands in the holy place and bless the LORD;* the LORD who made
heaven and earth bless you out of Zion.

Psalm 134

The Request for Presence
O God, come to my assistance.
O Lord, make haste to help me.

The Greeting
Your statutes have been like songs to me* wherever I have lived as a stranger.
I remember your Name in the night, O LORD,* and dwell upon your law.
This is how it has been with me,* because I have kept your commandments.

Psalm 119:54–56

The Refrain for the Night Watch
The LORD grants his loving-kindness in the daytime;* in the night season his song
is with me, a prayer to the God of my life.

Psalm 42:10

The Psalm   *You, O LORD, Are Gracious and Full of Compassion*
I will thank you, O LORD my God, with all my heart,* and glorify your Name for
evermore.

For great is your love toward me;* you have delivered me from the nethermost Pit.
The arrogant rise up against me, O God, and a band of violent men seeks my life;*
  they have not set you before their eyes.
But you, O LORD, are gracious and full of compassion,* slow to anger, and full of
  kindness and truth.
Turn to me and have mercy upon me;* give your strength to your servant; and save
  the child of your handmaid.

Psalm 86:12–16

The Refrain

The LORD grants his loving-kindness in the daytime;* in the night season his song
  is with me, a prayer to the God of my life.

A Reading

For let us either stand in awe of the wrath to come, or show regard for the grace
  which is at present displayed—one of these two things. Only let us in one or
  another be found in Christ Jesus unto the true life.

St. Ignatius, Bishop of Antioch (ca. 35–107 CE), The Epistles, XI

The Refrain

The LORD grants his loving-kindness in the daytime;* in the night season his song
  is with me, a prayer to the God of my life.

The Litany

Father, I pray for your holy catholic Church;
  That we all may be one.
Grant that every member of the Church may truly and humbly serve you;
  That your Name may be glorified by all people.
I pray for all who govern and hold authority in the nations of the world;
  That there may be justice and peace on the earth.
Have compassion on those who suffer from any grief or trouble;
  That they may be delivered from their distress.
Give to the departed eternal rest.
  Let light perpetual shine upon them.
I praise you for your saints who have entered into joy;
  May I also come to share in your heavenly kingdom.

The Thanksgiving

Lord, you now have set your servant free to go in peace as you have promised; for
  these eyes of mine have seen the Savior whom you have prepared for all the
  world to see: A Light to enlighten the nations, and the glory of your people
  Israel. *Amen.*

Nunc Dimittis

The Final Petition

Now guide me waking, O Lord, and guard me sleeping; that awake I may watch with Christ, and asleep, I may rest in peace. *Amen.*

The Office of Dawn

Observed on the Hour or Half-Hour Between 4:30 and 7:30 a.m.

The Call to Prayer

Worship the LORD, O Jerusalem;* praise your God, O Zion;
For he has strengthened the bars of your gates.

Psalm 147:13–14a

The Request for Presence

My soul waits for the LORD, more than watchmen for the morning,* more than watchmen for the morning.

Psalm 130:5

The Greeting

Glory be to the Father, and the Son, and the Holy Spirit.
As it was in the beginning, it is now
And ever shall be, world without end. *Amen.*

Gloria Patri

The Hymn

Spirit of God, descend upon my heart,
wean it from earth, through all its pulses move;
stoop to my weakness, mighty as Thou art,
and make me love you as I ought to love.
I ask no dream, no prophet ecstasies,
no sudden rending of the veil of clay.
No angel visitant, no opening skies:
but take the dimness of my soul ~~above.~~ *a w a y.*
Teach me to love you as your angels love,
one holy passion filling all my frame;
the baptism of the heaven-descended dove
my heart an altar, and your love the flame.

George Croly

The Psalm   The LORD Takes Pleasure in His People

Let Israel rejoice in his Maker;* let the children of Zion be joyful in their King.
Let them praise his Name in the dance;* let them sing praise to him with timbrel and harp.
For the LORD takes pleasure in his people* and adorns the poor with victory.
Let the faithful rejoice in triumph;* let them be joyful on their beds.

Psalm 149:2–5

68

The Gloria in Excelsis

Glory to God in the highest, and on earth peace to people of good will.
> We praise you.
> We bless you.
> We adore you.
> We glorify you.
We give thanks to you for your great glory.

The Small Verse

May the God of steadfastness and encouragement grant you to live in such
> harmony with one another, in accord with Jesus Christ, that together with one
> accord you may with one voice glorify the God and Father of our Lord Jesus
> Christ.

Romans 15:5–6

The Lord's Prayer

The Final Blessing

May the LORD bless us and keep us and cause His face to shine upon us from this
> day forth and forever more. *Amen.*

⇛

Saturday, Month of February

The Office of Midnight   **Observed on the Hour or Half-Hour
Between 10:30 p.m.✧ and 1:30 a.m.**

The Call to Prayer

I will cry aloud to God;* I will cry aloud, and he will hear me.

Psalm 77:1

The Request for Presence

O LORD, let my prayer be set forth in your sight as incense,* the lifting up of my
> hands as the evening sacrifice.

Psalm 141:2, adapted

The Greeting

Our Father, Yours are the kingdom, the power, and the glory forever.

The Canticle   **The First Song of Isaiah**
Ecce, Deus

Surely, it is God who saves me;*
  I will trust in him and not be afraid.
For the Lord is my stronghold and my sure defense,*
  and he will be my Savior.
Therefore you shall draw water with rejoicing*
  from the springs of salvation.
And on that day you shall say,*
  Give thanks to the Lord and call upon his Name;
Make his deeds known among the peoples;*
  see that they remember that his Name is exalted.
Sing praises of the Lord, for he has done great things,*
  and this is known in all the world.
Cry aloud, inhabitants of Zion, ring out your joy,*
  for the great one in the midst of you is the Holy One of Israel.

Isaiah 12:2–6

The Psalm   **Put Your Trust in the LORD**

Do not fret yourself because of evildoers;* do not be jealous of those who do
  wrong.
For they shall soon wither like the grass,* and like the green grass fade away.
Put your trust in the LORD and do good;* dwell in the land and feed on its riches.
Take delight in the LORD,* and he shall give you your heart's desire.
Commit your way to the LORD and put your trust in him,* and he will bring it to
  pass.
He will make your righteousness as clear as the light* and your just dealing as the
  noonday.
Be still before the LORD* and wait patiently for him.

Psalm 37:1–7

The Gloria

The Small Verse

How beautiful upon the mountains are the feet of him who brings good tidings,
  who publishes peace, who brings good tidings, who publishes salvation, who
  says to Zion, "Your God reigns."

Isaiah 52:7

The Final Thanksgiving

I will greatly rejoice in the LORD, my soul shall exult in my God; for he has
  clothed me with the garments of salvation, he has covered me with the robe of
  righteousness, as a bridegroom decks himself with a garland, and as a bride
  adorns herself with her jewels.

Isaiah 61:10

70

The Petition

May the Lord GOD, father of all mercy, grant us who dwell here a peaceful night
  and a perfect end. *Amen.*

The Office of the Night Watch　　　　Observed on the Hour or Half-Hour
Between 1:30 and 4:30 a.m.

The Call to Prayer

Behold now, bless the LORD, all you servants of the LORD,* you that stand by night
  in the house of the LORD.
Lift up your hands in the holy place and bless the LORD;* the LORD who made
  heaven and earth bless you out of Zion.

Psalm 134

The Request for Presence

O God, come to my assistance.
O Lord, make haste to help me.

The Greeting

To you I lift up my eyes,* to you enthroned in the heavens.

Psalm 123:1–3

The Refrain for the Night Watch

Yours is the day, yours also the night;* you established the moon and the sun.

Psalm 74:15

The Psalm　　　　　　　*My Mouth Will Proclaim Your Faithfulness*

Your love, O LORD, for ever will I sing;* from age to age my mouth will proclaim
  your faithfulness.
For I am persuaded that your love is established for ever;* you have set your
  faithfulness firmly in the heavens.
"I have made a covenant with my chosen one;* I have sworn an oath to David my
  servant:
'I will establish your line for ever,* and preserve your throne for all generations.'"
The heavens bear witness to your wonders, O LORD,* and to your faithfulness in
  the assembly of the holy ones;
For who in the skies can be compared to the LORD?* who is like the LORD among
  the gods?
God is much to be feared in the council of the holy ones,* great and terrible to all
  those round about him.
Who is like you, LORD God of hosts?* O mighty LORD, your faithfulness is all
  around you.

Psalm 89:1–8

71

The Refrain
Yours is the day, yours also the night;* you established the moon and the sun.

A Reading
Don't blame God for evil. It would make more sense to blame the sun for
darkness.

William Law (18th c.), Mystical Writings

The Refrain
Yours is the day, yours also the night;* you established the moon and the sun.

The Litany
Grant, Almighty God, that all who confess your Name may be united in your truth,
live together in your love, and reveal your glory in the world.
Lord, in your mercy, hear my prayer.
Guide the people of this land, and of all the nations, in the ways of justice and
peace; that we may honor one another and serve the common good.
Lord, in your mercy, hear my prayer.
Give us all a reverence for the earth as your own creation, that we may use its
resources rightly in the service of others and to your honor and glory.
Lord, in your mercy, hear my prayer.
Bless all whose lives are closely linked with mine, and grant that I may serve
Christ in them, and love even as he loves me.
Lord, in your mercy, hear my prayer.
Comfort and heal all those who suffer in body, mind, or spirit; give them courage
and hope in their troubles, and bring them the joy of your salvation.
Lord, in your mercy, hear my prayer.
I commend to your mercy all who have died, that your will for them may be
fulfilled; and I pray that I may share with all your saints in your eternal
kingdom.
Lord, in your mercy, hear my prayer.

The Thanksgiving
Lord, you now have set your servant free to go in peace as you have promised; for
these eyes of mine have seen the Savior whom you have prepared for all the
world to see: A Light to enlighten the nations, and the glory of your people
Israel.

Nunc Dimittis

The Final Petition
Behold now, bless the Lord, all you servants of the Lord,* you that stand by night
in the house of the Lord.
Lift up your hands in the holy place and bless the Lord;* the Lord who made
heaven and earth bless you out of Zion.

Psalm 134

The Office of Dawn   **Observed on the Hour or Half-Hour**
                                                Between 4:30 and 7:30 a.m.

The Call to Prayer
Sing to the LORD with thanksgiving;* make music to our God upon the harp.

Psalm 147:7

The Request for Presence
My soul waits for the LORD, more than watchmen for the morning,* more than
    watchmen for the morning.

Psalm 130:5

The Greeting
Glory be to the Father, and the Son, and the Holy Spirit.
As it was in the beginning, it is now
And ever shall be, world without end. *Amen.*

Gloria Patri

The Hymn
Forward through the ages,
in unbroken line,
move the faithful spirits
at the call divine;
gifts in differing measures,
hearts of one accord,
manifold in service,
one the sure reward.
Wider grows the kingdom,
reign of love and light;
for it we must labor,
until our faith is sight.
Prophets have proclaimed it,
martyrs testified,
poets sung its glory,
heroes for it died.
Not alone we conquer,
not alone we fall;
in each loss or triumph
lose or triumph all.
Bound by God's far purpose
in one living whole,
move we on together
to the shining goal.

Frederick Lucian Hosmer

The Psalm   *Old and Young Together Praise the Name of the LORD*
Praise the LORD from the earth,* you sea-monsters and all deeps;
Fire and hail, snow and fog,* tempestuous wind, doing his will;
Mountains and all hills,* fruit trees and all cedars;
Wild beasts and all cattle,* creeping things and winged birds;
Kings of the earth and all peoples,* princes and all rulers of the world;
Young men and maidens,* old and young together.
Let them praise the Name of the LORD.

Psalm 148:7–13a

The Gloria in Excelsis
Glory to God in the highest, and on earth peace to people of good will.
    We praise you.
    We bless you.
    We adore you.
    We glorify you.
We give thanks to you for your great glory.

The Small Verse
You shall eat in plenty and be satisfied, and praise the name of the LORD your God,
    who has dealt wondrously with you. And my people shall never again be put to
    shame. You shall know that I am in the midst of Israel, and that I, the LORD, am
    your God and there is none else. And people shall never again be put to shame.

Joel 2:26–27

The Lord's Prayer

The Final Blessing
May the LORD bless us and keep us and cause His face to shine upon us from this
    day forth and forever more. *Amen.*

The Gloria
Glory be to God the Father, God the Son, and God the Holy Spirit. As it was in the beginning, so it is now and so it shall ever be, world without end. Alleluia. *Amen.* ✤

The Lord's Prayer
Our Father, who art in heaven, hallowed be your Name.
May your kingdom come, and your will be done, on earth as in heaven.
Give us today our daily bread.
Forgive us our sins as we forgive those who sin against us.
Lead us not into temptation, but deliver us from evil;
for yours are the kingdom and the power and the glory
forever and ever. *Amen.*

The following major holy days occur in March:
The Feast of St. Joseph: *March 19*
The Feast of the Annunciation of Our Lord Jesus Christ to the Blessed Virgin Mary: *March 25*

Prayer for use in the observation of a holy day:
Almighty God, by your Holy Spirit you have made us one with your saints in heaven and on earth: Grant that in my earthly pilgrimage, I may always be supported by this fellowship of love and prayer, and know myself to be surrounded by their witness to your power and mercy. I ask this for the sake of Jesus Christ, in whom all my intercessions are acceptable through the Spirit, and who lives and reigns forever and ever. *Amen.*

✤ *Alleluia* (or *Hallelujah)* is always omitted during Lent.
Likewise, the *Gloria* is omitted during Lent by many Christian communities.

✤ The Office of Midnight is always taken from the prayers for the day nearest to the hour of actual observation. Thus, if the office is to be observed at 10:30 p.m. on Sunday, the prayers will be taken from the Monday offices, and so forth.

MARCH

Sunday, Month of March

The Office of Midnight   **Observed on the Hour or Half-Hour Between 10:30 p.m.✢ and 1:30 a.m.**

The Call to Prayer
He is our God, the God of our salvation;* God is the LORD, by whom we escape death.

Psalm 68:19

The Request for Presence
O LORD, let my prayer be set forth in your sight as incense,* the lifting up of my hands as the evening sacrifice.

Psalm 141:2, adapted

The Greeting
Our Father Who art in Heaven, hallowed be Your name.

The Canticle   *The Song of Zechariah*
Benedictus Dominus Deus

Blessed be the Lord, the God of Israel;*
    he has come to his people and set them free.
He has raised up for us a mighty savior,*
    born of the house of his servant David.
Through his holy prophets he promised of old, that he would save us from our enemies,*
    from the hands of all who hate us.
He promised to show mercy to our fathers*
    and to remember his holy covenant.
This was the oath he swore to our father Abraham,*
    to set us free from the hands of our enemies,
Free to worship him without fear,*
    holy and righteous in his sight all the days of our life.

Luke 1:68–75

The Psalm   *The LORD Has Ordained the Blessing*
Oh, how good and pleasant it is,* when brethren live together in unity!
It is like fine oil upon the head* that runs down upon the beard,
Upon the beard of Aaron,* and runs down upon the collar of his robe.
It is like the dew of Hermon* that falls upon the hills of Zion.
For there the LORD has ordained the blessing:* life for evermore.

Psalm 133:1–5

The Gloria

The Small Verse
He will guard the feet of his faithful ones; but the wicked shall be cut off in
darkness; for not by might shall a man prevail.

1 Samuel 2:9

The Final Thanksgiving
I will greatly rejoice in the LORD, my soul shall exult in my God; for he has
clothed me with the garments of salvation, he has covered me with the robe of
righteousness, as a bridegroom decks himself with a garland, and as a bride
adorns herself with her jewels.

Isaiah 61:10

The Petition
May the Lord GOD, father of all mercy, grant us who dwell here a peaceful night
and a perfect end. *Amen.*

The Office of the Night Watch   Observed on the Hour or Half-Hour Between 1:30 and 4:30 a.m.

The Call to Prayer
Behold now, bless the LORD, all you servants of the LORD,* you that stand by night
in the house of the LORD.
Lift up your hands in the holy place and bless the LORD;* the LORD who made
heaven and earth bless you out of Zion.

Psalm 134

The Request for Presence
O God, come to my assistance.
O Lord, make haste to help me.

The Greeting
Blessed are you, O LORD;* instruct me in your statutes.

Psalm 119:12

The Refrain for the Night Watch
I commune with my heart in the night;* I ponder and search my mind.

Psalm 77:6

The Psalm   *Give Thanks to the LORD*
Hallelujah! Give thanks to the LORD, for he is good,* for his mercy endures for
ever.

Who can declare the mighty acts of the Lord* or show forth all his praise?
Happy are those who act with justice* and always do what is right!
Remember me, O Lord, with the favor you have for your people,* and visit me
    with your saving help;
That I may see the prosperity of your elect and be glad with the gladness of your
    people,* that I may glory with your inheritance.

Psalm 106:1–5

The Refrain
I commune with my heart in the night;* I ponder and search my mind.

A Reading
Greater benefits have we obtained through the ineffable grace of Christ than we
    have lost through the malice of Satan. Those whom the raging foe had thrust
    from their first peaceful dwelling, the Son of God has united to Himself and
    has placed them at the right hand of the Father, with whom He lives and reigns
    in unity with the Holy Spirit through endless ages. *Amen.*

Pope St. Leo I (d. 461 ce), Homily

The Refrain
I commune with my heart in the night;* I ponder and search my mind.

The Litany
For the holy Church of God, that it may be filled with truth and love, and be found
    without fault at the day of your coming, I pray to you, O Lord.
        Lord, in your mercy, hear my prayer.
For all who fear God and believe in you, Lord Christ, that our divisions may cease,
    and that all may be one as you and the Father are one, I pray to you, O Lord.
        Lord, in your mercy, hear my prayer.
For those who do not yet believe, and for those who have lost their faith, that they
    may receive the light of the Gospel, I pray to you, O Lord.
        Lord, in your mercy, hear my prayer.
For my enemies and those who wish me harm, and for all whom I have injured or
    offended, I pray to you, O Lord.
        Lord, in your mercy, hear my prayer.
For all who have commended themselves to my prayers; for my family, friends,
    and neighbors; that being freed from anxiety, they may live in joy, peace, and
    health, I pray to you, O Lord.
        Lord, in your mercy, hear my prayer.
For myself; for the forgiveness of my sins, and for the grace of the Holy Spirit to
    amend my life, I pray to you, O Lord.
        Lord, in your mercy, hear my prayer.

The Thanksgiving

Lord, you now have set your servant free to go in peace as you have promised; for
these eyes of mine have seen the Savior whom you have prepared for all the
world to see: A Light to enlighten the nations, and the glory of your people
Israel. *Amen.*

Nunc Dimittis

The Final Petition

Now guide me waking, O Lord, and guard me sleeping; that awake I may watch
with Christ, and asleep, I may rest in peace. *Amen.*

The Office of Dawn   Observed on the Hour or Half-Hour Between 4:30 and 7:30 a.m.

The Call to Prayer

Let everything that has breath* praise the LORD. Hallelujah!

Psalm 150:6

The Request for Presence

My soul waits for the LORD, more than watchmen for the morning,* more than
watchmen for the morning.

Psalm 130:5

The Greeting

Glory be to the Father, and the Son, and the Holy Spirit.
As it was in the beginning, it is now
And ever shall be, world without end. *Amen.*

Gloria Patri

The Hymn

Take time to be holy, speak oft with your Lord;
Abide in Him always, and feed on His word.
Make friends of God's children, help those who are weak,
Forgetting in nothing His blessing to seek.
Take time to be holy, the world rushes on;
Spend much time in secret, with Jesus alone.
By looking to Jesus, like Him we shall be;
Your friends in your conduct His likeness will see.
Take time to be holy, be calm in your soul,
Each thought and each motive beneath His control.
Thus led by His Spirit to fountains of love,
We soon will be fitted for service above.

William Longstaff

81

The Psalm   ***The LORD Shall Reign for Ever***

Happy are they who have the God of Jacob for their help!* whose hope is in the
   LORD their God;
Who made heaven and earth, the seas, and all that is in them;* who keeps his
   promise for ever;
Who gives justice to those who are oppressed,* and food to those who hunger.
The LORD loves the righteous; the LORD cares for the stranger;* he sustains the
   orphan and widow, but frustrates the way of the wicked.
The LORD shall reign for ever,* your God, O Zion, throughout all generations.
   Hallelujah!

Psalm 146:4–6, 8–9

The Gloria in Excelsis

Glory to God in the highest, and on earth peace to people of good will.
   We praise you.
   We bless you.
   We adore you.
   We glorify you.
We give thanks to you for your great glory.

The Small Verse

And the LORD said to Moses, "Say to all the congregation of the people of Israel,
   You shall be holy; for I, the LORD your God, am holy."

Leviticus 19:1

The Lord's Prayer

The Final Blessing

May the LORD bless us and keep us and cause His face to shine upon us from this
   day forth and forever more. *Amen.*

Monday, Month of March

The Office of Midnight   **Observed on the Hour or Half-Hour
                                            Between 10:30 p.m.✛ and 1:30 a.m.**

The Call to Prayer

To you, O LORD, I lift up my soul; my God, I put my trust in you;* let me not be
   humiliated, nor let my enemies triumph over me.

Psalm 25:1

The Request for Presence

O LORD, let my prayer be set forth in your sight as incense,* the lifting up of my
hands as the evening sacrifice.

Psalm 141:2, adapted

The Greeting

Our Father, may Your kingdom come on earth as in Heaven.

The Canticle

A Song of Creation—Part Three
Benedicite, omnia opera Domini

Glorify the Lord, all you works of the Lord,*
praise him and highly exalt him for ever.
In the firmament of his power, glorify the Lord,*
praise him and highly exalt him for ever.
Let the people of God glorify the Lord,*
praise him and highly exalt him for ever.
Glorify the Lord, O priests and servants of the Lord,*
praise him and highly exalt him for ever.
Glorify the Lord, O spirits and souls of the righteous,*
praise him and highly exalt him for ever.
You that are holy and humble of heart, glorify the Lord,*
praise him and highly exalt him for ever.
Let us glorify the Lord: Father, Son, and Holy Spirit;*
praise him and highly exalt him for ever.
In the firmament of his power, glorify the Lord,*
praise him and highly exalt him for ever.

Song of the Three Young Men, 62–68

The Psalm

My Heart Is Firmly Fixed

My heart is firmly fixed, O God, my heart is fixed;* I will sing and make melody.
Wake up, my spirit; awake, lute and harp;* I myself will waken the dawn.
I will confess you among the peoples, O LORD;* I will sing praises to you among
the nations.
For your loving-kindness is greater than the heavens,* and your faithfulness
reaches to the clouds.
Exalt yourself above the heavens, O God,* and your glory over all the earth.
So that those who are dear to you may be delivered,* save with your right hand
and answer me.

Psalm 108:1–6

The Gloria

The Small Verse

"See now that I, even I, am he, and there is no god beside me; I kill and I make
alive; I wound and I heal; and there is none that can deliver out of my hand."

Deuteronomy 32:39

The Final Thanksgiving

I will greatly rejoice in the LORD, my soul shall exult in my God; for he has
clothed me with the garments of salvation, he has covered me with the robe of
righteousness, as a bridegroom decks himself with a garland, and as a bride
adorns herself with her jewels.

Isaiah 61:10

The Office of the Night Watch   Observed on the Hour or Half-Hour
Between 1:30 and 4:30 a.m.

The Call to Prayer

Behold now, bless the LORD, all you servants of the LORD,* you that stand by night
in the house of the LORD.
Lift up your hands in the holy place and bless the LORD;* the LORD who made
heaven and earth bless you out of Zion.

Psalm 134

The Request for Presence

O God, come to my assistance.
O Lord, make haste to help me.

The Greeting

Hosannah, LORD, hosannah!* LORD, send us now success.

Psalm 118:25

The Refrain for the Night Watch

You shall not be afraid of any terror by night,* nor of the arrow that flies by day;

Psalm 91:5

The Psalm   *Your Love, O LORD, Upheld Me*

If the LORD had not come to my help,* I should soon have dwelt in the land of
silence.
As often as I said, "My foot has slipped,"* your love, O LORD, upheld me.
When many cares fill my mind,* your consolations cheer my soul.

Psalm 94:17–19

The Refrain

You shall not be afraid of any terror by night,* nor of the arrow that flies by day;

A Reading

In what way did He come but this, "The Word was made flesh and dwelt among
us"? Now when we speak, in order that what we have in our mind may enter
through the ear into the mind of a hearer, the word which we have in our hearts

becomes an outward sound and is called speech; and yet our thought does not lose itself in the sound, but remains complete in itself, taking the form of speech without being modified in its own nature by the change. In just this way, the Divine Word, though suffering no change of nature, yet became flesh, that He might dwell among us.

St. Augustine (ca. 410 CE), Concerning a General View of
the Subjects Treated in Holy Scripture, bk I, chap. 13

The Refrain
You shall not be afraid of any terror by night,* nor of the arrow that flies by day;

The Litany
For the peace of the world, that a spirit of respect and forbearance may grow among nations and peoples, I pray to you, O Lord.
> *Lord, hear my prayer.*

For those in positions of public trust, that they may serve justice, and promote the dignity and freedom of every person, I pray to you, O Lord.
> *Lord, hear my prayer.*

For the poor, the persecuted, the sick, and all who suffer; for refugees, prisoners, and all who are in danger; that they may be relieved and protected, I pray to you, O Lord.
> *Lord, hear my prayer.*

For the forgiveness of my sins, and for the grace of the Holy Spirit to amend my life, I pray to you, O Lord.
> *Lord, hear my prayer.*

For all who have died in the communion of your Church, and those whose faith is known to you alone, that, with all the saints, they may have rest in that place where there is no pain or grief, but life eternal, I pray to you, O Lord.
> *Lord, hear my prayer.*

Rejoicing in the fellowship of the ever-blessed Virgin Mary and all the saints, I commend my self and all your faithful to Christ our God.
> *To you, O Lord our God.*

The Thanksgiving
Lord, you now have set your servant free to go in peace as you have promised; for these eyes of mine have seen the Savior whom you have prepared for all the world to see: A Light to enlighten the nations, and the glory of your people Israel. *Amen.*

Nunc Dimittis

The Final Petition
Now guide me waking, O Lord, and guard me sleeping; that awake I may watch with Christ, and asleep, I may rest in peace. *Amen.*

The Office of Dawn **Observed on the Hour or Half-Hour**
Between 4:30 and 7:30 a.m.

The Call to Prayer
Worship the LORD, O Jerusalem;* praise your God, O Zion;
For he has strengthened the bars of your gates.

Psalm 147:13–14a

The Request for Presence
My soul waits for the LORD, more than watchmen for the morning,* more than
watchmen for the morning.

Psalm 130:5

The Greeting
Glory be to the Father, and the Son, and the Holy Spirit.
As it was in the beginning, it is now
And ever shall be, world without end. *Amen.*

Gloria Patri

The Hymn
I am yours, O Lord, I have heard your voice,
and it told your love for me;
but I long to rise in the arms of faith
and be closer drawn to thee.
Consecrate me now to your service, Lord,
by the power of grace divine;
let my soul look up with a steadfast hope,
and my will be lost in thine.
There are depths of love I cannot know
til I cross the narrow sea;
there are heights of joy that I may not reach
until I rest in peace with thee.
Draw me nearer, nearer, blessed Lord,
to the cross where you once died.
Draw me nearer, nearer, blessed Lord,
to your precious, bleeding side.

Fanny J. Crosby

The Psalm *He Gives Snow Like Wool*
The LORD sends out his command to the earth,* and his word runs very swiftly.
He gives snow like wool;* he scatters hoarfrost like ashes.
He scatters his hail like bread crumbs;* who can stand against his cold?
He sends forth his word and melts them;* he blows with his wind, and the waters
flow.

Psalm 147:16–19

86

The Gloria in Excelsis

Glory to God in the highest, and on earth peace to people of good will.
>We praise you.
>We bless you.
>We adore you.
>We glorify you.

We give thanks to you for your great glory.

The Small Verse

And Mary said, "My soul magnifies the Lord, and my spirit rejoices in God my
>Savior, for he has regarded the low estate of his handmaiden. For behold,
>henceforth all generations will call me blessed; for he who is mighty has done
>great things for me, and holy is his name. And his mercy is on those who fear
>him from generation to generation."

Luke 1:46–50

The Lord's Prayer

The Final Blessing

May the LORD bless us and keep us and cause His face to shine upon us from this
>day forth and forever more. *Amen.*

꒳

Tuesday, Month of March

The Office of Midnight   **Observed on the Hour or Half-Hour
Between 10:30 p.m.✢ and 1:30 a.m.**

The Call to Prayer

It is a good thing to give thanks to the LORD,* and to sing praises to your Name,
>O Most High;
To tell of your loving-kindness early in the morning* and of your faithfulness in
>the night season;

Psalm 92:1–2

The Request for Presence

O LORD, let my prayer be set forth in your sight as incense,* the lifting up of my
>hands as the evening sacrifice.

Psalm 141:2, adapted

87

The Greeting
Our Father, may Your will be done, on earth as in Heaven.

The Canticle   **The Third Song of Isaiah**
Surge, illuminare

Arise, shine, for your light has come,*
    and the glory of the Lord has dawned upon you.
For behold, darkness covers the land;*
    deep gloom enshrouds the peoples.
But over you the Lord will rise,*
    and his glory will appear upon you.
Nations will stream to your light,*
    and kings to the brightness of your dawning.
Your gates will always be open;*
    by day or night they will never be shut.
They will call you, The City of the Lord,*
    The Zion of the Holy One of Israel.
Violence will no more be heard in your land,*
    ruin or destruction within your borders.
You will call your walls, Salvation,*
    and all your portals, Praise.
The sun will no more be your light by day;*
    by night you will not need the brightness of the moon.
The Lord will be your everlasting light,*
    and your God will be your glory.

Isaiah 60:1–3, 11a, 14c, 18–19

The Psalm   **Mercy and Truth Have Met Together**
Show us your mercy, O LORD,* and grant us your salvation.
I will listen to what the LORD God is saying,* for he is speaking peace to his
    faithful people and to those who turn their hearts to him.
Truly, his salvation is very near to those who fear him,* that his glory may dwell
    in our land.
Mercy and truth have met together;* righteousness and peace have kissed each
    other.
Truth shall spring up from the earth,* and righteousness shall look down from
    heaven.
The LORD will indeed grant prosperity,* and our land will yield its increase.
Righteousness shall go before him,* and peace shall be a pathway for his feet.

Psalm 85:7–13

The Gloria

88

The Small Verse
And he said to them, "Go unto all the world and preach the gospel to the whole
creation."

Mark 16:15

The Final Thanksgiving
I will greatly rejoice in the LORD, my soul shall exult in my God; for he has
clothed me with the garments of salvation, he has covered me with the robe of
righteousness, as a bridegroom decks himself with a garland, and as a bride
adorns herself with her jewels.

Isaiah 61:10

The Petition
May the Lord GOD, father of all mercy, grant us who dwell here a peaceful night
and a perfect end. *Amen*

The Office of the Night Watch   Observed on the Hour or Half-Hour Between 1:30 and 4:30 a.m.

The Call to Prayer
Behold now, bless the LORD, all you servants of the LORD,* you that stand by night
in the house of the LORD.
Lift up your hands in the holy place and bless the LORD;* the LORD who made
heaven and earth bless you out of Zion.

Psalm 134

The Request for Presence
O God, come to my assistance.
O Lord, make haste to help me.

The Greeting
Out of Zion, perfect in its beauty,* God reveals himself in glory.

Psalm 50:2

The Refrain for the Night Watch
It is a good thing to give thanks to the LORD,* and to sing praises to your Name,
O Most High;
To tell of your loving-kindness early in the morning* and of your faithfulness in
the night season.

Psalm 92:1–2

The Psalm   *I Will Yet Give Thanks to My God*
Send out your light and your truth, that they may lead me,* and bring me to your
holy hill and to your dwelling;

That I may go to the altar of God, to the God of my joy and gladness;* and on the
harp I will give thanks to you, O God my God.
Why are you so full of heaviness, O my soul?* and why are you so disquieted
within me?
Put your trust in God;* for I will yet give thanks to him, who is the help of my
countenance, and my God.

Psalm 43:3–6

The Refrain
It is a good thing to give thanks to the LORD,* and to sing praises to your Name,
O Most High;
To tell of your loving-kindness early in the morning* and of your faithfulness in
the night season.

A Reading
I don't think we can have virtue or the fullness of grace if we don't live in the cell
of our heart and soul. Only in this inner private place do we gain the treasure
that is life and health for us. Here in this secret place we're given the sacred
nothingness that is a holy, intimate knowledge of ourselves and of God.

Catherine of Siena, Letters

The Refrain
It is a good thing to give thanks to the LORD,* and to sing praises to your Name,
O Most High;
To tell of your loving-kindness early in the morning* and of your faithfulness in
the night season.

The Litany
For all people in their daily life and work;
*For my family, friends, and neighbors, and for those who are alone, I pray
to you, Lord God.*
For this community, the nation, and the world;
For all who work for justice, freedom, and peace, I pray to you, Lord God.
For the just and proper use of your creation;
*For the victims of hunger, fear, injustice, and oppression, I pray to you,
Lord God.*
For all who are in danger, sorrow, or any kind of trouble;
*For those who minister to the sick, the friendless, and the needy, I pray to
you, Lord God.*
For the peace and unity of the Church of God;
*For all who proclaim the Gospel, and all who seek the Truth, I pray to you,
Lord God.*
Hear me, Lord;
For your mercy is great.

The Thanksgiving

Lord, you now have set your servant free to go in peace as you have promised; for
these eyes of mine have seen the Savior whom you have prepared for all the
world to see: A Light to enlighten the nations, and the glory of your people
Israel. *Amen.*

Nunc Dimittis

The Final Petition

Now guide me waking, O Lord, and guard me sleeping; that awake I may watch
with Christ, and asleep, I may rest in peace. *Amen.*

The Office of Dawn   **Observed on the Hour or Half-Hour
Between 4:30 and 7:30 a.m.**

The Call to Prayer

Hallelujah! Praise the Lord from the heavens;* praise him in the heights.

Psalm 148:1

The Request for Presence

My soul waits for the Lord, more than watchmen for the morning,* more than
watchmen for the morning.

Psalm 130:5

The Greeting

Glory be to the Father, and the Son, and the Holy Spirit.
As it was in the beginning, it is now
And ever shall be, world without end. *Amen.*

Gloria Patri

The Hymn

Marvelous grace of our loving Lord,
grace that exceeds our sin and our guilt!
Yonder on Calvary's mount outpoured,
there where the blood of the Lamb was spilt.
Sin and despair, like the sea waves cold,
threaten the soul with infinite loss;
grace that is greater, yes, grace untold,
points to the refuge, the mighty cross.
Marvelous, infinite, matchless grace,
freely bestowed on all who believe!
You who are longing to see his face,
will you this moment that grace receive?
Grace, grace, God's grace,

91

grace that will pardon and cleanse within;
grace, grace, God's grace,
grace that is greater than all our sin!

Julia H. Johnston

The Psalm   *Praise Him, All His Host*

Praise the Lord from the heavens;* praise him in the heights.
Praise him, all you angels of his;* praise him, all his host.
Praise him, sun and moon;* praise him, all you shining stars.
Praise him, heaven of heavens,* and you waters above the heavens.
Let them praise the Name of the Lord;* for he commanded, and they were
    created.
He made them stand fast for ever and ever;* he gave them a law which shall not
    pass away.

Psalm 148:1b–6

The Gloria in Excelsis

Glory to God in the highest, and on earth peace to people of good will.
    We praise you.
    We bless you.
    We adore you.
    We glorify you.
We give thanks to you for your great glory.

The Small Verse

Then Jonah prayed to the Lord his God from the belly of the fish, saying, "I called
    to the Lord, out of my distress, and he answered me; out of the belly of Sheol I
    cried, and thou didst hear my voice. The waters closed in over me, the deep
    was round about me; weeds were wrapped around my head at the roots of the
    mountains, yet thou didst bring up my life from the Pit, O Lord, my God."

Jonah 2:1ff

The Lord's Prayer

The Final Blessing

May the Lord bless us and keep us and cause His face to shine upon us from this
    day forth and forever more. *Amen.*

Wednesday, Month of March

The Office of Midnight   **Observed on the Hour or Half-Hour**
Between 10:30 p.m.✠ and 1:30 a.m.

The Call to Prayer

Behold now, bless the LORD, all you servants of the LORD,* you that stand by night
    in the house of the LORD.
Lift up your hands in the holy place and bless the LORD;* the LORD who made
    heaven and earth bless you out of Zion.

Psalm 134

The Request for Presence

O LORD, let my prayer be set forth in your sight as incense,* the lifting up of my
    hands as the evening sacrifice.

Psalm 141:2, adapted

The Greeting

Our Father, give us this day our daily bread.

The Canticle   *The Song of Simeon*
Nunc Dimittis

Lord, you now have set your servant free*
    to go in peace as you have promised;
For these eyes of mine have seen the Savior,*
    whom you have prepared for all the world to see:
A Light to enlighten the nations,*
    and the glory of your people Israel.
Glory to the Father, and to the Son, and to the Holy Spirit:*
    as it was in the beginning, is now, and will be for ever. *Amen.*

Luke 2:29–32

The Psalm   *The LORD Heard Me*

I will bless the LORD at all times;* his praise shall ever be in my mouth.
I will glory in the LORD;* let the humble hear and rejoice.
Proclaim with me the greatness of the LORD;* let us exalt his Name together.
I sought the LORD, and he answered me* and delivered me out of all my terror.
Look upon him and be radiant,* and let not your faces be ashamed.
I called in my affliction and the LORD heard me* and saved me from all my
    troubles.
The angel of the LORD encompasses those who fear him,* and he will deliver them.
Taste and see that the LORD is good;* happy are they who trust in him!
Fear the LORD, you that are his saints,* for those who fear him lack nothing.

93

The young lions lack and suffer hunger,* but those who seek the LORD lack
    nothing that is good.

Psalm 34:1–10

The Gloria

The Small Verse
For this reason I bow my knees before the Father, from whom every family on
    earth is named.

Romans 3:14, 15

The Final Thanksgiving
I will greatly rejoice in the LORD, my soul shall exult in my God; for he has
    clothed me with the garments of salvation, he has covered me with the robe of
    righteousness, as a bridegroom decks himself with a garland, and as a bride
    adorns herself with her jewels.

Isaiah 61:10

The Petition
May the Lord GOD, father of all mercy, grant us who dwell here a peaceful night
    and a perfect end. *Amen.*

The Office of the Night Watch — Observed on the Hour or Half-Hour Between 1:30 and 4:30 a.m.

The Call to Prayer
Behold now, bless the LORD, all you servants of the LORD,* you that stand by night
    in the house of the LORD.
Lift up your hands in the holy place and bless the LORD;* the LORD who made
    heaven and earth bless you out of Zion.

Psalm 134

The Request for Presence
O God, come to my assistance.
O Lord, make haste to help me.

The Greeting
I cry out to you, O LORD;* I say, "You are my refuge, my portion in the land of the
    living."

Psalm 142:5

The Refrain for the Night Watch
Behold now, bless the LORD, all you servants of the LORD,* you that stand by night
    in the house of the LORD.

Psalm 134:1

The Psalm
Redeem Me, O Lord

I will wash my hands in innocence, O Lord,* that I may go in procession round
  your altar,
Singing aloud a song of thanksgiving* and recounting all your wonderful deeds.
Lord, I love the house in which you dwell* and the place where your glory abides.
Do not sweep me away with sinners,* nor my life with those who thirst for blood,
Whose hands are full of evil plots,* and their right hand full of bribes.
As for me, I will live with integrity;* redeem me, O Lord, and have pity on me.
My foot stands on level ground;* in the full assembly I will bless the Lord.

Psalm 26:6–12

The Refrain
Behold now, bless the Lord, all you servants of the Lord,* you that stand by night
  in the house of the Lord.

A Reading
. . . Even as the sun has many rays, yet one light; and the tree many boughs, yet its
  strength is one, seated in the deep-lodged root; and as when many streams flow
  down from one source, though a multiplicity of waters seem to be diffused,
  unity is preserved in the source itself. Thus so, the Church, flooded with the
  light of the Lord, puts forth her rays through the whole world with yet one light
  which is spread upon all places. . . . She stretches forth her branches over the
  universal earth, in the riches of plenty, and pours abroad her bountiful and
  onward stream; yet there is one head, one source, one mother, abundant in the
  results of her fruitfulness.

St. Cyprian (d. 258 CE), The Homilies, adapted

The Refrain
Behold now, bless the Lord, all you servants of the Lord,* you that stand by night
  in the house of the Lord.

The Litany
For the peace from above, for the loving-kindness of God, and for the salvation of
  my soul, I pray to the Lord.
  Lord, have mercy.
For the peace of the world, for the welfare of the Holy Church of God, and for the
  unity of all peoples, I pray to the Lord.
  Lord, have mercy.
For my city [town, village], for every city and community, and for those who live
  in them, I pray to the Lord.
  Lord, have mercy.
For seasonable weather, and for an abundance of the fruits of the earth, I pray to
  the Lord.
  Lord, have mercy.

For the good earth which God has given us, and for the wisdom and will to
conserve it, I pray to the Lord.
Lord, have mercy.
For deliverance from all danger, violence, oppression, and degradation, I pray to
the Lord.
Lord, have mercy.
For the absolution and remission of my sins and offenses, I pray to the Lord.
Lord, have mercy.
Defend me, deliver me, and in your compassion protect me, O Lord, by your grace.
Lord, have mercy.

The Thanksgiving
Lord, you now have set your servant free to go in peace as you have promised; for
these eyes of mine have seen the Savior whom you have prepared for all the
world to see: A Light to enlighten the nations, and the glory of your people
Israel. *Amen.*

Nunc Dimittis

The Final Petition
Now guide me waking, O Lord, and guard me sleeping; that awake I may watch
with Christ, and asleep, I may rest in peace. *Amen.*

The Office of Dawn · Observed on the Hour or Half-Hour Between 4:30 and 7:30 a.m.

The Call to Prayer
Hallelujah! Sing to the LORD a new song;* sing his praise in the congregation of
the faithful.

Psalm 149:1

The Request for Presence
My soul waits for the LORD, more than watchmen for the morning,* more than
watchmen for the morning.

Psalm 130:5

The Greeting
Glory be to the Father, and the Son, and the Holy Spirit.
As it was in the beginning, it is now
And ever shall be, world without end. *Amen.*

Gloria Patri

The Hymn
Come down, O Love divine,
seek here this soul of mine,

and visit it with your own ardor glowing;
O Comforter, draw near,
within my heart appear,
and kindle it, your holy flame bestowing.
O let it freely burn,
'til earthly passions turn
to dust and ashes in its heat consuming;
and let your glorious light
shine ever on my sight,
and clothe me round, the while my path illuming.

Bianco of Siena, translated by Richard F. Littledale

The Psalm   *Praise the LORD from the Earth*
Praise the LORD from the earth,* you sea-monsters and all deeps;
Fire and hail, snow and fog,* tempestuous wind, doing his will;
Mountains and all hills,* fruit trees and all cedars;
Wild beasts and all cattle,* creeping things and winged birds;
Kings of the earth and all peoples,* princes and all rulers of the world;
Young men and maidens,* old and young together.
Let them praise the Name of the LORD,*

Psalm 148:7–13a

The Gloria in Excelsis
Glory to God in the highest, and on earth peace to people of good will.
   We praise you.
   We bless you.
   We adore you.
   We glorify you.
We give thanks to you for your great glory.

The Small Verse
"If you take away from the midst of you the yoke, the pointing of the finger, and
   speaking wickedness, if you pour yourself out for the hungry and satisfy the
   desire of the afflicted, then shall your light rise in the darkness and your gloom
   be as the noonday."

Isaiah 58:9b–10

The Lord's Prayer

The Final Blessing
May the LORD bless us and keep us and cause His face to shine upon us from this
   day forth and forever more. *Amen.*

97

Thursday, Month of March

The Office of Midnight   **Observed on the Hour or Half-Hour**
Between 10:30 p.m.✝ and 1:30 a.m.

The Call to Prayer
But I will call upon God,* and the LORD will deliver me.
In the evening, in the morning, and at noonday, I will complain and lament,* and
    he will hear my voice.
He will bring me safely back . . .
God, who is enthroned of old, will hear me.

Psalm 55:17 ff

The Request for Presence
O LORD, let my prayer be set forth in your sight as incense,* the lifting up of my
    hands as the evening sacrifice.

Psalm 141:2, adapted

The Greeting
Our Father, forgive us our sins as we forgive those who have sinned against us.

The Canticle   ***The Song of Mary***
Magnificat

My soul proclaims the greatness of the Lord, my spirit rejoices in God my
    Savior;*
    for he has looked with favor on his lowly servant.
From this day all generations will call me blessed:*
    the Almighty has done great things for me, and holy is his Name.
He has mercy on those who fear him*
    in every generation.
He has shown the strength of his arm,*
    he has scattered the proud in their conceit.
He has cast down the mighty from their thrones,*
    and has lifted up the lowly.
He has filled the hungry with good things,*
    and the rich he has sent away empty.
He has come to the help of his servant Israel,*
    for he has remembered his promise of mercy,
The promise he made to our fathers,*
    to Abraham and his children for ever.
Glory to the Father, and to the Son, and to the Holy Spirit:*
    as it was in the beginning, is now, and will be for ever. *Amen.*

Luke 1:46–55

The Psalm   *From the Heavens He Beheld the Earth*
Let this be written for a future generation,* so that a people yet unborn may praise
  the LORD.
For the LORD looked down from his holy place on high;* from the heavens he
  beheld the earth;
That he might hear the groan of the captive* and set free those condemned to die;

Psalm 102:18–22

The Gloria

The Small Verse
"I have loved you," says the LORD. But you say, "How hast thou loved us?"

Malachi 1:2

The Final Thanksgiving
I will greatly rejoice in the LORD, my soul shall exult in my God; for he has
  clothed me with the garments of salvation, he has covered me with the robe of
  righteousness, as a bridegroom decks himself with a garland, and as a bride
  adorns herself with her jewels.

Isaiah 61:10

The Petition
May the Lord GOD, father of all mercy, grant us who dwell here a peaceful night
  and a perfect end. *Amen.*

The Office of the Night Watch   **Observed on the Hour or Half-Hour**
Between 1:30 and 4:30 a.m.

The Call to Prayer
Behold now, bless the LORD, all you servants of the LORD,* you that stand by night
  in the house of the LORD.
Lift up your hands in the holy place and bless the LORD;* the LORD who made
  heaven and earth bless you out of Zion.

Psalm 134

The Request for Presence
O God, come to my assistance.
O Lord, make haste to help me.

The Greeting
Your righteousness, O God, reaches to the heavens;* you have done great things;
  who is like you, O God?

Psalm 71:19

The Refrain for the Night Watch

Darkness is not dark to you; the night is as bright as the day;* darkness and light
to you are both alike.

Psalm 139:11

The Psalm   We Will Bless the LORD

May you be blessed by the LORD,* the maker of heaven and earth.
The heaven of heavens is the LORD's,* but he entrusted the earth to its peoples.
The dead do not praise the LORD,* nor all those who go down into silence;
But we will bless the LORD,* from this time forth for evermore. Hallelujah!

Psalm 115:15–18

The Refrain

Darkness is not dark to you; the night is as bright as the day;* darkness and light
to you are both alike.

A Reading

A good host does not bring his guest to his house before he has prepared the feast;
but when he has made all due preparation and decked with their proper
adornments his house, his couches, his table, then he brings his guest home
because all things that are suitable for his refreshment are in readiness. In the
same manner the rich and munificent Entertainer, when He had decked the
habitation with beauties of every kind and prepared this great and varied
banquet, then introduced humanity, assigning to us as our task not the
acquiring of what was not here, but the enjoyment of the things that are here;
and for that reason He gives us, as foundations, the instincts of a two-fold
nature, blending in us the Divine with the earthly, that by means of both we
may be naturally and properly disposed to each enjoyment: that is, enjoying
God by means of our more divine nature, and the good things of earth by the
sense in us that is akin to them.

St. Gregory, Bishop of Nyssa (ca. 330–395 CE), On the Making of Man, chap. 2

The Refrain

Darkness is not dark to you; the night is as bright as the day;* darkness and light
to you are both alike.

The Litany

O God the Father, Creator of heaven and earth,
Have mercy upon me.
O God the Son, Redeemer of the world,
Have mercy upon me.
O God the Holy Spirit, Sanctifier of the faithful,
Have mercy upon me.
O holy, blessed, and glorious Trinity, one God,
Have mercy upon me.

Remember not, Lord Christ, my offenses, nor the offenses of my forefathers; neither reward me according to my sins. Spare me, good Lord, spare your people, whom you have redeemed with your most precious blood, and by your mercy preserve us, for ever.
> *Spare us, good Lord.*

The Thanksgiving

Lord, you now have set your servant free to go in peace as you have promised; for these eyes of mine have seen the Savior whom you have prepared for all the world to see: A Light to enlighten the nations, and the glory of your people Israel. *Amen.*

Nunc Dimittis

The Final Petition

Now guide me waking, O Lord, and guard me sleeping; that awake I may watch with Christ, and asleep, I may rest in peace. *Amen.*

The Office of Dawn   **Observed on the Hour or Half-Hour Between 4:30 and 7:30 a.m.**

The Call to Prayer

Hallelujah! Praise the LORD, O my soul!* I will praise the LORD as long as I live; I will sing praises to my God while I have my being.

Psalm 146:1

The Request for Presence

My soul waits for the LORD, more than watchmen for the morning,* more than watchmen for the morning.

Psalm 130:5

The Greeting

Glory be to the Father, and the Son, and the Holy Spirit.
As it was in the beginning, it is now
And ever shall be, world without end. *Amen.*

Gloria Patri

The Hymn

Sing praise to God who reigns above,
the God of all creation,
the God of power, the God of love,
the God of our salvation.
With healing balm my soul is filled
and every faithless murmur stilled:

To God all praise and glory.
Thus all my toilsome way along,
I sing aloud your praises,
that earth may hear the grateful song
my voice unwearied raises.
Be joyful in the Lord, my heart,
both soul and body bear your part:
To God all praise and glory.

Johann J. Schutz, translated by Frances E. Cox

The Psalm   *The Lord Has Pleasure in Those Who Fear Him*
He covers the heavens with clouds * and prepares rain for the earth;
He makes grass to grow upon the mountains* and green plants to serve mankind.
He provides food for flocks and herds* and for the young ravens when they cry.
He is not impressed by the might of a horse;* he has no pleasure in the strength of
a man;
But the Lord has pleasure in those who fear him,* in those who await his gracious
favor.

Psalm 147:8–12

The Gloria in Excelsis
Glory to God in the highest, and on earth peace to people of good will.
    We praise you.
    We bless you.
    We adore you.
    We glorify you.
We give thanks to you for your great glory.

The Small Verse
If we live by the Spirit, let us also walk by the Spirit.

Galatians 5:25

The Lord's Prayer

The Final Blessing
May the Lord bless us and keep us and cause His face to shine upon us from this
day forth and forever more. *Amen.*

༃

Friday, Month of March

The Office of Midnight

Observed on the Hour or Half-Hour Between 10:30 p.m.✠ and 1:30 a.m.

The Call to Prayer

Had you desired it, I would have offered sacrifice,* but you take no delight in
burnt-offerings.
The sacrifice of God is a troubled spirit;* a broken and contrite heart, O God, you
will not despise.

Psalm 51:17–18

The Request for Presence

O LORD, let my prayer be set forth in your sight as incense,* the lifting up of my
hands as the evening sacrifice.

Psalm 141:2, adapted

The Greeting

Our Father, lead us not into temptation, but deliver us from evil.

The Canticle

A Song of Penitence
Kyrie Pantokrator

O Lord and Ruler of the hosts of heaven,*
    God of Abraham, Isaac, and Jacob, and of all their righteous offspring:
You made the heavens and the earth,*
    with all their vast array.
All things quake with fear at your presence;*
    they tremble because of your power.
But your merciful promise is beyond all measure;*
    it surpasses all that our minds can fathom.
O Lord, you are full of compassion,*
    long-suffering, and abounding in mercy.
You hold back your hand;*
    you do not punish as we deserve.
In your great goodness, Lord, you have promised forgiveness to sinners,*
    that they may repent of their sin and be saved.

Prayer of Manasseh 1–2, 4, 6–7

The Psalm

Cleanse Me from My Sin

Have mercy on me, O God, according to your loving-kindness;* in your great
compassion blot out my offenses.
Wash me through and through from my wickedness* and cleanse me from my sin.
For I know my transgressions,* and my sin is ever before me.

103

Against you only have I sinned* and done what is evil in your sight.
And so you are justified when you speak* and upright in your judgment.
Indeed, I have been wicked from my birth,* a sinner from my mother's womb.
For behold, you look for truth deep within me,* and will make me understand
wisdom secretly.
Purge me from my sin, and I shall be pure;* wash me, and I shall be clean indeed.
Make me hear of joy and gladness,* that the body you have broken may rejoice.
Hide your face from my sins* and blot out all my iniquities.

Psalm 51:1–10

The Gloria

The Small Verse
. . . and when he saw the wagon which Joseph had sent to carry him, the spirit of
their father Jacob revived; and Israel said, "It is enough; Joseph my son is
alive; and I will go and see him before I die."

Genesis 45:27b–28

The Final Thanksgiving
I will greatly rejoice in the LORD, my soul shall exult in my God; for he has
clothed me with the garments of salvation, he has covered me with the robe of
righteousness, as a bridegroom decks himself with a garland, and as a bride
adorns herself with her jewels.

Isaiah 61:10

The Petition
May the Lord GOD, father of all mercy, grant us who dwell here a peaceful night
and a perfect end. *Amen.*

The Office of the Night Watch Observed on the Hour or Half-Hour
Between 1:30 and 4:30 a.m.

The Call to Prayer
Behold now, bless the LORD, all you servants of the LORD,* you that stand by night
in the house of the LORD.
Lift up your hands in the holy place and bless the LORD;* the LORD who made
heaven and earth bless you out of Zion.

Psalm 134

The Request for Presence
O God, come to my assistance.
O Lord, make haste to help me.

The Greeting

I will thank you, O LORD my God, with all my heart,* and glorify your Name for
evermore.

Psalm 86:12

The Refrain for the Night Watch

I will bless the LORD who gives me counsel;* my heart teaches me, night after night.

Psalm 16:7

The Psalm   *One Day Tells Its Tale to Another*

The heavens declare the glory of God,* and the firmament shows his handiwork.
One day tells its tale to another,* and one night imparts knowledge to another.
Although they have no words or language,* and their voices are not heard,
Their sound has gone out into all lands,* and their message to the ends of the
world.

Psalm 19:1–4

The Refrain

I will bless the LORD who gives me counsel;* my heart teaches me, night after
night.

A Reading

Whenever his thoughts urged him to pass judgment on something he saw, he
would say to himself, "Agathon, it is not your business to do that." In this way,
he always recalled his spirit to himself.

The Sayings of the Desert Fathers (4th c. CE)

The Refrain

I will bless the LORD who gives me counsel;* my heart teaches me, night after night.

The Litany

From all evil and wickedness; from sin; from the crafts and assaults of the devil;
and from everlasting damnation,
Good Lord, deliver me.
From all blindness of heart; from pride, vainglory, and hypocrisy; from envy,
hatred, and malice; and from all want of charity,
Good Lord, deliver me.
From all inordinate and sinful affections; and from all the deceits of the world, the
flesh, and the devil,
Good Lord, deliver me.
From all false doctrine, heresy, and schism; from hardness of heart, and contempt
of your Word and commandment,
Good Lord, deliver me.

105

By the mystery of your holy Incarnation; by your holy Nativity and submission to
the Law; by your Baptism, Fasting, and Temptation,
> *Good Lord, deliver me.*
In all time of tribulation; in all time of prosperity; in the hour of death, and in the
day of judgment,
> *Good Lord, deliver me.*

The Thanksgiving
Lord, you now have set your servant free to go in peace as you have promised; for
these eyes of mine have seen the Savior whom you have prepared for all the
world to see: A Light to enlighten the nations, and the glory of your people
Israel. *Amen.*

Nunc Dimittis

The Final Petition
Now guide me waking, O Lord, and guard me sleeping; that awake I may watch
with Christ, and asleep, I may rest in peace. *Amen.*

The Office of Dawn   Observed on the Hour or Half-Hour
Between 4:30 and 7:30 a.m.

The Call to Prayer
Hallelujah! How good it is to sing praises to our God!* how pleasant it is to honor
him with praise!

Psalm 147:1

The Request for Presence
My soul waits for the LORD, more than watchmen for the morning,* more than
watchmen for the morning.

Psalm 130:5

The Greeting
Glory be to the Father, and the Son, and the Holy Spirit.
As it was in the beginning, it is now
And ever shall be, world without end. *Amen.*

Gloria Patri

The Hymn
There is a place of quiet rest,
near to the heart of God.
A place where sin cannot molest,
near to the heart of God.
There is a place of comfort sweet,

near to the heart of God.
A place where we our Savior meet,
near to the heart of God.
There is a place of full release,
near to the heart of God.
A place where all is joy and peace,
near to the heart of God.

Cleland B. McAfee

The Psalm   *The LORD Takes Pleasure in His People*

Let Israel rejoice in his Maker;* let the children of Zion be joyful in their King.
Let them praise his Name in the dance;* let them sing praise to him with timbrel
    and harp.
For the LORD takes pleasure in his people* and adorns the poor with victory.
Let the faithful rejoice in triumph;* let them be joyful on their beds.

Psalm 149:2–5

The Gloria in Excelsis

Glory to God in the highest, and on earth peace to people of good will.
    We praise you.
    We bless you.
    We adore you.
    We glorify you.
We give thanks to you for your great glory.

The Small Verse

The LORD said to Moses, "Say to Aaron and his sons, Thus you shall bless the
    people of Israel: you shall say to them,
"The LORD bless you and keep you: The LORD make his face to shine upon you and
    be gracious to you: The LORD lift up his countenance upon you, and give you
    peace.
"So shall they put my name upon the people of Israel, and I will bless them."

Numbers 6:22–27

The Lord's Prayer

The Final Blessing

May the LORD bless us and keep us and cause His face to shine upon us from this
    day forth and forever more. *Amen.*

Saturday, Month of March

The Office of Midnight   **Observed on the Hour or Half-Hour**
                                    Between 10:30 p.m.✠ and 1:30 a.m.

The Call to Prayer
Bless God in the congregation;* bless the LORD, you that are of the fountain of
    Israel.

Psalm 68:26

The Request for Presence
O LORD, let my prayer be set forth in your sight as incense,* the lifting up of my
    hands as the evening sacrifice.

Psalm 141:2, adapted

The Greeting
Our Father, Yours are the kingdom, the power, and the glory forever.

The Canticle   ***Glory to God***
                                                     Gloria in excelsis

Glory to God in the highest,
    and peace to his people on earth.
Lord God, heavenly King, almighty God and Father,
    we worship you, we give you thanks, we praise you for your glory.
Lord Jesus Christ, only Son of the Father, Lord God, Lamb of God,
you take away the sin of the world:
    have mercy on us;
you are seated at the right hand of the Father:
    receive our prayer.
For you alone are the Holy One, you alone are the Lord, you alone are the Most
    High,
    Jesus Christ, with the Holy Spirit, in the glory of God the Father. *Amen.*

The Psalm   ***Who Is Like You, O God?***
Your righteousness, O God, reaches to the heavens;* you have done great things;
    who is like you, O God?
You have showed me great troubles and adversities,* but you will restore my life
    and bring me up again from the deep places of the earth.
You strengthen me more and more;* you enfold and comfort me,
Therefore I will praise you upon the lyre for your faithfulness, O my God;* I will
    sing to you with the harp, O Holy One of Israel.
My lips will sing with joy when I play to you,* and so will my soul, which you
    have redeemed.

My tongue will proclaim your righteousness all day long,* for they are ashamed
and disgraced who sought to do me harm.

Psalm 71:19–24

The Gloria

The Small Verse
When the king of Israel saw them, he said to Elisha, "My father, shall I slay them?
Shall I slay them?" He answered, "You shall not slay them. Would you slay
those whom you have taken captive with your sword and with your bow? Set
bread and water before them, that they may eat and drink and go to their
master."

2 Kings 6:21–22

The Final Thanksgiving
I will greatly rejoice in the LORD, my soul shall exult in my God; for he has
clothed me with the garments of salvation, he has covered me with the robe of
righteousness, as a bridegroom decks himself with a garland, and as a bride
adorns herself with her jewels.

Isaiah 61:10

The Petition
May the Lord GOD, father of all mercy, grant us who dwell here a peaceful night
and a perfect end. *Amen.*

The Office of the Night Watch   Observed on the Hour or Half-Hour Between 1:30 and 4:30 a.m.

The Call to Prayer
Behold now, bless the LORD, all you servants of the LORD,* you that stand by night
in the house of the LORD.
Lift up your hands in the holy place and bless the LORD;* the LORD who made
heaven and earth bless you out of Zion.

Psalm 134

The Request for Presence
O God, come to my assistance.
O Lord, make haste to help me.

The Greeting
Deliver me, O LORD, by your hand* from those whose portion in life is this world;

Psalm 17:14

The Refrain for the Night Watch

Happy are they who have not walked in the counsel of the wicked,* nor lingered
in the way of sinners, nor sat in the seats of the scornful!
Their delight is in the law of the LORD,* and they meditate on his law day and night.

Psalm 1:1–2

The Psalm
I Will Declare the Mysteries of Ancient Times

Hear my teaching, O my people;* incline your ears to the words of my mouth.
I will open my mouth in a parable;* I will declare the mysteries of ancient times.
That which we have heard and known, and what our forefathers have told us,* we
will not hide from their children.
We will recount to generations to come the praiseworthy deeds and the power of
the LORD,* and the wonderful works he has done.

Psalm 78:1–4

The Refrain

Happy are they who have not walked in the counsel of the wicked,* nor lingered
in the way of sinners, nor sat in the seats of the scornful!
Their delight is in the law of the LORD,* and they meditate on his law day and
night.

A Reading

Let your children be partakers of true Christian training; let them learn of how great
avail humility is with God—how much the spirit of pure affection can prevail
with Him—how excellent and great His fear is, and how it saves all those who
walk in it with a pure mind. For He is a Searcher of the thoughts and desires of
the heart; His breath is in us; and when He pleases, He will take it away.

Clement of Rome (ca. 96 CE), Letter to the Corinthians XXI, 94–95

The Refrain

Happy are they who have not walked in the counsel of the wicked,* nor lingered
in the way of sinners, nor sat in the seats of the scornful!
Their delight is in the law of the LORD,* and they meditate on his law day and
night.

The Litany

That it may please you to bless and keep all your people,
I beseech you to hear me, good Lord.
That it may please you to send laborers into your harvest and to draw all
humankind into your kingdom,
I beseech you to hear me, good Lord.
That it may please you to give to all people increase of grace to hear and receive
your Word, and to bring forth the fruits of the Spirit,
I beseech you to hear me, good Lord.

That it may please you to bring into the way of truth all such as have erred, and are deceived,
> *I beseech you to hear me, good Lord.*

That it may please you to give me a heart to love and fear you, and diligently to live after your commandments,
> *I beseech you to hear me, good Lord.*

The Thanksgiving

Lord, you now have set your servant free to go in peace as you have promised; for these eyes of mine have seen the Savior whom you have prepared for all the world to see: A Light to enlighten the nations, and the glory of your people Israel. *Amen.*

Nunc Dimittis

The Final Petition

Now guide me waking, O Lord, and guard me sleeping; that awake I may watch with Christ, and asleep, I may rest in peace. *Amen.*

The Office of Dawn

Observed on the Hour or Half-Hour Between 4:30 and 7:30 a.m.

The Call to Prayer

Let everything that has breath* praise the LORD. Hallelujah!

Psalm 150:6

The Request for Presence

My soul waits for the LORD, more than watchmen for the morning,* more than watchmen for the morning.

Psalm 130:5

The Greeting

Glory be to the Father, and the Son, and the Holy Spirit.
As it was in the beginning, it is now
And ever shall be, world without end. *Amen.*

Gloria Patri

The Hymn

Love divine, all loves excelling,
Joy of heaven to earth come down;
fix in us your humble dwelling;
all your faithful mercies crown!
Jesus, thou art all compassion,
pure unbounded love Thou art;
visit us with your salvation;

III

enter every trembling heart.
Breathe, O breathe your loving Spirit,
into every troubled breast!
Let us all in you inherit;
let us find that second rest.
Take away our bent to sinning;
Alpha and Omega be;
end of faith, as its beginning,
set our hearts at liberty.
Finish, then, your new creation;
pure and spotless let us be.
Let us see your great salvation
perfectly restored in you;
changed from glory into glory,
til in heaven we take our place,
til we cast our crowns before you
lost in wonder, love, and praise.

Charles Wesley

The Psalm   *Let Everything That Has Breath Praise the LORD*

Praise him for his mighty acts;* praise him for his excellent greatness.
Praise him with the blast of the ram's-horn;* praise him with lyre and harp.
Praise him with timbrel and dance;* praise him with strings and pipe.
Praise him with resounding cymbals;* praise him with loud-clanging cymbals.
Let everything that has breath* praise the LORD. Hallelujah!

Psalm 150:2–6

The Gloria in Excelsis

Glory to God in the highest, and on earth peace to people of good will.
    We praise you.
    We bless you.
    We adore you.
    We glorify you.
We give thanks to you for your great glory.

The Small Verse

So we know and believe the love God has for us. God is love, and he who abides
    in love, abides in God, and God abides in him.

I John 4:16

The Lord's Prayer

The Final Blessing

May the LORD bless us and keep us and cause His face to shine upon us from this
    day forth and forever more. *Amen.*

The Gloria

Glory be to God the Father, God the Son, and God the Holy Spirit. As it was in the beginning, so it is now and so it shall ever be, world without end. Alleluia. *Amen.* ✤

The Lord's Prayer

Our Father, who art in heaven, hallowed be your Name.
May your kingdom come, and your will be done, on earth as in heaven.
Give us today our daily bread.
Forgive us our sins as we forgive those who sin against us.
Lead us not into temptation, but deliver us from evil;
for yours are the kingdom and the power and the glory
forever and ever. *Amen.*

The following major holy day occurs in April:
The Feast of St. Mark, the Evangelist: *April 25*

Prayer for use in the observation of a holy day:
Almighty God, by your Holy Spirit you have made us one with your saints in heaven and on earth: Grant that in my earthly pilgrimage, I may always be supported by this fellowship of love and prayer, and know myself to be surrounded by their witness to your power and mercy. I ask this for the sake of Jesus Christ, in whom all my intercessions are acceptable through the Spirit, and who lives and reigns forever and ever. *Amen.*

✤ *Alleluia* (or *Hallelujah*) is always omitted during Lent.
Likewise, the *Gloria* is omitted during Lent by many Christian communities.

✛ The Office of Midnight is always taken from the prayers for the day nearest to the hour of actual observation. Thus, if the office is to be observed at 10:30 p.m. on Sunday, the prayers will be taken from the Monday offices, and so forth.

APRIL

Sunday, Month of April

The Office of Midnight

Observed on the Hour or Half-Hour Between 10:30 p.m.✛ and 1:30 a.m.

The Call to Prayer

In his might he rules for ever; his eyes keep watch over the nations;* let no rebel rise up against him.
Bless our God, you peoples;* make the voice of his praise to be heard;

Psalm 66:7–8

The Request for Presence

O LORD, let my prayer be set forth in your sight as incense,* the lifting up of my hands as the evening sacrifice.

Psalm 141:2, adapted

The Greeting

Our Father Who art in Heaven, hallowed be Your name forever.

The Canticle

The Song of Moses
Cantemus Domino

I will sing to the Lord, for he is lofty and uplifted;*
    the horse and its rider has he hurled into the sea.
The Lord is my strength and my refuge;*
    the Lord has become my Savior.
This is my God and I will praise him,*
    the God of my people and I will exalt him.
The Lord is a mighty warrior;*
    Yahweh is his Name.
Who can be compared with you, O Lord, among the gods?*
    who is like you, glorious in holiness, awesome in renown, and worker of wonders?
With your constant love you led the people you redeemed;*
    with your might you brought them in safety to your holy dwelling.
You will bring them in and plant them*
    on the mount of your possession,
The resting-place you have made for yourself, O Lord,*
    the sanctuary, O Lord, that your hand has established.
The Lord shall reign*
    for ever and for ever.

Exodus: 15:1–6, 11–13, 17–18

The Psalm   **LORD, Hide Not Your Face from Me**

LORD, hear my prayer, and let my cry come before you;* hide not your face from
    me in the day of my trouble.
Incline your ear to me;* when I call, make haste to answer me,
For my days drift away like smoke,* and my bones are hot as burning coals.
My heart is smitten like grass and withered,* so that I forget to eat my bread.
Because of the voice of my groaning* I am but skin and bones.
I have become like a vulture in the wilderness,* like an owl among the ruins.
I lie awake and groan;* I am like a sparrow, lonely on a house-top.

Psalm 102: 1–7

The Gloria

The Small Verse

For thus says the Lord GOD: Behold, I, I myself will search for my sheep, and will
    seek them out.

Ezekiel 34: 11

The Final Thanksgiving

I will greatly rejoice in the LORD, my soul shall exult in my God; for he has
    clothed me with the garments of salvation, he has covered me with the robe of
    righteousness, as a bridegroom decks himself with a garland, and as a bride
    adorns herself with her jewels.

Isaiah 61: 10

The Petition

May the Lord GOD, father of grace and mercy, grant all who dwell here a peaceful
    night and a perfect end. *Amen.*

The Office of the Night Watch   **Observed on the Hour or Half-Hour**
                                          Between 1:30 and 4:30 a.m.

The Call to Prayer

Behold now, bless the LORD, all you servants of the LORD,* you that stand by night
    in the house of the LORD.
Lift up your hands in the holy place and bless the LORD;* the LORD who made
    heaven and earth bless you out of Zion.

Psalm 134

The Request for Presence

O God, come to my assistance.
O Lord, make haste to help me.

The Greeting

It is a good thing to give thanks to the LORD,* and to sing praises to your Name,
    O Most High;
To tell of your loving-kindness early in the morning* and of your faithfulness in
    the night season;

Psalm 92:1–2

The Refrain for the Night Watch

The heavens declare the glory of God,* and the firmament shows his handiwork.
One day tells its tale to another,* and one night imparts knowledge to another.

Psalm 19:1–2

The Psalm   The LORD Does Wonders for the Faithful

Answer me when I call, O God, defender of my cause;* you set me free when I
    am hard-pressed; have mercy on me and hear my prayer.
"You mortals, how long will you dishonor my glory;* how long will you worship
    dumb idols and run after false gods?"
Know that the LORD does wonders for the faithful;* when I call upon the LORD, he
    will hear me.
Tremble, then, and do not sin;* speak to your heart in silence upon your bed.

Psalm 4:1–4

The Refrain

The heavens declare the glory of God,* and the firmament shows his handiwork.
One day tells its tale to another,* and one night imparts knowledge to another.

A Reading

O holy Apostles, how shall we thank you, you who have labored so much for us!
    I am filled with admiration whenever I think of you, Peter. When I remember
    you, Paul, I am moved to tears. My lips are mute when I consider your
    sufferings: How many prisons you have sanctified! How many chains you have
    adorned! How many pains you have suffered! . . . You bore Christ in your
    hearts and refreshed the Christian communities through your sermons. Praised
    be the work of your tongues.

St. John Chrysostom, Bishop of Constantinople (ca. 347–407 CE), Homily

The Refrain

The heavens declare the glory of God,* and the firmament shows his handiwork.
One day tells its tale to another,* and one night imparts knowledge to another.

The Litany

That it may please you to show your mercy to all prisoners and captives, the
    homeless and the hungry, and all who are desolate and oppressed,
    I beseech you to hear me, good Lord.

That it may please you to give and preserve to our use the bountiful fruits of the earth, so that in due time all may enjoy them,
> *I beseech you to hear me, good Lord.*

That it may please you to inspire all your people, in our several callings, to do the work which you gave us to do with singleness of heart as your servants, and for the common good,
> *I beseech you to hear me, good Lord.*

That it may please you to visit the lonely; to strengthen all who suffer in mind, body, and spirit; and to comfort with your presence those who are failing and infirm,
> *I beseech you to hear me, good Lord.*

That it may please you to strengthen such as do stand; to comfort and help the weak-hearted; to raise up those who fall; and finally to beat down Satan under our feet,
> *I beseech you to hear me, good Lord.*

That it may please you to grant to all the faithful departed eternal life and peace,
> *I beseech you to hear me, good Lord.*

That it may please you to grant that, in the fellowship of all your saints, I may attain to your heavenly kingdom,
> *Son of God, I beseech you to hear me.*
> *Son of God, I beseech you to hear me.*

The Thanksgiving

Lord, you now have set your servant free to go in peace as you have promised; for these eyes of mine have seen the Savior whom you have prepared for all the world to see: A Light to enlighten the nations, and the glory of your people Israel. *Amen.*

Nunc Dimittis

The Final Petition

Now guide me waking, O Lord, and guard me sleeping; that awake I may watch with Christ, and asleep, I may rest in peace. *Amen.*

The Office of Dawn   **Observed on the Hour or Half-Hour Between 4:30 and 7:30 a.m.**

The Call to Prayer

Hallelujah! Praise the LORD, O my soul* I will praise the LORD as long as I live;
I will sing praises to my God while I have my being.

Psalm 146:1

The Request for Presence

My soul waits for the LORD, more than watchmen for the morning,* more than watchmen for the morning.

Psalm 130:5

119

The Greeting

Glory be to the Father, and to the Son, and to the Holy Spirit.
As it was in the beginning, it is now
And ever shall be, world without end. *Amen.*

Gloria Patri

The Hymn

Holy God, we praise Your Name
Lord of all we bow before You;
all on earth Your scepter claim,
all in heaven above adore You;
Infinite Your vast domain,
everlasting is Your reign.
Hark, the loud celestial hymn
angel choirs above are raising;
Cherubim and Seraphim
in unceasing chorus praising,
fill the heavens with sweet accord;
Holy, Holy, Holy Lord!
Lo, the Apostolic train
join, Your sacred name to hallow:
prophets swell the loud refrain,
and the white-robed Martyrs follow;
and, from morn till set of sun,
through the Church the song goes on.
Holy Father, Holy Son,
Holy Spirit, Three we name You,
While in essence only One,
undivided God we claim You:
and, adoring, bend the knee
while we own the mystery.

Te Deum, translated by Msgr. Hugh Thomas Henry

The Psalm   *Praise the Name of the LORD*

Praise the LORD from the earth,* you sea-monsters and all deeps;
Fire and hail, snow and fog,* tempestuous wind, doing his will;
Mountains and all hills,* fruit trees and all cedars;
Wild beasts and all cattle,* creeping things and winged birds;
Kings of the earth and all peoples,* princes and all rulers of the world;
Young men and maidens,* old and young together.
Let them praise the Name of the LORD,*

Psalm 148:7–13a

The Gloria in Excelsis

Glory to God in the highest, and on earth peace to people of good will.
> We praise you.
> We bless you.
> We adore you.
> We glorify you.

We give thanks to you for your great glory

The Small Verse

The Apostle wrote, saying: I have been crucified with Christ; it is no longer I who
> live, but Christ who lives in me; and the life I now live in the flesh I live by
> faith in the Son of God who loved me and gave himself for me.

Galatians 2:20

The Lord's Prayer

The Final Blessing

May the LORD bless us and keep us and cause His face to shine upon us from this
> day forth and forever more. *Amen.*

࿋

Monday, Month of April

The Office of Midnight

**Observed on the Hour or Half-Hour
Between 10:30 p.m.✠ and 1:30 a.m.**

The Call to Prayer

Enter his gates with thanksgiving; go into his courts with praise;* give thanks to
> him and call upon his Name.

Psalm 100:3

The Request for Presence

O LORD, let my prayer be set forth in your sight as incense,* the lifting up of my
> hands as the evening sacrifice.

Psalm 141:2, adapted

The Greeting

Our Father, may Your kingdom come on earth as in Heaven.

The Canticle   **A Song of Creation—Part One**
Benedicite, omnia opera Domini

Glorify the Lord, all you works of the Lord,*
    praise him and highly exalt him for ever.
In the firmament of his power, glorify the Lord,*
    praise him and highly exalt him for ever.
Glorify the Lord, you angels and all powers of the Lord,*
    heavens and all waters above the heavens.
Sun and moon and stars of the sky, glorify the Lord,*
    praise him and highly exalt him for ever.
Glorify the Lord, every shower of rain and fall of dew,*
    all winds and fire and heat.
Winter and Summer, glorify the Lord,*
    praise him and highly exalt him for ever.
Glorify the Lord, O chill and cold,*
    drops of dew and flakes of snow.
Frost and cold, ice and sleet, glorify the Lord,*
    praise him and highly exalt him for ever.
Glorify the Lord, O nights and days,*
    O shining light and enfolding dark.
Storm clouds and thunderbolts, glorify the Lord,*
    praise him and highly exalt him for ever.

Song of the Three Young Men, 35-51

The Psalm   **What Is Man That You Should Be Mindful of Him**

O Lord our Governor,* how exalted is your Name in all the world!
Out of the mouths of infants and children* your majesty is praised above the
    heavens.
You have set up a stronghold against your adversaries,* to quell the enemy and the
    avenger.
When I consider your heavens, the work of your fingers,* the moon and the stars
    you have set in their courses,
What is man that you should be mindful of him?* the son of man that you should
    seek him out?
You have made him but little lower than the angels;* you adorn him with glory
    and honor;
You give him mastery over the works of your hands;* you put all things under his
    feet:
All sheep and oxen,* even the wild beasts of the field,
The birds of the air, the fish of the sea,* and whatsoever walks in the paths of the sea.
O Lord our Governor,* how exalted is your Name in all the world!

Psalm 8

The Gloria

122

The Small Verse
And who knows whether you have not come to the kingdom for such a time as this?

Esther 4:14b

The Final Thanksgiving
I will greatly rejoice in the LORD, my soul shall exult in my God; for he has
clothed me with the garments of salvation, he has covered me with the robe of
righteousness, as a bridegroom decks himself with a garland, and as a bride
adorns herself with her jewels.

Isaiah 61:10

The Petition
May the Lord GOD, father of grace and mercy, grant all who dwell here a peaceful
night and a perfect end. *Amen.*

The Office of the Night Watch   Observed on the Hour or Half-Hour
Between 1:30 and 4:30 a.m.

The Call to Prayer
Behold now, bless the LORD, all you servants of the LORD,* you that stand by night
in the house of the LORD.
Lift up your hands in the holy place and bless the LORD;* the LORD who made
heaven and earth bless you out of Zion.

Psalm 134

The Request for Presence
O God, come to my assistance.
O Lord, make haste to help me.

The Greeting
The LORD lives! Blessed is my Rock!* Exalted is the God of my salvation!

Psalm 18:46

The Refrain for the Night Watch
The LORD grants his loving-kindness in the daytime;* in the night season his song
is with me, a prayer to the God of my life.

Psalm 42:10

The Psalm   *How Manifold Are Your Works*
Bless the LORD, O my soul;* O LORD my God, how excellent is your greatness!
you are clothed with majesty and splendor.
You wrap yourself with light as with a cloak* and spread out the heavens like a
curtain.

You lay the beams of your chambers in the waters above;* you make the clouds
your chariot; you ride on the wings of the wind.
You make the winds your messengers* and flames of fire your servants.
You have set the earth upon its foundations,* so that it never shall move at any time.
You covered it with the Deep as with a mantle;* the waters stood higher than the
mountains.
At your rebuke they fled;* at the voice of your thunder they hastened away.
They went up into the hills and down to the valleys beneath,* to the places you
had appointed for them.
O LORD, how manifold are your works!* in wisdom you have made them all; the
earth is full of your creatures.

Psalm 104: 1–8, 25

The Refrain
The LORD grants his loving-kindness in the daytime;* in the night season his song
is with me, a prayer to the God of my life.

A Reading
For although it be good to think upon the kindness of God, and to love Him and to
praise Him for it, yet it is far better to think upon the naked "being" of Him,
and to love Him and praise Him for Himself.

Anonymous (14th c. English), The Cloud of Unknowing

The Refrain
The LORD grants his loving-kindness in the daytime;* in the night season his song
is with me, a prayer to the God of my life.

The Litany
For the peace from above, for the loving-kindness of God, and for the salvation of
my soul, I pray to the Lord.
Lord, have mercy.
For the peace of the world, for the welfare of the Holy Church of God, and for the
unity of all peoples, I pray to the Lord.
Lord, have mercy.
For the leaders of the nations and for all in authority, I pray to the Lord.
Lord, have mercy.
For the aged and infirm, for the widowed and orphans, and for the sick and the
suffering, I pray to the Lord.
Lord, have mercy.
For the poor and the oppressed, for the unemployed and the destitute, for prisoners
and captives, and for all who remember and care for them, I pray to the Lord.
Lord, have mercy.
For all who have died in the hope of the resurrection, and for all the departed,
I pray to the Lord.
Lord, have mercy.

The Thanksgiving

Lord, you now have set your servant free to go in peace as you have promised; for
these eyes of mine have seen the Savior whom you have prepared for all the
world to see: A Light to enlighten the nations, and the glory of your people
Israel. *Amen*

Nunc Dimittis

The Final Petition

Now guide me waking, O Lord, and guard me sleeping; that awake I may watch
with Christ, and asleep, I may rest in peace. *Amen.*

The Office of Dawn

**Observed on the Hour or Half-Hour
Between 4:30 and 7:30 a.m.**

The Call to Prayer

Sing to the LORD with thanksgiving;* make music to our God upon the harp.

Psalm 147:7

The Request for Presence

My soul waits for the LORD, more than watchmen for the morning,* more than
watchmen for the morning.

Psalm 130:5

The Greeting

Glory be to the Father, and the Son, and the Holy Spirit.
As it was in the beginning, it is now
And ever shall be, world without end. *Amen.*

Gloria Patri

The Hymn

O Zion, haste, your mission high fulfilling,
To tell to all the world that God is light,
That He who made all nations is not willing
One soul should perish, lost in shades of night.
Proclaim to every people, tongue, and nation
That God, in Whom they live and move, is love;
Tell how He stooped to save His lost creation,
And died on earth that we might live above.
Give of your sons and daughters to bear the messages glorious;
Give of your wealth to speed them on their way;
Pour out your soul for them in prayer victorious;
O Zion, haste to bring the brighter day.

Mary A. Thomson, adapted

125

The Psalm   The LORD Takes Pleasure in His People

Let Israel rejoice in his Maker;* let the children of Zion be joyful in their King.
Let them praise his Name in the dance;* let them sing praise to him with timbrel
  and harp.
For the LORD takes pleasure in his people* and adorns the poor with victory.
Let the faithful rejoice in triumph;* let them be joyful on their beds.

Psalm 149:2–5

The Gloria in Excelsis

Glory to God in the highest, and on earth peace to people of good will.
  We praise you.
  We bless you.
  We adore you.
  We glorify you.
We give thanks to you for your great glory.

The Small Verse

For if while we were enemies we were reconciled to God by the death of his Son,
  much more, now that we are, shall we be saved by his life.

Romans 5:10

The Lord's Prayer

The Final Blessing

May the LORD bless us and keep us and cause His face to shine upon us from this
  day forth and forever more. *Amen.*

♫

Tuesday, Month of April

The Office of Midnight   Observed on the Hour or Half-Hour
                                Between 10:30 p.m.✢ and 1:30 a.m.

The Call to Prayer

Praise God, from whom all blessings flow; praise him, all creatures here below;
  praise him above, you heavenly hosts; praise Father, Son, and Holy Ghost.

Doxology

The Request for Presence

O LORD, let my prayer be set forth in your sight as incense,* the lifting up of my
hands as the evening sacrifice.

Psalm 141:2, adapted

The Greeting

Our Father, may Your will be done, on earth as in Heaven.

The Canticle   The First Song of Isaiah
Ecce, Deus

Surely, it is God who saves me;*
    I will trust in him and not be afraid.
For the Lord is my stronghold and my sure defense,*
    and he will be my Savior.
Therefore you shall draw water with rejoicing*
    from the springs of salvation.
And on that day you shall say,*
    Give thanks to the Lord and call upon his Name;
Make his deeds known among the peoples;*
    see that they remember that his Name is exalted.
Sing praises of the Lord, for he has done great things,*
    and this is known in all the world.
Cry aloud, inhabitants of Zion, ring out your joy,*
    for the great one in the midst of you is the Holy One of Israel.

Isaiah 12:2–6

The Psalm   The Law of the LORD Is Perfect

The law of the LORD is perfect and revives the soul;* the testimony of the LORD is
    sure and gives wisdom to the innocent.
The statutes of the LORD are just and rejoice the heart;* the commandment of the
    LORD is clear and gives light to the eyes.
The fear of the LORD is clean and endures for ever;* the judgments of the LORD are
    true and righteous altogether.
More to be desired are they than gold, more than much fine gold,* sweeter far
    than honey, than honey in the comb.
By them also is your servant enlightened,* and in keeping them there is great
    reward.

Psalm 19:7–11

The Gloria

The Small Verse

If your enemy is hungry, give him bread to eat; and if he is thirsty, give him water to
    drink; for you will heap coals of fire on his head, and the Lord will reward you.

Proverbs 25:21–22

The Final Thanksgiving

I will greatly rejoice in the LORD, my soul shall exult in my God; for he has
clothed me with the garments of salvation, he has covered me with the robe of
righteousness, as a bridegroom decks himself with a garland, and as a bride
adorns herself with her jewels.

Isaiah 61:10

The Petition

May the Lord GOD, father of grace and mercy, grant all who dwell here a peaceful
night and a perfect end. *Amen.*

The Office of the Night Watch   Observed on the Hour or Half-Hour
Between 1:30 and 4:30 a.m.

The Call to Prayer

Behold now, bless the LORD, all you servants of the LORD,* you that stand by night
in the house of the LORD.
Lift up your hands in the holy place and bless the LORD;* the LORD who made
heaven and earth bless you out of Zion.

Psalm 134

The Request for Presence

O God, come to my assistance.
O Lord, make haste to help me.

The Greeting

Those who trust in the LORD are like Mount Zion,* which cannot be moved, but
stands fast for ever.

Psalm 125:1

The Refrain for the Night Watch

Yours is the day, yours also the night;* you established the moon and the sun.

Psalm 74:15

The Psalm   The LORD Will Make Your Enemies Your Footstool

The LORD said to my Lord, "Sit at my right hand,* until I make your enemies your
footstool."
The LORD will send the scepter of your power out of Zion,* saying, "Rule over
your enemies round about you.
Princely state has been yours from the day of your birth;* in the beauty of holiness
have I begotten you, like dew from the womb of the morning."
The LORD has sworn and he will not recant:* "You are a priest for ever after the
order of Melchizedek."

Psalm 110:1–4

The Refrain
Yours is the day, yours also the night;* you established the moon and the sun.

A Reading
But as far as the substance of the resurrection body is concerned, it will even then still be "flesh." This is why the body of Christ is named as "flesh" after His resurrection. Wherefore the apostle also says, "What is sown as a natural body [*corpus animale*] rises as a spiritual body [*corpus spirituale*]." For there will then (after the resurrection) be such concord between flesh and spirit—i.e., the spirit quickening the servant flesh without any need for sustenance therefrom—that there will be no further conflict within ourselves. And just as there will be no more external enemies to bear with, so neither will we have to bear with ourselves as enemies within.

St. Augustine (ca. 410 CE), The Reality of the Resurrection

The Refrain
Yours is the day, yours also the night;* you established the moon and the sun.

The Litany
Father, I pray for your holy catholic Church;
> *That we all may be one.*

Grant that every member of the Church may truly and humbly serve you;
> *That your Name may be glorified by all people.*

I pray for all who govern and hold authority in the nations of the world;
> *That there may be justice and peace on the earth.*

Have compassion on those who suffer from any grief or trouble;
> *That they may be delivered from their distress.*

Give to the departed eternal rest.
> *Let light perpetual shine upon them.*

I praise you for your saints who have entered into joy;
> *May I also come to share in your heavenly kingdom.*

The Thanksgiving
Lord, you now have set your servant free to go in peace as you have promised; for these eyes of mine have seen the Savior whom you have prepared for all the world to see: A Light to enlighten the nations, and the glory of your people Israel. *Amen.*

Nunc Dimittis

The Final Petition
Now guide me waking, O Lord, and guard me sleeping; that awake I may watch with Christ, and asleep, I may rest in peace. *Amen.*

The Office of Dawn

Observed on the Hour or Half-Hour Between 4:30 and 7:30 a.m.

The Call to Prayer

Worship the LORD. O Jerusalem;* praise your God, O Zion;
For he has strengthened the bars of your gates.

Psalm 147:13–14a

The Request for Presence

My soul waits for the LORD, more than watchmen for the morning,* more than
watchmen for the morning.

Psalm 130:5

The Greeting

Glory be to the Father, and the Son, and the Holy Spirit.
As it was in the beginning, it is now
And ever shall be, world without end. *Amen.*

Gloria Patri

The Hymn

Sun of my soul, my Saviour dear,
It is not night if You are near;
Oh may no earth-born cloud arise
Ever to hide You from my eyes!
Abide with me from morn till eve,
For without You I cannot live;
And abide with me when night is nigh,
For without You I dare not die.
Come now and bless us as we wake,
Ere through the world our way we make,
Till in the ocean of Thy love
We lose ourselves in heaven above.

John Keble, adapted

The Psalm   *He Gives Snow Like Wool*

The LORD sends out his command to the earth,* and his word runs very swiftly.
He gives snow like wool;* he scatters hoarfrost like ashes.
He scatters his hail like bread crumbs;* who can stand against his cold?
He sends forth his word and melts them;* he blows with his wind, and the waters flow.

Psalm 147:13–19

The Gloria in Excelsis

Glory to God in the highest, and on earth peace to people of good will.
We praise you.
We bless you.

We adore you.
We glorify you.
We give thanks to you for your great glory.

The Small Verse

This is the message we have heard from him and proclaim to you, that God is light
and in him is no darkness at all. If we say we have fellowship with him while
we walk in darkness, we lie and do not live according to the truth; but if we
walk in the light, as he is in the light, we have fellowship with one another.

1 John 1:5–7a

The Lord's Prayer

The Final Blessing

May the LORD bless us and keep us and cause His face to shine upon us from this
day forth and forever more. *Amen.*

Wednesday, Month of April

The Office of Midnight

**Observed on the Hour or Half-Hour
Between 10:30 p.m.✝ and 1:30 a.m.**

The Call to Prayer

Sing to God, sing praises to his Name; exalt him who rides upon the heavens;*
YAHWEH is his Name, rejoice before him!

Psalm 68:4

The Request for Presence

O LORD, let my prayer be set forth in your sight as incense,* the lifting up of my
hands as the evening sacrifice.

Psalm 141:2, adapted

The Greeting

Our Father, give us this day our daily bread.

The Canticle

A Song of Creation—Part Two
Benedicite, omnia opera Domini

Glorify the Lord, all you works of the Lord,*
praise him and highly exalt him for ever.
In the firmament of his power, glorify the Lord,*
praise him and highly exalt him for ever.

Let the earth glorify the Lord,*
  praise him and highly exalt him for ever.
Glorify the Lord, O mountains and hills, and all that grows upon the earth,*
  praise him and highly exalt him for ever.
Glorify the Lord, O springs of water, seas, and streams,*
  O whales and all that move in the waters.
All birds of the air, glorify the Lord,*
  praise him and highly exalt him for ever.
Glorify the Lord, O beasts of the wild,*
  and all you flocks and herds.
O men and women everywhere, glorify the Lord,*
  praise him and highly exalt him for ever.

Song of the Three Young Men, 52–61

The Psalm   *May God Give Us His Blessing*
May God be merciful to us and bless us,* show us the light of his countenance and
  come to us.
Let your ways be known upon earth,* your saving health among all nations.
Let the peoples praise you, O God;* let all the peoples praise you.
Let the nations be glad and sing for joy,* for you judge the peoples with equity
  and guide all the nations upon earth.
Let the peoples praise you, O God;* let all the peoples praise you.
The earth has brought forth her increase;* may God, our own God, give us his
  blessing.

Psalm 67:1–6

The Gloria

The Small Verse
But God, who is rich in mercy, out of the great love with which he loved us, even
  when we were dead through our trespasses, made us alive together with Christ
  (by grace you have been saved).

Ephesians 2:4–5

The Final Thanksgiving
I will greatly rejoice in the LORD, my soul shall exult in my God; for he has
  clothed me with the garments of salvation, he has covered me with the robe of
  righteousness, as a bridegroom decks himself with a garland, and as a bride
  adorns herself with her jewels.

Isaiah 61:10

The Petition
May the Lord GOD, father of grace and mercy, grant all who dwell here a peaceful
  night and a perfect end. *Amen*

132

The Office of the Night Watch   **Observed on the Hour or Half-Hour**
Between 1:30 and 4:30 a.m.

The Call to Prayer
Behold now, bless the LORD, all you servants of the LORD,* you that stand by night
  in the house of the LORD.
Lift up your hands in the holy place and bless the LORD;* the LORD who made
  heaven and earth bless you out of Zion.

Psalm 134

The Request for Presence
O God, come to my assistance.
O Lord, make haste to help me.

The Greeting
For you are the LORD, most high over all the earth;* you are exalted far above all
  gods.

Psalm 97:9

The Refrain for the Night Watch
I commune with my heart in the night;* I ponder and search my mind.

Psalm 77:6

The Psalm   *How Priceless Is Your Love, O God*
Your love, O LORD, reaches to the heavens,* and your faithfulness to the clouds.
Your righteousness is like the strong mountains, your justice like the great deep;*
  you save both man and beast, O LORD.
How priceless is your love, O God!* your people take refuge under the shadow of
  your wings.
They feast upon the abundance of your house;* you give them drink from the river
  of your delights.
For with you is the well of life,* and in your light we see light.
Continue your loving-kindness to those who know you,* and your favor to those
  who are true of heart.

Psalm 36:5–10

The Refrain
I commune with my heart in the night;* I ponder and search my mind.

A Reading
Christ, be with me, Christ, before me, Christ, behind me,
Christ in me, Christ beneath me, Christ above me,
Christ on my right, Christ on my left,
Christ where I lie, Christ where I sit, Christ where I arise,

133

Christ in the heart of everyone who thinks of me,
Christ in the mouth of everyone who speaks of me,
Christ in every eye that sees me,
Christ in every ear that hears me.
   Salvation is of the Lord,
   Salvation is of the Lord,
   Salvation is of the Christ,
   May your salvation, O Lord, be ever with us.

St. Patrick (389–461 CE)

The Refrain
I commune with my heart in the night;* I ponder and search my mind.

The Litany
Grant, Almighty God, that all who confess your Name may be united in your truth,
   live together in your love, and reveal your glory in the world. ˏ
   Lord, in your mercy, hear my prayer.
Guide the people of this land, and of all the nations, in the ways of justice and
   peace; that we may honor one another and serve the common good.
   Lord, in your mercy, hear my prayer.
Give us all a reverence for the earth as your own creation, that we may use its
   resources rightly in the service of others and to your honor and glory.
   Lord, in your mercy, hear my prayer.
Bless all whose lives are closely linked with mine, and grant that I may serve
   Christ in them, and love even as he loves me.
   Lord, in your mercy, hear my prayer.
Comfort and heal all those who suffer in body, mind, or spirit; give them courage
   and hope in their troubles, and bring them the joy of your salvation.
   Lord, in your mercy, hear my prayer.
I commend to your mercy all who have died, that your will for them may be
   fulfilled; and I pray that I may share with all your saints in your eternal
   kingdom.
   Lord, in your mercy, hear my prayer.

The Thanksgiving
Lord, you now have set your servant free to go in peace as you have promised; for
   these eyes of mine have seen the Savior whom you have prepared for all the
   world to see: A Light to enlighten the nations, and the glory of your people
   Israel. *Amen.*

Nunc Dimittis

The Final Petition
Now guide me waking, O Lord, and guard me sleeping; that awake I may watch
   with Christ, and asleep, I may rest in peace. *Amen.*

134

The Office of Dawn

Observed on the Hour or Half-Hour
Between 4:30 and 7:30 a.m.

The Call to Prayer

Hallelujah! Sing to the LORD a new song;* sing his praise in the congregation of
the faithful.

Psalm 149:1

The Request for Presence

My soul waits for the LORD, more than watchmen for the morning,* more than
watchmen for the morning.

Psalm 130:5

The Greeting

Glory be to the Father, and the Son, and the Holy Spirit.
As it was in the beginning, it is now
And ever shall be, world without end. *Amen.*

Gloria Patri

The Hymn

Jesu, the very thought of Thee,
with sweetness fills my breast,
but sweeter still Your face to see,
and in Your presence rest.
Nor voice can sing, nor heart can frame,
nor can the memory find
a sweeter sound than Your blest Name,
O Savior of mankind!
Jesu, our only joy be Thou.
As You our prize wilt be:
Jesu, be all our glory now,
and through eternity. *Amen.*

St. Bernard (11th c. Latin), translated by Fr. Edward Casawall

The Psalm

Praise Him for His Mighty Acts

Praise him for his mighty acts;* praise him for his excellent greatness.
Praise him with the blast of the ram's-horn;* praise him with lyre and harp.
Praise him with timbrel and dance;* praise him with strings and pipe.
Praise him with resounding cymbals;* praise him with loud-clanging cymbals.
Let everything that has breath* praise the LORD. Hallelujah!

Psalm 150:2–6

The Gloria in Excelsis

Glory to God in the highest, and on earth peace to people of good will.
We praise you.
We bless you.

135

We adore you.
We glorify you.
We give thanks to you for your great glory.

The Small Verse
And Jesus said: Peace I leave with you; my peace I give to you; not as the world
gives do I give to you. Let not your hearts be troubled, neither let them be
afraid.

John 14:27

The Lord's Prayer

The Final Blessing
May the LORD bless us and keep us and cause His face to shine upon us from this
day forth and forever more. *Amen.*

༈

Thursday, Month of April

The Office of Midnight   **Observed on the Hour or Half-Hour
                                     Between 10:30 p.m.✛ and 1:30 a.m.**

The Call to Prayer
I will sing of mercy and justice;* to you, O LORD, will I sing praises.

Psalm 101:1

The Request for Presence
O LORD, let my prayer be set forth in your sight as incense,* the lifting up of my
hands as the evening sacrifice.

Psalm 141:2, adapted

The Greeting
Our Father, forgive us our sins as we forgive those who have sinned against us.

The Canticle   *A Song of Penitence*
                                            Kyrie Pantokrator

And now, O Lord, I bend the knee of my heart,*
    and make my appeal, sure of your gracious goodness.
I have sinned, O Lord, I have sinned,*
    and I know my wickedness only too well.
Therefore I make this prayer to you:*
    Forgive me, Lord, forgive me.

Do not let me perish in my sin,*
    nor condemn me to the depths of the earth.
For you, O Lord, are the God of those who repent,*
    and in me you will show forth your goodness.
Unworthy as I am, you will save me, in accordance with your great mercy,*
    and I will praise you without ceasing all the days of my life.
For all the powers of heaven sing your praises,*
    and yours is the glory to ages of ages. *Amen.*

Prayer of Manasseh 11–15

The Psalm   *Wait Upon the Lord*

O Lord, I am not proud;* I have no haughty looks.
I do not occupy myself with great matters,* or with things that are too hard for me.
But I still my soul and make it quiet, like a child upon its mother's breast;* my
    soul is quieted within me.
O Israel, wait upon the Lord,* from this time forth for evermore.

Psalm 131

The Gloria

The Small Verse
He was despised and rejected by men; a man of sorrows, and acquainted with
    grief; and as one from whom men hide their faces he was despised, and we
    esteemed him not.

Isaiah 53:3

The Final Thanksgiving
I will greatly rejoice in the Lord, my soul shall exult in my God; for he has
    clothed me with the garments of salvation, he has covered me with the robe of
    righteousness, as a bridegroom decks himself with a garland, and as a bride
    adorns herself with her jewels.

Isaiah 61:10

The Petition
May the Lord God, father of grace and mercy, grant all who dwell here a peaceful
    night and a perfect end. *Amen.*

The Office of the Night Watch   Observed on the Hour or Half-Hour
Between 1:30 and 4:30 a.m.

The Call to Prayer
Behold now, bless the Lord, all you servants of the Lord,* you that stand by night
    in the house of the Lord.

137

Lift up your hands in the holy place and bless the LORD;* the LORD who made
heaven and earth bless you out of Zion.

Psalm 134

The Request for Presence
O God, come to my assistance.
O Lord, make haste to help me.

The Greeting
Out of Zion, perfect in its beauty,* God reveals himself in glory.
Let the heavens declare the rightness of his cause;* for God himself is judge.

Psalm 50:2, 6

The Refrain for the Night Watch
You shall not be afraid of any terror by night,* nor of the arrow that flies by day;

Psalm 91: 5

The Psalm   Show How Upright the LORD Is
The righteous shall flourish like a palm tree,* and shall spread abroad like a cedar
of Lebanon.
Those who are planted in the house of the LORD* shall flourish in the courts of our
God;
They shall still bear fruit in old age;* they shall be green and succulent;
That they may show how upright the LORD is,* my Rock, in whom there is no fault.

Psalm 92:11–14

The Refrain
You shall not be afraid of any terror by night,* nor of the arrow that flies by day;

A Reading
But above all Thy Heart, sweet Jesus my God, was wounded so that by a visible
wound we would be enabled to see the invisible wound of Thy love. For how
could the ardor of this Thy love be better shown than by this, that not only Thy
body, but even Thy very Heart was pierced with a lance? Truly the wounds of
the flesh showed forth the wounds of the spirit. Who is there who would not
love a heart so wounded? Who would not love one so loving?

St. Bonaventure (ca. 1217–74), Sermons

The Refrain
You shall not be afraid of any terror by night,* nor of the arrow that flies by day;

The Litany
For the holy Church of God, that it may be filled with truth and love, and be found
without fault at the day of your coming, I pray to you, O Lord.
Lord, in your mercy, hear my prayer

For all who fear God and believe in you, Lord Christ, that our divisions may cease, and that all may be one as you and the Father are one, I pray to you, O Lord.
Lord, in your mercy, hear my prayer.

For those who do not yet believe, and for those who have lost their faith, that they may receive the light of the Gospel, I pray to you, O Lord.
Lord, in your mercy, hear my prayer.

For my enemies and those who wish me harm, and for all whom I have injured or offended, I pray to you, O Lord.
Lord, in your mercy, hear my prayer.

For all who have commended themselves to my prayers; for my family, friends, and neighbors; that being freed from anxiety, they may live in joy, peace, and health, I pray to you, O Lord.
Lord, in your mercy, hear my prayer.

For myself; for the forgiveness of my sins, and for the grace of the Holy Spirit to amend my life, I pray to you, O Lord.
Lord, in your mercy, hear my prayer

The Thanksgiving

Lord, you now have set your servant free to go in peace as you have promised; for these eyes of mine have seen the Savior whom you have prepared for all the world to see: A Light to enlighten the nations, and the glory of your people Israel. *Amen.*

Nunc Dimittis

The Final Petition

Now guide me waking, O Lord, and guard me sleeping; that awake I may watch with Christ, and asleep, I may rest in peace. *Amen.*

The Office of Dawn
Observed on the Hour or Half-Hour Between 4:30 and 7:30 a.m.

The Call to Prayer

Let everything that has breath* praise the LORD. Hallelujah!

Psalm 150:6

The Request for Presence

My soul waits for the LORD, more than watchmen for the morning,* more than watchmen for the morning.

Psalm 130:5

The Greeting

Glory be to the Father, and to the Son, and to the Holy Spirit.
As it was in the beginning, it is now
And ever shall be, world without end. *Amen.*

Gloria Patri

The Hymn

All glory, laud and honor
to you, Redeemer, King,
to whom the lips of children
made sweet hosannas ring.
The company of angels
are praising you on high,
and we with all creation
in chorus make reply.
All glory, laud, and honor
to you, Redeemer, King,
to whom the lips of children
make sweet hosannas ring.

Theodulph of Orleans (9th c. Latin), translated by John Mason Neale

The Psalm   *He Commanded and They Were Created*

Praise the LORD from the heavens;* praise him in the heights.
Praise him, all you angels of his;* praise him, all his host.
Praise him, sun and moon;* praise him, all you shining stars.
Praise him, heaven of heavens,* and you waters above the heavens.
Let them praise the Name of the LORD;* for he commanded, and they were created.
He made them stand fast for ever and ever;* he gave them a law which shall not
　pass away.

Psalm 148:1b–6

The Gloria in Excelsis

Glory to God in the highest, and on earth peace to people of good will.
　We praise you.
　We bless you.
　We adore you.
　We glorify you.
We give thanks to you for your great glory

The Small Verse

Jesus said: A new commandment I give to you that you love one another; even as
　I have loved you, that you should also love one another. By this will all men
　know that you are my disciples, if you have love one for another.

John 13:34–35

The Lord's Prayer

The Final Blessing

May the LORD bless us and keep us and cause His face to shine upon us from this
　day forth and forever more. *Amen.*

Friday, Month of April

The Office of Midnight **Observed on the Hour or Half-Hour Between 10:30 p.m.✟ and 1:30 a.m.**

The Call to Prayer
Accept, O LORD, the willing tribute of my lips,* and teach me your judgments.

Psalm 119:108

The Request for Presence
O LORD, let my prayer be set forth in your sight as incense,* the lifting up of my hands as the evening sacrifice.

Psalm 141:2, adapted

The Greeting
Our Father, lead us not into temptation, but deliver us from evil.

The Canticle ***A Song of Penitence***
Kyrie Pantokrator

O Lord and Ruler of the hosts of heaven,*
  God of Abraham, Isaac, and Jacob, and of all their righteous offspring:
You made the heavens and the earth,*
  with all their vast array.
All things quake with fear at your presence;*
  they tremble because of your power.
But your merciful promise is beyond all measure;*
  it surpasses all that our minds can fathom.
O Lord, you are full of compassion,*
  long-suffering, and abounding in mercy.
You hold back your hand;*
  you do not punish as we deserve.
In your great goodness, Lord, you have promised forgiveness to sinners,*
  that they may repent of their sin and be saved.

Prayer of Manasseh 1–2, 4, 6–7

The Psalm ***LORD, You Laid the Foundations of the Earth***
And I said, "O my God, do not take me away in the midst of my days;* your years endure throughout all generations.
In the beginning, O LORD, you laid the foundations of the earth,* and the heavens are the work of your hands;
They shall perish, but you will endure; they all shall wear out like a garment;* as clothing you will change them, and they shall be changed;
But you are always the same,* and your years will never end.
The children of your servants shall continue,* and their offspring shall stand fast in your sight."

Psalm 102:24–28

141

The Gloria

The Small Verse
For the mountains may depart and the hills be removed, but my steadfast love
  shall not depart from you, and my covenant of peace shall not be removed,
  says the LORD, who has compassion on you.

Isaiah 54:10

The Final Thanksgiving
I will greatly rejoice in the LORD, my soul shall exult in my God; for he has
  clothed me with the garments of salvation, he has covered me with the robe of
  righteousness, as a bridegroom decks himself with a garland, and as a bride
  adorns herself with her jewels.

Isaiah 61:10

The Petition
May the Lord GOD, father of grace and mercy, grant all who dwell here a peaceful
  night and a perfect end. *Amen.*

The Office of the Night Watch — Observed on the Hour or Half-Hour Between 1:30 and 4:30 a.m.

The Call to Prayer
Behold now, bless the LORD, all you servants of the LORD,* you that stand by night
  in the house of the LORD.
Lift up your hands in the holy place and bless the LORD;* the LORD who made
  heaven and earth bless you out of Zion.

Psalm 134

The Request for Presence
O God, come to my assistance.
O Lord, make haste to help me.

The Greeting
I love you, O LORD my strength,* O LORD my stronghold, my crag, and my haven.
My God, my rock in whom I put my trust,* my shield, the horn of my salvation,
  and my refuge; you are worthy of praise.

Psalm 18:1–2

The Refrain for the Night Watch
It is a good thing to give thanks to the LORD,* and to sing praises to your Name,
  O Most High;
To tell of your loving-kindness early in the morning* and of your faithfulness in
  the night season.

Psalm 92:1–2

The Psalm   The LORD, My Refuge and My Stronghold

He who dwells in the shelter of the Most High,* abides under the shadow of the
    Almighty.
He shall say to the LORD, "You are my refuge and my stronghold,* my God in
    whom I put my trust."
He shall deliver you from the snare of the hunter* and from the deadly pestilence.
He shall cover you with his pinions, and you shall find refuge under his wings;*
    his faithfulness shall be a shield and buckler.
You shall not be afraid of any terror by night,* nor of the arrow that flies by day;
Of the plague that stalks in the darkness,* nor of the sickness that lays waste at
    mid-day.
A thousand shall fall at your side and ten thousand at your right hand,* but it shall
    not come near you.

Psalm 91:1–7

The Refrain

It is a good thing to give thanks to the LORD,* and to sing praises to your Name,
    O Most High;
To tell of your loving-kindness early in the morning* and of your faithfulness in
    the night season.

A Reading

God deliver us from saying, "We are not angels," or "We are not saints," whenever
    we commit some imperfection. We may not be; but what a good thing it is for
    us to reflect that we can be if we will only try and if God gives us His hand! Do
    not be afraid that He will fail to do His part if we do not fail to do ours. And
    since we come here for no other reason, let us put our hands to the plough, as
    they say. . . . We must have a holy boldness, for God helps the strong, being no
    respecter of persons.

St. Teresa of Avila (1562 CE), The Way of Perfection

The Refrain

It is a good thing to give thanks to the LORD,* and to sing praises to your Name,
    O Most High;
To tell of your loving-kindness early in the morning* and of your faithfulness in
    the night season.

The Litany

For the peace of the world, that a spirit of respect and forbearance may grow
    among nations and peoples, I pray to you, O Lord.
    Lord, hear my prayer.
For those in positions of public trust, that they may serve justice, and promote the
    dignity and freedom of every person, I pray to you, O Lord.
    Lord, hear my prayer.

For the poor, the persecuted, the sick, and all who suffer; for refugees, prisoners, and all who are in danger; that they may be relieved and protected, I pray to you, O Lord.
Lord, hear my prayer.
For the forgiveness of my sins, and for the grace of the Holy Spirit to amend my life, I pray to you, O Lord.
Lord, hear my prayer.
For all who have died in the communion of your Church, and those whose faith is known to you alone, that, with all the saints, they may have rest in that place where there is no pain or grief, but life eternal, I pray to you, O Lord.
Lord, hear my prayer
Rejoicing in the fellowship of the ever-blessed Virgin Mary and all the saints, I commend my self and all your faithful to Christ our God.
To you, O Lord our God.

The Thanksgiving

Lord, you now have set your servant free to go in peace as you have promised; for these eyes of mine have seen the Savior whom you have prepared for all the world to see: A Light to enlighten the nations, and the glory of your people Israel. *Amen.*

Nunc Dimittis

The Final Petition

Now guide me waking, O Lord, and guard me sleeping; that awake I may watch with Christ, and asleep, I may rest in peace. *Amen.*

The Office of Dawn   Observed on the Hour or Half-Hour Between 4:30 and 7:30 a.m.

The Call to Prayer

Hallelujah! Praise the LORD from the heavens;* praise him in the heights.

Psalm 148:1

The Request for Presence

My soul waits for the LORD, more than watchmen for the morning,* more than watchmen for the morning.

Psalm 130:5

The Greeting

Glory be to the Father, and the Son, and the Holy Spirit.
As it was in the beginning, it is now
And ever shall be, world without end. *Amen.*

Gloria Patri

The Hymn

I need you every hour, most gracious Lord;
no tender voice like yours can peace afford.

144

I need you, O, I need you; every hour I need you.
O bless me now, my Saviour, as I come to you.
I need you every hour, most Holy One;
now make me yours indeed, most blessed Son.
I need you, O, I need you; every hour I need you.
O bless me now, my Saviour, as I come to you.
I need you every hour; teach me your will;
and your rich promises in me fulfill.
I need you, O, I need you; every hour I need you.
O bless me now, my Saviour, as I come to you.

Annie S. Hawks

The Psalm   *He Covers the Heavens with Clouds*

He covers the heavens with clouds* and prepares rain for the earth;
He makes grass to grow upon the mountains* and green plants to serve mankind.
He provides food for flocks and herds* and for the young ravens when they cry.
He is not impressed by the might of a horse;* he has no pleasure in the strength of a man;
But the LORD has pleasure in those who fear him,* in those who await his gracious favor.

Psalm 147:8–12

The Gloria in Excelsis

Glory to God in the highest, and on earth peace to people of good will.
    We praise you.
    We bless you.
    We adore you.
    We glorify you.
We give thanks to you for your great glory.

The Small Verse

And being found in human form, he humbled himself and became obedient unto death, even death on a cross. Therefore God has highly exalted him and bestowed on him the name which is above every name, that at the name of Jesus every knee should bow, in heaven and on earth and under the earth, and every tongue confess that Jesus Christ is Lord, to the glory of God the Father.

Philippians 2:8–11

The Lord's Prayer

The Final Blessing

May the Lord, bless us and keep us and cause His face to shine upon us from this day forth and forever more. *Amen.*

Saturday, Month of April

The Office of Midnight

Observed on the Hour or Half-Hour
Between 10:30 p.m.✣ and 1:30 a.m.

The Call to Prayer
I consider the days of old;* I remember the years long past;
I commune with my heart in the night;* I ponder and search my mind.

Psalm 77:5–6

The Request for Presence
O LORD, let my prayer be set forth in your sight as incense,* the lifting up of my
hands as the evening sacrifice.

Psalm 141:2, adapted

The Greeting
Our Father, Yours are the kingdom, the power, and the glory forever.

The Canticle

The Song of Zechariah
Benedictus Dominus Deus

Blessed be the Lord, the God of Israel;*
he has come to his people and set them free.
He has raised up for us a mighty savior,*
born of the house of his servant David . . .
You, my child, shall be called the prophet of the Most High,*
for you will go before the Lord to prepare his way,
To give his people knowledge of salvation*
by the forgiveness of their sins.
In the tender compassion of our God*
the dawn from on high shall break upon us,
To shine on those who dwell in darkness and the shadow of death,*
and to guide our feet into the way of peace.
Glory to the Father, and to the Son, and to the Holy Spirit:*
as it was in the beginning, is now, and will be for ever. *Amen.*

Luke 1:68–69, 76–79

The Psalm

Delight in the Law of the LORD
Happy are they who have not walked in the counsel of the wicked,* nor lingered
in the way of sinners, nor sat in the seats of the scornful!
Their delight is in the law of the LORD,* and they meditate on his law day and night.
They are like trees planted by streams of water, bearing fruit in due season, with
leaves that do not wither;* everything they do shall prosper.
It is not so with the wicked;* they are like chaff which the wind blows away.

146

Therefore the wicked shall not stand upright when judgment comes,* nor the sinner in the council of the righteous.
For the LORD knows the way of the righteous,* but the way of the wicked is doomed.

Psalm 1

The Gloria

The Small Verse
Owe no man anything, except to love one another; for he who loves his neighbor has fulfilled the law.

Romans 13:8

The Final Thanksgiving
I will greatly rejoice in the LORD, my soul shall exult in my God; for he has clothed me with the garments of salvation, he has covered me with the robe of righteousness, as a bridegroom decks himself with a garland, and as a bride adorns herself with her jewels.

Isaiah 61:10

The Petition
May the Lord GOD, father of grace and mercy, grant all who dwell here a peaceful night and a perfect end. *Amen.*

The Office of the Night Watch   Observed on the Hour or Half-Hour Between 1:30 and 4:30 a.m.

The Call to Prayer
Behold now, bless the LORD, all you servants of the LORD,* you that stand by night in the house of the LORD.
Lift up your hands in the holy place and bless the LORD;* the LORD who made heaven and earth bless you out of Zion.

Psalm 134

The Request for Presence
O God, come to my assistance.
O Lord, make haste to help me.

The Greeting
You, O LORD, are my lamp;* my God, you make my darkness bright.

Psalm 18:29

The Refrain for the Night Watch
Behold now, bless the LORD, all you servants of the LORD,* you that stand by night in the house of the LORD.

Psalm 134:1

147

The Psalm — *O Lord, Let the Ungodly Know They Are But Mortal*

The ungodly have fallen into the pit they dug,* and in the snare they set is their own foot caught.

The LORD is known by his acts of justice;* the wicked are trapped in the works of their own hands.

The wicked shall be given over to the grave,* and also all the peoples that forget God.

For the needy shall not always be forgotten,* and the hope of the poor shall not perish for ever.

Rise up, O LORD, let not the ungodly have the upper hand;* let them be judged before you.

Put fear upon them, O LORD;* let the ungodly know they are but mortal.

Psalm 9:15–20

The Refrain

Behold now, bless the LORD, all you servants of the LORD,* you that stand by night in the house of the LORD.

A Reading

It is of her womb that we are born; our nourishing is from her milk, our quickening from her breath. The Spouse of Christ cannot become adulterate, she who is undefiled and chaste, owning but one home and guarding with virtuous modesty the sanctity of one chamber. She it is who keeps us for God and appoints unto the Kingdom those she has bourne. He can no longer have God for a Father who has not the Church for a Mother.

St. Cyprian, Bishop of Carthage (14 September 258), Homily

The Refrain

Behold now, bless the LORD, all you servants of the LORD,* you that stand by night in the house of the LORD.

The Litany

For all people in their daily life and work;
For my family, friends, and neighbors, and for those who are alone, I pray to you, Lord God.

For this community, the nation, and the world;
For all who work for justice, freedom, and peace, I pray to you, Lord God.

For the just and proper use of your creation;
For the victims of hunger, fear, injustice, and oppression, I pray to you, Lord God.

For all who are in danger, sorrow, or any kind of trouble;
For those who minister to the sick, the friendless, and the needy, I pray to you, Lord God.

148

For the peace and unity of the Church of God;
For all who proclaim the Gospel, and all who seek the Truth, I pray to you,
Lord God.
Hear me, Lord;
For your mercy is great.

The Thanksgiving

Lord, you now have set your servant free to go in peace as you have promised; for
these eyes of mine have seen the Savior whom you have prepared for all the
world to see: A Light to enlighten the nations, and the glory of your people
Israel. *Amen.*

Nunc Dimittis

The Final Petition

Now guide me waking, O Lord, and guard me sleeping; that awake I may watch
with Christ, and asleep, I may rest in peace. *Amen.*

The Office of Dawn   Observed on the Hour or Half-Hour
                                         Between 4:30 and 7:30 a.m.

The Call to Prayer

Hallelujah! How good it is to sing praises to our God!* How pleasant it is to honor
him with praise!

Psalm 147:1

The Request for Presence

My soul waits for the LORD, more than watchmen for the morning,* more than
watchmen for the morning.

Psalm 130:5

The Greeting

Glory be to the Father, and to the Son, and to the Holy Spirit.
As it was in the beginning, it is now
And ever shall be, world without end. *Amen.*

Gloria Patri

The Hymn

For all the saints, who from their labors rest,
who you by faith before the world confessed
your name, O Jesus, be forever blest.
Alleluia, Alleluia!
You were their rock, their fortress, and their might;
you, Lord, their captain in the well-fought fight;

149

you in the darkness drear, their one true light.
Alleluia, Alleluia!
O blest communion, fellowship divine!
We feebly struggle, they in glory shine;
yet all are one in you, for all are thine.
Alleluia, Alleluia! Amen!

William W. How

The Psalm   *Happy Are They Whose Hope Is in the LORD*

Happy are they who have the God of Jacob for their help!* whose hope is in the
    LORD their God;
Who made heaven and earth, the seas, and all that is in them;* who keeps his
    promise for ever;
Who gives justice to those who are oppressed,* and food to those who hunger.
The LORD loves the righteous; the LORD cares for the stranger;* he sustains the
    orphan and widow, but frustrates the way of the wicked.
The LORD shall reign for ever,* your God, O Zion, throughout all generations.
    Hallelujah!

Psalm 146:4–6, 8–9

The Gloria in Excelsis

Glory to God in the highest, and on earth peace to people of good will.
    We praise you.
    We bless you.
    We adore you.
    We glorify you.
We give thanks to you for your great glory

The Small Verse

There is one body and one Spirit, just as you were called to the one hope that
    belongs to your call, one Lord, one faith, one baptism, one God and Father of
    us all, who is above all and through all and in all. But grace was given to each
    of us according to the measure of Christ's gifts.

Ephesians 4:4–7

The Lord's Prayer

The Final Blessing

May the LORD bless us and keep us and cause His face to shine upon us from this
    day forth and forever more. *Amen.*

The Gloria
Glory be to God the Father, God the Son, and God the Holy Spirit. As it was
in the beginning, so it is now and so it shall ever be, world without end.
Alleluia. *Amen.*

The Lord's Prayer
Our Father, who art in heaven, hallowed be your Name.
May your kingdom come, and your will be done, on earth as in heaven.
Give us today our daily bread.
Forgive us our sins as we forgive those who sin against us.
Lead us not into temptation, but deliver us from evil;
for yours are the kingdom and the power and the glory
forever and ever. *Amen*

The following major holy days occur in May:
The Feast of St. Phillip and St. James, Apostles: *May 1*
The Feast of the Visitation of the Blessed Virgin Mary: *May 31*

Prayer for use in the observation of a holy day:
Almighty God, by your Holy Spirit you have made us one with your saints in
heaven and on earth: Grant that in my earthly pilgrimage, I may always be
supported by this fellowship of love and prayer, and know myself to be
surrounded by their witness to your power and mercy. I ask this for the sake of
Jesus Christ, in whom all my intercessions are acceptable through the
Spirit, and who lives and reigns forever and ever. *Amen.*

✣ The Office of Midnight is always taken from the prayers for the day nearest
to the hour of actual observation. Thus, if the office is to be observed at 10:30 p.m.
on Sunday, the prayers will be taken from the Monday offices, and so forth.

MAY

Sunday, Month of May

The Office of Midnight   **Observed on the Hour or Half-Hour**
                                     Between 10:30 p.m.✚ and 1:30 a.m.

The Call to Prayer
Sing to the LORD with the harp,* with the harp and the voice of song.
With trumpets and the sound of the horn* shout with joy before the King, the
LORD.

Psalm 98:6–7

The Request for Presence
O LORD, let my prayer be set forth in your sight as incense,* the lifting up of my
hands as the evening sacrifice.

Psalm 141:2, adapted

The Greeting
Our Father Who art in Heaven, hallowed be Your name.

The Canticle   *You Are God*
                                                  Te Deum laudamus

You are God: we praise you;
You are the Lord; we acclaim you;
You are the eternal Father:
All creation worships you.
To you all angels, all the powers of heaven,
Cherubim and Seraphim, sing in endless praise:
    Holy, holy, holy Lord, God of power and might,
    heaven and earth are full of your glory.
The glorious company of apostles praise you.
The noble fellowship of prophets praise you.
The white-robed army of martyrs praise you.
Throughout the world the holy Church acclaims you;
    Father, of majesty unbounded,
    your true and only Son, worthy of all worship,
    and the Holy Spirit, advocate and guide.
You, Christ, are the king of glory,
the eternal Son of the Father.
When you became man to set us free
you did not shun the Virgin's womb.
You overcame the sting of death
and opened the kingdom of heaven to all believers.
You are seated at God's right hand in glory.

We believe that you will come and be our judge.
Come then, Lord, and help your people,
bought with the price of your own blood,
and bring us with your saints
to glory everlasting.

The Psalm   *Who Is Like the LORD*

Hallelujah! Give praise, you servants of the LORD;* praise the Name of the LORD.
Let the Name of the LORD be blessed,* from this time forth for evermore.
From the rising of the sun to its going down* let the Name of the LORD be praised.
The LORD is high above all nations,* and his glory above the heavens.
Who is like the LORD our God, who sits enthroned on high* but stoops to behold
    the heavens and the earth?
He takes up the weak out of the dust* and lifts up the poor from the ashes.
He sets them with the princes,* with the princes of his people.
He makes the woman of a childless house* to be a joyful mother of children.

Psalm 113

The Gloria

The Small Verse

Let a man examine himself and so eat of the bread and drink of the cup. For any
    one who eats and drinks without discerning the body eats and drinks judgment
    upon himself.

1 Corinthians 11:28–29

The Final Thanksgiving

I will greatly rejoice in the LORD, my soul shall exult in my God; for he has
    clothed me with the garments of salvation, he has covered me with the robe of
    righteousness, as a bridegroom decks himself with a garland, and as a bride
    adorns herself with her jewels.

Isaiah 61:10

The Petition

May the Lord GOD, father of all mercy, grant us who dwell here a peaceful night
    and a perfect end. *Amen.*

The Office of the Night Watch   Observed on the Hour or Half-Hour
Between 1:30 and 4:30 a.m.

The Call to Prayer

Behold now, bless the LORD, all you servants of the LORD,* you that stand by night
    in the house of the LORD.

Lift up your hands in the holy place and bless the LORD;* the LORD who made
heaven and earth bless you out of Zion.

Psalm 134

The Request for Presence
O God, come to my assistance.
O Lord, make haste to help me.

The Greeting
For you are my hope, O Lord GOD,* my confidence since I was young.
I have been sustained by you ever since I was born; from my mother's womb you
have been my strength;* my praise shall be always of you.

Psalm 71:5–6

The Refrain for the Night Watch
Darkness is not dark to you; the night is as bright as the day;* darkness and light
to you are both alike.

Psalm 139:11

The Psalm   God Is My Shield and Defense
God is my shield and defense;* he is the savior of the true in heart.
God is a righteous judge;* God sits in judgment every day.
If they will not repent, God will whet his sword;* he will bend his bow and make
it ready.
He has prepared his weapons of death;* he makes his arrows shafts of fire.
Look at those who are in labor with wickedness,* who conceive evil, and give
birth to a lie.
They dig a pit and make it deep* and fall into the hole that they have made.
Their malice turns back upon their own head;* their violence falls on their own
scalp.
I will bear witness that the LORD is righteous;* I will praise the Name of the LORD
Most High.

Psalm 7:11–18

The Refrain
Darkness is not dark to you; the night is as bright as the day;* darkness and light
to you are both alike.

A Reading
What good does it do to speak learnedly about the Trinity if, lacking humanity,
you displease the Trinity? Indeed, it is not learning that makes one holy and
just, but a virtuous life makes us pleasing to God. I would rather feel contrition
than know how to define it. For what would it profit us to know the whole
Bible by heart and the principles of the philosophers, if we live without grace

and the love of God? Vanity of vanities and all is vanity, except to love God and serve him alone.

Thomas à Kempis (ca. 1421 CE), Imitation of Christ

The Refrain
Darkness is not dark to you; the night is as bright as the day;* darkness and light to you are both alike.

The Litany
For the peace from above, for the loving-kindness of God, and for the salvation of my soul, I pray to the Lord.
Lord, have mercy.
For the peace of the world, for the welfare of the Holy Church of God, and for the unity of all peoples, I pray to the Lord.
Lord, have mercy.
For my city [town, village], for every city and community, and for those who live in them, I pray to the Lord.
Lord, have mercy.
For seasonable weather, and for an abundance of the fruits of the earth, I pray to the Lord.
Lord, have mercy.
For the good earth which God has given us, and for the wisdom and will to conserve it, I pray to the Lord.
Lord, have mercy.
For deliverance from all danger, violence, oppression, and degradation, I pray to the Lord.
Lord, have mercy.
For the absolution and remission of my sins and offenses, I pray to the Lord.
Lord, have mercy.
Defend me, deliver me, and in your compassion protect me, O Lord, by your grace.
Lord, have mercy.

The Thanksgiving
Lord, you now have set your servant free to go in peace as you have promised; for these eyes of mine have seen the Savior whom you have prepared for all the world to see: A Light to enlighten the nations, and the glory of your people Israel. *Amen.*

Nunc Dimittis

The Final Petition
Now guide me waking, O Lord, and guard me sleeping; that awake I may watch with Christ, and asleep, I may rest in peace. *Amen.*

157

The Office of Dawn   **Observed on the Hour or Half-Hour**
Between 4:30 and 7:30 a.m.

The Call to Prayer
Let everything that has breath* praise the LORD. Hallelujah!

Psalm 150:6

The Request for Presence
My soul waits for the LORD, more than watchmen for the morning,* more than
watchmen for the morning.

Psalm 130:5

The Greeting
Glory be to the Father, and the Son, and the Holy Spirit.
As it was in the beginning, it is now
And ever shall be, world without end. *Amen.*

Gloria Patri

The Hymn
Holy, holy, holy! Lord God Almighty!
Early in the morning our song shall rise to Thee;
Holy, holy, holy! Merciful and Mighty!
God in Three Persons, blessed Trinity!
Holy, holy, holy! all the saints adore Thee,
Casting down their golden crowns around the glassy sea.
Cherubim and seraphim falling down before Thee,
Which wert, and art, and evermore shalt be.
Holy, holy, holy, Lord God Almighty!
All Thy works shall praise Thy Name in earth and sky and sea;
Holy, holy, holy! Merciful and Mighty!
God in Three Persons, blessed Trinity!

Reginald Heber

The Psalm   *Praise the Name of the LORD*
Praise the LORD from the heavens;* praise him in the heights.
Praise him, all you angels of his;* praise him, all his host.
Praise him, sun and moon;* praise him, all you shining stars.
Praise him, heaven of heavens,* and you waters above the heavens.
Let them praise the Name of the LORD;* for he commanded, and they were
created.
He made them stand fast for ever and ever;* he gave them a law which shall not
pass away.

Psalm 148:1b–6

The Gloria in Excelsis

Glory to God in the highest, and on earth peace to people of good will.
>We praise you.
>We bless you.
>We adore you.
>We glorify you.

We give thanks to you for your great glory

The Small Verse

Jesus taught us, saying: Therefore I tell you, every sin and blasphemy will be forgiven men, but the blasphemy against the Spirit will not be forgiven. And whoever says a word against the Son of man will be forgiven; but whoever speaks against the Holy Spirit will not be forgiven, either in this age or in the age to come.

Matthew 12:31–32

The Lord's Prayer

The Final Blessing

May the LORD bless us and keep us and cause His face to shine upon us from this day forth and forever more. *Amen.*

☙

Monday, Month of May

The Office of Midnight

Observed on the Hour or Half-Hour Between 10:30 p.m.✠ and 1:30 a.m.

The Call to Prayer

Let the words of my mouth and the meditation of my heart be acceptable in your sight,* O LORD, my strength and my redeemer.

Psalm 19:14

The Request for Presence

O LORD, let my prayer be set forth in your sight as incense, the lifting up of my hands as the evening sacrifice.

Psalm 141:2, adapted

The Greeting

Our Father, may Your kingdom come on earth as in Heaven.

The Canticle   *A Song of Creation—Part Two*
                                            Benedicite, omnia opera Domini

Glorify the Lord, all you works of the Lord,*
  praise him and highly exalt him for ever.
In the firmament of his power, glorify the Lord,*
  praise him and highly exalt him forever.
Let the earth glorify the Lord,*
  praise him and highly exalt him for ever.
Glorify the Lord, O mountains and hills, and all that grows upon the earth,*
  praise him and highly exalt him for ever.
Glorify the Lord, O springs of water, seas, and streams,*
  O whales and all that move in the waters.
All birds of the air, glorify the Lord,*
  praise him and highly exalt him for ever.
Glorify the Lord, O beasts of the wild,*
  and all you flocks and herds.
O men and women everywhere, glorify the Lord,*
  praise him and highly exalt him for ever.

                                    Song of the Three Young Men, 52–61

The Psalm   *Sing Praise to the LORD*
The LORD will be a refuge for the oppressed,* a refuge in time of trouble.
Those who know your Name will put their trust in you,* for you never forsake
  those who seek you, O LORD.
Sing praise to the LORD who dwells in Zion;* proclaim to the peoples the things he
  has done.

                                            Psalm 9:7–11

The Gloria

The Small Verse
Do not be fainthearted in your prayers, nor neglect to give alms.

                                            Sirach 7:10

The Final Thanksgiving
I will greatly rejoice in the LORD, my soul shall exult in my God; for he has
  clothed me with the garments of salvation, he has covered me with the robe of
  righteousness, as a bridegroom decks himself with a garland, and as a bride
  adorns herself with her jewels.

                                            Isaiah 61:10

The Petition
May the Lord GOD, father of all mercy, grant us who dwell here a peaceful night
  and a perfect end. *Amen.*

The Office of the Night Watch   **Observed on the Hour or Half-Hour**
Between 1:30 and 4:30 a.m.

The Call to Prayer

Behold now, bless the LORD, all you servants of the LORD,* you that stand by night
in the house of the LORD.
Lift up your hands in the holy place and bless the LORD;* the LORD who made
heaven and earth bless you out of Zion.

Psalm 134

The Request for Presence

O God, come to my assistance.
O Lord, make haste to help me.

The Greeting

To you, O LORD, I lift up my soul; my God, I put my trust in you;* let me not be
humiliated, nor let my enemies triumph over me.

Psalm 25:1

The Refrain for the Night Watch

I will bless the LORD who gives me counsel;* my heart teaches me, night after
night.

Psalm 16:7

The Psalm   Bless the LORD, O My Soul

As a father cares for his children,* so does the LORD care for those who fear him.
For he himself knows whereof we are made;* he remembers that we are but dust.
Our days are like the grass;* we flourish like a flower of the field;
When the wind goes over it, it is gone,* and its place shall know it no more.
But the merciful goodness of the LORD endures for ever on those who fear him,*
and his righteousness on children's children;
On those who keep his covenant* and remember his commandments and do them.
The LORD has set his throne in heaven,* and his kingship has dominion over all.
Bless the LORD, you angels of his, you mighty ones who do his bidding,* and
hearken to the voice of his word.
Bless the LORD, all you his hosts,* you ministers of his who do his will.
Bless the LORD, all you works of his, in all places of his dominion;* bless the
LORD, O my soul.

Psalm 103:13–22

The Refrain

I will bless the LORD who gives me counsel;* my heart teaches me, night after
night.

A Reading
And yet God—although nothing worthy of His greatness can be said of Him—has condescended to accept the worship of our mouths, and has desired us through the medium of our own words to rejoice in His praise.

St. Augustine (ca. 410 CE), Handbook on Faith, Hope, and Love

The Refrain
I will bless the LORD who gives me counsel;* my heart teaches me, night after night.

The Litany
O God the Father, Creator of heaven and earth,
Have mercy upon me.
O God the Son, Redeemer of the world,
Have mercy upon me.
O God the Holy Spirit, Sanctifier of the faithful,
Have mercy upon me.
O holy, blessed, and glorious Trinity, one God,
Have mercy upon me.
Remember not, Lord Christ, my offenses, nor the offenses of my forefathers; neither reward me according to my sins. Spare me, good Lord, spare your people, whom you have redeemed with your most precious blood, and by your mercy preserve us, for ever.
Spare us, good Lord.

The Thanksgiving
Lord, you now have set your servant free to go in peace as you have promised; for these eyes of mine have seen the Savior whom you have prepared for all the world to see: A Light to enlighten the nations, and the glory of your people Israel. *Amen.*

Nunc Dimittis

The Final Petition
Now guide me waking, O Lord, and guard me sleeping; that awake I may watch with Christ, and asleep, I may rest in peace. *Amen.*

The Office of Dawn   Observed on the Hour or Half-Hour Between 4:30 and 7:30 a.m.

The Call to Prayer
Hallelujah! Sing to the LORD a new song;* sing his praise in the congregation of the faithful.

Psalm 149:1

The Request for Presence

My soul waits for the LORD, more than watchmen for the morning,* more than
watchmen for the morning.

Psalm 130:5

The Greeting

Glory be to the Father, and the Son, and the Holy Spirit.
As it was in the beginning, it is now
And ever shall be, world without end. *Amen.*

Gloria Patri

The Hymn

Come, let us use the grace divine,
and all with one accord,
in a perpetual covenant join
ourselves to Christ the Lord;
Give up ourselves, thru Jesus' power,
his name to glorify;
and promise, in this sacred hour,
for God to live and die.
The covenant we this moment make
be ever kept in mind;
we will no more our God forsake,
or cast these words behind.
We never will throw off the fear
of God who hears our vow;
and if you are well pleased to hear,
come, Lord, and meet us now.

Charles Wesley

The Psalm   The LORD Shall Reign For Ever

Happy are they who have the God of Jacob for their help!* whose hope is in the
LORD their God;
Who made heaven and earth, the seas, and all that is in them;* who keeps his
promise for ever;
Who gives justice to those who are oppressed,* and food to those who hunger.
The LORD loves the righteous; the LORD cares for the stranger;* he sustains the
orphan and widow, but frustrates the way of the wicked.
The LORD shall reign for ever,* your God, O Zion, throughout all generations.
Hallelujah!

Psalm 146:4-6, 8-9

The Gloria in Excelsis

Glory to God in the highest, and on earth peace to people of good will.
We praise you.

163

We bless you.
We adore you.
We glorify you.
We give thanks to you for your great glory.

The Small Verse
Put on then, as God's chosen ones, holy and beloved, compassion, kindness,
lowliness, meekness, and patience, forbearing one another and, if one has a
complaint against another, forgiving each other; as the Lord has forgiven you,
so you also must forgive.

Colossians 3:12–13

The Lord's Prayer

The Final Blessing
May the LORD bless us and keep us and cause His face to shine upon us from this
day forth and forever more. *Amen.*

Tuesday, Month of May

The Office of Midnight   **Observed on the Hour or Half-Hour
Between 10:30 p.m.✢ and 1:30 a.m.**

The Call to Prayer
I will call upon the LORD,* and so shall I be saved from my enemies.

Psalm 18:3

The Request for Presence
O LORD, let my prayer be set forth in your sight as incense,* the lifting up of my
hands as the evening sacrifice.

Psalm 141:2, adapted

The Greeting
Our Father, may Your will be done on earth as in Heaven.

The Canticle   **The Second Song of Isaiah**
Quaerite Dominum

Seek the Lord while he wills to be found;*
    call upon him when he draws near.

Let the wicked forsake their ways*
    and the evil ones their thoughts;
And let them turn to the Lord, and he will have compassion,*
    and to our God, for he will richly pardon.
For my thoughts are not your thoughts,*
    nor your ways my ways, says the Lord.
For as the heavens are higher than the earth,*
    so are my ways higher than your ways, and my thoughts than your thoughts.
or as rain and snow fall from the heavens*
    and return not again, but water the earth,
Bringing forth life and giving growth,*
    seed for sowing and bread for eating,
So is my word that goes forth from my mouth;*
    it will not return to me empty;
But it will accomplish that which I have purposed,*
    and prosper in that for which I sent it.

Isaiah 55:6–11

The Psalm   ***God Girds Me About with Strength***
You, O LORD, are my lamp;* my God, you make my darkness bright.
With you I will break down an enclosure;* with the help of my God I will scale
    any wall.
As for God, his ways are perfect; the words of the LORD are tried in the fire;* he is
    a shield to all who trust in him.
For who is God, but the LORD?* who is the Rock, except our God?
It is God who girds me about with strength* and makes my way secure.
He makes me sure-footed like a deer* and lets me stand firm on the heights.

Psalm 18:29–34

The Gloria

The Small Verse
And he answered them, "Go and tell John what you have seen and heard: the blind
    receive their sight, the lame walk, lepers are cleansed, and the deaf hear, the
    dead are raised up, the poor have good news preached to them. And blessed is
    he who takes no offense at me."

Luke 7:22–23

The Final Thanksgiving
I will greatly rejoice in the LORD, my soul shall exult in my God; for he has
    clothed me with the garments of salvation, he has covered me with the robe of
    righteousness, as a bridegroom decks himself with a garland, and as a bride
    adorns herself with her jewels.

Isaiah 61:10

The Petition

May the Lord GOD, father of all mercy, grant us who dwell here a peaceful night and a perfect end. *Amen.*

The Office of the Night Watch　　　　**Observed on the Hour or Half-Hour Between 1:30 and 4:30 a.m.**

The Call to Prayer

Behold now, bless the LORD, all you servants of the LORD,* you that stand by night in the house of the LORD.
Lift up your hands in the holy place and bless the LORD;* the LORD who made heaven and earth bless you out of Zion.

Psalm 134

The Request for Presence

O God, come to my assistance.
O Lord, make haste to help me.

The Greeting

Who is like you, LORD God of hosts?* O mighty LORD, your faithfulness is all around you.

Psalm 89:8

The Refrain for the Night Watch

Happy are they who have not walked in the counsel of the wicked,* nor lingered in the way of sinners, nor sat in the seats of the scornful!
Their delight is in the law of the LORD,* and they meditate on his law day and night.

Psalm 1:1–2

The Psalm　　　　*O LORD, Teach Me Your Paths*

To you, O LORD, I lift up my soul; my God, I put my trust in you;* let me not be humiliated, nor let my enemies triumph over me.
Let none who look to you be put to shame;* let the treacherous be disappointed in their schemes.
Show me your ways, O LORD,* and teach me your paths.
Lead me in your truth and teach me,* for you are the God of my salvation; in you have I trusted all the day long.

Psalm 25:1–4

The Refrain

Happy are they who have not walked in the counsel of the wicked,* nor lingered in the way of sinners, nor sat in the seats of the scornful!
Their delight is in the law of the LORD,* and they meditate on his law day and night.

A Reading

Therefore, if you would stand and not fall, cease never in your intent, but beat evermore on this cloud of unknowing that is betwixt you and your God with a sharp dart of longing love, and be loathe to think on anything less than God, and go not forth from that exercise for anything that happens. For this only is the work that destroys the root and ground of sin.

Anonymous (14th c.), The Cloud of Unknowing

The Refrain

Happy are they who have not walked in the counsel of the wicked,* nor lingered in the way of sinners, nor sat in the seats of the scornful!
Their delight is in the law of the LORD,* and they meditate on his law day and night.

The Litany

From all evil and wickedness; from sin; from the crafts and assaults of the devil; and from everlasting damnation,
Good Lord, deliver me.
From all blindness of heart; from pride, vainglory, and hypocrisy; from envy, hatred, and malice; and from all want of charity,
Good Lord, deliver me.
From all inordinate and sinful affections; and from all the deceits of the world, the flesh, and the devil,
Good Lord, deliver me.
From all false doctrine, heresy, and schism; from hardness of heart, and contempt of your Word and commandment,
Good Lord, deliver me.
By the mystery of your holy Incarnation; by your holy Nativity and submission to the Law; by your Baptism, Fasting, and Temptation,
Good Lord, deliver me.
In all time of tribulation; in all time of prosperity; in the hour of death, and in the day of judgment,
Good Lord, deliver me.

The Thanksgiving

Lord, you now have set your servant free to go in peace as you have promised; for these eyes of mine have seen the Savior whom you have prepared for all the world to see: A Light to enlighten the nations, and the glory of your people Israel. *Amen.*

Nunc Dimittis

The Final Petition

Now guide me waking, O Lord, and guard me sleeping; that awake I may watch with Christ, and asleep, I may rest in peace. *Amen.*

The Office of Dawn   **Observed on the Hour or Half-Hour**
Between 4:30 and 7:30 a.m.

The Call to Prayer
Hallelujah! Praise the LORD, O my soul!* I will praise the Lord as long as I live; I
will sing praises to my God while I have my being.

Psalm 146:1

The Request for Presence
My soul waits for the LORD, more than watchmen for the morning,* more than
watchmen for the morning.

Psalm 130:5

The Greeting
Glory be to the Father, and the Son, and the Holy Spirit.
As it was in the beginning, it is now
And ever shall be, world without end. *Amen.*

Gloria Patri

The Hymn
O strength and stay upholding all creation,
Who ever does Himself unmoved abide,
yet day by day the light in due gradation
from hour to hour through all its changes guide;
Grant to life's day a calm, unclouded ending,
an eve untouched by shadows of decay,
the brightness of a holy deathbed blending
with dawning glories of the eternal day.
Hear us, O Father, gracious and forgiving
and You, O Christ, the coeternal Word,
Who with the Holy Spirit by all things living
now and to endless ages are adored. *Amen.*

St. Ambrose, translated by J. Ellerton and F. J. A. Hort

The Psalm   *The LORD Sends Out His Command to the Earth*
The LORD sends out his command to the earth,* and his word runs very swiftly.
He gives snow like wool;* he scatters hoarfrost like ashes.
He scatters his hail like bread crumbs;* who can stand against his cold?
He sends forth his word and melts them;* he blows with his wind, and the waters
flow.

Psalm 147:16–19

The Gloria in Excelsis
Glory to God in the highest, and on earth peace to people of good will.
We praise you.
We bless you.

We adore you.
We glorify you.
We give thanks to you for your great glory.

The Small Verse
There is one body and one Spirit, just as you were called to the one hope that
belongs to your call, one Lord, one faith, one baptism, one God and Father of
us all, who is above all and through all and in all. But grace was given to each
of us according to the measure of Christ's gift.

Ephesians 4:4–7

The Lord's Prayer

The Final Blessing
May the LORD bless us and keep us and cause His face to shine upon us from this
day forth and forever more. *Amen.*

Wednesday, Month of May

The Office of Midnight   **Observed on the Hour or Half-Hour**
Between 10:30 p.m.✠ and 1:30 a.m.

The Call to Prayer
"Who can ascend the hill of the LORD?"* and who can stand in his holy place?"
"Those who have clean hands and a pure heart,* who have not pledged themselves
to falsehood, nor sworn by what is a fraud."

Psalm 24:3–4

The Request for Presence
O LORD, let my prayer be set forth in your sight as incense,* the lifting up of my
hands as the evening sacrifice.

Psalm 141:2, adapted

The Greeting
Our Father, give us this day our daily bread.

The Canticle   ***The Song of the Redeemed***
Magna et mirabilia
O ruler of the universe, Lord God, great deeds are they that you have done,*
surpassing human understanding.
Your ways are ways of righteousness and truth,*
O King of all the ages. Who can fail to do you homage, Lord,

and sing the praises of your Name?*
for you only are the Holy One.
All nations will draw near and fall down before you,*
because your just and holy works have been revealed.
Glory to the Father, and to the Son, and to the Holy Spirit:*
as it was in the beginning, is now, and will be for ever. *Amen.*

Revelation 15:3–4

The Psalm   The Lord Is My Shepherd

The LORD is my shepherd;* I shall not be in want.
He makes me lie down in green pastures* and leads me beside still waters.
He revives my soul* and guides me along right pathways for his Name's sake.
Though I walk through the valley of the shadow of death, I shall fear no evil;* for
you are with me; your rod and your staff, they comfort me.
You spread a table before me in the presence of those who trouble me;* you have
anointed my head with oil, and my cup is running over.
Surely your goodness and mercy shall follow me all the days of my life,* and I
will dwell in the house of the LORD for ever.

Psalm 23

The Gloria

The Small Verse

And he who sat upon the throne said, "Behold, I make all things new." Also he
said, "Write this, for these words are trustworthy and true." And he said to me,
"It is done! I am the Alpha and the Omega, the beginning and the end."

Revelation 21:5–6

The Final Thanksgiving

I will greatly rejoice in the LORD, my soul shall exult in my God; for he has
clothed me with the garments of salvation, he has covered me with the robe of
righteousness, as a bridegroom decks himself with a garland, and as a bride
adorns herself with her jewels.

Isaiah 61:10

The Petition

May the Lord GOD, father of all mercy, grant us who dwell here a peaceful night
and a perfect end. *Amen.*

The Office of the Night Watch   Observed on the Hour or Half-Hour
Between 1:30 and 4:30 a.m.

The Call to Prayer

Behold now, bless the LORD, all you servants of the LORD,* you that stand by night
in the house of the LORD.

Lift up your hands in the holy place and bless the LORD;* the LORD who made heaven and earth bless you out of Zion.

Psalm 134

The Request for Presence
O God, come to my assistance.
O Lord, make haste to help me.

The Greeting
Exalt yourself above the heavens, O God,* and your glory over all the earth.
So that those who are dear to you may be delivered,* save with your right hand and answer me.

Psalm 108:5–6

The Refrain for the Night Watch
The heavens declare the glory of God,* and the firmament shows his handiwork.
One day tells its tale to another,* and one night imparts knowledge to another.

Psalm 19:1–2

The Psalm   *You Know My Sitting Down and My Rising Up*
LORD, you have searched me out and known me;* you know my sitting down and my rising up; you discern my thoughts from afar.
You trace my journeys and my resting-places* and are acquainted with all my ways.
Indeed, there is not a word on my lips,* but you, O LORD, know it altogether.
You press upon me behind and before* and lay your hand upon me.
Such knowledge is too wonderful for me;* it is so high that I cannot attain to it.
Where can I go then from your Spirit?* where can I flee from your presence?

Psalm 139:1–6

The Refrain
The heavens declare the glory of God,* and the firmament shows his handiwork.
One day tells its tale to another,* and one night imparts knowledge to another.

A Reading
It is, of course, the One who, when he was teaching prayer, strongly emphasized this sentence which he put into his prayer, saying: "For if you forgive others their trespasses, your Heavenly Father will also forgive you your trespasses. But if you do not forgive others, neither will your Father forgive you your offenses." Anyone who is not awakened by such great thundering as that is not asleep, but dead! And yet such a word has power to awaken even the dead.

St. Augustine (ca. 410 CE), Handbook on Faith, Hope, and Love

The Refrain
The heavens declare the glory of God,* and the firmament shows his handiwork.
One day tells its tale to another,* and one night imparts knowledge to another.

The Litany
That it may please you to bless and keep all your people,
I beseech you to hear me, good Lord.
That it may please you to send laborers into your harvest and to draw all
humankind into your kingdom,
I beseech you to hear me, good Lord.
That it may please you to give to all people increase of grace to hear and receive
your Word, and to bring forth the fruits of the Spirit,
I beseech you to hear me, good Lord.
That it may please you to bring into the way of truth all such as have erred, and
are deceived,
I beseech you to hear me, good Lord.
That it may please you to give me a heart to love and fear you, and diligently to
live after your commandments,
I beseech you to hear me, good Lord.

The Thanksgiving
Lord, you now have set your servant free to go in peace as you have promised; for
these eyes of mine have seen the Savior whom you have prepared for all the
world to see: A Light to enlighten the nations, and the glory of your people
Israel. *Amen.*

Nunc Dimittis

The Final Petition
Now guide me waking, O Lord, and guard me sleeping; that awake I may watch
with Christ, and asleep, I may rest in peace. *Amen.*

The Office of Dawn   **Observed on the Hour or Half-Hour
Between 4:30 and 7:30 a.m.**

The Call to Prayer
Hallelujah! How good it is to sing praises to our God!* how pleasant it is to honor
him with praise!

Psalm 147:1

The Request for Presence
My soul waits for the LORD, more than watchmen for the morning,* more than
watchmen for the morning.

Psalm 130:5

The Greeting
Glory be to the Father, and the Son, and the Holy Spirit.
As it was in the beginning, it is now
And ever shall be, world without end. *Amen.*

Gloria Patri

The Hymn

God moves in a mysterious way
his wonders to perform;
he plants his footsteps in the sea,
and rides upon the storm.
Deep in unfathomable mines
of never-failing skill,
he treasures up his bright designs,
and works his sovereign will.
You fearful saints, fresh courage take,
the clouds you so much dread
are big with mercy, and shall break
in blessings on your head.

William Cowper

The Psalm   *Let Everything That Has Breath Praise the* LORD

Praise him for his mighty acts;* praise him for his excellent greatness.
Praise him with the blast of the ram's-horn;* praise him with lyre and harp.
Praise him with timbrel and dance;* praise him with strings and pipe.
Praise him with resounding cymbals;* praise him with loud-clanging cymbals.
Let everything that has breath* praise the LORD. Hallelujah!

Psalm 150:2–6

The Gloria in Excelsis

Glory to God in the highest, and on earth peace to people of good will.
    We praise you.
    We bless you.
    We adore you.
    We glorify you.
We give thanks to you for your great glory.

The Small Verse

Jesus said: All things have been delivered to me by my Father; and no one knows
    the Son except the Father, and no one knows the Father except the Son and
    those to whom the Son chooses to reveal him.

Matthew 11:27

The Lord's Prayer

The Final Blessing

May the LORD bless us and keep us and cause His face to shine upon us from this
    day forth and forever more. *Amen.*

Thursday, Month of May

The Office of Midnight   **Observed on the Hour or Half-Hour Between 10:30 p.m.✙ and 1:30 a.m.**

The Call to Prayer
In God, whose word I praise, in God I trust and will not be afraid,* for what can flesh do to me?

Psalm 56:4

The Request for Presence
O LORD, let my prayer be set forth in your sight as incense, the lifting up of my hands as the evening sacrifice.

Psalm 141:2, adapted

The Greeting
Our Father, forgive us our sins as we forgive those who have sinned against us.

The Canticle   Song of Praise
Benedictus es, Domine

Glory to you, Lord God of our fathers;*
  you are worthy of praise; glory to you.
Glory to you for the radiance of you holy Name;*
  we will praise you and highly exalt you for ever.
Glory to you in the splendor of you temple;*
  on the throne of your majesty, glory to you.
Glory to you, seated between the Cherubim;*
  we will praise you and highly exalt you for ever.
Glory to you, beholding the depths;*
  in the high vault of heaven, glory to you.
Glory to you, Father, Son, and Holy Spirit;*
  we will praise you and highly exalt you for ever.

Song of the Three Young Men, 29–34

The Psalm   God Is My King from Ancient Times
Yet God is my King from ancient times,* victorious in the midst of the earth.
You divided the sea by your might* and shattered the heads of the dragons upon the waters;
You crushed the heads of Leviathan* and gave him to the people of the desert for food.
You split open spring and torrent;* you dried up ever-flowing rivers.
Yours is the day, yours also the night;* you established the moon and the sun.
You fixed all the boundaries of the earth;* you made both summer and winter.

Psalm 74:11–17

174

The Gloria

The Small Verse
It is a fearful thing to fall into the hands of the living God.

Hebrews 10:31

The Final Thanksgiving
I will greatly rejoice in the LORD, my soul shall exult in my God; for he has
  clothed me with the garments of salvation, he has covered me with the robe of
  righteousness, as a bridegroom decks himself with a garland, and as a bride
  adorns herself with her jewels.

Isaiah 61:10

The Petition
May the Lord GOD, father of all mercy, grant us who dwell here a peaceful night
  and a perfect end. *Amen.*

The Office of the Night Watch   **Observed on the Hour or Half-Hour**
                                                        Between 1:30 and 4:30 a.m.

The Call to Prayer
Behold now, bless the LORD, all you servants of the LORD,* you that stand by night
  in the house of the LORD.
Lift up your hands in the holy place and bless the LORD;* the LORD who made
  heaven and earth bless you out of Zion.

Psalm 134

The Request for Presence
O God, come to my assistance.
O Lord, make haste to help me.

The Greeting
But I put my trust in your mercy;* my heart is joyful because of your saving help.
I will sing to the LORD, for he has dealt with me richly;* I will praise the Name of
  the Lord Most High.

Psalm 13:5–6

The Refrain for the Night Watch
The LORD grants his loving-kindness in the daytime;* in the night season his song
  is with me, a prayer to the God of my life.

Psalm 42:10

The Psalm   ***The LORD Has Heard My Supplication***
I grow weary because of my groaning;* every night I drench my bed and flood my
  couch with tears.

My eyes are wasted with grief* and worn away because of all my enemies.
Depart from me, all evildoers,* for the LORD has heard the sound of my weeping.
The LORD has heard my supplication;* the LORD accepts my prayer.

Psalm 6:6–9

The Refrain

The LORD grants his loving-kindness in the daytime;* in the night season his song
is with me, a prayer to the God of my life.

A Reading

Our heart must be kept with all carefulness both by day and night, and no place be
given to the devil; but every effort must be used that the ministers of God—that
is, those spirits who were sent to minister to those who are called to be the
heirs of salvation—may find a place within us and be delighted to enter into
the guest-chamber of our soul and, dwelling within us, may guide us by their
counsel; if indeed they do find the habitation of our heart adorned by the
practice of virtue and holiness.

Origen (ca. 185–254 CE), translated by Rufinus, De Principiis

The Refrain

The LORD grants his loving-kindness in the daytime;* in the night season his song
is with me, a prayer to the God of my life.

The Litany

That it may please you to show your mercy to all prisoners and captives, the
homeless and the hungry, and all who are desolate and oppressed,
  I beseech you to hear me, good Lord.
That it may please you to give and preserve to our use the bountiful fruits of the
earth, so that in due time all may enjoy them,
  I beseech you to hear me, good Lord.
That it may please you to inspire all your people, in our several callings, to do the
work which you gave us to do with singleness of heart as your servants, and for
the common good,
  I beseech you to hear me, good Lord.
That it may please you to visit the lonely; to strengthen all who suffer in mind,
body, and spirit; and to comfort with your presence those who are failing and
infirm,
  I beseech you to hear me, good Lord.
That it may please you to strengthen such as do stand; to comfort and help the
weak-hearted; to raise up those who fall; and finally to beat down Satan under
our feet,
  I beseech you to hear me, good Lord.
That it may please you to grant to all the faithful departed eternal life and peace,
  I beseech you to hear me, good Lord.

That it may please you to grant that, in the fellowship of all your saints, I may attain to your heavenly kingdom,

> *Son of God, I beseech you to hear me.*
> *Son of God, I beseech you to hear me.*

The Thanksgiving

Lord, you now have set your servant free to go in peace as you have promised; for these eyes of mine have seen the Savior whom you have prepared for all the world to see: A Light to enlighten the nations, and the glory of your people Israel. *Amen.*

Nunc Dimittis

The Final Petition

Now guide me waking, O Lord, and guard me sleeping; that awake I may watch with Christ, and asleep, I may rest in peace. *Amen.*

The Office of Dawn

Observed on the Hour or Half-Hour Between 4:30 and 7:30 a.m.

The Call to Prayer

Worship the LORD, O Jerusalem;* praise your God, O Zion;
For he has strengthened the bars of your gates.

Psalm 147:13–14a

The Request for Presence

My soul waits for the LORD, more than watchmen for the morning,* more than watchmen for the morning.

Psalm 130:5

The Greeting

Glory be to the Father, and the Son, and the Holy Spirit.
As it was in the beginning, it is now
And ever shall be, world without end. *Amen.*

Gloria Patri

The Hymn

The God of Abraham praise, Who reigns enthroned above;
Ancient of everlasting days, and God of Love;
Jehovah, great I AM! by earth and Heav'n confessed;
I bow and bless the sacred Name forever blessed.
He by Himself has sworn; I on His oath depend,
I shall, on eagle wings upborne, to Heaven ascend.
I shall behold His face; I shall His power adore,

177

And sing the wonders of His grace forevermore.
Before the great Three-in-One all exulting stand;
And tell the wonders He hath done, through His almighty hand:
The list'ning spheres attend, and swell the growing fame;
And sing, in songs which never end, the wondrous Name.
The whole triumphant host give thanks to God on high;
"Hail, Father, Son, and Holy Ghost," they ever cry.
Hail, Abraham's God, and mine! (I join the heav'nly lays,)
All might and majesty are Yours, and endless praise.

The Yigdal of Daniel ben Judah (ca. 1400 CE), adapted

The Psalm   *He Covers the Heavens With Clouds*
He covers the heavens with clouds* and prepares rain for the earth;
He makes grass to grow upon the mountains* and green plants to serve mankind.
He provides food for flocks and herds* and for the young ravens when they cry.
He is not impressed by the might of a horse;* he has no pleasure in the strength of
a man;
But the LORD has pleasure in those who fear him,* in those who await his gracious
favor.

Psalm 147:8–12

The Gloria in Excelsis
Glory to God in the highest, and on earth peace to people of good will.
We praise you.
We bless you.
We adore you.
We glorify you.
We give thanks to you for your great glory.

The Small Verse
Jesus said to those who questioned him: "Your father Abraham rejoiced that he
was to see my day; he saw it and was glad." The Jews then said to him, "You
are not yet fifty years old, and have you seen Abraham?" Jesus said to them,
"Truly, truly, I say to you, before Abraham was, I am."

John 8:56–58

The Lord's Prayer

The Final Blessing
May the LORD bless us and keep us and cause His face to shine upon us from this
day forth and forever more. *Amen.*

178

Friday, Month of May

The Office of Midnight

Observed on the Hour or Half-Hour Between 10:30 p.m.✝ and 1:30 a.m.

The Call to Prayer

Happy are they whose way is blameless,* who walk in the law of the LORD!
Happy are they who observe his decrees* and seek him with all their hearts!
Who never do any wrong,* but always walk in his ways.

Psalm 119:1–3

The Request for Presence

O LORD, let my prayer be set forth in your sight as incense,* the lifting up of my
　hands as the evening sacrifice.

Psalm 141:2, adapted

The Greeting

Our Father, lead us not into temptation, but deliver us from evil.

The Canticle

A Song of Penitence
Kyrie Pantokrator

O Lord and Ruler of the hosts of heaven,*
　God of Abraham, Isaac, and Jacob, and of all their righteous offspring:
You made the heavens and the earth,*
　with all their vast array.
All things quake with fear at your presence;*
　they tremble because of your power.
But your merciful promise is beyond all measure;*
　it surpasses all that our minds can fathom.
O Lord, you are full of compassion,*
　long-suffering, and abounding in mercy.
You hold back your hand;*
　you do not punish as we deserve. In your great goodness, Lord,
you have promised forgiveness to sinners,*
　that they may repent of their sin and be saved.

Prayer of Manasseh 1–2, 4, 6–7

The Psalm

The LORD Is My Strength and My Shield

Blessed is the LORD!* for he has heard the voice of my prayer.
The LORD is my strength and my shield;* my heart trusts in him, and I have been
　helped;
Therefore my heart dances for joy,* and in my song will I praise him.
The LORD is the strength of his people,* a safe refuge for his anointed.
Save your people and bless your inheritance;* shepherd them and carry them for ever.

Psalm 28:7–11

179

The Gloria

The Small Verse
Heal me, O LORD, and I shall be healed; save me, and I shall be saved; for thou art
my praise.

Jeremiah 17:14

The Final Thanksgiving
I will greatly rejoice in the LORD, my soul shall exult in my God; for he has
clothed me with the garments of salvation, he has covered me with the robe of
righteousness, as a bridegroom decks himself with a garland, and as a bride
adorns herself with her jewels.

Isaiah 61:10

The Petition
May the Lord GOD, father of all mercy, grant us who dwell here a peaceful night
and a perfect end. *Amen.*

The Office of the Night Watch   Observed on the Hour or Half-Hour
Between 1:30 and 4:30 a.m.

The Call to Prayer
Behold now, bless the LORD, all you servants of the LORD,* you that stand by night
in the house of the LORD.
Lift up your hands in the holy place and bless the LORD;* the LORD who made
heaven and earth bless you out of Zion.

Psalm 134

The Request for Presence
O God, come to my assistance.
O Lord, make haste to help me.

The Greeting
I am bound by the vow I made to you, O God;* I will present to you
thank-offerings;
For you have rescued my soul from death and my feet from stumbling,* that I may
walk before God in the light of the living.

Psalm 56:11–12

The Refrain for the Night Watch
Yours is the day, yours also the night;* you established the moon and the sun.

Psalm 74:15

180

The Psalm   *You Delivered Them*

My God, my God, why have you forsaken me?* and are so far from my cry and
   from the words of my distress?

O my God, I cry in the daytime, but you do not answer;* by night as well, but I
   find no rest.

Yet you are the Holy One,* enthroned upon the praises of Israel.

Our forefathers put their trust in you;* they trusted, and you delivered them.

They cried out to you and were delivered;* they trusted in you and were not put to
   shame.

Psalm 22:1–5

The Refrain

Yours is the day, yours also the night;* you established the moon and the sun.

A Reading

Perhaps you will say, "What difference is there between being tempted as such
   and falling or entering into temptation?" Well, if one is overcome of evil—and
   we will be overcome unless we struggle against it ourselves and unless God
   protects us with His shield—that one has entered into temptation, and is in it,
   and is brought under it like one who is held captive. But if one withstands and
   endures, then he or she is indeed tempted, but has not entered into temptation
   or fallen under it. Thus Jesus was led up of the Spirit, not to enter into
   temptation, but "to be tempted of the devil."

Dionysius, the Great, Bishop of Alexandria (d. ca. 264 CE),
Exposition of Luke XXII

The Refrain

Yours is the day, yours also the night;* you established the moon and the sun.

The Litany

For the peace from above, for the loving-kindness of God, and for the salvation of
   my soul, I pray to the Lord.
   Lord, have mercy.

For the peace of the world, for the welfare of the Holy Church of God, and for the
   unity of all peoples, I pray to the Lord.
   Lord, have mercy.

For the leaders of the nations and for all in authority, I pray to the Lord.
   Lord, have mercy.

For the aged and infirm, for the widowed and orphans, and for the sick and the
   suffering, I pray to the Lord.
   Lord, have mercy.

For the poor and the oppressed, for the unemployed and the destitute, for prisoners
   and captives, and for all who remember and care for them, I pray to the Lord.
   Lord, have mercy.

For all who have died in the hope of the resurrection, and for all the departed, I
    pray to the Lord.
    Lord, have mercy.

The Thanksgiving

Lord, you now have set your servant free to go in peace as you have promised; for
    these eyes of mine have seen the Savior whom you have prepared for all the
    world to see: A Light to enlighten the nations, and the glory of your people
    Israel. *Amen.*

Nunc Dimittis

The Final Petition

Now guide me waking, O Lord, and guard me sleeping; that awake I may watch
    with Christ, and asleep, I may rest in peace. *Amen.*

The Office of Dawn — Observed on the Hour or Half-Hour Between 4:30 and 7:30 a.m.

The Call to Prayer

Sing to the LORD with thanksgiving; * make music to our God upon the harp.

Psalm 147:7

The Request for Presence

My soul waits for the LORD, more than watchmen for the morning,* more than
    watchmen for the morning.

Psalm 130:5

The Greeting

Glory be to the Father, and the Son, and the Holy Spirit.
As it was in the beginning, it is now
And ever shall be, world without end. *Amen.*

Gloria Patri

The Hymn

Beneath the cross of Jesus
I fain would take my stand,
the shadow of a mighty rock
within a weary land;
a home within the wilderness,
a rest upon the way,
from the burning of the noontide heat,
and the burden of the day.
Upon that cross of Jesus
mine eye at times can see
the very dying form of One

who suffered there for me;
and from my stricken heart with tears
two wonders I confess:
the wonders of redeeming love
and my unworthiness.
I take, O cross, your shadow
for my abiding place;
I ask no other sunshine than
the sunshine of his face;
content to let the world go by,
to know no gain nor loss,
my sinful self my only shame,
my glory all the cross.

Elizabeth C. Clephane

The Psalm   *Praise the Name of the LORD*
Praise the LORD from the earth,* you sea-monsters and all deeps;
Fire and hail, snow and fog,* tempestuous wind, doing his will;
Mountains and all hills,* fruit trees and all cedars;
Wild beasts and all cattle,* creeping things and winged birds;
Kings of the earth and all peoples,* princes and all rulers of the world;
Young men and maidens,* old and young together.
Let them praise the Name of the LORD,*

Psalm 148:7–13a

The Gloria in Excelsis
Glory to God in the highest, and on earth peace to people of good will.
 We praise you.
 We bless you.
 We adore you.
 We glorify you.
We give thanks to you for your great glory.

The Small Verse
Then Jesus told his disciples, "If any man would come after me, let him deny
 himself and take up his cross and follow me, For whoever would save his life
 will lose it, and whoever loses his life for my sake will find it."

Matthew 16:24–25

The Lord's Prayer

The Final Blessing
May the LORD bless us and keep us and cause His face to shine upon us from this
 day forth and forever more. *Amen.*

183

Saturday, Month of May

The Office of Midnight   Observed on the Hour or Half-Hour
Between 10:30 p.m.✝ and 1:30 a.m.

The Call to Prayer
Sing to the LORD, you servants of his;* give thanks for the remembrance of his
holiness.

Psalm 30:4

The Request for Presence
O LORD, let my prayer be set forth in your sight as incense,* the lifting up of my
hands as the evening sacrifice.

Psalm 141:2, adapted

The Greeting
Our Father, Yours are the kingdom, the power, and the glory forever.

The Canticle   *The First Song of Isaiah*

Ecce, Deus

Surely, it is God who saves me;*
  I will trust in him and not be afraid.
For the Lord is my stronghold and my sure defense,*
  and he will be my Savior.
Therefore you shall draw water with rejoicing*
  from the springs of salvation.
And on that day you shall say,*
  Give thanks to the Lord and call upon his Name;
Make his deeds known among the peoples;*
  see that they remember that his Name is exalted.
Sing praises of the Lord, for he has done great things,*
  and this is known in all the world.
Cry aloud, inhabitants of Zion, ring out your joy,*
  for the great one in the midst of you is the Holy One of Israel.

Isaiah 12:2–6

The Psalm   *I Will Confess My Transgressions to the LORD*
Happy are they whose transgressions are forgiven,* and whose sin is put away!
Happy are they to whom the LORD imputes no guilt,* and in whose spirit there is
  no guile!
While I held my tongue, my bones withered away,* because of my groaning all
  day long.
For your hand was heavy upon me day and night;* my moisture was dried up as in
  the heat of summer.

184

Then I acknowledged my sin to you,* and did not conceal my guilt.
I said, "I will confess my transgressions to the LORD."* Then you forgave me the
    guilt of my sin.
Therefore all the faithful will make their prayers to you in time of trouble;* when
    the great waters overflow, they shall not reach them.

Psalm 32:1–7

The Gloria

The Small Verse
And he said to them, "Therefore every scribe who has been trained in the kingdom
    of heaven is like a householder who brings out of his treasure what is new and
    what is old."

Matthew 13:53

The Final Thanksgiving
I will greatly rejoice in the LORD, my soul shall exult in my God; for he has
    clothed me with the garments of salvation, he has covered me with the robe of
    righteousness, as a bridegroom decks himself with a garland, and as a bride
    adorns herself with her jewels.

Isaiah 61:10

The Petition
May the Lord GOD, father of all mercy, grant us who dwell here a peaceful night
    and a perfect end. *Amen.*

The Office of the Night Watch   Observed on the Hour or Half-Hour
Between 1:30 and 4:30 a.m.

The Call to Prayer
Behold now, bless the LORD, all you servants of the LORD,* you that stand by night
    in the house of the LORD.
Lift up your hands in the holy place and bless the LORD;* the LORD who made
    heaven and earth bless you out of Zion.

Psalm 134

The Request for Presence
O God, come to my assistance.
O Lord, make haste to help me.

The Greeting
For your Name's sake, O LORD,* forgive my sin, for it is great.

Psalm 25:10

185

The Refrain for the Night Watch
I commune with my heart in the night;* I ponder and search my mind.

Psalm 77:6

The Psalm   Those Who Keep in My Way Will I Show the Salvation of God
Consider this well, you who forget God,* lest I rend you and there be none to
deliver you.
Whoever offers me the sacrifice of thanksgiving honors me;* but to those who
keep in my way will I show the salvation of God."

Psalm 50:23–24

The Refrain
I commune with my heart in the night;* I ponder and search my mind.

A Reading
If we do not venture to approach men who are in power, except with humility and
reverence, when we wish to ask a favor, how much must we beseech the Lord
God of all things with all humility and purity of devotion? And let us be
assured that it is not in many words, but in purity of heart and tears of
compunction that we are heard. For this reason, prayer ought to be short and
pure, unless, perhaps, it is lengthened by the inspiration of the divine grace.

The Rule of St. Benedict, chap. VII

The Refrain
I commune with my heart in the night;* I ponder and search my mind.

The Litany
Father, I pray for your holy catholic Church;
> *That we all may be one.*

Grant that every member of the Church may truly and humbly serve you;
> *That your Name may be glorified by all people.*

I pray for all who govern and hold authority in the nations of the world;
> *That there may be justice and peace on the earth.*

Have compassion on those who suffer from any grief or trouble;
> *That they may be delivered from their distress.*

Give to the departed eternal rest.
> *Let light perpetual shine upon them.*

I praise you for your saints who have entered into joy;
> *May I also come to share in your heavenly kingdom.*

The Thanksgiving
Lord, you now have set your servant free to go in peace as you have promised; for
these eyes of mine have seen the Savior whom you have prepared for all the world
to see: A Light to enlighten the nations, and the glory of your people Israel. *Amen.*

Nunc Dimittis

186

The Final Petition
Now guide me waking, O Lord, and guard me sleeping; that awake I may watch with Christ, and asleep, I may rest in peace. *Amen.*

The Office of Dawn   Observed on the Hour or Half-Hour
                                        Between 4:30 and 7:30 a.m.

The Call to Prayer
Worship the LORD, O Jerusalem;* praise your God, O Zion;
For he has strengthened the bars of your gates.

Psalm 147:13–14a

The Request for Presence
My soul waits for the LORD, more than watchmen for the morning,* more than watchmen for the morning.

Psalm 130:5

The Greeting
Glory be to the Father, and the Son, and the Holy Spirit.
As it was in the beginning, it is now
And ever shall be, world without end. *Amen.*

Gloria Patri

The Hymn
Breathe on me, Breath of God,
fill me with life anew,
that I may love what you love,
and do what you would do.
Breathe on me, Breath of God,
until my heart is pure,
until with you I will one will,
to do and to endure.
Breathe on me, Breath of God,
so shall I never die,
but live with you the perfect life
of Heaven's eternity.

Edwin Hatch

The Psalm   The LORD Takes Pleasure in His People
Let Israel rejoice in his Maker;* let the children of Zion be joyful in their King.
Let them praise his Name in the dance;* let them sing praise to him with timbrel and harp.

187

For the LORD takes pleasure in his people* and adorns the poor with victory.
Let the faithful rejoice in triumph;* let them be joyful on their beds.

Psalm 149:2–5

The Gloria in Excelsis
Glory to God in the highest, and on earth peace to people of good will.
  We praise you.
  We bless you.
  We adore you.
  We glorify you.
We give thanks to you for your great glory.

The Small Verse
Jesus said to them again, "Peace be with you. As the Father has sent me, even so I
  send you." And he breathed on them, and said to them, "Receive the holy
  Spirit. If you forgive the sins of any, they are forgiven; if you retain the sins of
  any, they are retained."

John 20:21–14

The Lord's Prayer

The Final Blessing
May the LORD bless us and keep us and cause His face to shine upon us from this
  day forth and forever more. *Amen.*

The Gloria
Glory be to God the Father, God the Son, and God the Holy Spirit. As it was in the beginning, so it is now and so it shall ever be, world without end. Alleluia. *Amen.*

The Lord's Prayer
Our Father, who art in heaven, hallowed be your Name.
May your kingdom come, and your will be done, on earth as in heaven.
Give us today our daily bread.
Forgive us our sins as we forgive those who sin against us.
Lead us not into temptation, but deliver us from evil;
for yours are the kingdom and the power and the glory
forever and ever. Amen

The following major holy days occur in June:
The Feast of St. Barnabas: *June 11*
The Feast of St. Peter and St. Paul: *June 29*

Prayer for use in the observation of a holy day:
Almighty God, by your Holy Spirit you have made us one with your saints in heaven and on earth: Grant that in my earthly pilgrimage, I may always be supported by this fellowship of love and prayer, and know myself to be surrounded by their witness to your power and mercy. I ask this for the sake of Jesus Christ, in whom all my intercessions are acceptable through the Spirit, and who lives and reigns forever and ever. *Amen.*

✣ The Office of Midnight is always taken from the prayers for the day nearest to the hour of actual observation. Thus, if the office is to be observed at 10:30 p.m. on Sunday, the prayers will be taken from the Monday offices, and so forth.

JUNE

Sunday, Month of June

The Office of Midnight   **Observed on the Hour or Half-Hour**
                                    Between 10:30 p.m.✢ and 1:30 a.m.

The Call to Prayer
Let the Name of the LORD be blessed,* from this time forth for evermore.
From the rising of the sun to its going down* let the Name of the LORD be praised.
Psalm 113:2–3

The Request for Presence
O LORD, let my prayer be set forth in your sight as incense,* the lifting up of my
    hands as the evening sacrifice
Psalm 141:2, adapted

The Greeting
Our Father Who art in Heaven, hallowed be Your name.

The Canticle   *The Song of Zechariah*
                                                  Benedictus Dominus Deus

Blessed be the Lord, the God of Israel;*
    he has come to his people and set them free.
He has raised up for us a mighty savior,*
    born of the house of his servant David.
Through his holy prophets he promised of old, that he would save us from our
    enemies,*
    from the hands of all who hate us.
He promised to show mercy to our fathers*
    and to remember his holy covenant.
This was the oath he swore to our father Abraham,*
    to set us free from the hands of our enemies,
Free to worship him without fear,*
    holy and righteous in his sight all the days of our life.
Luke 1:68–75

The Psalm   *All His Commandments Are Sure*
Hallelujah! I will give thanks to the LORD with my whole heart,* in the assembly
    of the upright, in the congregation.
Great are the deeds of the LORD!* they are studied by all who delight in them.
His work is full of majesty and splendor,* and his righteousness endures for ever.
The works of his hands are faithfulness and justice;* all his commandments are
    sure.
They stand fast for ever and ever,* because they are done in truth and equity.

He sent redemption to his people; he commanded his covenant for ever;* holy and awesome is his Name.

The fear of the LORD is the beginning of wisdom;* those who act accordingly have a good understanding; his praise endures for ever.

Psalm 111:1–3, 7–10

The Gloria

The Small Verse

The sun shall be no more your light by day, nor for brightness shall the moon give light to you by night; but the LORD will be your everlasting light, and your God will be your glory.

Isaiah 60:19

The Final Thanksgiving

I will greatly rejoice in the LORD, my soul shall exult in my God; for he has clothed me with the garments of salvation, he has covered me with the robe of righteousness, as a bridegroom decks himself with a garland, and as a bride adorns herself with her jewels.

Isaiah 61:10

The Petition

May the Lord GOD, father of all mercy, grant us who dwell here a peaceful night and a perfect end. *Amen.*

The Office of the Night Watch   Observed on the Hour or Half-Hour Between 1:30 and 4:30 a.m.

The Call to Prayer

Behold now, bless the LORD, all you servants of the LORD,* you that stand by night in the house of the LORD.

Lift up your hands in the holy place and bless the LORD;* the LORD who made heaven and earth bless you out of Zion.

Psalm 134

The Request for Presence

O God, come to my assistance.
O Lord, make haste to help me.

The Greeting

"You are my God, and I will thank you;* you are my God, and I will exalt you."

Psalm 118:28

The Refrain for the Night Watch
You shall not be afraid of any terror by night,* nor of the arrow that flies by day;

Psalm 91:5

The Psalm   *Your Word Is Everlasting*
In your loving-kindness, revive me,* that I may keep the decrees of your mouth.
O LORD, your word is everlasting;* it stands firm in the heavens.
Your faithfulness remains from one generation to another;* you established the
    earth, and it abides.
By your decree these continue to this day,* for all things are your servants.
If my delight had not been in your law,* I should have perished in my affliction.
I will never forget your commandments,* because by them you give me life.
I am yours; oh, that you would save me!* for I study your commandments.

Psalm 119:88–94

The Refrain
You shall not be afraid of any terror by night,* nor of the arrow that flies by day;

A Reading
All our power is of God; I say *of God*! From Him we have life; from Him we have
    strength; by power derived and conceived from Him, we do, while yet in this
    world, foreknow the indications of things to come. Only remember, let fear be
    the keeper of innocence in order that the Lord, who of His mercy has flowed
    into our hearts in an access of celestial grace, may be kept by righteous
    submissiveness in the hostelry of a grateful mind so that the assurance we have
    gained may not beget carelessness, and the old enemy creep up on us again.

Cyprian, Bishop of Carthage (d. ca. 258), The Epistles

The Refrain
You shall not be afraid of any terror by night,* nor of the arrow that flies by day;

The Litany
Grant, Almighty God, that all who confess your Name may be united in your truth,
    live together in your love, and reveal your glory in the world.
    Lord, in your mercy, hear my prayer.
Guide the people of this land, and of all the nations, in the ways of justice and
    peace; that we may honor one another and serve the common good.
    Lord, in your mercy, hear my prayer.
Give us all a reverence for the earth as your own creation, that we may use its
    resources rightly in the service of others and to your honor and glory.
    Lord, in your mercy, hear my prayer.
Bless all whose lives are closely linked with mine, and grant that I may serve
    Christ in them, and love even as he loves me.
    Lord, in your mercy, hear my prayer.

Comfort and heal all those who suffer in body, mind, or spirit; give them courage and hope in their troubles, and bring them the joy of your salvation.
Lord, in your mercy, hear my prayer.
I commend to your mercy all who have died, that your will for them may be fulfilled; and I pray that I may share with all your saints in your eternal kingdom.
Lord, in your mercy, hear my prayer.

The Thanksgiving
Lord, you now have set your servant free to go in peace as you have promised; for these eyes of mine have seen the Savior whom you have prepared for all the world to see: A Light to enlighten the nations, and the glory of your people Israel. *Amen.*

Nunc Dimittis

The Final Petition
Now guide me waking, O Lord, and guard me sleeping; that awake I may watch with Christ, and asleep, I may rest in peace. *Amen.*

The Office of Dawn · Observed on the Hour or Half-Hour Between 4:30 and 7:30 a.m.

The Call to Prayer
Let everything that has breath* praise the LORD. Hallelujah!

Psalm 150:6

The Request for Presence
My soul waits for the LORD, more than watchmen for the morning,* more than watchmen for the morning.

Psalm 130:5

The Greeting
Glory be to the Father, and the Son, and the Holy Spirit.
As it was in the beginning, it is now
And ever shall be, world without end. *Amen.*

Gloria Patri

The Hymn
Blest be the tie that binds
our hearts in Christian love;
the fellowship of kindred minds
is like to that above.
Before our Father's throne

we pour our ardent prayers;
our fears, our hopes, our aims are one,
our comforts and our cares.
We share each other's woes,
our mutual burdens bear;
and often for each other flows
the sympathizing tear.

John Fawcett

The Psalm   *Let Everything That Has Breath Praise the* LORD
Praise him for his mighty acts;* praise him for his excellent greatness.
Praise him with the blast of the ram's-horn;* praise him with lyre and harp.
Praise him with timbrel and dance;* praise him with strings and pipe.
Praise him with resounding cymbals;* praise him with loud-clanging cymbals.
Let everything that has breath* praise the LORD. Hallelujah!

Psalm 150: 2–6

The Gloria in Excelsis
Glory to God in the highest, and on earth peace to people of good will.
>We praise you.
>We bless you.
>We adore you.
>We glorify you.
We give thanks to you for your great glory.

The Small Verse
The cup of blessing which we bless, is it not a participation in the blood of Christ?
The bread which we break, is it not a participation in the body of Christ?
Because there is one bread, we who are many are one body, for we all partake
of the one bread.

1 Corinthians 10:16–17

The Lord's Prayer

The Final Blessing
May the LORD bless us and keep us and cause His face to shine upon us from this
day forth and forever more. *Amen.*

Monday, Month of June

The Office of Midnight

Observed on the Hour or Half-Hour
Between 10:30 p.m.✣ and 1:30 a.m.

The Call to Prayer
Proclaim with me the greatness of the LORD;* let us exalt his Name together.

Psalm 33:1

The Request for Presence
O LORD, let my prayer be set forth in your sight as incense,* the lifting up of my
hands as the evening sacrifice.

Psalm 141:2, adapted

The Greeting
Our Father, may Your kingdom come on earth as in Heaven.

The Canticle

A Song of Creation—Part Three
Benedicite, omnia opera Domini

Glorify the Lord, all you works of the Lord,*
  praise him and highly exalt him for ever.
In the firmament of his power, glorify the Lord,*
  praise him and highly exalt him for ever.
Let the people of God glorify the Lord,*
  praise him and highly exalt him for ever.
Glorify the Lord, O priests and servants of the Lord,*
  praise him and highly exalt him for ever.
Glorify the Lord, O spirits and souls of the righteous,*
  praise him and highly exalt him for ever.
You that are holy and humble of heart, glorify the Lord,*
  praise him and highly exalt him for ever.
Let us glorify the Lord: Father, Son, and Holy Spirit;*
  praise him and highly exalt him for ever.
In the firmament of his power, glorify the Lord,*
  praise him and highly exalt him for ever.

Song of the Three Young Men, 62–68

The Psalm

My Heart Is Firmly Fixed

Exalt yourself above the heavens, O God,* and your glory over all the earth.
My heart is firmly fixed, O God, my heart is fixed;* I will sing and make melody.
Wake up, my spirit; awake, lute and harp;* I myself will waken the dawn.
I will confess you among the peoples, O LORD;* I will sing praise to you among
  the nations.

197

For your loving-kindness is greater than the heavens,* and your faithfulness
reaches to the clouds.
Exalt yourself above the heavens, O God,* and your glory over all the earth.

Psalm 57:6–11

The Gloria

The Small Verse
But love your enemies, and do good, and lend, expecting nothing in return; and
your reward will be great, and you will be sons of the Most High; for he is kind
to the ungrateful and the selfish. Be merciful, even as your Father is merciful.

Luke 6: 35–36

The Final Thanksgiving
I will greatly rejoice in the Lord, my soul shall exult in my God; for he has clothed
me with the garments of salvation, he has covered me with the robe of
righteousness, as a bridegroom decks himself with a garland, and as a bride
adorns herself with her jewels.

Isaiah 61:10

The Office of the Night Watch   Observed on the Hour or Half-Hour
Between 1:30 and 4:30 a.m.

The Call to Prayer
Behold now, bless the LORD, all you servants of the LORD,* you that stand by night
in the house of the LORD.
Lift up your hands in the holy place and bless the LORD;* the LORD who made
heaven and earth bless you out of Zion.

Psalm 134

The Request for Presence
O God, come to my assistance.
O Lord, make haste to help me.

The Greeting
Be exalted, O LORD, in your might;* we will sing and praise your power.

Psalm 21:14

The Refrain for the Night Watch
It is a good thing to give thanks to the LORD,* and to sing praises to your Name,
O Most High;
To tell of your loving-kindness early in the morning* and of your faithfulness in
the night season.

Psalm 92:1–2

The Psalm   *How Deep I Find Your Thoughts*

How deep I find your thoughts, O God!* how great is the sum of them!

If I were to count them, they would be more in number than the sand;* to count
them all, my life span would need to be like yours.

Psalm 139:16–17

The Refrain

It is a good thing to give thanks to the LORD,* and to sing praises to your Name,
O Most High;

To tell of your loving-kindness early in the morning* and of your faithfulness in
the night season.

A Reading

Thus the Father and the Son and the Holy Spirit, and each of these by Himself, is
God; and at the same time, they are all one God; and each of them by Himself
is a complete substance, and yet they are all one substance. The Father is not
the Son nor the Holy Spirit; the Son is not the Father nor the Holy Spirit; the
Holy Spirit is not the Father nor the Son; but the Father is only Father, the Son
is only Son, and the Holy Spirit is only Holy Spirit. To all three belong the
same eternity, the same unchangeableness, the same majesty, the same power.
In the Father is unity, in the Son equality, in the Holy Spirit the harmony of
unity and equality; and these three attributes are all one because of the Father,
all equal because of the Son, and all harmonious because of the Holy Spirit.

St. Augustine (ca. 410 CE), On Christian Doctrine

The Refrain

It is a good thing to give thanks to the LORD,* and to sing praises to your Name,
O Most High;

To tell of your loving-kindness early in the morning* and of your faithfulness in
the night season.

The Litany

For the peace of the world, that a spirit of respect and forbearance may grow
among nations and peoples, I pray to you, O Lord.
Lord, hear my prayer.

For those in positions of public trust, that they may serve justice, and promote the
dignity and freedom of every person, I pray to you, O Lord.
Lord, hear my prayer.

For the poor, the persecuted, the sick, and all who suffer; for refugees, prisoners,
and all who are in danger; that they may be relieved and protected, I pray to
you, O Lord.
Lord, hear my prayer.

For the forgiveness of my sins, and for the grace of the Holy Spirit to amend my
life, I pray to you, O Lord.
Lord, hear my prayer.

For all who have died in the communion of your Church, and those whose faith is
known to you alone, that, with all the saints, they may have rest in that place
where there is no pain or grief, but life eternal, I pray to you, O Lord.
Lord, hear my prayer
Rejoicing in the fellowship of the ever-blessed Virgin Mary and all the saints, I
commend my self and all your faithful to Christ our God.
To you, O Lord our God.

The Thanksgiving

Lord, you now have set your servant free to go in peace as you have promised; for
these eyes of mine have seen the Savior whom you have prepared for all the
world to see: A Light to enlighten the nations, and the glory of your people
Israel. *Amen.*

Nunc Dimittis

The Final Petition

Now guide me waking, O Lord, and guard me sleeping; that awake I may watch
with Christ, and asleep, I may rest in peace. *Amen.*

The Office of Dawn Observed on the Hour or Half-Hour
Between 4:30 and 7:30 a.m.

The Call to Prayer

Hallelujah! How good it is to sing praises to our God!* how pleasant it is to honor
him with praise!

Psalm 147:1

The Request for Presence

My soul waits for the LORD, more than watchmen for the morning,* more than
watchmen for the morning.

Psalm 130:5

The Greeting

Glory be to the Father, and the Son, and the Holy Spirit.
As it was in the beginning, it is now
And ever shall be, world without end. *Amen.*

Gloria Patri

The Hymn

O God of truth, O Lord of might,
Who orders time and change aright,
and sends the early morning ray,
and lights the glow of perfect day.

200

Extinguish, Lord, each sinful fire,
and banish every ill desire;
and while You keep the body whole,
shed forth your peace upon the soul
Almighty Father, hear my cry
through Jesus Christ, our Lord most high
who with the Holy Spirit and Thee
does live and reign eternally. *Amen.*

Attributed to St. Ambrose, translated by J. M. Neale

The Psalm   The LORD Sends Out His Command to the Earth

The LORD sends out his command to the earth,* and his word runs very swiftly.
He gives snow like wool;* he scatters hoarfrost like ashes.
He scatters his hail like bread crumbs;* who can stand against his cold?
He sends forth his word and melts them;* he blows with his wind, and the waters
flow.

Psalm 147:16–19

The Gloria in Excelsis

Glory to God in the highest, and on earth peace to people of good will.
    We praise you.
    We bless you.
    We adore you.
    We glorify you.
We give thanks to you for your great glory.

The Small Verse

So, whether you eat or drink, or whatever you do, do all to the glory of God. Give
no offense to Jews or to Greeks or to the church of God.

I Corinthians 10:31–32

The Lord's Prayer

The Final Blessing

May the LORD bless us and keep us and cause His face to shine upon us from this
day forth and forever more. *Amen.*

Tuesday, Month of June

The Office of Midnight   **Observed on the Hour or Half-Hour**
                                                  Between 10:30 p.m.✢ and 1:30 a.m.

The Call to Prayer
I will call upon the Most High God,* the God who maintains my cause.

Psalm 57:2

The Request for Presence
O LORD, let my prayer be set forth in your sight as incense,* the lifting up of my hands as the evening sacrifice.

Psalm 141:2, adapted

The Greeting
Our Father, may Your will be done, on earth as in Heaven.

The Canticle   *The Third Song of Isaiah*

Surge, illuminare

Arise, shine, for your light has come,*
   and the glory of the Lord has dawned upon you.
For behold, darkness covers the land;*
   deep gloom enshrouds the peoples.
But over you the Lord will rise,*
   and his glory will appear upon you.
Nations will stream to your light,*
   and kings to the brightness of your dawning.
Your gates will always be open;*
   by day or night they will never be shut.
They will call you, The City of the Lord,*
   The Zion of the Holy One of Israel.
Violence will no more be heard in your land,*
   ruin or destruction within your borders.
You will call your walls, Salvation,*
   and all your portals, Praise.
The sun will no more be your light by day;*
   by night you will not need the brightness of the moon.
The Lord will be your everlasting light,*
   and your God will be your glory.

Isaiah 60:1–3, 11a, 14c, 18–19

The Psalm   *Light Shines in the Darkness for the Upright*
Light shines in the darkness for the upright;* the righteous are merciful and full of compassion.

202

It is good for them to be generous in lending* and to manage their affairs with justice.
For they will never be shaken;* the righteous will be kept in everlasting remembrance.
They will not be afraid of any evil rumors;* their heart is right; they put their trust in the Lord.
Their heart is established and will not shrink,

Psalm 112:4–8a

The Gloria

The Small Verse
Continue steadfastly in prayer, being watchful in it with thanksgiving.

Colossians 3: 2

The Final Thanksgiving
I will greatly rejoice in the LORD, my soul shall exult in my God; for he has clothed me with the garments of salvation, he has covered me with the robe of righteousness, as a bridegroom decks himself with a garland, and as a bride adorns herself with her jewels.

Isaiah 61:10

The Petition
May the Lord GOD, father of all mercy, grant us who dwell here a peaceful night and a perfect end. *Amen.*

The Office of the Night Watch   Observed on the Hour or Half-Hour
Between 1:30 and 4:30 a.m.

The Call to Prayer
Behold now, bless the LORD, all you servants of the LORD,* you that stand by night in the house of the LORD.
Lift up your hands in the holy place and bless the LORD;* the LORD who made heaven and earth bless you out of Zion.

Psalm 134

The Request for Presence
O God, come to my assistance.
O Lord, make haste to help me.

The Greeting
Blessed is the LORD!* for he has heard the voice of my prayer.

Psalm 28:7

The Refrain for the Night Watch

Behold now, bless the LORD, all you servants of the LORD,* you that stand by night in the house of the LORD.

Psalm 134:1

The Psalm   The LORD Is in His Holy Temple

In the LORD have I taken refuge;* how then can you say to me, "Fly away like a bird to the hilltop;

For see how the wicked bend the bow and fit their arrows to the string,* to shoot from ambush at the true of heart.

When the foundations are being destroyed,* what can the righteous do?"

The LORD is in his holy temple;* the LORD's throne is in heaven.

His eyes behold the inhabited world;* his piercing eye weighs our worth.

The LORD weighs the righteous as well as the wicked,* but those who delight in violence he abhors.

Upon the wicked he shall rain coals of fire and burning sulphur;* a scorching wind shall be their lot.

For the LORD is righteous; he delights in righteous deeds;* and the just shall see his face.

Psalm 11

The Refrain

Behold now, bless the LORD, all you servants of the LORD,* you that stand by night in the house of the LORD.

A Reading

The woman who washed and anointed Christ's feet did so to express love and not to earn it. The things we do demonstrate our loving response to love already received.

William Tyndale, The Parable

The Refrain

Behold now, bless the LORD, all you servants of the LORD,* you that stand by night in the house of the LORD.

The Litany

For all people in their daily life and work;
For my family, friends, and neighbors, and for those who are alone, I pray to you, Lord God.

For this community, the nation, and the world;
For all who work for justice, freedom, and peace, I pray to you, Lord God.

For the just and proper use of your creation;
For the victims of hunger, fear, injustice, and oppression, I pray to you, Lord God.

For all who are in danger, sorrow, or any kind of trouble;
For those who minister to the sick, the friendless, and the needy, I pray to you, Lord God.
For the peace and unity of the Church of God;
For all who proclaim the Gospel, and all who seek the Truth, I pray to you, Lord God.
Hear me, Lord;
For your mercy is great.

The Thanksgiving

Lord, you now have set your servant free to go in peace as you have promised; for these eyes of mine have seen the Savior whom you have prepared for all the world to see: A Light to enlighten the nations, and the glory of your people Israel. *Amen.*

Nunc Dimittis

The Final Petition

Now guide me waking, O Lord, and guard me sleeping; that awake I may watch with Christ, and asleep, I may rest in peace. *Amen.*

The Office of Dawn

Observed on the Hour or Half-Hour Between 4:30 and 7:30 a.m.

The Call to Prayer

Hallelujah! Sing to the LORD a new song;* Sing his praise in the congregation of the faithful.

Psalm 149:1

The Request for Presence

My soul waits for the LORD, more than watchmen for the morning,* more than watchmen for the morning.

Psalm 130:5

The Greeting

Glory be to the Father, and the Son, and the Holy Spirit.
As it was in the beginning, it is now
And ever shall be, world without end. *Amen.*

Gloria Patri

The Hymn

Hosanna, loud hosanna, the little children sang,
through pillared court and temple the lovely anthem rang.
To Jesus, who had blessed them close folded to his breast,
the children sang their praises, the simplest and the best.

205

"Hosanna in the highest!" now that ancient song we sing,
for Christ is our Redeemer, the Lord of heaven our King.
O may we, like them, ever praise him with heart and life and voice,
and in his blissful presence eternally rejoice!

Jeanette Threlfall

The Psalm   *Happy Are They Whose Hope Is in the Lord Their God*

Happy are they who have the God of Jacob for their help!* whose hope is in the
   Lord their God;
Who made heaven and earth, the seas, and all that is in them;* who keeps his
   promise for ever;
Who gives justice to those who are oppressed,* and food to those who hunger.
The Lord loves the righteous; the Lord cares for the stranger;* he sustains the
   orphan and widow, but frustrates the way of the wicked.
The Lord shall reign for ever,* your God, O Zion, throughout all generations.
   Hallelujah!

Psalm 146:4–6, 8–9

The Gloria in Excelsis

Glory to God in the highest, and on earth peace to people of good will.
   We praise you.
   We bless you.
   We adore you.
   We glorify you.
We give thanks to you for your great glory.

The Small Verse

And round the throne, on each side of the throne, are four living creatures, full of
   eyes in front and behind, the first living creature like a lion, the second living
   creature like an ox, the third living creature with the face of a man, and the
   fourth living creature like a flying eagle. And the four living creatures, each of
   them with six wings, are full of eyes all round and within, and day and night
   they never cease to sing, "Holy, holy, holy, is the Lord God Almighty, who was
   and is and is to come!"

Revelation 4:6b–8

The Lord's Prayer

The Final Blessing

May the Lord bless us and keep us and cause His face to shine upon us from this
   day forth and forever more. *Amen.*

Wednesday, Month of June

The Office of Midnight　　　　**Observed on the Hour or Half-Hour Between 10:30 p.m.✣ and 1:30 a.m.**

The Call to Prayer
Not to us, O LORD, not to us, but to your Name give glory;* because of your love and because of your faithfulness.

Psalm 115:1

The Request for Presence
O LORD, let my prayer be set forth in your sight as incense,* the lifting up of my hands as the evening sacrifice.

Psalm 141:2, adapted

The Greeting
Our Father, give us this day our daily bread.

The Canticle　　　　　　　　　　　　*The Song of Simeon*
Nunc Dimittis

Lord, you now have set your servant free*
　to go in peace as you have promised;
For these eyes of mine have seen the Savior,*
　whom you have prepared for all the world to see:
A Light to enlighten the nations,*
　and the glory of your people Israel.
Glory to the Father, and to the Son, and to the Holy Spirit:*
　as it was in the beginning, is now, and will be for ever. *Amen.*

Luke 2:29–32

The Psalm　　　　　　　　*Our God Is Full of Compassion*
I love the LORD, because he has heard the voice of my supplication,* because he has inclined his ear to me whenever I called upon him.
The cords of death entangled me; the grip of the grave took hold of me;* I came to grief and sorrow.
Then I called upon the Name of the LORD:* "O LORD, I pray you, save my life."
Gracious is the LORD and righteous;* our God is full of compassion.
The LORD watches over the innocent;* I was brought very low, and he helped me.
Turn again to your rest, O my soul,* for the LORD has treated you well.

Psalm 116:1–6

The Gloria

The Small Verse
Behold my servant, whom I uphold, my chosen, in whom my soul delights; I have put my Spirit upon him, he will bring forth justice to the nations. He will not

207

cry or lift up his voice. Or make it heard in the street; a bruised reed he will not
break, and a dimly burning wick he will not quench; he will faithfully bring
forth justice. He will not fail or be discouraged till he has established justice in
the earth; and the coastlands wait for his law.

Isaiah 42:1–4

The Final Thanksgiving
I will greatly rejoice in the LORD, my soul shall exult in my God; for he has
clothed me with the garments of salvation, he has covered me with the robe of
righteousness, as a bridegroom decks himself with a garland, and as a bride
adorns herself with her jewels.

Isaiah 61:10

The Petition
May the Lord GOD, father of all mercy, grant us who dwell here a peaceful night
and a perfect end. *Amen.*

The Office of the Night Watch   Observed on the Hour or Half-Hour
Between 1:30 and 4:30 a.m.

The Call to Prayer
Behold now, bless the LORD, all you servants of the LORD,* you that stand by night
in the house of the LORD.
Lift up your hands in the holy place and bless the LORD;* the LORD who made
heaven and earth bless you out of Zion.

Psalm 134

The Request for Presence
O God, come to my assistance.
O Lord, make haste to help me.

The Greeting
Restore us, O God of hosts;* show the light of your countenance, and we shall be
saved.

Psalm 80:3

The Refrain for the Night Watch
Darkness is not dark to you; the night is as bright as the day;* darkness and light
to you are both alike.

Psalm 139:11

The Psalm   *Give Light to My Eyes*
Look upon me and answer me, O LORD my God;* give light to my eyes, lest I
sleep in death;

Lest my enemy say, "I have prevailed over him,"* and my foes rejoice that I have
  fallen.
But I put my trust in your mercy;* my heart is joyful because of your saving help.
I will sing to the LORD, for he has dealt with me richly;* I will praise the Name of
  the Lord Most High.

Psalm 13:3–6

The Refrain
Darkness is not dark to you; the night is as bright as the day;* darkness and light
  to you are both alike.

A Reading
God, whose whole being is goodness, whose will is power and whose every act is
  mercy, designated in the very beginning the remedy His good will had ordained
  for our redemption. . . . When the fulness of time ordained for this redemption
  had come, our Lord Jesus descended from His heavenly throne, though not
  abandoning His Father's glory, and came into this world. In the natural order
  His birth had no precedent; it was a new order because the Invisible had
  become visible; it was a new order because the Incomprehensible had willed to
  be comprehended; it was a new order that the Eternal should begin in time; that
  the Lord of the universe should permit the dignity of His majesty to be
  overshadowed and assume the form of a servant; that God, infinitely distant
  from suffering, should deign to become human with all humanity's suffering;
  that the Immortal should humble Himself under the laws of death.

Pope St. Leo I (d. 461 CE), Homily

The Refrain
Darkness is not dark to you; the night is as bright as the day;* darkness and light
  to you are both alike.

The Litany
For the peace from above, for the loving-kindness of God, and for the salvation of
  my soul, I pray to the Lord.
  Lord, have mercy.
For the peace of the world, for the welfare of the Holy Church of God, and for the
  unity of all peoples, I pray to the Lord.
  Lord, have mercy.
For my city [town, village], for every city and community, and for those who live
  in them, I pray to the Lord.
  Lord, have mercy.
For seasonable weather, and for an abundance of the fruits of the earth, I pray to
  the Lord.
  Lord, have mercy.
For the good earth which God has given us, and for the wisdom and will to
  conserve it, I pray to the Lord.
  Lord, have mercy.

For deliverance from all danger, violence, oppression, and degradation, I pray to the Lord.
Lord, have mercy.
For the absolution and remission of my sins and offenses, I pray to the Lord.
Lord, have mercy.
Defend me, deliver me, and in your compassion protect me, O Lord, by your grace.
Lord, have mercy.

The Thanksgiving

Lord, you now have set your servant free to go in peace as you have promised; for these eyes of mine have seen the Savior whom you have prepared for all the world to see: A Light to enlighten the nations, and the glory of your people Israel. *Amen.*

Nunc Dimittis

The Final Petition

Now guide me waking, O Lord, and guard me sleeping; that awake I may watch with Christ, and asleep, I may rest in peace. *Amen.*

The Office of Dawn   Observed on the Hour or Half-Hour Between 4:30 and 7:30 a.m.

The Call to Prayer

Hallelujah! Praise the LORD, O my soul!* I will praise the LORD as long as I live; I will sing praises to my God while I have my being.

Psalm 146:1

The Request for Presence

My soul waits for the LORD, more than watchmen for the morning,* more than watchmen for the morning.

Psalm 130:5

The Greeting

Glory be to the Father, and the Son, and the Holy Spirit.
As it was in the beginning, it is now
And ever shall be, world without end. *Amen.*

Gloria Patri

The Hymn

Come, thou Fount of every blessing,
tune my heart to sing your grace;
streams of mercy, never ceasing,
call for songs of loudest praise.
Teach me some melodious sonnet,
sung by flaming tongues above.
Praise the mount! I'm fixed upon it,

mount of your redeeming love.
O to grace how great a debtor
daily I'm constrained to be!
Let your goodness, like a fetter,
bind my wandering heart to thee.
Prone to wander, Lord, I feel it,
prone to leave the God I love;
here's my heart, O take and seal it,
seal it for your courts above.

Robert Robinson

The Psalm   *Praise the Lord All You Angels of His*

Praise the Lord from the heavens;* praise him in the heights.
Praise him, all you angels of his;* praise him, all his host.
Praise him, sun and moon;* praise him, all you shining stars.
Praise him, heaven of heavens,* and you waters above the heavens.
Let them praise the Name of the Lord;* for he commanded, and they were
    created.
He made them stand fast for ever and ever;* he gave them a law which shall not
    pass away.

Psalm 148: 1b–6

The Gloria in Excelsis

Glory to God in the highest, and on earth peace to people of good will.
    We praise you.
    We bless you.
    We adore you.
    We glorify you.
We give thanks to you for your great glory.

The Small Verse

For everything created by God is good, and nothing is to be rejected if it is
    received with thanksgiving; for then it is consecrated by the word of God and
    prayer.

1 Timothy 4:4–5

The Lord's Prayer

The Final Blessing

May the Lord bless us and keep us and cause His face to shine upon us from this
    day forth and forever more. *Amen.*

Thursday, Month of June

The Office of Midnight **Observed on the Hour or Half-Hour**
Between 10:30 p.m.✢ and 1:30 a.m.

The Call to Prayer
Come now and look upon the works of the LORD,* what awesome things he has
done on earth.

Psalm 46:9

The Request for Presence
O LORD, let my prayer be set forth in your sight as incense,* the lifting up of my
hands as the evening sacrifice.

Psalm 141:2, adapted

The Greeting
Our Father, forgive us our sins as we forgive those who have sinned against us.

The Canticle *The Song of Mary*
Magnificat

My soul proclaims the greatness of the Lord, my spirit rejoices in God my
Savior;*
for he has looked with favor on his lowly servant.
From this day all generations will call me blessed:*
the Almighty has done great things for me, and holy is his Name.
He has mercy on those who fear him *
in every generation.
He has shown the strength of his arm,*
he has scattered the proud in their conceit.
He has cast down the mighty from their thrones,*
and has lifted up the lowly.
He has filled the hungry with good things,*
and the rich he has sent away empty.
He has come to the help of his servant Israel,*
for he has remembered his promise of mercy,
The promise he made to our fathers,*
to Abraham and his children for ever.
Glory to the Father, and to the Son, and to the Holy Spirit:*
as it was in the beginning, is now, and will be for ever. *Amen.*

Luke 1:46–55

The Psalm *The LORD Has Done Great Things for Us*
When the LORD restored the fortunes of Zion,* then were we like those who dream.
Then was our mouth filled with laughter,* and our tongue with shouts of joy.

212

Then they said among the nations,* "The LORD has done great things for them."
The LORD has done great things for us,* and we are glad indeed.
Restore our fortunes, O LORD,* like the watercourses of the Negev.
Those who sowed with tears* will reap with songs of joy.
Those who go out weeping, carrying the seed,* will come again with joy,
  shouldering their sheaves.

Psalm 126

The Gloria

The Small Verse
Examine yourselves, to see whether you are holding to your faith. Test yourselves.
  Do you not realize that Jesus Christ is in you?—unless indeed you fail to meet
  the test!

2 Corinthians 13:5

The Final Thanksgiving
I will greatly rejoice in the LORD, my soul shall exult in my God; for he has
  clothed me with the garments of salvation, he has covered me with the robe of
  righteousness, as a bridegroom decks himself with a garland, and as a bride
  adorns herself with her jewels.

Isaiah 61:10

The Petition
May the Lord GOD, father of all mercy, grant us who dwell here a peaceful night
  and a perfect end. *Amen.*

The Office of the Night Watch   Observed on the Hour or Half-Hour
Between 1:30 and 4:30 a.m.

The Call to Prayer
Behold now, bless the LORD, all you servants of the LORD,* you that stand by night
  in the house of the LORD.
Lift up your hands in the holy place and bless the LORD;* the LORD who made
  heaven and earth bless you out of Zion.

Psalm 134

The Request for Presence
O God, come to my assistance.
O Lord, make haste to help me.

The Greeting
My mouth shall recount your mighty acts and saving deeds all day long;* though I
  cannot know the number of them.

Psalm 71:15

213

The Refrain for the Night Watch
I will bless the LORD who gives me counsel;* my heart teaches me, night after night.
Psalm 16:7

The Psalm   *Create in Me a Clean Heart*
Create in me a clean heart, O God,* and renew a right spirit within me.
Cast me not away from your presence* and take not your holy Spirit from me.
Give me the joy of your saving help again* and sustain me with your bountiful
    Spirit.
I shall teach your ways to the wicked,* and sinners shall return to you.
Psalm 51:11–14

The Refrain
I will bless the LORD who gives me counsel;* my heart teaches me, night after
    night.

A Reading
I am of the opinion that there is a certain limit to the powers of human nature,
    although there may be a Paul (of whom it is said, "He is a chosen vessel unto
    Me"), or a Peter (against whom the gates of Hell shall not prevail), or a Moses
    ("the friend of God"); yet not one of them could sustain, without destruction to
    himself, the whole simultaneous assault of the opposing powers of evil, unless
    indeed the might of Him alone were to work in him, the might of Him who
    said, "Be of good cheer. I have overcome the world."
Origen (ca. 185–254 CE), translated by Rufinus, De Principiis

The Refrain
I will bless the LORD who gives me counsel;* my heart teaches me, night after night.

The Litany
O God the Father, Creator of heaven and earth,
    Have mercy upon me.
O God the Son, Redeemer of the world,
    Have mercy upon me.
O God the Holy Spirit, Sanctifier of the faithful,
    Have mercy upon me.
O holy, blessed, and glorious Trinity, one God,
    Have mercy upon me.
Remember not, Lord Christ, my offenses, nor the offenses of my forefathers;
    neither reward me according to my sins. Spare me, good Lord, spare your
    people, whom you have redeemed with your most precious blood, and by your
    mercy preserve us, for ever.
    Spare us, good Lord.

The Thanksgiving

Lord, you now have set your servant free to go in peace as you have promised; for these eyes of mine have seen the Savior whom you have prepared for all the world to see: A Light to enlighten the nations, and the glory of your people Israel. *Amen.*

Nunc Dimittis

The Final Petition

Now guide me waking, O Lord, and guard me sleeping; that awake I may watch with Christ, and asleep, I may rest in peace. *Amen.*

The Office of Dawn   Observed on the Hour or Half-Hour Between 4:30 and 7:30 a.m.

The Call to Prayer

Hallelujah! How good it is to sing praises to our God!* how pleasant it is to honor him with praise!

Psalm 147:1

The Request for Presence

My soul waits for the Lord, more than watchmen for the morning,* more than watchmen for the morning.

Psalm 130:5

The Greeting

Glory be to the Father, and the Son, and the Holy Spirit.
As it was in the beginning, it is now
And ever shall be, world without end. *Amen.*

Gloria Patri

The Hymn

Forth in your name, O Lord, I go,
my daily labor to pursue;
you, only you, resolved to know
in all I think or speak or do.
The task your wisdom has assigned,
O let me cheerfully fulfill;
in all my works your presence find,
and prove your good and perfect will.
For you delightfully employ
whatever your bounteous grace has given;
and run my course with even joy,
and closely walk with you to heaven.

Charles Wesley

The Psalm   ***The L**ord **Has Pleasure in Those Who Await His Gracious Favor***
He covers the heavens with clouds* and prepares rain for the earth;
He makes grass to grow upon the mountains* and green plants to serve mankind.
He provides food for flocks and herds* and for the young ravens when they cry.
He is not impressed by the might of a horse;* he has no pleasure in the strength of
    a man;
But the Lord has pleasure in those who fear him,* in those who await his gracious
    favor.

Psalm 147:8–12

The Gloria in Excelsis
Glory to God in the highest, and on earth peace to people of good will.
    We praise you.
    We bless you.
    We adore you.
    We glorify you.
We give thanks to you for your great glory.

The Small Verse
Come to me, all who labor and are heavy laden, and I will give you rest. Take my
    yoke upon you, and learn from me; for I am gentle and lowly in heart, and you
    will find rest for your souls. For my yoke is easy, and my burden is light.

Matthew 11:28–30

The Lord's Prayer

The Final Blessing
May the Lord bless us and keep us and cause His face to shine upon us from this
    day forth and forever more. *Amen.*

༃

Friday, Month of June

The Office of Midnight   **Observed on the Hour or Half-Hour**
                                                Between 10:30 p.m.✢ and 1:30 a.m.

The Call to Prayer
The Lord is near to those who call upon him,* to all who call upon him faithfully.

Psalm 145:19

The Request for Presence

O LORD, let my prayer be set forth in your sight as incense,* the lifting up of my hands as the evening sacrifice.

Psalm 141:2, adapted

The Greeting

Our Father, lead us not into temptation, but deliver us from evil.

The Canticle   A Song of Penitence
Kyrie Pantokrator

O Lord and Ruler of the hosts of heaven,*
    God of Abraham, Isaac, and Jacob, and of all their righteous offspring:
You made the heavens and the earth,*
    with all their vast array.
All things quake with fear at your presence;*
    they tremble because of your power.
But your merciful promise is beyond all measure;*
    it surpasses all that our minds can fathom.
O Lord, you are full of compassion,*
    long-suffering, and abounding in mercy.
You hold back your hand;*
    you do not punish as we deserve.
In your great goodness, Lord, you have promised forgiveness to sinners,*
    that they may repent of their sin and be saved.

Prayer of Manasseh 1–2, 4, 6–7

The Psalm   The LORD Will Save Those Whose Spirits Are Crushed

The eyes of the LORD are upon the righteous,* and his ears are open to their cry.
The face of the LORD is against those who do evil,* to root out the remembrance of them from the earth.
The righteous cry, and the LORD hears them* and delivers them from all their troubles.
The LORD is near to the brokenhearted* and will save those whose spirits are crushed.
Many are the troubles of the righteous,* but the LORD will deliver him out of them all.
He will keep safe all his bones;* not one of them shall be broken.
Evil shall slay the wicked,* and those who hate the righteous will be punished.
The LORD ransoms the life of his servants,* and none will be punished who trust in him.

Psalm 34:15–22

The Gloria

The Small Verse
What then shall we say to this? If God is for us, who is against us?

Romans 8:31

The Final Thanksgiving
I will greatly rejoice in the LORD, my soul shall exult in my God; for he has
clothed me with the garments of salvation, he has covered me with the robe of
righteousness, as a bridegroom decks himself with a garland, and as a bride
adorns herself with her jewels.

Isaiah 61:10

The Petition
May the Lord GOD, father of all mercy, grant us who dwell here a peaceful night
and a perfect end. *Amen.*

The Office of the Night Watch   Observed on the Hour or Half-Hour

Between 1:30 and 4:30 a.m.

The Call to Prayer
Behold now, bless the LORD, all you servants of the LORD,* you that stand by night
in the house of the LORD.
Lift up your hands in the holy place and bless the LORD;* the LORD who made
heaven and earth bless you out of Zion.

Psalm 134

The Request for Presence
O God, come to my assistance.
O Lord, make haste to help me.

The Greeting
Whom have I in heaven but you?* and having you I desire nothing upon earth.

Psalm 73:25

The Refrain for the Night Watch
Happy are they who have not walked in the counsel of the wicked,* nor lingered
in the way of sinners, nor sat in the seats of the scornful!
Their delight is in the law of the LORD,* and they meditate on his law day and night.

Psalm 1:1–2

The Psalm   *I Have Put My Hope in Your Word*
Let those who fear you turn to me,* and also those who know your decrees.
Let my heart be sound in your statutes,* that I may not be put to shame.
My soul has longed for your salvation;* I have put my hope in your word.

My eyes have failed from watching for your promise,* and I say, "When will you comfort me?"

Psalm 119:79–82

The Refrain
Happy are they who have not walked in the counsel of the wicked,* nor lingered in the way of sinners, nor sat in the seats of the scornful!
Their delight is in the law of the LORD,* and they meditate on his law day and night.

A Reading
Suppose, then, we were wanderers in a strange country, and could not live happily away from our fatherland, and that we felt wretched in our wandering, and wishing to put an end to our misery, determined to return home. We find, however, that we must make use of some mode of conveyance, either by land or water, in order to reach that fatherland. . . . But then the beauty of the country through which we pass, and the very pleasure of the motion, charm our hearts and turn these which we ought to use into objects of enjoyment instead; and we become unwilling as a result to hasten to the end of our journey. . . . Such is the picture of our condition in this life. . . . If we wish to return to our Father's home, this world must be used, not enjoyed.

St. Augustine (ca. 410 CE), On Christian Doctrine

The Refrain
Happy are they who have not walked in the counsel of the wicked,* nor lingered in the way of sinners, nor sat in the seats of the scornful!
Their delight is in the law of the LORD,* and they meditate on his law day and night.

The Litany
From all evil and wickedness; from sin; from the crafts and assaults of the devil; and from everlasting damnation,
Good Lord, deliver me.
From all blindness of heart; from pride, vainglory, and hypocrisy; from envy, hatred, and malice; and from all want of charity,
Good Lord, deliver me.
From all inordinate and sinful affections; and from all the deceits of the world, the flesh, and the devil,
Good Lord, deliver me.
From all false doctrine, heresy, and schism; from hardness of heart, and contempt of your Word and commandment,
Good Lord, deliver me.
By the mystery of your holy Incarnation; by your holy Nativity and submission to the Law; by your Baptism, Fasting, and Temptation,
Good Lord, deliver me.

In all time of tribulation; in all time of prosperity; in the hour of death, and in the
day of judgment,
> Good Lord, deliver me.

The Thanksgiving
Lord, you now have set your servant free to go in peace as you have promised; for
these eyes of mine have seen the Savior whom you have prepared for all the
world to see: A Light to enlighten the nations, and the glory of your people
Israel. *Amen.*

Nunc Dimittis

The Final Petition
Now guide me waking, O Lord, and guard me sleeping; that awake I may watch
with Christ, and asleep, I may rest in peace. *Amen.*

The Office of Dawn   **Observed on the Hour or Half-Hour
Between 4:30 and 7:30 a.m.**

The Call to Prayer
Worship the LORD, O Jerusalem;* praise your God, O Zion;
For he has strengthened the bars of your gates.

Psalm 147:13–14a

The Request for Presence
My soul waits for the LORD, more than watchmen for the morning,* more than
watchmen for the morning.

Psalm 130:5

The Greeting
Glory be to the Father, and the Son, and the Holy Spirit.
As it was in the beginning, it is now
And ever shall be, world without end. *Amen.*

Gloria Patri

The Hymn
Fairest Lord Jesus, Ruler of all nature,
O Thou of God and man the Son,
Thee will I cherish, Thee will I honor,
Thou, my soul's glory, joy and crown.
Fair are the meadows, fairer still the woodlands,
Robed in the blooming garb of spring;
Jesus is fairer, Jesus is purer,
Who makes the woeful heart to sing.
Fair is the sunshine, fairer still the moonlight,

And all the twinkling starry host;
Jesus shines brighter, Jesus shines purer
Than all the angels heaven can boast.

17th c. German Jesuit, translated by Joseph A. Seiss

The Psalm   *The LORD Adorns the Poor with Victory*

Let Israel rejoice in his Maker;* let the children of Zion be joyful in their King.
Let them praise his Name in the dance;* let them sing praise to him with timbrel
and harp.
For the LORD takes pleasure in his people* and adorns the poor with victory.
Let the faithful rejoice in triumph;* let them be joyful on their beds.

Psalm 149:2–5

The Gloria in Excelsis

Glory to God in the highest, and on earth peace to people of good will.
　　We praise you.
　　We bless you.
　　We adore you.
　　We glorify you.
We give thanks to you for your great glory.

The Small Verse

Jesus taught us, saying: Truly, truly, I say to you, if any one keeps my word, he
will never see death.

John 8:51

The Lord's Prayer

The Final Blessing

May the LORD bless us and keep us and cause His face to shine upon us from this
day forth and forever more. *Amen.*

℘

Saturday, Month of June

The Office of Midnight   **Observed on the Hour or Half-Hour**
Between 10:30 p.m.✢ and 1:30 a.m.

The Call to Prayer

Happy are the people whose strength is in you!* whose hearts are set on the
pilgrims' way.

For one day in your courts is better than a thousand in my own room,* and to stand
at the threshold of the house of my God than to dwell in the tents of the wicked.

Psalm 84:4, 9

The Request for Presence

O LORD, let my prayer be set forth in your sight as incense,* the lifting up of my
hands as the evening sacrifice.

Psalm 141:2, adapted

The Greeting

Our Father, Yours are the kingdom, the power, and the glory forever.

The Canticle   Glory to God
Gloria in excelsis

Glory to God in the highest,
and peace to his people on earth.
Lord God, heavenly King,
almighty God and Father,
    we worship you, we give you thanks,
    we praise you for your glory.
Lord Jesus Christ, only Son of the Father,
Lord God, Lamb of God,
    you take away the sin of the world: have mercy on us;
    you are seated at the right hand of the Father: receive our prayer.
For you alone are the Holy One, you alone are the Lord, you alone are the Most High,
Jesus Christ, with the Holy Spirit, in the glory of God the Father. *Amen.*

The Psalm   LORD, How Great Are Your Works

It is a good thing to give thanks to the LORD,* and to sing praises to your Name, O
Most High;
To tell of your loving-kindness early in the morning* and of your faithfulness in
the night season;
On the psaltery, and on the lyre,* and to the melody of the harp.
For you have made me glad by your acts, O LORD;* and I shout for joy because of
the works of your hands.
LORD, how great are your works!* your thoughts are very deep.

Psalm 92:1–5

The Gloria

The Small Verse

He told them another parable. "The kingdom of heaven is like leaven which a
woman took and hid in three measures of flour, till it was all leavened."

Matthew 13:33

222

The Final Thanksgiving
I will greatly rejoice in the Lord, my soul shall exult in my God; for he has clothed me with the garments of salvation, he has covered me with the robe of righteousness, as a bridegroom decks himself with a garland, and as a bride adorns herself with her jewels.

Isaiah 61:10

The Petition
May the Lord God, father of all mercy, grant us who dwell here a peaceful night and a perfect end. *Amen.*

The Office of the Night Watch   Observed on the Hour or Half-Hour
Between 1:30 and 4:30 a.m.

The Call to Prayer
Behold now, bless the Lord, all you servants of the Lord,* you that stand by night in the house of the Lord.
Lift up your hands in the holy place and bless the Lord;* the Lord who made heaven and earth bless you out of Zion.

Psalm 134

The Request for Presence
O God, come to my assistance.
O Lord, make haste to help me.

The Greeting
Awesome things will you show us in your righteousness, O God of our salvation,*
     O Hope of all the ends of the earth and of the seas that are far away.

Psalm 65:5

The Refrain for the Night Watch
The heavens declare the glory of God,* and the firmament shows his handiwork.
One day tells its tale to another,* and one night imparts knowledge to another.

Psalm 19:1–2

The Psalm   For the Lord Listens to the Needy
I will praise the Name of God in song;* I will proclaim his greatness with thanksgiving.
This will please the Lord more than an offering of oxen,* more than bullocks with horns and hoofs.
The afflicted shall see and be glad;* you who seek God, your heart shall live.
For the Lord listens to the needy,* and his prisoners he does not despise.
Let the heavens and the earth praise him,* the seas and all that moves in them;

Psalm 69:32–36

The Refrain
The heavens declare the glory of God,* and the firmament shows his handiwork.
One day tells its tale to another,* and one night imparts knowledge to another.

A Reading
When we pray, "Give us this day our daily bread," we are, in a measure, shutting
tomorrow out of our prayer. We do not live in tomorrow but in today. We do not
seek tomorrow's grace or tomorrow's bread. They thrive best, and get most out
of life, who live in the living present. They pray best who pray for today's
needs, not for tomorrow's, which may render our prayers unnecessary and
redundant by not existing at all. . . . There is no storing tomorrow's grace or
tomorrow's praying; neither is there any laying-up of today's grace to meet
tomorrow's necessities. We cannot have tomorrow's grace, we cannot eat
tomorrow's bread, we cannot do tomorrow's praying.

Edward Bounds, The Necessity of Prayer

The Refrain
The heavens declare the glory of God,* and the firmament shows his handiwork.
One day tells its tale to another,* and one night imparts knowledge to another.

The Litany
That it may please you to bless and keep all your people,
  I beseech you to hear me, good Lord.
That it may please you to send laborers into your harvest and to draw all
humankind into your kingdom,
  I beseech you to hear me, good Lord.
That it may please you to give to all people increase of grace to hear and receive
your Word, and to bring forth the fruits of the Spirit,
  I beseech you to hear me, good Lord.
That it may please you to bring into the way of truth all such as have erred, and
are deceived,
  I beseech you to hear me, good Lord.
That it may please you to give me a heart to love and fear you, and diligently to
live after your commandments,
  I beseech you to hear me, good Lord.

The Thanksgiving
Lord, you now have set your servant free to go in peace as you have promised; for
these eyes of mine have seen the Savior whom you have prepared for all the
world to see: A Light to enlighten the nations, and the glory of your people
Israel. *Amen.*

Nunc Dimittis

The Final Petition

Now guide me waking, O Lord, and guard me sleeping; that awake I may watch
with Christ, and asleep, I may rest in peace. *Amen.*

The Office of Dawn

**Observed on the Hour or Half-Hour
Between 4:30 and 7:30 a.m.**

The Call to Prayer

Sing to the LORD with thanksgiving; * make music to our God upon the harp.

Psalm 147:7

The Request for Presence

My soul waits for the LORD, more than watchmen for the morning,* more than
watchmen for the morning.

Psalm 130:5

The Greeting

Glory be to the Father, and the Son, and the Holy Spirit.
As it was in the beginning, it is now
And ever shall be, world without end. *Amen.*

Gloria Patri

The Hymn

Come, Holy Spirit, who ever One
are with the Father and the Son,
this is the hour, our souls possess
with Your full flood of holiness.
Let flesh and heart and lips and mind,
sound forth our witness to mankind;
and love light up our mortal frame,
til others catch the living flame.
Grant this, O Father, ever One
with Christ, Your sole-begotten Son,
and Holy Spirit, Whom all adore,
reigning and blest forevermore.

Latin—attributed to St. Ambrose, translated by Henry, Cardinal Newman

The Psalm
Praise the LORD from the Earth

Praise the LORD from the earth,* you sea-monsters and all deeps;
Fire and hail, snow and fog,* tempestuous wind, doing his will;
Mountains and all hills,* fruit trees and all cedars;
Wild beasts and all cattle,* creeping things and winged birds;
Kings of the earth and all peoples,* princes and all rulers of the world;

225

Young men and maidens,* old and young together.
Let them praise the Name of the LORD,

Psalm 148:7–13a

The Gloria in Excelsis
Glory to God in the highest, and on earth peace to people of good will.
  We praise you.
  We bless you.
  We adore you.
  We glorify you.
We give thanks to you for your great glory.

The Small Verse
Jesus said to them: I have yet many things to say to you, but you can not bear
  them now. When the Spirit of truth comes, he will guide you into all the truth;
  for he will not speak on his own authority, but whatever he hears, he will
  speak, and he will declare to you the things that are to come.

John 16:12–13

The Lord's Prayer

The Final Blessing
May the LORD bless us and keep us and cause His face to shine upon us from this
  day forth and forever more. *Amen.*

The Gloria

Glory be to God the Father, God the Son, and God the Holy Spirit. As it was in the beginning, so it is now and so it shall ever be, world without end. Alleluia. *Amen.*

The Lord's Prayer

Our Father, who art in heaven, hallowed be your Name.
May your kingdom come, and your will be done, on earth as in heaven.
Give us today our daily bread.
Forgive us our sins as we forgive those who sin against us.
Lead us not into temptation, but deliver us from evil;
for yours are the kingdom and the power and the glory
forever and ever. *Amen*

The following major holy days occur in July:

The Feast of St. Mary Magdalene: *July 22*
The Feast of St. James and St. John: *July 25*

Prayer for use in the observation of a holy day:

Almighty God, by your Holy Spirit you have made us one with your saints in heaven and on earth: Grant that in my earthly pilgrimage, I may always be supported by this fellowship of love and prayer, and know myself to be surrounded by their witness to your power and mercy. I ask this for the sake of Jesus Christ, in whom all my intercessions are acceptable through the Spirit, and who lives and reigns forever and ever. *Amen.*

✤ The Office of Midnight is always taken from the prayers for the day nearest to the hour of actual observation. Thus, if the office is to be observed at 10:30 p.m. on Sunday, the prayers will be taken from the Monday offices, and so forth.

JULY

Sunday, Month of July

The Office of Midnight   **Observed on the Hour or Half-Hour**
Between 10:30 p.m.✚ and 1:30 a.m.

The Call to Prayer
Rejoice in the LORD, you righteous,* and give thanks to his holy Name.

Psalm 97:12

The Request for Presence
O LORD, let my prayer be set forth in your sight as incense,* the lifting up of my
hands as the evening sacrifice.

Psalm 141:2, adapted

The Greeting
Our Father Who art in Heaven, hallowed be Your name forever.

The Canticle   *The Song of Moses*
Cantemus Domino

I will sing to the Lord, for he is lofty and uplifted;*
    the horse and its rider has he hurled into the sea.
The Lord is my strength and my refuge;*
    the Lord has become my Savior.
This is my God and I will praise him,*
    the God of my people and I will exalt him.
The Lord is a mighty warrior;*
    Yahweh is his Name.
Who can be compared with you, O Lord, among the gods?*
    who is like you, glorious in holiness, awesome in renown, and worker of
    wonders?
With your constant love you led the people you redeemed;*
    with your might you brought them in safety to your holy dwelling.
You will bring them in and plant them*
    on the mount of your possession,
The resting-place you have made for yourself, O Lord,*
    the sanctuary, O Lord, that your hand has established.
The Lord shall reign*
    for ever and for ever.

Exodus: 15:1–6, 11–13, 17–18

The Psalm   *God Makes My Way Secure*
It is God who girds me about with strength* and makes my way secure.
He makes me sure-footed like a deer* and lets me stand firm on the heights.

230

He trains my hands for battle* and my arms for bending even a bow of bronze.
You have given me your shield of victory;* your right hand also sustains me; your
  loving care makes me great.
You lengthen my stride beneath me,* and my ankles do not give way.

Psalm 18:33–37

The Gloria

The Small Verse
There is neither Jew nor Greek, there is neither slave nor free, there is neither male
  nor female; for you are all one in Christ Jesus.

Galatians 3:28

The Final Thanksgiving
I will greatly rejoice in the LORD, my soul shall exult in my God; for he has
  clothed me with the garments of salvation, he has covered me with the robe of
  righteousness, as a bridegroom decks himself with a garland, and as a bride
  adorns herself with her jewels.

Isaiah 61:10

The Petition
May the Lord GOD, father of grace and mercy, grant all who dwell here a peaceful
  night and a perfect end. *Amen.*

The Office of the Night Watch   Observed on the Hour or Half-Hour
                                          Between 1:30 and 4:30 a.m.

The Call to Prayer
Behold now, bless the LORD, all you servants of the LORD,* you that stand by night
  in the house of the LORD.
Lift up your hands in the holy place and bless the LORD;* the LORD who made
  heaven and earth bless you out of Zion.

Psalm 134

The Request for Presence
O God, come to my assistance.
O Lord, make haste to help me.

The Greeting
Let all who seek you rejoice and be glad in you;* let those who love your
  salvation say for ever, "Great is the LORD!"

Psalm 70:4

231

The Refrain for the Night Watch

The LORD grants his loving-kindness in the daytime;* in the night season his song is with me, a prayer to the God of my life.

Psalm 42:10

The Psalm   Make Your Way Straight before Me

Lead me, O LORD, in your righteousness, because of those who lie in wait for me;* make your way straight before me.

For there is no truth in their mouth;* there is destruction in their heart;

Their throat is an open grave;* they flatter with their tongue.

Declare them guilty, O God;* let them fall, because of their schemes.

Because of their many transgressions cast them out,* for they have rebelled against you.

But all who take refuge in you will be glad;* they will sing out their joy for ever.

You will shelter them,* so that those who love your Name may exult in you.

For you, O LORD, will bless the righteous;* you will defend them with your favor as with a shield.

Psalm 5:8–15

The Refrain

The LORD grants his loving-kindness in the daytime;* in the night season his song is with me, a prayer to the God of my life.

A Reading

Let us do what the prophet said: "I said, I will take heed of my ways, that I sin not with my tongue: I have set a guard to my mouth. I was dumb, and was humbled, and kept silence even from good things." (Ps. 38[39]:2–3) Here the prophet shows that, if at times we ought to refrain from useful speech for the sake of silence, how much more ought we to abstain from evil words on account of the punishment due to sin.

The Rule of St. Benedict

The Refrain

The LORD grants his loving-kindness in the daytime;* in the night season his song is with me, a prayer to the God of my life.

The Litany

That it may please you to show your mercy to all prisoners and captives, the homeless and the hungry, and all who are desolate and oppressed,

I beseech you to hear me, good Lord.

That it may please you to give and preserve to our use the bountiful fruits of the earth, so that in due time all may enjoy them,

I beseech you to hear me, good Lord.

That it may please you to inspire all your people, in our several callings, to do the work which you gave us to do with singleness of heart as your servants, and for the common good,

I beseech you to hear me, good Lord.

That it may please you to visit the lonely; to strengthen all who suffer in mind, body, and spirit; and to comfort with your presence those who are failing and infirm,
> *I beseech you to hear me, good Lord.*

That it may please you to strengthen such as do stand; to comfort and help the weak-hearted; to raise up those who fall; and finally to beat down Satan under our feet,
> *I beseech you to hear me, good Lord.*

That it may please you to grant to all the faithful departed eternal life and peace,
> *I beseech you to hear me, good Lord.*

That it may please you to grant that, in the fellowship of all your saints, I may attain to your heavenly kingdom,
> *Son of God, I beseech you to hear me.*
> *Son of God, I beseech you to hear me.*

The Thanksgiving

Lord, you now have set your servant free to go in peace as you have promised; for these eyes of mine have seen the Savior whom you have prepared for all the world to see: A Light to enlighten the nations, and the glory of your people Israel. *Amen.*

Nunc Dimittis

The Final Petition

Now guide me waking, O Lord, and guard me sleeping; that awake I may watch with Christ, and asleep, I may rest in peace. *Amen.*

The Office of Dawn

Observed on the Hour or Half-Hour Between 4:30 and 7:30 a.m.

The Call to Prayer

Let everything that has breath* praise the LORD. Hallelujah!

Psalm 150:6

The Request for Presence

My soul waits for the LORD, more than watchmen for the morning,* more than watchmen for the morning.

Psalm 130:5

The Greeting

Glory be to the Father, and the Son, and the Holy Spirit.
As it was in the beginning, it is now
And ever shall be, world without end. *Amen.*

Gloria Patri

The Hymn

God of our fathers, whose almighty hand
leads forth in beauty all the starry band
of shining worlds in splendor through the skies,
our grateful songs before your throne arise.
Your love divine has led us in the past,
in this free land by you our lot is cast;
be then our ruler, guardian, guide, and stay,
your word our law, your paths our chosen way.
From war's alarms, from deadly pestilence,
be your strong arm our ever sure defense;
your true religion in our hearts increase,
your bounteous goodness nourish us in peace.
Refresh your people on their toilsome way,
lead us from night to never-ending day;
fill all our lives with love and grace divine,
and glory, laud, and praise be ever thine.

Daniel Crane Roberts

The Psalm   The LORD Cares for the Stranger

Happy are they who have the God of Jacob for their help!* whose hope is in the
   LORD their God;
Who made heaven and earth, the seas, and all that is in them;* who keeps his
   promise for ever;
Who gives justice to those who are oppressed,* and food to those who hunger.
The LORD loves the righteous; the LORD cares for the stranger;* he sustains the
   orphan and widow, but frustrates the way of the wicked.
The LORD shall reign for ever,* your God, O Zion, throughout all generations.
   Hallelujah!

Psalm 146:4–6, 8–9

The Gloria in Excelsis

Glory to God in the highest, and on earth peace to people of good will.
   We praise you.
   We bless you.
   We adore you.
   We glorify you.
We give thanks to you for your great glory.

The Small Verse

Thus says the LORD: Listen to me, my people, and give ear to me, my nation; for a
   law will go forth from me, and my justice for a light to the peoples. My
   deliverance draws near speedily, my salvation has gone forth, and my arm will
   rule the peoples; the coastlands wait for me, and for my arm they hope.

Isaiah 51:4–5

234

The Lord's Prayer

The Final Blessing
May the LORD bless us and keep us and cause His face to shine upon us from this
day forth and forever more. *Amen.*

♋

Monday, Month of July

The Office of Midnight   **Observed on the Hour or Half-Hour
Between 10:30 p.m.✛ and 1:30 a.m.**

The Call to Prayer
Let us come before his presence with thanksgiving* and raise a loud shout to him
with psalms.

Psalm 95:2

The Request for Presence
O LORD, let my prayer be set forth in your sight as incense,* the lifting up of my
hands as the evening sacrifice.

Psalm 141:2, adapted

The Greeting
Our Father, may Your kingdom come on earth as in Heaven.

The Canticle   *A Song of Creation—Part One*
Benedicite, omnia opera Domini

Glorify the Lord, all you works of the Lord,*
    praise him and highly exalt him for ever.
In the firmament of his power, glorify the Lord,*
    praise him and highly exalt him for ever.
Glorify the Lord, you angels and all powers of the Lord,*
    O heavens and all waters above the heavens.
Sun and moon and stars of the sky, glorify the Lord,*
    praise him and highly exalt him for ever.
Glorify the Lord, every shower of rain and fall of dew,*
    all winds and fire and heat.
Winter and Summer, glorify the Lord,*
    praise him and highly exalt him for ever.
Glorify the Lord, O chill and cold,*
    drops of dew and flakes of snow.

Frost and cold, ice and sleet, glorify the Lord,*
praise him and highly exalt him for ever.
Glorify the Lord, O nights and days,*
O shining light and enfolding dark.
Storm clouds and thunderbolts, glorify the Lord,*
praise him and highly exalt him for ever.

Song of the Three Young Men, 35–51

The Psalm   *Put Your Trust in God*

As the deer longs for the water-brooks,* so longs my soul for you, O God.
My soul is athirst for God, athirst for the living God;* when shall I come to appear
before the presence of God?
My tears have been my food day and night,* while all day long they say to me,
"Where now is your God?"
I pour out my soul when I think on these things:* how I went with the multitude
and led them into the house of God,
With the voice of praise and thanksgiving,* among those who keep holy-day.
Why are you so full of heaviness, O my soul?* and why are you so disquieted
within me?
Put your trust in God;* for I will yet give thanks to him, who is the help of my
countenance, and my God.

Psalm 42:1–7

The Gloria

The Small Verse

With joy you will draw water from the wells of salvation. And you will say in that
day: "Give thanks to the LORD, call upon his name; make known his deeds
among the nations, proclaim that his name is exalted.

Isaiah 12:3–4

The Final Thanksgiving

I will greatly rejoice in the LORD, my soul shall exult in my God; for he has
clothed me with the garments of salvation, he has covered me with the robe of
righteousness, as a bridegroom decks himself with a garland, and as a bride
adorns herself with her jewels.

Isaiah 61:10

The Petition

May the Lord GOD, father of grace and mercy, grant all who dwell here a peaceful
night and a perfect end. *Amen.*

236

The Office of the Night Watch

Observed on the Hour or Half-Hour Between 1:30 and 4:30 a.m.

The Call to Prayer
Behold now, bless the Lord, all you servants of the Lord,* you that stand by night in the house of the Lord.
Lift up your hands in the holy place and bless the Lord;* the Lord who made heaven and earth bless you out of Zion.

Psalm 134

The Request for Presence
O God, come to my assistance.
O Lord, make haste to help me.

The Greeting
My lips will sing with joy when I play to you,* and so will my soul, which you have redeemed.

Psalm 71:23

The Refrain for the Night Watch
Yours is the day, yours also the night;* you established the moon and the sun.

Psalm 74:15

The Psalm   *Hide Me under the Shadow of Your Wings*
I call upon you, O God, for you will answer me;* incline your ear to me and hear my words.
Show me your marvelous loving-kindness,* O Savior of those who take refuge at your right hand from those who rise up against them.
Keep me as the apple of your eye;* hide me under the shadow of your wings,

Psalm 17:6–8

The Refrain
Yours is the day, yours also the night;* you established the moon and the sun.

A Reading
Now it seems to me that when God has brought someone to a clear knowledge of the world and of its nature and of the fact that another world (or let us say, another kingdom) exists, and that there is a great difference between the one and the other, and of what it is to love the Creator and what to love the creature (this must be discovered by experience, for it is a very different matter from merely thinking about it and believing it); when one, then, understands by sight and experience what can be gained by the one practice and lost by the other, and what the Creator is and what the creature, and many other things which the Lord teaches to those who are willing to devote themselves to being taught by

237

Him in prayer. . . . then one loves very differently from those of us who have
not advanced thus far.

Teresa of Avila (1562 CE), The Way of Perfection

The Refrain
Yours is the day, yours also the night;* you established the moon and the sun.

The Litany
For the peace from above, for the loving-kindness of God, and for the salvation of
my soul, I pray to the Lord.
Lord, have mercy.
For the peace of the world, for the welfare of the Holy Church of God, and for the
unity of all peoples, I pray to the Lord.
Lord, have mercy.
For the leaders of the nations and for all in authority, I pray to the Lord.
Lord, have mercy.
For the aged and infirm, for the widowed and orphans, and for the sick and the
suffering, I pray to the Lord.
Lord, have mercy.
For the poor and the oppressed, for the unemployed and the destitute, for prisoners
and captives, and for all who remember and care for them, I pray to the Lord.
Lord, have mercy.
For all who have died in the hope of the resurrection, and for all the departed, I
pray to the Lord.
Lord, have mercy.

The Thanksgiving
Lord, you now have set your servant free to go in peace as you have promised; for
these eyes of mine have seen the Savior whom you have prepared for all the
world to see: A Light to enlighten the nations, and the glory of your people
Israel. *Amen.*

Nunc Dimittis

The Final Petition
Now guide me waking, O Lord, and guard me sleeping; that awake I may watch
with Christ, and asleep, I may rest in peace. *Amen.*

The Office of Dawn   **Observed on the Hour or Half-Hour
Between 4:30 and 7:30 a.m.**

The Call to Prayer
Worship the LORD, O Jerusalem;* praise your God, O Zion;
For he has strengthened the bars of your gates.

Psalm 147:13–14a

The Request for Presence
My soul waits for the LORD, more than watchmen for the morning,* more than
watchmen for the morning.

Psalm 130:5

The Greeting
Glory be to the Father, and the Son, and the Holy Spirit.
As it was in the beginning, it is now
And ever shall be, world without end. *Amen.*

Gloria Patri

The Hymn
Christ for the world we sing, the world to Christ we bring,
with loving zeal;
the poor, and them that mourn, the faint and overborne, sin-sick and sorrow-worn,
whom Christ can heal.
Christ for the world we sing, the world to Christ we bring
with one accord;
with us the work to share, with us reproach to dare, with us the cross to bear,
for Christ our Lord.
Christ for the world we sing, the world to Christ we bring,
with joyful song;
the newborn souls, whose days inspired with hope and praise,
to Christ belong.

Samuel Wolcott, adapted

The Psalm   He Gives Snow Like Wool
The LORD sends out his command to the earth,* and his word runs very swiftly.
He gives snow like wool;* he scatters hoarfrost like ashes.
He scatters his hail like bread crumbs;* who can stand against his cold?
He sends forth his word and melts them;* he blows with his wind, and the waters
flow.

Psalm 147:16–19

The Gloria in Excelsis
Glory to God in the highest, and on earth peace to people of good will.
We praise you.
We bless you.
We adore you.
We glorify you.
We give thanks to you for your great glory.

The Small Verse
And Jesus came and said to them, "All authority in heaven and on earth has been
given to me. Go therefore and make disciples of all nations, baptizing them in

the name of the Father and of the Son and of the Holy Spirit, teaching them to observe all that I have commanded you; and lo, I am with you always, to the close of the age."

Matthew 28:18–20

The Lord's Prayer

The Final Blessing
May the LORD bless us and keep us and cause His face to shine upon us from this day forth and forever more. *Amen.*

ॐ

Tuesday, Month of July

The Office of Midnight　　　　　**Observed on the Hour or Half-Hour Between 10:30 p.m.✛ and 1:30 a.m.**

The Call to Prayer
The Lord is in his holy temple; let all the earth keep silence before him.

Traditional

The Request for Presence
O LORD, let my prayer be set forth in your sight as incense,* the lifting up of my hands as the evening sacrifice.

Psalm 141:2, adapted

The Greeting
Our Father, may Your will be done, on earth as in Heaven.

The Canticle　　　　　　　　　　**The First Song of Isaiah**
Ecce, Deus

Surely, it is God who saves me;*
 I will trust in him and not be afraid.
For the Lord is my stronghold and my sure defense,*
 and he will be my Savior.
Therefore you shall draw water with rejoicing*
 from the springs of salvation.
And on that day you shall say,*
 Give thanks to the Lord and call upon his Name;
Make his deeds known among the peoples;*
 see that they remember that his Name is exalted.

Sing praises of the Lord, for he has done great things,*
and this is known in all the world.
Cry aloud, inhabitants of Zion, ring out your joy,*
for the great one in the midst of you is the Holy One of Israel.

Isaiah 12:2–6

The Psalm   *I Have Made the Lord GOD My Refuge*
Whom have I in heaven but you?* and having you I desire nothing upon earth.
Though my flesh and my heart should waste away,* God is the strength of my
heart and my portion for ever.
Truly, those who forsake you will perish;* you destroy all who are unfaithful.
But it is good for me to be near God;* I have made the Lord GOD my refuge.

Psalm 73:25–28

The Gloria

The Small Verse
See what love the Father has given us, that we should be called children of God;
and so we are.

I John 3:Ia

The Final Thanksgiving
I will greatly rejoice in the LORD, my soul shall exult in my God; for he has
clothed me with the garments of salvation, he has covered me with the robe of
righteousness, as a bridegroom decks himself with a garland, and as a bride
adorns herself with her jewels.

Isaiah 61:10

The Petition
May the Lord GOD, father of grace and mercy, grant all who dwell here a peaceful
night and a perfect end. *Amen.*

The Office of the Night Watch   **Observed on the Hour or Half-Hour**
                                       Between 1:30 and 4:30 a.m.

The Call to Prayer
Behold now, bless the LORD, all you servants of the LORD,* you that stand by night
in the house of the LORD.
Lift up your hands in the holy place and bless the LORD;* the LORD who made
heaven and earth bless you out of Zion.

Psalm 134

The Request for Presence
O God, come to my assistance.
O Lord, make haste to help me.

The Greeting

Happy are the people whose strength is in you!* whose hearts are set on the pilgrims' way.

Psalm 84:4

The Refrain for the Night Watch

I commune with my heart in the night;* I ponder and search my mind.

Psalm 77:6

The Psalm   Your Decrees Are My Study

I have more understanding than all my teachers,* for your decrees are my study.
I am wiser than the elders,* because I observe your commandments.
I restrain my feet from every evil way,* that I may keep your word.
I do not shrink from your judgments,* because you yourself have taught me.

Psalm 119:99–102

The Refrain

I commune with my heart in the night;* I ponder and search my mind.

A Reading

And just as he who ministers to a bodily hurt in some cases applies contraries, as cold to hot, moist to dry, etc., and in some cases applies likes, as a round cloth to a round wound, or an oblong cloth to an oblong wound . . . in the same way the wisdom of God in healing humanity has applied Himself to the cure, being Himself healer and medicine both in one. Seeing then that humanity fell through pride, He restored us through humility. We were ensnared by the wisdom of the serpent; we are set free by the foolishness of God. . . . On the other hand, He came as a human being to save us who are humanity, as a mortal to save us who are mortals, and by death to save us who were dead.

St. Augustine (ca. 410 CE), On Christian Doctrine

The Refrain

I commune with my heart in the night;* I ponder and search my mind.

The Litany

Father, I pray for your holy catholic Church;
That we all may be one.
Grant that every member of the Church may truly and humbly serve you;
That your Name may be glorified by all people.
I pray for all who govern and hold authority in the nations of the world;
That there may be justice and peace on the earth.
Have compassion on those who suffer from any grief or trouble;
That they may be delivered from their distress.
Give to the departed eternal rest.
Let light perpetual shine upon them.

I praise you for your saints who have entered into joy;
May I also come to share in your heavenly kingdom.

The Thanksgiving

Lord, you now have set your servant free to go in peace as you have promised; for these eyes of mine have seen the Savior whom you have prepared for all the world to see: A Light to enlighten the nations, and the glory of your people Israel. *Amen.*

Nunc Dimittis

The Final Petition

Now guide me waking, O Lord, and guard me sleeping; that awake I may watch with Christ, and asleep, I may rest in peace. *Amen.*

The Office of Dawn

Observed on the Hour or Half-Hour Between 4:30 and 7:30 a.m.

The Call to Prayer

Hallelujah! Praise the LORD from the heavens;* praise him in the heights.

Psalm 148:1

The Request for Presence

My soul waits for the LORD, more than watchmen for the morning,* more than watchmen for the morning.

Psalm 130:5

The Greeting

Glory be to the Father, and the Son, and the Holy Spirit.
As it was in the beginning, it is now
And ever shall be, world without end. *Amen.*

Gloria Patri

The Hymn

Faith of our fathers, living still,
in spite of dungeon, fire, and sword;
O how our hearts beat high with joy
whene'er we hear that glorious word!
Faith of our fathers, holy faith!
We will be true to you till death.
Faith of our fathers, we will love
both friend and foe in all our strife;
and preach you, too, as love knows how
by kindly words and virtuous life.

Faith of our fathers, holy faith!
We will be true to you till death.

Frederick W. Faber

The Psalm   ***Praise the Lord from the Heavens***
Praise the Lord from the heavens;* praise him in the heights.
Praise him, all you angels of his;* praise him, all his host.
Praise him, sun and moon;* praise him, all you shining stars.
Praise him, heaven of heavens,* and you waters above the heavens.
Let them praise the Name of the Lord;* for he commanded, and they were
    created.
He made them stand fast for ever and ever;* he gave them a law which shall not
    pass away.

Psalm 148:1b–6

The Gloria in Excelsis
Glory to God in the highest, and on earth peace to people of good will.
    We praise you.
    We bless you.
    We adore you.
    We glorify you.
We give thanks to you for your great glory.

The Small Verse
And behold, the Lord passed by, and a great and strong wind rent the mountains,
    and broke in pieces the rocks before the Lord, but the Lord was not in the
    wind; and after the wind an earthquake, but the Lord was not in the
    earthquake; and after the earthquake a fire, but the Lord was not in the fire;
    and after the fire a still small voice. . . .

I Kings 19:11b–12

The Lord's Prayer

The Final Blessing
May the Lord bless us and keep us and cause His face to shine upon us from this
    day forth and forever more. *Amen.*

244

Wednesday, Month of July

The Office of Midnight   **Observed on the Hour or Half-Hour**
Between 10:30 p.m.✢ and 1:30 a.m.

The Call to Prayer
And in the temple of the LORD* all are crying, "Glory!"

Psalm 29:9

The Request for Presence
O LORD, let my prayer be set forth in your sight as incense,* the lifting up of my
    hands as the evening sacrifice.

Psalm 141:2, adapted

The Greeting
Our Father, give us this day our daily bread.

The Canticle   *A Song of Creation—Part Two*
Benedicite, omnia opera Domini

Glorify the Lord, all you works of the Lord,*
    praise him and highly exalt him for ever.
In the firmament of his power, glorify the Lord,*
    praise him and highly exalt him for ever.
Let the earth glorify the Lord,*
    praise him and highly exalt him for ever.
Glorify the Lord, O mountains and hills, and all that grows upon the earth,*
    praise him and highly exalt him for ever.
Glorify the Lord, O springs of water, seas, and streams,*
    O whales and all that move in the waters.
All birds of the air, glorify the Lord,*
    praise him and highly exalt him for ever.
Glorify the Lord, O beasts of the wild,*
    and all you flocks and herds.
O men and women everywhere, glorify the Lord,*
    praise him and highly exalt him for ever.

Song of the Three Young Men, 52–61

The Psalm   *The LORD's Will Stands Fast For Ever*
By the word of the LORD were the heavens made,* by the breath of his mouth all
    the heavenly hosts.
He gathers up the waters of the ocean as in a water-skin* and stores up the depths
    of the sea.
Let all the earth fear the LORD;* let all who dwell in the world stand in awe of him.
For he spoke, and it came to pass;* he commanded, and it stood fast.

245

The LORD brings the will of the nations to naught;* he thwarts the designs of the
 peoples.
But the LORD's will stands fast for ever,* and the designs of his heart from age to age.

Psalm 33:6–11

The Gloria

The Small Verse
Jesus taught us saying: The kingdom of heaven is like treasure hidden in a field,
 which a man found and covered up; then in his joy he goes and sells all that he
 has and buys that field.

Matthew 13:44

The Final Thanksgiving
I will greatly rejoice in the LORD, my soul shall exult in my God; for he has
 clothed me with the garments of salvation, he has covered me with the robe of
 righteousness, as a bridegroom decks himself with a garland, and as a bride
 adorns herself with her jewels.

Isaiah 61:10

The Petition
May the Lord GOD, father of grace and mercy, grant all who dwell here a peaceful
 night and a perfect end. *Amen.*

The Office of the Night Watch — Observed on the Hour or Half-Hour Between 1:30 and 4:30 a.m.

The Call to Prayer
Behold now, bless the LORD, all you servants of the LORD,* you that stand by night
 in the house of the LORD.
Lift up your hands in the holy place and bless the LORD;* the LORD who made
 heaven and earth bless you out of Zion.

Psalm 134

The Request for Presence
O God, come to my assistance.
O Lord, make haste to help me.

The Greeting
May God give us his blessing,*and may all the ends of the earth stand in awe of him.

Psalm 67:7

The Refrain for the Night Watch
You shall not be afraid of any terror by night,* nor of the arrow that flies by day;

Psalm 91:5

246

The Psalm   *My Eyes Are upon the Faithful*

My eyes are upon the faithful in the land, that they may dwell with me,* and only
those who lead a blameless life shall be my servants.

Those who act deceitfully shall not dwell in my house,* and those who tell lies
shall not continue in my sight.

I will soon destroy all the wicked in the land,* that I may root out all evildoers
from the city of the LORD.

Psalm 101:6–8

The Refrain

You shall not be afraid of any terror by night,* nor of the arrow that flies by day;

A Reading

. . . We are not to suppose either that those things which are in our own power can
be done without the help of God, or that those which are in God's hand can be
brought to completion without the intervention of our acts and desires and
intentions.

Origen (ca. 185–254 CE), translated by Rufinus, De Principiis

The Refrain

You shall not be afraid of any terror by night,* nor of the arrow that flies by day;

The Litany

Grant, Almighty God, that all who confess your Name may be united in your truth,
live together in your love, and reveal your glory in the world.
Lord, in your mercy, hear my prayer.

Guide the people of this land, and of all the nations, in the ways of justice and
peace; that we may honor one another and serve the common good.
Lord, in your mercy, hear my prayer.

Give us all a reverence for the earth as your own creation, that we may use its
resources rightly in the service of others and to your honor and glory.
Lord, in your mercy, hear my prayer.

Bless all whose lives are closely linked with mine, and grant that I may serve
Christ in them, and love even as he loves me.
Lord, in your mercy, hear my prayer.

Comfort and heal all those who suffer in body, mind, or spirit; give them courage
and hope in their troubles, and bring them the joy of your salvation.
Lord, in your mercy, hear my prayer.

I commend to your mercy all who have died, that your will for them may be
fulfilled; and I pray that I may share with all your saints in your eternal
kingdom.
Lord, in your mercy, hear my prayer.

The Thanksgiving

Lord, you now have set your servant free to go in peace as you have promised; for
these eyes of mine have seen the Savior whom you have prepared for all the

247

world to see: A Light to enlighten the nations, and the glory of your people Israel. *Amen.*

Nunc Dimittis

The Final Petition
Now guide me waking, O Lord, and guard me sleeping; that awake I may watch with Christ, and asleep, I may rest in peace. *Amen.*

The Office of Dawn   Observed on the Hour or Half-Hour
Between 4:30 and 7:30 a.m.

The Call to Prayer
Hallelujah! Sing to the LORD a new song;* sing his praise in the congregation of the faithful.

Psalm 149:1

The Request for Presence
My soul waits for the LORD, more than watchmen for the morning,* more than watchmen for the morning.

Psalm 130:5

The Greeting
Glory be to the Father, and the Son, and the Holy Spirit.
As it was in the beginning, it is now
And ever shall be, world without end. *Amen.*

Gloria Patri

The Hymn
Sweet hour of prayer! sweet hour of prayer!
That calls me from a world of care,
And bids me at my Father's throne
Make all my wants and wishes known.
In seasons of distress and grief,
My soul has often found relief
And oft escaped the tempter's snare
By your return, sweet hour of prayer!
Sweet hour of prayer! sweet hour of prayer!
Your wings shall my petition bear
To Him whose truth and faithfulness
Engage the waiting soul to bless.
And since He bids me seek His face,
Believe His Word and trust His grace,
I'll cast on Him my every care,
And wait for you, sweet hour of prayer!

William B. Bradbury

248

The Psalm
Praise the Name of the LORD

Praise the LORD from the earth,* you sea-monsters and all deeps;
Fire and hail, snow and fog,* tempestuous wind, doing his will;
Mountains and all hills,* fruit trees and all cedars;
Wild beasts and all cattle,* creeping things and winged birds;
Kings of the earth and all peoples,* princes and all rulers of the world;
Young men and maidens,* old and young together.
Let them praise the Name of the LORD,*

Psalm 148:7–13a

The Gloria in Excelsis
Glory to God in the highest, and on earth peace to people of good will.
 We praise you.
 We bless you.
 We adore you.
 We glorify you.
We give thanks to you for your great glory.

The Small Verse
The Apostle wrote us, saying: Rejoice always, pray constantly, give thanks in all
 circumstances; for this is the will of God in Christ Jesus for you.

1 Thessalonians 5:16–18

The Lord's Prayer

The Final Blessing
May the LORD bless us and keep us and cause His face to shine upon us from this
 day forth and forever more. *Amen.*

☞

Thursday, Month of July

The Office of Midnight
**Observed on the Hour or Half-Hour
Between 10:30 p.m.✛ and 1:30 a.m.**

The Call to Prayer
Into your hands, O Lord, I commend my spirit; for you have redeemed me,
 O Lord, O God of truth. Keep me, O Lord, as the apple of your eye; hide me
 under the shadow of your wings.

The Book of Common Prayer

249

The Request for Presence

O LORD, let my prayer be set forth in your sight as incense,* the lifting up of my hands as the evening sacrifice.

Psalm 141:2, adapted

The Greeting

Our Father, forgive us our sins as we forgive those who have sinned against us.

The Canticle   A Song of Penitence

Kyrie Pantokrator

And now, O Lord, I bend the knee of my heart,*
   and make my appeal, sure of your gracious goodness.
I have sinned, O Lord, I have sinned,*
   and I know my wickedness only too well.
Therefore I make this prayer to you:*
   Forgive me, Lord, forgive me.
Do not let me perish in my sin,*
   nor condemn me to the depths of the earth.
For you, O Lord, are the God of those who repent,*
   and in me you will show forth your goodness.
Unworthy as I am, you will save me, in accordance with your great mercy,*
   and I will praise you without ceasing all the days of my life.
For all the powers of heaven sing your praises,*
   and yours is the glory to ages of ages. *Amen.*

Prayer of Manasseh 11–15

The Psalm   Rejoice in the LORD

You are my hiding-place; you preserve me from trouble;* you surround me with shouts of deliverance.
"I will instruct you and teach you in the way that you should go;* I will guide you with my eye.
Do not be like horse or mule, which have no understanding;* who must be fitted with bit and bridle, or else they will not stay near you."
Great are the tribulations of the wicked;* but mercy embraces those who trust in the LORD.
Be glad, you righteous, and rejoice in the LORD;* shout for joy, all who are true of heart.

Psalm 32:8–12

The Gloria

The Small Verse

Truly, truly, I say to you, he who hears my word and believes him who sent me, has eternal life; he does not come into judgment, but has passed from death to life.

John 5: 24

The Final Thanksgiving

I will greatly rejoice in the LORD, my soul shall exult in my God; for he has clothed me with the garments of salvation, he has covered me with the robe of righteousness, as a bridegroom decks himself with a garland, and as a bride adorns herself with her jewels.

Isaiah 61:10

The Petition

May the Lord GOD, father of grace and mercy, grant all who dwell here a peaceful night and a perfect end. *Amen.*

The Office of the Night Watch

Observed on the Hour or Half-Hour Between 1:30 and 4:30 a.m.

The Call to Prayer

Behold now, bless the LORD, all you servants of the LORD,* you that stand by night in the house of the LORD.
Lift up your hands in the holy place and bless the LORD;* the LORD who made heaven and earth bless you out of Zion.

Psalm 134

The Request for Presence

O God, come to my assistance.
O Lord, make haste to help me.

The Greeting

The earth has brought forth her increase;* may God, our own God, give us his blessing.

Psalm 57:6

The Refrain for the Night Watch

It is a good thing to give thanks to the LORD,* and to sing praises to your Name, O Most High;
To tell of your loving-kindness early in the morning* and of your faithfulness in the night season.

Psalm 92:1–2

The Psalm   *I Will Not Know Evil*

I will sing of mercy and justice;* to you, O LORD, will I sing praises.
I will strive to follow a blameless course; oh, when will you come to me?* I will walk with sincerity of heart within my house.
I will set no worthless thing before my eyes;* I hate the doers of evil deeds; they shall not remain with me.
A crooked heart shall be far from me;* I will not know evil.

Psalm 101:1–4

251

The Refrain

It is a good thing to give thanks to the LORD,* and to sing praises to your Name,
O Most High;
To tell of your loving-kindness early in the morning* and of your faithfulness in
the night season.

A Reading

This is the meaning of the statement, "The works of the Lord are great, well-
considered in all his acts of will"—that in a strange and ineffable fashion even
that which is done against his will is not done without his will. For it would not
be done without his allowing it—and surely his permission is not unwilling but
willing—nor would he who is good allow the evil to be done, unless in his
omnipotence he could bring good even out of evil.

St. Augustine (ca. 410 CE), Handbook on Faith, Hope, and Love

The Refrain

It is a good thing to give thanks to the LORD,* and to sing praises to your Name,
O Most High;
To tell of your loving-kindness early in the morning* and of your faithfulness in
the night season.

The Litany

For the holy Church of God, that it may be filled with truth and love, and be found
without fault at the day of your coming, I pray to you, O Lord.
> *Lord, in your mercy, hear my prayer*

For all who fear God and believe in you, Lord Christ, that our divisions may cease,
and that all may be one as you and the Father are one, I pray to you, O Lord.
> *Lord, in your mercy, hear my prayer.*

For those who do not yet believe, and for those who have lost their faith, that they
may receive the light of the Gospel, I pray to you, O Lord.
> *Lord, in your mercy, hear my prayer.*

For my enemies and those who wish me harm, and for all whom I have injured or
offended, I pray to you, O Lord.
> *Lord, in your mercy, hear my prayer.*

For all who have commended themselves to my prayers; for my family, friends,
and neighbors; that being freed from anxiety, they may live in joy, peace, and
health, I pray to you, O Lord.
> *Lord, in your mercy, hear my prayer.*

For myself; for the forgiveness of my sins, and for the grace of the Holy Spirit to
amend my life, I pray to you, O Lord.
> *Lord, in your mercy, hear my prayer*

The Thanksgiving

Lord, you now have set your servant free to go in peace as you have promised; for
these eyes of mine have seen the Savior whom you have prepared for all the

world to see: A Light to enlighten the nations, and the glory of your people Israel. *Amen.*

Nunc Dimittis

The Final Petition

Now guide me waking, O Lord, and guard me sleeping; that awake I may watch with Christ, and asleep, I may rest in peace. *Amen.*

The Office of Dawn

Observed on the Hour or Half-Hour Between 4:30 and 7:30 a.m.

The Call to Prayer

Hallelujah! Praise the LORD, O my soul!* I will praise the LORD as long as I live; I will sing praises to my God while I have my being.

Psalm 146:1

The Request for Presence

My soul waits for the LORD, more than watchmen for the morning,* more than watchmen for the morning.

Psalm 130:5

The Greeting

Glory be to the Father, and the Son, and the Holy Spirit.
As it was in the beginning, it is now
And ever shall be, world without end. *Amen.*

Gloria Patri

The Hymn

Crown him with many crowns,
the Lamb upon his throne,
Hark! how the heavenly anthem drowns
all music but its own.
Awake, my soul, and sing
of him who died for you,
and hail him as your matchless King
through all eternity.
Crown him the Lord of life,
who triumphed o'er the grave,
and rose victorious in the strife
for those he came to save.
His glories now we sing,
who died, and rose on high,
who died, eternal life to bring,
and lives that death may die.

Matthew Bridges and Godfrey Thring

253

The Psalm   *He Prepares Rain for the Earth*

He covers the heavens with clouds* and prepares rain for the earth;
He makes grass to grow upon the mountains* and green plants to serve mankind.
He provides food for flocks and herds* and for the young ravens when they cry.
He is not impressed by the might of a horse;* he has no pleasure in the strength of
    a man;
But the LORD has pleasure in those who fear him,* in those who await his gracious
    favor.

Psalm 147:8–12

The Gloria in Excelsis

Glory to God in the highest, and on earth peace to people of good will.
    We praise you.
    We bless you.
    We adore you.
    We glorify you.
We give thanks to you for your great glory.

The Small Verse

And I will put my spirit within you, and cause you to walk in my statutes and be
    careful to obey my ordinances. You shall dwell in the land which I gave to your
    fathers; and you shall be my people, and I will be your God.

Ezekiel 36:27–28

The Lord's Prayer

The Final Blessing

May the LORD bless us and keep us and cause His face to shine upon us from this
    day forth and forever more. *Amen.*

ॐ

Friday, Month of July

The Office of Midnight   **Observed on the Hour or Half-Hour**
                                                Between 10:30 p.m.✣ and 1:30 a.m.

The Call to Prayer

God looks down from heaven upon us all,* to see if there is any who is wise, if
    there is one who seeks after God.

Psalm 53:2

The Request for Presence

O LORD, let my prayer be set forth in your sight as incense,* the lifting up of my hands as the evening sacrifice.

Psalm 141:2, adapted

The Greeting

Our Father, lead us not into temptation, but deliver us from evil.

The Canticle   A Song of Penitence
Kyrie Pantokrator

O Lord and Ruler of the hosts of heaven,*
   God of Abraham, Isaac, and Jacob, and of all their righteous offspring:
You made the heavens and the earth,*
   with all their vast array.
All things quake with fear at your presence;*
   they tremble because of your power.
But your merciful promise is beyond all measure;*
   it surpasses all that our minds can fathom.
O Lord, you are full of compassion,*
   long-suffering, and abounding in mercy.
You hold back your hand;*
   you do not punish as we deserve.
In your great goodness, Lord, you have promised forgiveness to sinners,*
   that they may repent of their sin and be saved.

Prayer of Manasseh 1–2, 4, 6–7

The Psalm   In God I Trust and Will Not Be Afraid

In God the LORD, whose word I praise, in God I trust and will not be afraid,* for what can mortals do to me?
I am bound by the vow I made to you, O God;* I will present to you thank-offerings;
For you have rescued my soul from death and my feet from stumbling,* that I may walk before God in the light of the living.

Psalm 56:10–12

The Gloria

The Small Verse

May the Lord Almighty grant me and those I love a peaceful night and a perfect end.

The Book of Common Prayer

The Final Thanksgiving

I will greatly rejoice in the LORD, my soul shall exult in my God; for he has clothed me with the garments of salvation, he has covered me with the robe of

righteousness, as a bridegroom decks himself with a garland, and as a bride adorns herself with her jewels.

Isaiah 61:10

The Petition
May the Lord GOD, father of grace and mercy, grant all who dwell here a peaceful night and a perfect end. *Amen.*

The Office of the Night Watch   Observed on the Hour or Half-Hour
Between 1:30 and 4:30 a.m.

The Call to Prayer
Behold now, bless the LORD, all you servants of the LORD,* you that stand by night in the house of the LORD.
Lift up your hands in the holy place and bless the LORD;* the LORD who made heaven and earth bless you out of Zion.

Psalm 134

The Request for Presence
O God, come to my assistance.
O Lord, make haste to help me.

The Greeting
Deliver me, O LORD, by your hand* from those whose portion in life is this world;

Psalm 17:14

The Refrain for the Night Watch
Behold now, bless the LORD, all you servants of the LORD,* you that stand by night in the house of the LORD.

Psalm 134:1

The Psalm   *My Soul in Silence Waits*
For God alone my soul in silence waits;* truly, my hope is in him.
He alone is my rock and my salvation,* my stronghold, so that I shall not be shaken.
In God is my safety and my honor;* God is my strong rock and my refuge.
Put your trust in him always, O people,* pour out your hearts before him, for God is our refuge.
God has spoken once, twice have I heard it,* that power belongs to God.

Psalm 62:6–9, 13

The Refrain
Behold now, bless the LORD, all you servants of the LORD,* you that stand by night in the house of the LORD.

256

A Reading

God's presence and activity are beyond our ability to comprehend. We can accept them with faith. We can be deeply thankful for them. But there is no way we can grasp them, describe them, explain them. . . . The closer we are to God, the less we know about God.

Pseudo-Macarius (4th c.), Homilies

The Refrain

Behold now, bless the LORD, all you servants of the LORD,* you that stand by night in the house of the LORD.

The Litany

For the peace of the world, that a spirit of respect and forbearance may grow among nations and peoples, I pray to you, O Lord.
Lord, hear my prayer.
For those in positions of public trust, that they may serve justice, and promote the dignity and freedom of every person, I pray to you, O Lord.
Lord, hear my prayer.
For the poor, the persecuted, the sick, and all who suffer; for refugees, prisoners, and all who are in danger; that they may be relieved and protected, I pray to you, O Lord.
Lord, hear my prayer.
For the forgiveness of my sins, and for the grace of the Holy Spirit to amend my life, I pray to you, O Lord.
Lord, hear my prayer.
For all who have died in the communion of your Church, and those whose faith is known to you alone, that, with all the saints, they may have rest in that place where there is no pain or grief, but life eternal, I pray to you, O Lord.
Lord, hear my prayer
Rejoicing in the fellowship of the ever-blessed Virgin Mary and all the saints, I commend my self and all your faithful to Christ our God.
To you, O Lord our God.

The Thanksgiving

Lord, you now have set your servant free to go in peace as you have promised; for these eyes of mine have seen the Savior whom you have prepared for all the world to see: A Light to enlighten the nations, and the glory of your people Israel. *Amen.*

Nunc Dimittis

The Final Petition

Now guide me waking, O Lord, and guard me sleeping; that awake I may watch with Christ, and asleep, I may rest in peace. *Amen.*

The Office of Dawn **Observed on the Hour or Half-Hour**
Between 4:30 and 7:30 a.m.

The Call to Prayer
Hallelujah! How good it is to sing praises to our God!* how pleasant it is to honor
him with praise!

Psalm 147:1

The Request for Presence
My soul waits for the LORD, more than watchmen for the morning,* more than
watchmen for the morning.

Psalm 130:5

The Greeting
Glory be to the Father, and the Son, and the Holy Spirit.
As it was in the beginning, it is now
And ever shall be, world without end. *Amen.*

Gloria Patri

The Hymn
The church's one foundation is Jesus Christ her Lord;
she is his new creation by water and the Word.
From heaven he came and sought her to be his holy bride;
with his own blood he bought her, and for her life he died.
Elect from every nation, yet one o'er all the earth;
her charter of salvation, one Lord, one faith, one birth;
one holy name she blesses, partakes one holy food,
and to one hope she presses, with every grace endued.
Mid toil and tribulation, and tumult of her war,
she waits the consummation of peace forevermore;
till, with the vision glorious, her longing eyes are blest,
and the great church victorious shall be the church at rest.

Samuel J. Stone

The Psalm **The LORD Adorns the Poor with Victory**
Let Israel rejoice in his Maker;* let the children of Zion be joyful in their King.
Let them praise his Name in the dance;* let them sing praise to him with timbrel
and harp.
For the LORD takes pleasure in his people* and adorns the poor with victory.
Let the faithful rejoice in triumph;* let them be joyful on their beds.

Psalm 149:2–5

The Gloria in Excelsis
Glory to God in the highest, and on earth peace to people of good will.
We praise you.

258

We bless you.
We adore you.
We glorify you.
We give thanks to you for your great glory.

The Small Verse

So then you are no longer strangers and sojourners, but you are fellow citizens
with the saints and members of the household of God, built upon the
foundation of the apostles and prophets, Jesus Christ himself being the
cornerstone. In whom the whole structure is joined together and grows into a
holy temple in the Lord; in whom you also are built into it for a dwelling place
of God in the Spirit.

Ephesians 2:19–22

The Lord's Prayer

The Final Blessing

May the LORD bless us and keep us and cause His face to shine upon us from this
day forth and forever more. *Amen.*

৯৸

Saturday, Month of July

The Office of Midnight   **Observed on the Hour or Half-Hour**
                                  Between 10:30 p.m.✠ and 1:30 a.m.

The Call to Prayer

Ascribe to the LORD the glory due his Name;* worship the LORD in the beauty of
holiness.

Psalm 29:2

The Request for Presence

O LORD, let my prayer be set forth in your sight as incense,* the lifting up of my
hands as the evening sacrifice.

Psalm 141:2, adapted

The Greeting

Our Father, Yours are the kingdom, the power, and the glory forever.

259

The Canticle

The Song of Zechariah
Benedictus Dominus Deus

Blessed be the Lord, the God of Israel;*
  he has come to his people and set them free.
He has raised up for us a mighty savior,*
  born of the house of his servant David
You, my child, shall be called the prophet of the Most High,*
  for you will go before the Lord to prepare his way,
To give his people knowledge of salvation*
  by the forgiveness of their sins.
In the tender compassion of our God*
  the dawn from on high shall break upon us,
To shine on those who dwell in darkness and the shadow of death,*
  and to guide our feet into the way of peace.
Glory to the Father, and to the Son, and to the Holy Spirit:*
  as it was in the beginning, is now, and will be for ever. *Amen.*

Luke 1:68–69, 76–79

The Psalm

Kingship Belongs to the Lord

All the ends of the earth shall remember and turn to the Lord,* and all the families
  of the nations shall bow before him.
For kingship belongs to the Lord;* he rules over the nations.
To him alone all who sleep in the earth bow down in worship;* all who go down to
  the dust fall before him.
My soul shall live for him; my descendants shall serve him;* they shall be known
  as the Lord's for ever.
They shall come and make known to a people yet unborn* the saving deeds that
  he has done.

Psalm 22 26–30

The Gloria

The Small Verse
Jesus said to us: Let not your hearts be troubled; believe in God, believe also in
  me.

John 14:1

The Final Thanksgiving
I will greatly rejoice in the Lord, my soul shall exult in my God; for he has clothed
  me with the garments of salvation, he has covered me with the robe of
  righteousness, as a bridegroom decks himself with a garland, and as a bride
  adorns herself with her jewels.

Isaiah 61:10

The Petition
May the Lord GOD, father of grace and mercy, grant all who dwell here a peaceful night and a perfect end. *Amen.*

The Office of the Night Watch   **Observed on the Hour or Half-Hour Between 1:30 and 4:30 a.m.**

The Call to Prayer
Behold now, bless the LORD, all you servants of the LORD,* you that stand by night in the house of the LORD.
Lift up your hands in the holy place and bless the LORD;* the LORD who made heaven and earth bless you out of Zion.

Psalm 134

The Request for Presence
O God, come to my assistance.
O Lord, make haste to help me.

The Greeting
Save us, O LORD our God, and gather us from among the nations,* that we may give thanks to your holy Name and glory in your praise.

Psalm 106:47

The Refrain for the Night Watch
Darkness is not dark to you; the night is as bright as the day;* darkness and light to you are both alike.

Psalm 139:11

The Psalm   *My Hope Is in You*
LORD, let me know my end and the number of my days,* so that I may know how short my life is.
You have given me a mere handful of days, and my lifetime is as nothing in your sight;* truly, even those who stand erect are but a puff of wind.
We walk about like a shadow, and in vain we are in turmoil;* we heap up riches and cannot tell who will gather them.
And now, what is my hope? * O Lord, my hope is in you.

Psalm 39:5–8

The Refrain
Darkness is not dark to you; the night is as bright as the day;* darkness and light to you are both alike.

A Reading

Many a time I wish I had held my peace and not associated with men. Why, indeed, do we converse and gossip among ourselves when we seldom do part from one another without a troubled conscience? We do so because we seek comfort from one another's conversation and wish to ease the mind wearied by diverse thoughts. Hence, we talk and think quite fondly of things we like very much or of things we dislike intensely. But, sad to say, we often talk vainly and to no purpose; for this external pleasure effectively bars inward and divine consolation. Therefore we must watch and pray lest time pass idly.

Thomas à Kempis (ca. 1421 CE), Reading the Holy Scripture

The Refrain

Darkness is not dark to you; the night is as bright as the day;* darkness and light to you are both alike.

The Litany

For all people in their daily life and work;
For my family, friends, and neighbors, and for those who are alone, I pray to you, Lord God.
For this community, the nation, and the world;
For all who work for justice, freedom, and peace, I pray to you, Lord God.
For the just and proper use of your creation;
For the victims of hunger, fear, injustice, and oppression, I pray to you, Lord God.
For all who are in danger, sorrow, or any kind of trouble;
For those who minister to the sick, the friendless, and the needy, I pray to you, Lord God.
For the peace and unity of the Church of God;
For all who proclaim the Gospel, and all who seek the Truth, I pray to you, Lord God.
Hear me, Lord;
For your mercy is great.

The Thanksgiving

Lord, you now have set your servant free to go in peace as you have promised; for these eyes of mine have seen the Savior whom you have prepared for all the world to see: A Light to enlighten the nations, and the glory of your people Israel. *Amen.*

Nunc Dimittis

The Final Petition

Now guide me waking, O Lord, and guard me sleeping; that awake I may watch with Christ, and asleep, I may rest in peace. *Amen.*

The Office of Dawn   **Observed on the Hour or Half-Hour**
Between 4:30 and 7:30 a.m.

The Call to Prayer
Let everything that has breath* praise the LORD. Hallelujah!

Psalm 150:6

The Request for Presence
My soul waits for the LORD, more than watchmen for the morning,* more than
watchmen for the morning.

Psalm 130:5

The Greeting
Glory be to the Father, and the Son, and the Holy Spirit.
As it was in the beginning, it is now
And ever shall be, world without end. *Amen.*

Gloria Patri

The Hymn
Hark, the loud celestial hymn
angel choirs above are raising;
Cherubim and Seraphim
In unceasing chorus praising,
fill the heavens with sweet accord:
Holy, Holy, Holy Lord!
Lo, the Apostolic train join,
Your sacred name to hallow;
prophets swell the loud refrain,
and the white-robed Martyrs follow;
and, from morn till set of sun,
through the Church the song goes on.
Holy Father, Holy Son,
Holy Spirit, Three we name You,
While in essence only One,
undivided God we claim You:
and, adoring, bend the knee
while we own the mystery.
Spare Your people, Lord, we pray,
by a thousand snares surrounded:
keep us without sin today,
never let us be confounded.
Lo, we put our trust in You;
never, Lord, abandon us.

Te Deum; Ignaz Frantz, translated by Fr. Clarence Alphonsus Walworth

The Psalm   *Praise the Lord*
Praise him for his mighty acts;* praise him for his excellent greatness.
Praise him with the blast of the ram's-horn;* praise him with lyre and harp.
Praise him with timbrel and dance;* praise him with strings and pipe.
Praise him with resounding cymbals;* praise him with loud-clanging cymbals.
Let everything that has breath* praise the Lord. Hallelujah!

Psalm 150:2–6

The Gloria in Excelsis
Glory to God in the highest, and on earth peace to people of good will.
> We praise you.
> We bless you.
> We adore you.
> We glorify you.
We give thanks to you for your great glory.

The Small Verse
Daniel said: "Blessed be the name of God for ever and ever, to whom belong
wisdom and might. He changes times and seasons; he removes kings and sets
up kings; he gives wisdom to the wise and knowledge to those who have
understanding; he reveals deep and mysterious things; he knows what is in the
darkness, and the light dwells with him. To thee, O God of my fathers, I give
thanks and praise."

Daniel 2:20–23

The Lord's Prayer

The Final Blessing
May the Lord bless us and keep us and cause His face to shine upon us from this
day forth and forever more. *Amen.*

The Gloria
Glory be to God the Father, God the Son, and God the Holy Spirit. As it was
in the beginning, so it is now and so it shall ever be, world without end.
Alleluia. *Amen.*

The Lord's Prayer
Our Father, who art in heaven, hallowed be your Name.
May your kingdom come, and your will be done, on earth as in heaven.
Give us today our daily bread.
Forgive us our sins as we forgive those who sin against us.
Lead us not into temptation, but deliver us from evil;
for yours are the kingdom and the power and the glory
forever and ever. *Amen*

The following major holy days occur in August:
The Transfiguration of our Lord Jesus Christ: *August 6*
The Feast of Mary, the Virgin: *August 15*
The Feast of St. Bartholomew: *August 24*

Prayer for use in the observation of a holy day:
Almighty God, by your Holy Spirit you have made us one with your saints in
heaven and on earth: Grant that in my earthly pilgrimage, I may always be
supported by this fellowship of love and prayer, and know myself to be
surrounded by their witness to your power and mercy. I ask this for the sake of
Jesus Christ, in whom all my intercessions are acceptable through the
Spirit, and who lives and reigns forever and ever. *Amen.*

✣ The Office of Midnight is always taken from the prayers for the day nearest
to the hour of actual observation. Thus, if the office is to be observed at 10:30 p.m.
on Sunday, the prayers will be taken from the Monday offices, and so forth.

AUGUST

Sunday, Month of August

The Office of Midnight   **Observed on the Hour or Half-Hour**
                                   Between 10:30 p.m.✠ and 1:30 a.m.

The Call to Prayer
Ascribe to the LORD, you families of the peoples;* ascribe to the LORD honor and
power.

Psalm 96:7

The Request for Presence
O LORD, let my prayer be set forth in your sight as incense,* the lifting up of my
hands as the evening sacrifice.

Psalm 141:2, adapted

The Greeting
Our Father Who art in Heaven, hallowed be Your name.

The Canticle   *You Are God*
                                                        Te Deum laudamus

You are God: we praise you;
You are the Lord; we acclaim you;
You are the eternal Father:
All creation worships you.
To you all angels, all the powers of heaven,
Cherubim and Seraphim, sing in endless praise:
    Holy, holy, holy Lord, God of power and might,
    heaven and earth are full of your glory.
The glorious company of apostles praise you.
The noble fellowship of prophets praise you.
The white-robed army of martyrs praise you.
Throughout the world the holy Church acclaims you;
    Father, of majesty unbounded,
    your true and only Son, worthy of all worship,
    and the Holy Spirit, advocate and guide.
You, Christ, are the king of glory,
the eternal Son of the Father.
When you became man to set us free
you did not shun the Virgin's womb.
You overcame the sting of death
And opened the kingdom of heaven to all believers.
You are seated at God's right hand in glory.
We believe that you will come and be our judge.
    Come then, Lord, and help your people,

268

bought with the price of your own blood,
and bring us with your saints
to glory everlasting.

The Psalm

Gracious and Upright Is the LORD

Gracious and upright is the LORD;* therefore he teaches sinners in his way.
He guides the humble in doing right* and teaches his way to the lowly.
All the paths of the LORD are love and faithfulness* to those who keep his
covenant and his testimonies.

Psalm 25:7–9

The Gloria

The Small Verse

But thou, our God, art kind and true, patient, and ruling all things in mercy. For
even if we sin, we are thine, knowing thy power; but we will not sin, because
we know that we are accounted thine. For to know thee is complete
righteousness, and to know thy power is the root of immortality.

Wisdom 15:1–3

The Final Thanksgiving

I will greatly rejoice in the LORD, my soul shall exult in my God; for he has
clothed me with the garments of salvation, he has covered me with the robe of
righteousness, as a bridegroom decks himself with a garland, and as a bride
adorns herself with her jewels.

Isaiah 61:10

The Petition

May the Lord GOD, father of all mercy, grant us who dwell here a peaceful night
and a perfect end. *Amen.*

The Office of the Night Watch

Observed on the Hour or Half-Hour Between 1:30 and 4:30 a.m.

The Call to Prayer

Behold now, bless the LORD, all you servants of the LORD,* you that stand by night
in the house of the LORD.
Lift up your hands in the holy place and bless the LORD;* the LORD who made
heaven and earth bless you out of Zion.

Psalm 134

The Request for Presence

O God, come to my assistance.
O Lord, make haste to help me.

The Greeting
For there is forgiveness with you;* therefore you shall be feared.

Psalm 130:3

The Refrain for the Night Watch
I will bless the LORD who gives me counsel;* my heart teaches me, night after night.

Psalm 16:7

The Psalm   The Earth Is the LORD'S
The earth is the LORD's and all that is in it,* the world and all who dwell therein.
For it is he who founded it upon the seas* and made it firm upon the rivers of the deep.
"Who can ascend the hill of the LORD?"* and who can stand in his holy place?"
"Those who have clean hands and a pure heart,* who have not pledged themselves
    to falsehood, nor sworn by what is a fraud.
They shall receive a blessing from the LORD* and a just reward from the God of
    their salvation."

Psalm 24:1–5

The Refrain
I will bless the LORD who gives me counsel;* my heart teaches me, night after
    night.

A Reading
I was convinced early in life that the most valuable religion is an inward life. It is
    a true love and reverence for God the Creator. It prompts good behavior toward
    other people and to all of God's creation. The human mind is capable of both
    abstract thought about God and affection for God that results from observing
    nature. It is not possible to love an unseen God while mistreating God's visible
    creation.

John Woolman, Journal

The Refrain
I will bless the LORD who gives me counsel;* my heart teaches me, night after night.

The Litany
For the peace from above, for the loving-kindness of God, and for the salvation of
    my soul, I pray to the Lord.
    Lord, have mercy.
For the peace of the world, for the welfare of the Holy Church of God, and for the
    unity of all peoples, I pray to the Lord.
    Lord, have mercy.
For my city [town, village], for every city and community, and for those who live
    in them, I pray to the Lord.
    Lord, have mercy.

For seasonable weather, and for an abundance of the fruits of the earth, I pray to the Lord.
Lord, have mercy.
For the good earth which God has given us, and for the wisdom and will to conserve it, I pray to the Lord.
Lord, have mercy.
For deliverance from all danger, violence, oppression, and degradation, I pray to the Lord.
Lord, have mercy.
For the absolution and remission of my sins and offenses, I pray to the Lord.
Lord, have mercy.
Defend me, deliver me, and in your compassion protect me, O Lord, by your grace.
Lord, have mercy.

The Thanksgiving

Lord, you now have set your servant free to go in peace as you have promised; for these eyes of mine have seen the Savior whom you have prepared for all the world to see: A Light to enlighten the nations, and the glory of your people Israel. *Amen.*

Nunc Dimittis

The Final Petition

Now guide me waking, O Lord, and guard me sleeping; that awake I may watch with Christ, and asleep, I may rest in peace. *Amen.*

The Office of Dawn

Observed on the Hour or Half-Hour Between 4:30 and 7:30 a.m.

The Call to Prayer

Hallelujah! Praise the LORD, O my soul* I will praise the LORD as long as I live; I will sing praises to my God while I have my being.

Psalm 146:1

The Request for Presence

My soul waits for the LORD, more than watchmen for the morning,* more than watchmen for the morning.

Psalm 130:5

The Greeting

Glory be to the Father, and to the Son, and to the Holy Spirit.
As it was in the beginning, it is now
And ever shall be, world without end. *Amen.*

Gloria Patri

The Hymn

Bread of the world in mercy broken,
wine of the soul in mercy shed,
by whom the words of life were spoken,
and in whose death our sins are dead:
Look on the heart by sorrow broken,
look on the tears by sinners shed;
and be your feast to us the token
that by your grace our souls are fed.

Reginald Heber

The Psalm   Praise the LORD from the Earth

Praise the LORD from the earth,* you sea-monsters and all deeps;
Fire and hail, snow and fog,* tempestuous wind, doing his will;
Mountains and all hills, * fruit trees and all cedars;
Wild beasts and all cattle,* creeping things and winged birds;
Kings of the earth and all peoples,* princes and all rulers of the world;
Young men and maidens,* old and young together.
Let them praise the Name of the LORD,*

Psalm 148: 7–13a

The Gloria in Excelsis

Glory to God in the highest, and on earth peace to people of good will.
  We praise you.
  We bless you.
  We adore you.
  We glorify you.
We give thanks to you for your great glory.

The Small Verse

Now as they were eating, Jesus took bread, and blessed, and broke it, and gave it
  to his disciples and said, "Take, eat; this is my body." And he took a cup, and
  when he had given thanks he gave it to them, saying, "Drink of it, all of you;
  for this is my blood of the covenant, which is poured out for many for the
  forgiveness of sins. I tell you I shall not drink again of this fruit of the vine
  until that day when I drink it new with you in my Father's kingdom."

Matthew 26:26–29

The Lord's Prayer

The Final Blessing

May the LORD bless us and keep us and cause His face to shine upon us from this
  day forth and forever more. *Amen.*

Monday, Month of August

The Office of Midnight

Observed on the Hour or Half-Hour Between 10:30 p.m.✛ and 1:30 a.m.

The Call to Prayer

Search for the LORD and his strength;* continually seek his face.

Psalm 105:4

The Request for Presence

O LORD, let my prayer be set forth in your sight as incense,* the lifting up of my
hands as the evening sacrifice.

Psalm 141:2, adapted

The Greeting

Our Father, may Your kingdom come on earth as in Heaven.

The Canticle

A Song of Creation—Part Two
Benedicite, omnia opera Domini

Glorify the Lord, all you works of the Lord,*
  praise him and highly exalt him for ever.
In the firmament of his power, glorify the Lord,*
  praise him and highly exalt him for ever.
Let the earth glorify the Lord,*
  praise him and highly exalt him for ever.
Glorify the Lord, O mountains and hills, and all that grows upon the earth,*
  praise him and highly exalt him for ever.
Glorify the Lord, O springs of water, seas, and streams,*
  O whales and all that move in the waters.
All birds of the air, glorify the Lord,*
  praise him and highly exalt him for ever.
Glorify the Lord, O beasts of the wild,*
  and all you flocks and herds.
O men and women everywhere, glorify the Lord,*
  praise him and highly exalt him for ever.

Song of the Three Young Men, 52–61

The Psalm

O LORD, You Are My Portion and My Cup

Protect me, O God, for I take refuge in you;* I have said to the LORD, "You are my
  Lord, my good above all other."
All my delight is upon the godly that are in the land,* upon those who are noble
  among the people.
But those who run after other gods* shall have their troubles multiplied.

Their libations of blood I will not offer,* nor take the names of their gods upon my
lips.
O Lord, you are my portion and my cup;* it is you who uphold my lot.

Psalm 16:1–5

The Gloria

The Small Verse
When the perishable puts on the imperishable, and the mortal puts on immortality,
then shall come to pass the saying that is written: "Death is swallowed up in
victory. O death, where is thy victory? O death, where is thy sting?"

1 Corinthians 15:54–55

The Final Thanksgiving
I will greatly rejoice in the Lord, my soul shall exult in my God; for he has
clothed me with the garments of salvation, he has covered me with the robe of
righteousness, as a bridegroom decks himself with a garland, and as a bride
adorns herself with her jewels.

Isaiah 61:10

The Petition
May the Lord God, father of all mercy, grant us who dwell here a peaceful night
and a perfect end. *Amen.*

The Office of the Night Watch — Observed on the Hour or Half-Hour Between 1:30 and 4:30 a.m.

The Call to Prayer
Behold now, bless the Lord, all you servants of the Lord,* you that stand by night
in the house of the Lord.
Lift up your hands in the holy place and bless the Lord;* the Lord who made
heaven and earth bless you out of Zion.

Psalm 134

The Request for Presence
O God, come to my assistance.
O Lord, make haste to help me.

The Greeting
You are to be praised, O God, in Zion... To you that hear prayer shall all flesh
come,* because of their transgressions.

Psalm 65:1–2

The Refrain for the Night Watch

Happy are they who have not walked in the counsel of the wicked,* nor lingered in the way of sinners, nor sat in the seats of the scornful!
Their delight is in the law of the LORD,* and they meditate on his law day and night.

Psalm 1:1–2

The Psalm   *You Are the LORD*

In sacrifice and offering you take no pleasure* (you have given me ears to hear you); Burnt-offering and sin-offering you have not required,* and so I said, "Behold, I come.
In the roll of the book it is written concerning me:* 'I love to do your will, O my God; your law is deep in my heart.'"
I proclaimed righteousness in the great congregation;* behold, I did not restrain my lips; and that, O LORD, you know.
Your righteousness have I not hidden in my heart; I have spoken of your faithfulness and your deliverance;* I have not concealed your love and faithfulness from the great congregation.
You are the LORD; do not withhold your compassion from me;* let your love and your faithfulness keep me safe for ever,

Psalm 40:7–12

The Refrain

Happy are they who have not walked in the counsel of the wicked,* nor lingered in the way of sinners, nor sat in the seats of the scornful!
Their delight is in the law of the LORD,* and they meditate on his law day and night.

A Reading

The law, if you use it aright, sends you to Christ. For since the law's aim is to justify humanity, and since it fails to effect this, it remits us to Him who can do so. Another way, again, of using the law lawfully is when we keep it, but as a thing superfluous. And how is a thing superfluous? As the bridle is properly used, not by the prancing horse that chomps it, but by the horse that wears it only for the sake of appearance; so he uses the law lawfully who governs himself, though not as constrained by the letter of it.

St. John Chrysostom, Bishop of Constantinople (ca. 347–407 CE),
Homily on the Epistle of St. Paul to Timothy

The Refrain

Happy are they who have not walked in the counsel of the wicked,* nor lingered in the way of sinners, nor sat in the seats of the scornful!
Their delight is in the law of the LORD,* and they meditate on his law day and night.

The Litany

O God the Father, Creator of heaven and earth,
Have mercy upon me.

O God the Son, Redeemer of the world,
Have mercy upon me.
O God the Holy Spirit, Sanctifier of the faithful,
Have mercy upon me.
O holy, blessed, and glorious Trinity, one God,
Have mercy upon me.
Remember not, Lord Christ, my offenses, nor the offenses of my forefathers;
neither reward me according to my sins. Spare me, good Lord, spare your
people, whom you have redeemed with your most precious blood, and by your
mercy preserve us, for ever.
Spare us, good Lord.

The Thanksgiving
Lord, you now have set your servant free to go in peace as you have promised; for
these eyes of mine have seen the Savior whom you have prepared for all the
world to see: A Light to enlighten the nations, and the glory of your people
Israel. *Amen.*

Nunc Dimittis

The Final Petition
Now guide me waking, O Lord, and guard me sleeping; that awake I may watch
with Christ, and asleep, I may rest in peace. *Amen.*

The Office of Dawn   Observed on the Hour or Half-Hour
Between 4:30 and 7:30 a.m.

The Call to Prayer
Sing to the LORD with thanksgiving;* make music to our God upon the harp.

Psalm 147:7

The Request for Presence
My soul waits for the LORD, more than watchmen for the morning,* more than
watchmen for the morning.

Psalm 130:5

The Greeting
Glory be to the Father, and the Son, and the Holy Spirit.
As it was in the beginning, it is now
And ever shall be, world without end. *Amen.*

Gloria Patri

The Hymn
My faith looks up to thee,
thou Lamb of Calvary,

Savior divine!
Now hear me while I pray,
take all my guilt away,
O let me from this day
be wholly thine!
May thy rich grace impart
strength to my fainting heart,
my zeal inspire!
As thou hast died for me,
O may my love to thee
pure, warm, and changeless be,
a living fire!

Ray Palmer

The Psalm   The LORD Adorns the Poor with Victory

Let Israel rejoice in his Maker;* let the children of Zion be joyful in their King.
Let them praise his Name in the dance;* let them sing praise to him with timbrel
and harp.
For the LORD takes pleasure in his people* and adorns the poor with victory.
Let the faithful rejoice in triumph;* let them be joyful on their beds.

Psalm 149:2–5

The Gloria in Excelsis

Glory to God in the highest, and on earth peace to people of good will.
We praise you.
We bless you.
We adore you.
We glorify you.
We give thanks to you for your great glory.

The Small Verse

But he said to them, "You are those who justify yourselves before men, but God
knows your hearts; for what is exalted among men is an abomination in the
sight of God."

Luke 16:15

The Lord's Prayer

The Final Blessing

May the LORD bless us and keep us and cause His face to shine upon us from this
day forth and forever more. *Amen.*

277

Tuesday, Month of August

The Office of Midnight

Observed on the Hour or Half-Hour Between 10:30 p.m.✢ and 1:30 a.m.

The Call to Prayer

The sacrifice of God is a troubled spirit;* a broken and contrite heart, O God, you will not despise.

Psalm 51:18

The Request for Presence

O LORD, let my prayer be set forth in your sight as incense,* the lifting up of my hands as the evening sacrifice.

Psalm 141:2, adapted

The Greeting

Our Father, may Your will be done, on earth as in Heaven.

The Canticle

The Second Song of Isaiah
Quaerite Dominum

Seek the Lord while he wills to be found;*
    call upon him when he draws near.
Let the wicked forsake their ways*
    and the evil ones their thoughts;
And let them turn to the Lord, and he will have compassion,*
    and to our God, for he will richly pardon.
For my thoughts are not your thoughts,*
    nor your ways my ways, says the Lord.
For as the heavens are higher than the earth,*
    so are my ways higher than your ways, and my thoughts than your thoughts.
For as rain and snow fall from the heavens*
    and return not again, but water the earth,
Bringing forth life and giving growth,*
    seed for sowing and bread for eating,
So is my word that goes forth from my mouth;*
    it will not return to me empty;
But it will accomplish that which I have purposed,*
    and prosper in that for which I sent it.

Isaiah 55:6–11

The Psalm

My Delight Is in Your Statutes

With my whole heart I seek you;* let me not stray from your commandments.
I treasure your promise in my heart,* that I may not sin against you.
Blessed are you, O LORD;* instruct me in your statutes.

278

With my lips will I recite* all the judgments of your mouth.
I have taken greater delight in the way of your decrees* than in all manner of riches.
I will meditate on your commandments* and give attention to your ways.
My delight is in your statutes;* I will not forget your word.

Psalm 119:10–16

The Gloria

The Small Verse
So Jesus proclaimed, as he taught in the temple, "You know me, and you know
where I come from? But I have not come of my own accord; he who sent me is
true, and him you do not know. I know him, for I have come from him, and he
sent me."

John 7:28–29

The Final Thanksgiving
I will greatly rejoice in the LORD, my soul shall exult in my God; for he has
clothed me with the garments of salvation, he has covered me with the robe of
righteousness, as a bridegroom decks himself with a garland, and as a bride
adorns herself with her jewels.

Isaiah 61:10

The Petition
May the Lord GOD, father of all mercy, grant us who dwell here a peaceful night
and a perfect end. *Amen.*

The Office of the Night Watch   Observed on the Hour or Half-Hour
Between 1:30 and 4:30 a.m.

The Call to Prayer
Behold now, bless the LORD, all you servants of the LORD,* you that stand by night
in the house of the LORD.
Lift up your hands in the holy place and bless the LORD;* the LORD who made
heaven and earth bless you out of Zion.

Psalm 134

The Request for Presence
O God, come to my assistance.
O Lord, make haste to help me.

The Greeting
Happy are they whom you choose and draw to your courts to dwell there!* they
will be satisfied by the beauty of your house, by the holiness of your temple.

Psalm 65:4

The Refrain for the Night Watch

The heavens declare the glory of God,* and the firmament shows his handiwork.
One day tells its tale to another,* and one night imparts knowledge to another.

Psalm 19:1–2

The Psalm   To You, O LORD, I Lift Up My Soul

Bow down your ear, O LORD, and answer me,* for I am poor and in misery.
Keep watch over my life, for I am faithful;* save your servant who puts his trust in
    you.
Be merciful to me, O LORD, for you are my God;* I call upon you all the day long.
Gladden the soul of your servant,* for to you, O LORD, I lift up my soul.
For you, O LORD, are good and forgiving,* and great is your love toward all who
    call upon you.

Psalm 86:1–5

The Refrain

The heavens declare the glory of God,* and the firmament shows his handiwork.
One day tells its tale to another,* and one night imparts knowledge to another.

A Reading

Now, wages for military service are paid as a just debt, not as a gift. Hence, he
    said, "The wages of sin is death," to show that death was not an unmerited
    punishment for sin, but a just debit. Yet a gift, unless it be gratuitous, is not
    grace. We are, therefore, to understand that even our merited goods are gifts
    from God, and when life eternal is given through them, what else do we have
    but "grace upon grace returned." (cf. John 1:16)

St. Augustine (ca. 410 CE), Handbook on Faith, Hope, and Love

The Refrain

The heavens declare the glory of God,* and the firmament shows his handiwork.
One day tells its tale to another,* and one night imparts knowledge to another.

The Litany

From all evil and wickedness; from sin; from the crafts and assaults of the devil;
    and from everlasting damnation,
    Good Lord, deliver me.
From all blindness of heart; from pride, vainglory, and hypocrisy; from envy,
    hatred, and malice; and from all want of charity,
    Good Lord, deliver me.
From all inordinate and sinful affections; and from all the deceits of the world, the
    flesh, and the devil,
    Good Lord, deliver me.
From all false doctrine, heresy, and schism; from hardness of heart, and contempt
    of your Word and commandment,
    Good Lord, deliver me.

By the mystery of your holy Incarnation; by your holy Nativity and submission to the Law; by your Baptism, Fasting, and Temptation,
> *Good Lord, deliver me.*

In all time of tribulation; in all time of prosperity; in the hour of death, and in the day of judgment,
> *Good Lord, deliver me.*

The Thanksgiving
Lord, you now have set your servant free to go in peace as you have promised; for these eyes of mine have seen the Savior whom you have prepared for all the world to see: A Light to enlighten the nations, and the glory of your people Israel. *Amen.*

Nunc Dimittis

The Final Petition
Now guide me waking, O Lord, and guard me sleeping; that awake I may watch with Christ, and asleep, I may rest in peace. *Amen.*

The Office of Dawn   Observed on the Hour or Half-Hour
Between 4:30 and 7:30 a.m.

The Call to Prayer
Worship the LORD, O Jerusalem;* praise your God, O Zion; For he has strengthened the bars of your gates.

Psalm 147:13–14a

The Request for Presence
My soul waits for the LORD, more than watchmen for the morning,* more than watchmen for the morning.

Psalm 130:5

The Greeting
Glory be to the Father, and the Son, and the Holy Spirit.
As it was in the beginning, it is now
And ever shall be, world without end. *Amen.*

Gloria Patri

The Hymn
Christ, from whom all blessings flow,
perfecting the saints below,
hear us, who your nature share,
who your mystic body are.
Move and actuate and guide,
diverse gifts to each divide;
placed according to your will,
let us all our work fulfill;

Many are we now, and one,
we who Jesus have put on;
there is neither bond nor free,
male nor female, Lord, in thee.

Charles Wesley

The Psalm   ***Who Can Stand Against His Cold***
The LORD sends out his command to the earth,* and his word runs very swiftly.
He gives snow like wool;* he scatters hoarfrost like ashes.
He scatters his hail like bread crumbs;* who can stand against his cold?
He sends forth his word and melts them;* he blows with his wind, and the waters flow.

Psalm 147:13–19

The Gloria in Excelsis
Glory to God in the highest, and on earth peace to people of good will.
    We praise you.
    We bless you.
    We adore you.
    We glorify you.
We give thanks to you for your great glory.

The Small Verse
Do you not know that you are God's temple and that God's spirit dwells in you? If
    any one destroys God's temple, God will destroy him. For God's temple is
    holy, and that temple you are.

1 Corinthians 3:16–17

The Lord's Prayer

The Final Blessing
May the LORD bless us and keep us and cause His face to shine upon us from this
    day forth and forever more. *Amen.*

⊰

Wednesday, Month of August

The Office of Midnight   **Observed on the Hour or Half-Hour
                                               Between 10:30 p.m.✛ and 1:30 a.m.**

The Call to Prayer
Into your hands I commend my spirit,* for you have redeemed me, O LORD,
    O God of truth.

Psalm 31:5

The Request for Presence
O LORD, let my prayer be set forth in your sight as incense,* the lifting up of my
hands as the evening sacrifice.

Psalm 141:2, adapted

The Greeting
Our Father, give us this day our daily bread.

The Canticle   The Song of the Redeemed
Magna et mirabilia
O ruler of the universe, Lord God, great deeds are they that you have done,*
surpassing human understanding.
Your ways are ways of righteousness and truth,*
O King of all the ages.
Who can fail to do you homage, Lord, and sing the praises of your Name?*
for you only are the Holy One.
All nations will draw near and fall down before you,*
because your just and holy works have been revealed.
Glory to the Father, and to the Son, and to the Holy Spirit:*
as it was in the beginning, is now, and will be for ever. *Amen.*

Revelation 15:3–4

The Psalm   Who May Abide upon Your Holy Hill
LORD, who may dwell in your tabernacle?* who may abide upon your holy hill?
Whoever leads a blameless life and does what is right,* who speaks the truth from
his heart.
There is no guile upon his tongue; he does no evil to his friend;* he does not heap
contempt upon his neighbor.
In his sight the wicked is rejected,* but he honors those who fear the LORD.
He has sworn to do no wrong* and does not take back his word.
He does not give his money in hope of gain,* nor does he take a bribe against the
innocent.
Whoever does these things* shall never be overthrown.

Psalm 15

The Gloria

The Small Verse
Jesus said to them, "I am the bread of life; he who comes to me shall not hunger,
and he who believes in me shall never thirst."

John 6:35

The Final Thanksgiving
I will greatly rejoice in the LORD, my soul shall exult in my God; for he has
clothed me with the garments of salvation, he has covered me with the robe of

righteousness, as a bridegroom decks himself with a garland, and as a bride adorns herself with her jewels.

Isaiah 61:10

The Petition
May the Lord GOD, father of all mercy, grant us who dwell here a peaceful night and a perfect end. *Amen.*

The Office of the Night Watch
Observed on the Hour or Half-Hour Between 1:30 and 4:30 a.m.

The Call to Prayer
Behold now, bless the LORD, all you servants of the LORD,* you that stand by night in the house of the LORD.
Lift up your hands in the holy place and bless the LORD;* the LORD who made heaven and earth bless you out of Zion.

Psalm 134

The Request for Presence
O God, come to my assistance.
O Lord, make haste to help me.

The Greeting
Blessed be the Lord GOD, the God of Israel,* who alone does wondrous deeds!
And blessed be his glorious Name for ever!* and may all the earth be filled with his glory. Amen. Amen.

Psalm 72:18–19

The Refrain for the Night Watch
The LORD grants his loving-kindness in the daytime;* in the night season his song is with me, a prayer to the God of my life.

Psalm 42:10

The Psalm   The LORD Loves the Gates of Zion
On the holy mountain stands the city he has founded;* the LORD loves the gates of Zion more than all the dwellings of Jacob.
Glorious things are spoken of you,* O city of our God.
I count Egypt and Babylon among those who know me;* behold Philistia, Tyre, and Ethiopia: in Zion were they born.
Of Zion it shall be said, "Everyone was born in her,* and the Most High himself shall sustain her."
The LORD will record as he enrolls the peoples,* "These also were born there."
The singers and the dancers will say,* "All my fresh springs are in you."

Psalm 87

The Refrain

The LORD grants his loving-kindness in the daytime;* in the night season his song
is with me, a prayer to the God of my life.

A Reading

Truth, not eloquence, is to be sought in reading Holy Scriptures; and every part
must be read in the spirit in which it was written. For in the Scriptures we
ought to seek profit rather than polished diction. Likewise we ought to read
simple and devout books as willingly as learned and profound ones. . . . If you
would profit from your endeavor, therefore, read with humility, simplicity, and
faith; and never seek a reputation for being learned. Seek willingly and listen
attentively to the words of the saints; do not be displeased with the sayings of
the ancients, for they were not made without purpose.

Thomas à Kempis (ca. 1421 CE), Imitation of Christ

The Refrain

The LORD grants his loving-kindness in the daytime;* in the night season his song
is with me, a prayer to the God of my life.

The Litany

That it may please you to bless and keep all your people,
  I beseech you to hear me, good Lord.
That it may please you to send laborers into your harvest and to draw all
humankind into your kingdom,
  I beseech you to hear me, good Lord.
That it may please you to give to all people increase of grace to hear and receive
your Word, and to bring forth the fruits of the Spirit,
  I beseech you to hear me, good Lord.
That it may please you to bring into the way of truth all such as have erred, and
are deceived,
  I beseech you to hear me, good Lord.
That it may please you to give me a heart to love and fear you, and diligently to
live after your commandments,
  I beseech you to hear me, good Lord.

The Thanksgiving

Lord, you now have set your servant free to go in peace as you have promised; for
these eyes of mine have seen the Savior whom you have prepared for all the
world to see: A Light to enlighten the nations, and the glory of your people
Israel. *Amen.*

Nunc Dimittis

The Final Petition

Now guide me waking, O Lord, and guard me sleeping; that awake I may watch
with Christ, and asleep, I may rest in peace. *Amen.*

The Office of Dawn   **Observed on the Hour or Half-Hour**
                                           Between 4:30 and 7:30 a.m.

The Call to Prayer
Hallelujah! Sing to the LORD a new song;* sing his praise in the congregation of
the faithful.

Psalm 149:1

The Request for Presence
My soul waits for the LORD, more than watchmen for the morning,* more than
watchmen for the morning.

Psalm 130:5

The Greeting
Glory be to the Father, and the Son, and the Holy Spirit.
As it was in the beginning, it is now
And ever shall be, world without end. *Amen.*

Gloria Patri

The Hymn
I love to tell the story
of unseen things above,
of Jesus and his glory,
of Jesus and his love.
I love to tell the story,
because I know 'tis true;
it satisfies my longings
as nothing else can do.
I love to tell the story,
for those who know it best
seem hungering and thirsting
to hear it like the rest.
And when, in scenes of glory,
I sing the new, new song,
'twill be the old, old story
that I have loved so long.

Katherine Hankey

The Psalm   *Praise the LORD*
Praise him for his mighty acts;* praise him for his excellent greatness.
Praise him with the blast of the ram's-horn;* praise him with lyre and harp.
Praise him with timbrel and dance;* praise him with strings and pipe.
Praise him with resounding cymbals;* praise him with loud-clanging cymbals.
Let everything that has breath * praise the LORD. Hallelujah!

Psalm 150:2–6

286

The Gloria in Excelsis
Glory to God in the highest, and on earth peace to people of good will.
    We praise you.
    We bless you.
    We adore you.
    We glorify you.
We give thanks to you for your great glory.

The Small Verse
The Psalmist wrote, saying: Give ear, O my people, to my teaching; incline your
ears to the words of my mouth! I will open my mouth in a parable; I will utter
dark sayings from old, things that we have heard and known. That our fathers
have told us. We will not hide them from their children. But tell to the coming
generation the glorious deeds of the LORD, and his might, and the wonders
which he has wrought.

Psalm 78:1–4

The Lord's Prayer

The Final Blessing
May the LORD bless us and keep us and cause His face to shine upon us from this
    day forth and forever more. *Amen.*

ॐ

Thursday, Month of August

The Office of Midnight   **Observed on the Hour or Half-Hour**
                                              Between 10:30 p.m.✢ and 1:30 a.m.

The Call to Prayer
Know this: The LORD himself is God;* he himself has made us, and we are his; we
are his people and the sheep of his pasture.

Psalm 100:2

The Request for Presence
O LORD, let my prayer be set forth in your sight as incense,* the lifting up of my
hands as the evening sacrifice.

Psalm 141:2, adapted

The Greeting
Our Father, forgive us our sins as we forgive those who have sinned against us.

The Canticle   *Song of Praise*
Benedictus es, Domine

Glory to you, Lord God of our fathers;*
  you are worthy of praise; glory to you.
Glory to you for the radiance of you holy Name;*
  we will praise you and highly exalt you for ever.
Glory to you in the splendor of you temple;*
  on the throne of your majesty, glory to you.
Glory to you, seated between the Cherubim;*
  we will praise you and highly exalt you for ever.
Glory to you, beholding the depths;*
  in the high vault of heaven, glory to you.
Glory to you, Father, Son, and Holy Spirit; *
  we will praise you and highly exalt you for ever.

Song of the Three Young Men, 29–34

The Psalm   *God Will Ransom My Life*

For the ransom of our life is so great,* that we should never have enough to pay it,
In order to live for ever and ever,* and never see the grave.
For we see that the wise die also; like the dull and stupid they perish* and leave
  their wealth to those who come after them.
Their graves shall be their homes for ever, their dwelling places from generation to
  generation,* though they call the lands after their own names.
Even though honored, they cannot live for ever;* they are like the beasts that perish.
Such is the way of those who foolishly trust in themselves,* and the end of those
  who delight in their own words.
Like a flock of sheep they are destined to die; Death is their shepherd;* they go
  down straightway to the grave.
Their form shall waste away,* and the land of the dead shall be their home.
But God will ransom my life;* he will snatch me from the grasp of death.

Psalm 49:7–15

The Gloria

The Small Verse

And then Jonah said to the LORD: "I had heard of thee by the hearing of the ear, but
  now my eye sees thee; therefore I despise myself, and repent in dust and ashes."

Jonah 42:5–6

The Final Thanksgiving

I will greatly rejoice in the LORD, my soul shall exult in my God; for he has
  clothed me with the garments of salvation, he has covered me with the robe of
  righteousness, as a bridegroom decks himself with a garland, and as a bride
  adorns herself with her jewels.

Isaiah 61:10

The Petition
May the Lord GOD, father of all mercy, grant us who dwell here a peaceful night and a perfect end. *Amen.*

The Office of the Night Watch   Observed on the Hour or Half-Hour
Between 1:30 and 4:30 a.m.

The Call to Prayer
Behold now, bless the LORD, all you servants of the LORD,* you that stand by night in the house of the LORD.
Lift up your hands in the holy place and bless the LORD;* the LORD who made heaven and earth bless you out of Zion.

Psalm 134

The Request for Presence
O God, come to my assistance.
O Lord, make haste to help me.

The Greeting
You, O LORD, are my lamp;* my God, you make my darkness bright.
With you I will break down an enclosure;* with the help of my God I will scale any wall.

Psalm 18:29–30

The Refrain for the Night Watch
Yours is the day, yours also the night;* you established the moon and the sun.

Psalm 74:15

The Psalm   *The LORD Bless You from Zion*
Happy are they all who fear the LORD,* and who follow in his ways!
You shall eat the fruit of your labor;* happiness and prosperity shall be yours.
Your wife shall be like a fruitful vine within your house,* your children like olive shoots round about your table.
The man who fears the LORD* shall thus indeed be blessed.
The LORD bless you from Zion,* and may you see the prosperity of Jerusalem all the days of your life.
May you live to see your children's children;* may peace be upon Israel.

Psalm 128

The Refrain
Yours is the day, yours also the night;* you established the moon and the sun.

A Reading
A man may go into the field and say his prayers and be aware of God; or he may be in church and be aware of God. But if he is more aware of God because he

289

is in a quiet place, that is his own deficiency and not due to God, Who is alike present in all things and all places, and is willing to give Himself everywhere, so far as lies in Him. He knows God rightly who knows Him everywhere.

Meister Eckhart (ca. 1260–1328 CE), The Sermons

The Refrain
Yours is the day, yours also the night;* you established the moon and the sun.

The Litany
That it may please you to show your mercy to all prisoners and captives, the homeless and the hungry, and all who are desolate and oppressed,
I beseech you to hear me, good Lord.
That it may please you to give and preserve to our use the bountiful fruits of the earth, so that in due time all may enjoy them,
I beseech you to hear me, good Lord.
That it may please you to inspire all your people, in our several callings, to do the work which you gave us to do with singleness of heart as your servants, and for the common good,
I beseech you to hear me, good Lord.
That it may please you to visit the lonely; to strengthen all who suffer in mind, body, and spirit; and to comfort with your presence those who are failing and infirm,
I beseech you to hear me, good Lord.
That it may please you to strengthen such as do stand; to comfort and help the weak-hearted; to raise up those who fall; and finally to beat down Satan under our feet,
I beseech you to hear me, good Lord.
That it may please you to grant to all the faithful departed eternal life and peace,
I beseech you to hear me, good Lord.
That it may please you to grant that, in the fellowship of all your saints, I may attain to your heavenly kingdom,
Son of God, I beseech you to hear me.
Son of God, I beseech you to hear me.

The Thanksgiving
Lord, you now have set your servant free to go in peace as you have promised; for these eyes of mine have seen the Savior whom you have prepared for all the world to see: A Light to enlighten the nations, and the glory of your people Israel. *Amen.*

Nunc Dimittis

The Final Petition
Now guide me waking, O Lord, and guard me sleeping; that awake I may watch with Christ, and asleep, I may rest in peace. *Amen.*

The Office of Dawn **Observed on the Hour or Half-Hour**
Between 4:30 and 7:30 a.m.

The Call to Prayer
Let everything that has breath* praise the LORD. Hallelujah!

Psalm 150:6

The Request for Presence
My soul waits for the LORD, more than watchmen for the morning,* more than
watchmen for the morning.

Psalm 130:5

The Greeting
Glory be to the Father, and to the Son, and to the Holy Spirit.
As it was in the beginning, it is now
And ever shall be, world without end. *Amen.*

Gloria Patri

The Hymn
Praise the Lord who reigns above
and keeps his court below;
praise the holy God of love
and all his greatness show;
praise him for his noble deeds,
praise him for his matchless power;
him from whom all good proceeds
let earth and heaven adore.
God, in whom they move and live,
let every creature sing,
glory to their Maker give,
and homage to their King.
Hallowed be your name beneath,
as in heaven, so on earth adored;
praise the Lord in every breath,
let all things praise the Lord.

Charles Wesley

The Psalm *Praise the LORD, Heaven of Heavens*
Hallelujah! Praise the LORD from the heavens;* praise him in the heights.
Praise him, all you angels of his;* praise him, all his host.
Praise him, sun and moon;* praise him, all you shining stars.
Praise him, heaven of heavens,* and you waters above the heavens.
Let them praise the Name of the LORD;* for he commanded, and they were created.
He made them stand fast for ever and ever;* he gave them a law which shall not
pass away.

Psalm 148:1–6

The Gloria in Excelsis
Glory to God in the highest, and on earth peace to people of good will.
  We praise you.
  We bless you.
  We adore you.
  We glorify you.
We give thanks to you for your great glory.

The Small Verse
The Apostle wrote, saying: For here we have no lasting city, but we seek the city
  which is to come. Through him then let us continually offer up a sacrifice of
  praise to God, that is, the fruit of our lips that acknowledge his name.
  Hebrews 13:14-15

The Lord's Prayer

The Final Blessing
May the LORD bless us and keep us and cause His face to shine upon us from this
  day forth and forever more. *Amen.*

☙

Friday, Month of August

The Office of Midnight   **Observed on the Hour or Half-Hour
                              Between 10:30 p.m.✝ and 1:30 a.m.**

The Call to Prayer
Fear the LORD, you that are his saints,* for those who fear him lack nothing
  Psalm 34:9

The Request for Presence
O LORD, let my prayer be set forth in your sight as incense,* the lifting up of my
  hands as the evening sacrifice.
  Psalm 141:2, adapted

The Greeting
Our Father, lead us not into temptation, but deliver us from evil.

The Canticle   *A Song of Penitence*
                                            Kyrie Pantokrator
O Lord and Ruler of the hosts of heaven,*
  God of Abraham, Isaac, and Jacob, and of all their righteous offspring:

292

You made the heavens and the earth,*
  with all their vast array.
All things quake with fear at your presence;*
  they tremble because of your power.
But your merciful promise is beyond all measure;*
  it surpasses all that our minds can fathom.
O Lord, you are full of compassion,*
  long-suffering, and abounding in mercy.
You hold back your hand;*
  you do not punish as we deserve.
In your great goodness, Lord, you have promised forgiveness to sinners,*
  that they may repent of their sin and be saved.

Prayer of Manasseh 1–2, 4, 6–7

The Psalm   Forgive Me All My Sin

For your Name's sake, O LORD,* forgive my sin, for it is great.
Who are they who fear the LORD?* he will teach them the way that they should
  choose.
They shall dwell in prosperity,* and their offspring shall inherit the land.
The LORD is a friend to those who fear him* and will show them his covenant.
My eyes are ever looking to the LORD,* for he shall pluck my feet out of the net.
Turn to me and have pity on me,* for I am left alone and in misery.
The sorrows of my heart have increased;* bring me out of my troubles.
Look upon my adversity and misery* and forgive me all my sin.

Psalm 25:10–17

The Gloria

The Small Verse
And he said to them, "Follow me, and I will make you fishers of men."

Matthew 4:19

The Final Thanksgiving
I will greatly rejoice in the LORD, my soul shall exult in my God; for he has
  clothed me with the garments of salvation, he has covered me with the robe of
  righteousness, as a bridegroom decks himself with a garland, and as a bride
  adorns herself with her jewels.

Isaiah 61:10

The Petition
May the Lord GOD, father of all mercy, grant us who dwell here a peaceful night
  and a perfect end. *Amen.*

The Office of the Night Watch   Observed on the Hour or Half-Hour
Between 1:30 and 4:30 a.m.

The Call to Prayer
Behold now, bless the LORD, all you servants of the LORD,* you that stand by night in the house of the LORD.
Lift up your hands in the holy place and bless the LORD;* the LORD who made heaven and earth bless you out of Zion.

Psalm 134

The Request for Presence
O God, come to my assistance.
O Lord, make haste to help me.

The Greeting
The LORD lives! Blessed is my Rock!* Exalted is the God of my salvation!

Psalm 18:46

The Refrain for the Night Watch
I commune with my heart in the night;* I ponder and search my mind.

Psalm 77:6

The Psalm   *Your Works Are Wonderful*
If I climb up to heaven, you are there;* if I make the grave my bed, you are there also.
If I take the wings of the morning* and dwell in the uttermost parts of the sea,
Even there your hand will lead me* and your right hand hold me fast.
If I say, "Surely the darkness will cover me,* and the light around me turn to night,"
Darkness is not dark to you; the night is as bright as the day;* darkness and light to you are both alike.
For you yourself created my inmost parts;* you knit me together in my mother's womb.
I will thank you because I am marvelously made;* your works are wonderful, and I know it well.

Psalm 139:7–13

The Refrain
I commune with my heart in the night;* I ponder and search my mind.

A Reading
For the passing and trivial sins of every day, from which no life is free—for them, the everyday prayer of the faithful makes satisfaction. For they can say the "Our Father, who art in heaven" who have already been reborn to such a Father

"by water and the Spirit." This prayer completely blots out our minor and everyday sins. The "Our Father" also blots out those sins which once made the life of the faithful wicked, but from which, now that they have changed for the better by repentance, they have departed. The condition of this is that just as they truly say, "Forgive us our debts," so also they truly say, "as we forgive our debtors;" that is, if what is said is also done, For to forgive a man who seeks forgiveness is indeed to give alms.

St. Augustine (ca. 1421 CE), Handbook on Faith, Hope, and Love

The Refrain
I commune with my heart in the night;* I ponder and search my mind.

The Litany
For the peace from above, for the loving-kindness of God, and for the salvation of my soul, I pray to the Lord.
> *Lord, have mercy.*

For the peace of the world, for the welfare of the Holy Church of God, and for the unity of all peoples, I pray to the Lord.
> *Lord, have mercy.*

For the leaders of the nations and for all in authority, I pray to the Lord.
> *Lord, have mercy.*

For the aged and infirm, for the widowed and orphans, and for the sick and the suffering, I pray to the Lord.
> *Lord, have mercy.*

For the poor and the oppressed, for the unemployed and the destitute, for prisoners and captives, and for all who remember and care for them, I pray to the Lord.
> *Lord, have mercy.*

For all who have died in the hope of the resurrection, and for all the departed, I pray to the Lord.
> *Lord, have mercy.*

The Thanksgiving
Lord, you now have set your servant free to go in peace as you have promised; for these eyes of mine have seen the Savior whom you have prepared for all the world to see: A Light to enlighten the nations, and the glory of your people Israel. *Amen.*

Nunc Dimittis

The Final Petition
Now guide me waking, O Lord, and guard me sleeping; that awake I may watch with Christ, and asleep, I may rest in peace. *Amen.*

The Office of Dawn   **Observed on the Hour or Half-Hour**
Between 4:30 and 7:30 a.m.

The Call to Prayer
Hallelujah! Praise the LORD from the heavens;* praise him in the heights.

Psalm 148:1

The Request for Presence
My soul waits for the LORD, more than watchmen for the morning,* more than
watchmen for the morning.

Psalm 130:5

The Greeting
Glory be to the Father, and the Son, and the Holy Spirit.
As it was in the beginning, it is now
And ever shall be, world without end. *Amen.*

Gloria Patri

The Hymn
Blessed assurance, Jesus is mine!
O what a foretaste of glory divine!
Heir of salvation, purchase of God,
born of his Spirit, washed in his blood.
This is my story, this is my song,
praising my Savior all the day long;
this is my story, this is my song,
praising my Savior all the day long.
Perfect submission, perfect delight,
visions of rapture now burst on my sight;
angels descending bring from above
echoes of mercy, whispers of love.

Fanny J. Crosby

The Psalm   *The LORD Has Pleasure in Those Who Fear Him*
He covers the heavens with clouds* and prepares rain for the earth;
He makes grass to grow upon the mountains* and green plants to serve mankind.
He provides food for flocks and herds* and for the young ravens when they cry.
He is not impressed by the might of a horse;* he has no pleasure in the strength of
a man;
But the LORD has pleasure in those who fear him,* in those who await his gracious
favor.

Psalm 147:8–12

The Gloria in Excelsis
Glory to God in the highest, and on earth peace to people of good will.
We praise you.

We bless you.
We adore you.
We glorify you.
We give thanks to you for your great glory.

The Small Verse
A new heart I will give you, and a new spirit I will put within you; and I will take
out of your flesh the heart of stone and give you a heart of flesh.

Ezekiel 36:26

The Lord's Prayer

The Final Blessing
May the Lord bless us and keep us and cause His face to shine upon us from this
day forth and forever more. *Amen.*

⸙

Saturday, Month of August

The Office of Midnight   Observed on the Hour or Half-Hour
Between 10:30 p.m.✝ and 1:30 a.m.

The Call to Prayer
Come, let us bow down, and bend the knee,* and kneel before the LORD our
Maker.
For he is our God, and we are the people of his pasture and the sheep of his hand.*
Oh, that today you would hearken to his voice!

Psalm 95:6–7

The Request for Presence
O LORD, let my prayer be set forth in your sight as incense,* the lifting up of my
hands as the evening sacrifice.

Psalm 141:2, adapted

The Greeting
Our Father, Yours are the kingdom, the power, and the glory forever.

The Canticle   The First Song of Isaiah
Ecce, Deus

Surely, it is God who saves me;*
I will trust in him and not be afraid.

For the Lord is my stronghold and my sure defense,*
and he will be my Savior.
Therefore you shall draw water with rejoicing*
from the springs of salvation.
And on that day you shall say,*
Give thanks to the Lord and call upon his Name;
Make his deeds known among the peoples;*
see that they remember that his Name is exalted.
Sing praises of the Lord, for he has done great things,*
and this is known in all the world.
Cry aloud, inhabitants of Zion, ring out your joy,*
for the great one in the midst of you is the Holy One of Israel.

Isaiah 12:2–6

The Psalm   *We Are Your People and the Sheep of Your Pasture*

Help us, O God our Savior, for the glory of your Name;* deliver us and forgive us
our sins, for your Name's sake.
Why should the heathen say, "Where is their God?"* Let it be known among the
heathen and in our sight that you avenge the shedding of your servants' blood.
Let the sorrowful sighing of the prisoners come before you,* and by your great
might spare those who are condemned to die.
May the revilings with which they reviled you, O Lord,* return seven-fold into
their bosoms.
For we are your people and the sheep of your pasture;* we will give you thanks
for ever and show forth your praise from age to age.

Psalm 79:9–13

The Gloria

The Small Verse

As he said this, a woman in the crowd raised her voice and said to him, "Blessed is
the womb that bore you, and the breasts that you sucked!" But he said to her,
"Blessed rather are those who hear the word of God and keep it!"

Luke 11:27–28

The Final Thanksgiving

I will greatly rejoice in the LORD, my soul shall exult in my God; for he has
clothed me with the garments of salvation, he has covered me with the robe of
righteousness, as a bridegroom decks himself with a garland, and as a bride
adorns herself with her jewels.

Isaiah 61:10

The Petition

May the Lord GOD, father of all mercy, grant us who dwell here a peaceful night
and a perfect end. *Amen.*

The Office of the Night Watch **Observed on the Hour or Half-Hour
Between 1:30 and 4:30 a.m.**

The Call to Prayer

Behold now, bless the LORD, all you servants of the LORD,* you that stand by night
in the house of the LORD.
Lift up your hands in the holy place and bless the LORD;* the LORD who made
heaven and earth bless you out of Zion.

Psalm 134

The Request for Presence

O God, come to my assistance.
O Lord, make haste to help me.

The Greeting

Let the words of my mouth and the meditation of my heart be acceptable in your
sight,* O LORD, my strength and my redeemer.

Psalm 19:14

The Refrain for the Night Watch

You shall not be afraid of any terror by night,* nor of the arrow that flies by day;

Psalm 91:5

The Psalm *Show Your Goodness, O LORD*

Those who trust in the LORD are like Mount Zion,* which cannot be moved, but
stands fast for ever.
The hills stand about Jerusalem;* so does the LORD stand round about his people,
from this time forth for evermore.
The scepter of the wicked shall not hold sway over the land allotted to the just,* so
that the just shall not put their hands to evil.
Show your goodness, O LORD, to those who are good* and to those who are true of
heart.
As for those who turn aside to crooked ways, the LORD will lead them away with
the evildoers;* but peace be upon Israel.

Psalm 125

The Refrain

You shall not be afraid of any terror by night,* nor of the arrow that flies by day;

A Reading

When the soul, in its gaze into heaven, has recognized its Author, it rises higher
than the sun, and far transcends all earthly power, and begins to be that which
it believes itself to be. . . . Be constant as well in prayer, therefore, as in
reading; now speak with God, now let God speak to you . . . and ceilings

299

enriched with gold, and houses adorned with mosaics of costly marble will seem mean to you so soon as you know that it is you yourself who is to be perfected and that dwelling which God has dwelt in as in a temple and in which the Holy Spirit has begun to make His abode is of more importance than all others.

Cyprian (d. 258 CE), Bishop of Carthage, The Epistles of Cyprian

The Refrain
You shall not be afraid of any terror by night,* nor of the arrow that flies by day;

The Litany
Father, I pray for your holy catholic Church;
> *That we all may be one.*

Grant that every member of the Church may truly and humbly serve you;
> *That your Name may be glorified by all people.*

I pray for all who govern and hold authority in the nations of the world;
> *That there may be justice and peace on the earth.*

Have compassion on those who suffer from any grief or trouble;
> *That they may be delivered from their distress.*

Give to the departed eternal rest.
> *Let light perpetual shine upon them.*

I praise you for your saints who have entered into joy;
> *May I also come to share in your heavenly kingdom.*

The Thanksgiving
Lord, you now have set your servant free to go in peace as you have promised; for these eyes of mine have seen the Savior whom you have prepared for all the world to see: A Light to enlighten the nations, and the glory of your people Israel. *Amen.*

Nunc Dimittis

The Final Petition
Now guide me waking, O Lord, and guard me sleeping; that awake I may watch with Christ, and asleep, I may rest in peace. *Amen.*

The Office of Dawn   **Observed on the Hour or Half-Hour**
Between 4:30 and 7:30 a.m.

The Call to Prayer
Hallelujah! How good it is to sing praises to our God!* How pleasant it is to honor him with praise!

Psalm 147:1

300

The Request for Presence
My soul waits for the LORD, more than watchmen for the morning,* more than
watchmen for the morning.

Psalm 130:5

The Greeting
Glory be to the Father, and to the Son, and to the Holy Spirit.
As it was in the beginning, it is now
And ever shall be, world without end. *Amen.*

Gloria Patri

The Hymn
O Jesus, Thou the beauty art
of angel worlds above!
Thy name is music to the heart,
enchanting it with love.
O my sweet Jesus! Hear the sighs
which unto Thee I send!
To Thee my inmost cries,
my being's hope and end.
O Jesu! Spotless Virgin flower!
Our life and joy! To Thee
be praise, beatitude and power,
through all eternity! Amen.

St. Bernard (11th c. Latin), translated by Fr. Edward Casawall

The Psalm   ***Happy Are They Whose Hope Is in the LORD Their God***
Happy are they who have the God of Jacob for their help!* whose hope is in the
    LORD their God;
Who made heaven and earth, the seas, and all that is in them;* who keeps his
    promise for ever;
Who gives justice to those who are oppressed,* and food to those who hunger.
The LORD loves the righteous; the LORD cares for the stranger;* he sustains the
    orphan and widow, but frustrates the way of the wicked.
The LORD shall reign for ever,* your God, O Zion, throughout all generations.
    Hallelujah!

Psalm 146:4–6; 8–9

The Gloria in Excelsis
Glory to God in the highest, and on earth peace to people of good will.
    We praise you.
    We bless you.
    We adore you.
    We glorify you.
We give thanks to you for your great glory.

301

The Small Verse
The lover sang: My beloved has gone down to his garden, to the bed of spices, to pasture his flock in the gardens, and to gather lilies. I am my beloved's and my beloved is mine; he pastures his flocks among the lilies.

Song of Songs 6: 1–3

The Lord's Prayer

The Final Blessing
May the LORD bless us and keep us and cause His face to shine upon us from this day forth and forever more. *Amen.*

The Gloria

Glory be to God the Father, God the Son, and God the Holy Spirit. As it was in the beginning, so it is now and so it shall ever be, world without end. Alleluia. *Amen.*

The Lord's Prayer

Our Father, who art in heaven, hallowed be your Name.
May your kingdom come, and your will be done, on earth as in heaven.
Give us today our daily bread.
Forgive us our sins as we forgive those who sin against us.
Lead us not into temptation, but deliver us from evil;
for yours are the kingdom and the power and the glory
forever and ever. *Amen*

The following major holy days occur in September:

Holy Cross Day: *September 14*
The Feast of St. Matthew: *September 21*
The Feast of St. Michael and All Angels: *September 29*

Prayer for use in the observation of a holy day:

Almighty God, by your Holy Spirit you have made us one with your saints in heaven and on earth: Grant that in my earthly pilgrimage, I may always be supported by this fellowship of love and prayer, and know myself to be surrounded by their witness to your power and mercy. I ask this for the sake of Jesus Christ, in whom all my intercessions are acceptable through the Spirit, and who lives and reigns forever and ever. *Amen.*

✣ The Office of Midnight is always taken from the prayers for the day nearest to the hour of actual observation. Thus, if the office is to be observed at 10:30 p.m. on Sunday, the prayers will be taken from the Monday offices, etc., etc.

SEPTEMBER

Sunday, Month of September

The Office of Midnight   **Observed on the Hour or Half-Hour
Between 10:30 p.m.✙ and 1:30 a.m.**

The Call to Prayer
O Lamb of God, that takest away the sins of the world, have mercy on us.
O Lamb of God, that takest away the sins of the world, have mercy on us.
O Lamb of God, that takest away the sins of the world, grant us thy peace.

The Book of Common Prayer

The Request for Presence
O LORD, let my prayer be set forth in your sight as incense,* the lifting up of my
   hands as the evening sacrifice.

Psalm 141:2, adapted

The Greeting
Our Father Who art in Heaven, hallowed be Your name.

The Canticle   *The Song of Zechariah*
Benedictus Dominus Deus

Blessed be the Lord, the God of Israel;*
   he has come to his people and set them free.
He has raised up for us a mighty savior,*
   born of the house of his servant David.
Through his holy prophets he promised of old, that he would save us from our
   enemies,*
   from the hands of all who hate us.
He promised to show mercy to our fathers*
   and to remember his holy covenant.
This was the oath he swore to our father Abraham,*
   to set us free from the hands of our enemies,
Free to worship him without fear,*
   holy and righteous in his sight all the days of our life.

Luke 1:68–75

The Psalm   *The LORD Upholds the Righteous*
The little that the righteous has* is better than great riches of the wicked.
For the power of the wicked shall be broken,* but the LORD upholds the righteous.
The LORD cares for the lives of the godly,* and their inheritance shall last for ever.
They shall not be ashamed in bad times,* and in days of famine they shall have
   enough.
As for the wicked, they shall perish,* and the enemies of the LORD, like the glory
   of the meadows, shall vanish; they shall vanish like smoke.

Psalm 37:17–21

The Gloria

The Small Verse

For from the rising of the sun to its setting my name is great among the nations, and in every place incense is offered to my name, and a pure offering; for my name is great among the nations, says the Lord of hosts.

Malachi 1:11

The Final Thanksgiving

I will greatly rejoice in the Lord, my soul shall exult in my God; for he has clothed me with the garments of salvation, he has covered me with the robe of righteousness, as a bridegroom decks himself with a garland, and as a bride adorns herself with her jewels.

Isaiah 61:10

The Petition

May the Lord God, father of all mercy, grant us who dwell here a peaceful night and a perfect end. *Amen.*

The Office of the Night Watch   Observed on the Hour or Half-Hour Between 1:30 and 4:30 a.m.

The Call to Prayer

Behold now, bless the Lord, all you servants of the Lord,* you that stand by night in the house of the Lord.
Lift up your hands in the holy place and bless the Lord;* the Lord who made heaven and earth bless you out of Zion.

Psalm 134

The Request for Presence

O God, come to my assistance.
O Lord, make haste to help me.

The Greeting

Not to us, O Lord, not to us, but to your Name give glory;* because of your love and because of your faithfulness.

Psalm 115:1

The Refrain for the Night Watch

It is a good thing to give thanks to the Lord,* and to sing praises to your Name, O Most High;
To tell of your loving-kindness early in the morning* and of your faithfulness in the night season.

Psalm 92:1–2

307

The Psalm   *Let Us Go to the House of the* Lord
I was glad when they said to me,* "Let us go to the house of the Lord."
Now our feet are standing* within your gates, O Jerusalem.
Jerusalem is built as a city* that is at unity with itself;
To which the tribes go up, the tribes of the Lord,* the assembly of Israel, to praise
   the Name of the Lord.
For there are the thrones of judgment,* the thrones of the house of David.

Psalm 122:1–5

The Refrain
It is a good thing to give thanks to the Lord,* and to sing praises to your Name,
   O Most High;
To tell of your loving-kindness early in the morning* and of your faithfulness in
   the night season.

A Reading
Brother Lawrence said: that when an occasion of practicing some virtue offered,
   he addressed himself to God, saying, "Lord, I cannot do this unless Thou
   enablest me," and that he then received strength more than sufficient;
That when he had failed in his duty, he only confessed his fault, saying to God, "I
   shall never do otherwise, if You leave me to myself; 'tis You must hinder my
   falling and mend what is amiss." And that after this, he gave himself no further
   uneasiness about it;
That we ought to act with God in the greatest simplicity, speaking to Him frankly
   and plainly, imploring His assistance in our affairs just as they happen, and that
   God never failed to grant it, as he himself had often experienced.

Brother Lawrence (ca. 1605–91 CE), The Practice of the Presence of God

The Refrain
It is a good thing to give thanks to the Lord,* and to sing praises to your Name,
   O Most High;
To tell of your loving-kindness early in the morning* and of your faithfulness in
   the night season.

The Litany
Grant, Almighty God, that all who confess your Name may be united in your truth,
   live together in your love, and reveal your glory in the world.
   Lord, in your mercy, hear my prayer.
Guide the people of this land, and of all the nations, in the ways of justice and
   peace; that we may honor one another and serve the common good.
   Lord, in your mercy, hear my prayer.
Give us all a reverence for the earth as your own creation, that we may use its
   resources rightly in the service of others and to your honor and glory.
   Lord, in your mercy, hear my prayer.

Bless all whose lives are closely linked with mine, and grant that I may serve
Christ in them, and love even as he loves me.
Lord, in your mercy, hear my prayer.
Comfort and heal all those who suffer in body, mind, or spirit; give them courage
and hope in their troubles, and bring them the joy of your salvation.
Lord, in your mercy, hear my prayer.
I commend to your mercy all who have died, that your will for them may be
fulfilled; and I pray that I may share with all your saints in your eternal
kingdom.
Lord, in your mercy, hear my prayer.

The Thanksgiving

Lord, you now have set your servant free to go in peace as you have promised; for
these eyes of mine have seen the Savior whom you have prepared for all the
world to see: A Light to enlighten the nations, and the glory of your people
Israel. *Amen.*

Nunc Dimittis

The Final Petition

Now guide me waking, O Lord, and guard me sleeping; that awake I may watch
with Christ, and asleep, I may rest in peace. *Amen.*

The Office of Dawn

**Observed on the Hour or Half-Hour
Between 4:30 and 7:30 a.m.**

The Call to Prayer

Let everything that has breath* praise the LORD. Hallelujah!

Psalm 150:6

The Request for Presence

My soul waits for the LORD, more than watchmen for the morning,* more than
watchmen for the morning.

Psalm 130:5

The Greeting

Glory be to the Father, and the Son, and the Holy Spirit.
As it was in the beginning, it is now
And ever shall be, world without end. *Amen.*

Gloria Patri

The Hymn

Holy God, we praise Your Name;
Lord of all we bow before You;
all on earth Your scepter claim,

all in heaven above adore You;
Infinite Your vast domain,
everlasting is Your reign.
Hark, the loud celestial hymn
angel choirs above are raising;
Cherubim and Seraphim
in unceasing chorus praising,
fill the heavens with sweet accord;
Holy, Holy, Holy Lord!
Holy Father, Holy Son,
Holy Spirit, Three we name You,
While in essence only One,
undivided God we claim You:
and, adoring, bend the knee
while we own the mystery.

Te Deum, translated by Msgr. Hugh Thomas Henry

The Psalm   Praise the Name of the LORD

Praise the LORD from the heavens;* praise him in the heights.
Praise him, all you angels of his;* praise him, all his host.
Praise him, sun and moon;* praise him, all you shining stars.
Praise him, heaven of heavens,* and you waters above the heavens.
Let them praise the Name of the LORD;* for he commanded, and they were
    created.
He made them stand fast for ever and ever;* he gave them a law which shall not
    pass away.

Psalm 148: 1b–6

The Gloria in Excelsis

Glory to God in the highest, and on earth peace to people of good will.
    We praise you.
    We bless you.
    We adore you.
    We glorify you.
We give thanks to you for your great glory.

The Small Verse

Lose your silver for the sake of a brother or a friend, and do not let it rust under a
    stone and be lost. Lay up your treasure according to the commandments of the
    Most High, and it will profit you more than gold.

Sirach 29: 10–11

The Lord's Prayer

The Final Blessing
May the LORD bless us and keep us and cause His face to shine upon us from this
    day forth and forever more. *Amen.*

৵

Monday, Month of September

The Office of Midnight   **Observed on the Hour or Half-Hour**
                                              Between 10:30 p.m.✢ and 1:30 a.m.

The Call to Prayer
Make a vow to the LORD your God and keep it;* let all around him bring gifts to
    him who is worthy to be feared.

Psalm 76:11

The Request for Presence
O LORD, let my prayer be set forth in your sight as incense,* the lifting up of my
    hands as the evening sacrifice.

Psalm 141:2, adapted

The Greeting
Our Father, may Your kingdom come on earth as in Heaven.

The Canticle   *A Song of Creation—Part Three*
                                        Benedicite, omnia opera Domini

Glorify the Lord, all you works of the Lord,*
    praise him and highly exalt him for ever.
In the firmament of his power, glorify the Lord,*
    praise him and highly exalt him for ever.
Let the people of God glorify the Lord,*
    praise him and highly exalt him for ever.
Glorify the Lord, O priests and servants of the Lord,*
    praise him and highly exalt him for ever.
Glorify the Lord, O spirits and souls of the righteous,*
    praise him and highly exalt him for ever.
You that are holy and humble of heart, glorify the Lord,*
    praise him and highly exalt him for ever.

Song of the Three Young Men, 62–68

The Psalm   *The LORD Is King*
The LORD is King; let the people tremble;* he is enthroned upon the cherubim; let
    the earth shake.

The LORD is great in Zion;* he is high above all peoples.
Let them confess his Name, which is great and awesome;* he is the Holy One.
"O mighty King, lover of justice, you have established equity;* you have executed
justice and righteousness in Jacob."
Proclaim the greatness of the LORD our God and fall down before his footstool;*
he is the Holy One.

Psalm 99:1–5

The Gloria

The Small Verse
And whatever you do, in word or deed, do everything in the name of the Lord
Jesus, giving thanks to God the Father through him.

Colossians 3:17

The Final Thanksgiving
I will greatly rejoice in the Lord, my soul shall exult in my God; for he has clothed
me with the garments of salvation, he has covered me with the robe of
righteousness, as a bridegroom decks himself with a garland, and as a bride
adorns herself with her jewels.

Isaiah 61:10

The Office of the Night Watch — Observed on the Hour or Half-Hour Between 1:30 and 4:30 a.m.

The Call to Prayer
Behold now, bless the LORD, all you servants of the LORD,* you that stand by night
in the house of the LORD.
Lift up your hands in the holy place and bless the LORD;* the LORD who made
heaven and earth bless you out of Zion.

Psalm 134

The Request for Presence
O God, come to my assistance.
O Lord, make haste to help me.

The Greeting
I will offer you the sacrifice of thanksgiving* and call upon the Name of the LORD.
Psalm 116:15

The Refrain for the Night Watch
Behold now, bless the LORD, all you servants of the LORD,* you that stand by night
in the house of the LORD.

Psalm 134:1

The Psalm   *Happy Are They Who Have God for Their Help*

Put not your trust in rulers, nor in any child of earth,* for there is no help in them.

When they breathe their last, they return to earth,* and in that day their thoughts
    perish.

Happy are they who have the God of Jacob for their help!* whose hope is in the
    Lord their God;

The Lord shall reign for ever,* your God, O Zion, throughout all generations.
    Hallelujah!

Psalm 146:2–4, 9

The Refrain

Behold now, bless the Lord, all you servants of the Lord,* you that stand by night
    in the house of the Lord.

A Reading

Let us urgently pray and groan with continual petitions, for know, beloved
    brethren, that I was not long ago warned of this in a vision—that is, that we
    were sleepy in our prayers and did not pray with watchfulness; and
    undoubtedly God who, "rebukes whom he loves; and when He rebukes,
    rebukes that He may amend" surely amends that He may preserve. Let us
    therefore strike off the bonds of sleep and pray with urgency and watchfulness
    . . . for the apostles ceased not to pray day and night; and the Lord Himself
    frequently and watchfully prayed, continuing all night in prayer. And assuredly
    what He prayed for, He prayed for on our behalf, since He was not a sinner.
    But if for us and our sins He both labored and watched and prayed, how much
    more ought we to be instant in prayer.

Cyprian, Bishop of Carthage (d. 258 CE), Epistle VII, to his clergy

The Refrain

Behold now, bless the Lord, all you servants of the Lord,* you that stand by night
    in the house of the Lord.

The Litany

For the holy Church of God, that it may be filled with truth and love, and be found
    without fault at the day of your coming, I pray to you, O Lord.
    Lord, in your mercy, hear my prayer

For all who fear God and believe in you, Lord Christ, that our divisions may cease,
    and that all may be one as you and the Father are one, I pray to you, O Lord.
    Lord, in your mercy, hear my prayer.

For those who do not yet believe, and for those who have lost their faith, that they
    may receive the light of the Gospel, I pray to you, O Lord.
    Lord, in your mercy, hear my prayer.

For my enemies and those who wish me harm, and for all whom I have injured or
    offended, I pray to you, O Lord.
    Lord, in your mercy, hear my prayer.

For all who have commended themselves to my prayers; for my family, friends, and neighbors; that being freed from anxiety, they may live in joy, peace, and health, I pray to you, O Lord.
Lord, in your mercy, hear my prayer.
For myself; for the forgiveness of my sins, and for the grace of the Holy Spirit to amend my life, I pray to you, O Lord.
Lord, in your mercy, hear my prayer

The Thanksgiving
Lord, you now have set your servant free to go in peace as you have promised; for these eyes of mine have seen the Savior whom you have prepared for all the world to see: A Light to enlighten the nations, and the glory of your people Israel. *Amen.*

Nunc Dimittis

The Final Petition
Now guide me waking, O Lord, and guard me sleeping; that awake I may watch with Christ, and asleep, I may rest in peace. *Amen.*

The Office of Dawn   Observed on the Hour or Half-Hour
Between 4:30 and 7:30 a.m.

The Call to Prayer
Hallelujah! Sing to the LORD a new song;* sing his praise in the congregation of the faithful.

Psalm 149:1

The Request for Presence
My soul waits for the LORD, more than watchmen for the morning,* more than watchmen for the morning.

Psalm 130:5

The Greeting
Glory be to the Father, and the Son, and the Holy Spirit.
As it was in the beginning, it is now
And ever shall be, world without end. *Amen.*

Gloria Patri

The Hymn
Savior, like a shepherd lead us,
much we need your tender care;
in your pleasant pastures feed us,
for our use your folds prepare.
Blessed Jesus, blessed Jesus!
You have bought us, yours we are.
Blessed Jesus, blessed Jesus!

You have bought us, yours we are.
Early let us seek your favor,
early let us do your will;
blessed Lord and only Savior,
with your love our being fill.
Blessed Jesus, blessed Jesus!
You have loved us, love us still.
Blessed Jesus, blessed Jesus!
You have loved us, love us still.

Dorothy A. Thrupp

The Psalm   The LORD Sustains the Orphan and Widow

Happy are they who have the God of Jacob for their help!* whose hope is in the
  LORD their God;
Who made heaven and earth, the seas, and all that is in them;* who keeps his
  promise for ever;
Who gives justice to those who are oppressed,* and food to those who hunger
The LORD loves the righteous; the LORD cares for the stranger;* he sustains the
  orphan and widow, but frustrates the way of the wicked.
The LORD shall reign for ever,* your God, O Zion, throughout all generations.
  Hallelujah!

Psalm 146:4–6, 8–9

The Gloria in Excelsis

Glory to God in the highest, and on earth peace to people of good will.
  We praise you.
  We bless you.
  We adore you.
  We glorify you.
We give thanks to you for your great glory.

The Small Verse

I will surely gather all of you, O Jacob, I will gather the remnant of Israel; I will
  set them together like sheep in a fold, like a flock in its pasture, a noisy
  multitude of men. He who opens the breach will go up before them; they will
  break through and pass the gate, going out by it. Their king will pass on before
  them, the Lord at their head.

Micah 2:12–13

The Lord's Prayer

The Final Blessing

May the Lord bless us and keep us and cause His face to shine upon us from this
  day forth and forever more. *Amen.*

315

Tuesday, Month of September

The Office of Midnight   **Observed on the Hour or Half-Hour**
Between 10:30 p.m.✢ and 1:30 a.m.

The Call to Prayer
Rejoice in the LORD, you righteous,* and give thanks to his holy Name.

Psalm 97:12

The Request for Presence
O LORD, let my prayer be set forth in your sight as incense,* the lifting up of my
hands as the evening sacrifice.

Psalm 141:2, adapted

The Greeting
Our Father, may Your will be done, on earth as in Heaven.

The Canticle   *The Third Song of Isaiah*
Surge, illuminare

Arise, shine, for your light has come,*
   and the glory of the Lord has dawned upon you.
For behold, darkness covers the land;*
   deep gloom enshrouds the peoples.
But over you the Lord will rise,*
   and his glory will appear upon you.
Nations will stream to your light,*
   and kings to the brightness of your dawning.
Your gates will always be open;*
   by day or night they will never be shut.
They will call you, The City of the Lord,*
   The Zion of the Holy One of Israel.
Violence will no more be heard in your land,*
   ruin or destruction within your borders.
You will call your walls, Salvation,*
   and all your portals, Praise.
The sun will no more be your light by day;*
   by night you will not need the brightness of the moon.
The Lord will be your everlasting light,*
   and your God will be your glory.

Isaiah 60:1–3, 11a, 14c, 18–19

The Psalm   *The Lord Chose David His Servant*
He chose instead the tribe of Judah* and Mount Zion, which he loved.
He built his sanctuary like the heights of heaven,* like the earth which he founded
   for ever.

He chose David his servant,* and took him away from the sheepfolds.

He brought him from following the ewes,* to be a shepherd over Jacob his people and over Israel his inheritance.

So he shepherded them with a faithful and true heart* and guided them with the skillfulness of his hands.

Psalm 78:68–72

The Gloria

The Small Verse

For as by a man came death, by a man has come also the resurrection of the dead. For as in Adam all die, so also in Christ shall all be made alive.

1 Corinthians 15:21–22

The Final Thanksgiving

I will greatly rejoice in the LORD, my soul shall exult in my God; for he has clothed me with the garments of salvation, he has covered me with the robe of righteousness, as a bridegroom decks himself with a garland, and as a bride adorns herself with her jewels.

Isaiah 61:10

The Petition

May the Lord GOD, father of all mercy, grant us who dwell here a peaceful night and a perfect end. *Amen.*

The Office of the Night Watch   Observed on the Hour or Half-Hour Between 1:30 and 4:30 a.m.

The Call to Prayer

Behold now, bless the LORD, all you servants of the LORD,* you that stand by night in the house of the LORD.

Lift up your hands in the holy place and bless the LORD;* the LORD who made heaven and earth bless you out of Zion.

Psalm 134

The Request for Presence

O God, come to my assistance.

O Lord, make haste to help me.

The Greeting

You are the God who works wonders* and have declared your power among the peoples.

Psalm 77:13

The Refrain for the Night Watch

Darkness is not dark to you; the night is as bright as the day;* darkness and light to you are both alike.

Psalm 139:11

The Psalm   *Blessed Be the LORD*

Blessed be the LORD my rock!* who trains my hands to fight and my fingers to battle;

My help and my fortress, my stronghold and my deliverer,* my shield in whom I trust, who subdues the peoples under me.

O LORD, what are we that you should care for us?* mere mortals that you should think of us?

We are like a puff of wind;* our days are like a passing shadow.

Psalm 144:1-4

The Refrain

Darkness is not dark to you; the night is as bright as the day;* darkness and light to you are both alike.

A Reading

No man appears in safety before the public eye unless he first relishes obscurity. No man is safe in speaking unless he loves to be silent. No man rules safely unless he is willing to be ruled. No man commands safely unless he has learned well how to obey. No man rejoices safely unless he has within him the testimony of a good conscience.

Thomas à Kempis (ca. 1421 CE), Imitation of Christ

The Refrain

Darkness is not dark to you; the night is as bright as the day;* darkness and light to you are both alike.

The Litany

For the peace of the world, that a spirit of respect and forbearance may grow among nations and peoples, I pray to you, O Lord.

    Lord, hear my prayer.

For those in positions of public trust, that they may serve justice, and promote the dignity and freedom of every person, I pray to you, O Lord.

    Lord, hear my prayer.

For the poor, the persecuted, the sick, and all who suffer; for refugees, prisoners, and all who are in danger; that they may be relieved and protected, I pray to you, O Lord.

    Lord, hear my prayer.

For the forgiveness of my sins, and for the grace of the Holy Spirit to amend my life, I pray to you, O Lord.

    Lord, hear my prayer.

318

For all who have died in the communion of your Church, and those whose faith is known to you alone, that, with all the saints, they may have rest in that place where there is no pain or grief, but life eternal, I pray to you, O Lord.
Lord, hear my prayer
Rejoicing in the fellowship of the ever-blessed Virgin Mary and all the saints, I commend my self and all your faithful to Christ our God.
To you, O Lord our God.

The Thanksgiving
Lord, you now have set your servant free to go in peace as you have promised; for these eyes of mine have seen the Savior whom you have prepared for all the world to see: A Light to enlighten the nations, and the glory of your people Israel. *Amen.*

Nunc Dimittis

The Final Petition
Now guide me waking, O Lord, and guard me sleeping; that awake I may watch with Christ, and asleep, I may rest in peace. *Amen.*

The Office of Dawn   Observed on the Hour or Half-Hour
Between 4:30 and 7:30 a.m.

The Call to Prayer
Hallelujah! Praise the LORD, O my soul!* I will praise the LORD as long as I live; I will sing praises to my God while I have my being.

Psalm 146:1

The Request for Presence
My soul waits for the LORD, more than watchmen for the morning,* more than watchmen for the morning.

Psalm 130:5

The Greeting
Glory be to the Father, and the Son, and the Holy Spirit.
As it was in the beginning, it is now
And ever shall be, world without end. *Amen.*

Gloria Patri

The Hymn
The voice of God is calling its summons in our day;
Isaiah heard in Zion, and we now hear God say:
"Whom shall I send to succor my people in their need?
Whom shall I send to loosen the bonds of shame and greed?

319

"I hear my people crying in slum and mine and mill;
No field or mart is silent, no city street is still.
I see my people falling in darkness and despair.
Whom shall I send to shatter the fetters which they bear?"
We heed, O Lord, your summons, and answer: Here are we!
Send us upon your errand, let us your servants be.
Our strength is dust and ashes, our years a passing hour;
but you can use our weakness to magnify your power.

John Haynes Holmes

The Psalm   *The LORD's Word Runs Very Swiftly*

The LORD sends out his command to the earth,* and his word runs very swiftly.
He gives snow like wool;* he scatters hoarfrost like ashes.
He scatters his hail like bread crumbs;* who can stand against his cold?
He sends forth his word and melts them;* he blows with his wind, and the waters
flow.

Psalm 147:16–19

The Gloria in Excelsis

Glory to God in the highest, and on earth peace to people of good will.
We praise you.
We bless you.
We adore you.
We glorify you.
We give thanks to you for your great glory.

The Small Verse

But how are men to call upon him in whom they have not believed? And how are
they to believe in him of whom they have never heard? And how are they to
hear without a preacher? And how can men preach unless they are sent? As it is
written, "How beautiful are the feet of those who preach good news!"

Romans 10:14–15

The Lord's Prayer

The Final Blessing

May the Lord bless us and keep us and cause His face to shine upon us from this
day forth and forever more. *Amen.*

Wednesday, Month of September

The Office of Midnight **Observed on the Hour or Half-Hour Between 10:30 p.m.✢ and 1:30 a.m.**

The Call to Prayer
Bless the LORD, O my soul,* and all that is within me, bless his holy Name.

Psalm 103:1

The Request for Presence
O LORD, let my prayer be set forth in your sight as incense,* the lifting up of my hands as the evening sacrifice.

Psalm 141:2, adapted

The Greeting
Our Father, give us this day our daily bread.

The Canticle *The Song of Simeon*
Nunc Dimittis

Lord, you now have set your servant free*
    to go in peace as you have promised;
For these eyes of mine have seen the Savior,*
    whom you have prepared for all the world to see:
A Light to enlighten the nations,*
    and the glory of your people Israel.
Glory to the Father, and to the Son, and to the Holy Spirit:*
    as it was in the beginning, is now, and will be for ever. *Amen.*

Luke 2:29–32

The Psalm *Light Has Sprung Up for the Righteous*
The heavens declare his righteousness,* and all the peoples see his glory.
Confounded be all who worship carved images and delight in false gods!* Bow
    down before him, all you gods.
Zion hears and is glad, and the cities of Judah rejoice,* because of your
    judgments, O LORD.
For you are the LORD, most high over all the earth;* you are exalted far above all gods.
The LORD loves those who hate evil;* he preserves the lives of his saints and
    delivers them from the hand of the wicked.
Light has sprung up for the righteous,* and joyful gladness for those who are
    truehearted.
Rejoice in the LORD, you righteous,* and give thanks to his holy Name.

Psalm 97:6–12

The Gloria

321

The Small Verse

For the grace of God has appeared for the salvation of all men, training us to
renounce irreligion and worldly passions, and to live sober, upright, and godly
lives in the world, awaiting our blessed hope, the appearing of the glory of our
great God and Savior, Jesus Christ.

Titus 3:11–13

The Final Thanksgiving

I will greatly rejoice in the LORD, my soul shall exult in my God; for he has
clothed me with the garments of salvation, he has covered me with the robe of
righteousness, as a bridegroom decks himself with a garland, and as a bride
adorns herself with her jewels.

Isaiah 61:10

The Petition

May the Lord GOD, father of all mercy, grant us who dwell here a peaceful night
and a perfect end. *Amen.*

The Office of the Night Watch   Observed on the Hour or Half-Hour Between 1:30 and 4:30 a.m.

The Call to Prayer

Behold now, bless the LORD, all you servants of the LORD,* you that stand by night
in the house of the LORD.
Lift up your hands in the holy place and bless the LORD;* the LORD who made
heaven and earth bless you out of Zion.

Psalm 134

The Request for Presence

O God, come to my assistance.
O Lord, make haste to help me.

The Greeting

In you, O LORD, have I taken refuge; let me never be put to shame;* deliver me in
your righteousness.

Psalm 31:1

The Refrain for the Night Watch

I will bless the LORD who gives me counsel;* my heart teaches me, night after night.

Psalm 16:7

The Psalm   Your Law Is My Love

Rulers have persecuted me without a cause,* but my heart stands in awe of your
word.

I am as glad because of your promise* as one who finds great spoils.
As for lies, I hate and abhor them,* but your law is my love.
Seven times a day do I praise you,* because of your righteous judgments.
Great peace have they who love your law;* for them there is no stumbling block.

Psalm 119:161–65

The Refrain
I will bless the LORD who gives me counsel;* my heart teaches me, night after night.

A Reading
"Cursed is everyone," as the divine eloquence testified, "who rests his hope in man." Thus, he who rests his hope in himself is bound by the bond of that curse. Therefore, we should seek from none other than the Lord God whatever it is that we hope to do well or hope to obtain as reward for our good works.

St. Augustine (ca. 410 CE), Handbook on Faith, Hope, and Love

The Refrain
I will bless the LORD who gives me counsel;* my heart teaches me, night after night.

The Litany
For all people in their daily life and work;
For my family, friends, and neighbors, and for those who are alone, I pray to you, Lord God.
For this community, the nation, and the world;
For all who work for justice, freedom, and peace, I pray to you, Lord God.
For the just and proper use of your creation;
For the victims of hunger, fear, injustice, and oppression, I pray to you, Lord God.
For all who are in danger, sorrow, or any kind of trouble;
For those who minister to the sick, the friendless, and the needy, I pray to you, Lord God.
For the peace and unity of the Church of God;
For all who proclaim the Gospel, and all who seek the Truth, I pray to you, Lord God.
Hear me, Lord;
For your mercy is great.

The Thanksgiving
Lord, you now have set your servant free to go in peace as you have promised; for these eyes of mine have seen the Savior whom you have prepared for all the world to see: A Light to enlighten the nations, and the glory of your people Israel. *Amen.*

Nunc Dimittis

The Final Petition
Now guide me waking, O Lord, and guard me sleeping; that awake I may watch with Christ, and asleep, I may rest in peace. *Amen.*

The Office of Dawn   Observed on the Hour or Half-Hour
                                         Between 4:30 and 7:30 a.m.

The Call to Prayer
Hallelujah! How good it is to sing praises to our God!* how pleasant it is to honor him with praise!

Psalm 147:1

The Request for Presence
My soul waits for the LORD, more than watchmen for the morning,* more than watchmen for the morning.

Psalm 130:5

The Greeting
Glory be to the Father, and the Son, and the Holy Spirit.
As it was in the beginning, it is now
And ever shall be, world without end. *Amen.*

Gloria Patri

The Hymn
Rejoice, the Lord is King!
Your Lord and King adore;
mortals, give thanks and sing,
and triumph evermore.
Lift up your heart, lift up your voice;
rejoice; again I say, rejoice.
Jesus the Savior reigns,
the God of truth and love;
when he had purged our stains,
he took his seat above.
Lift up your heart, lift up your voice;
rejoice, again I say, rejoice.

Charles Wesley

The Psalm   *Praise the LORD*
Praise him for his mighty acts;* praise him for his excellent greatness.
Praise him with the blast of the ram's-horn;* praise him with lyre and harp.
Praise him with timbrel and dance;* praise him with strings and pipe.
Praise him with resounding cymbals;* praise him with loud-clanging cymbals.
Let everything that has breath* praise the LORD. Hallelujah!

Psalm 150:2–6

324

The Gloria in Excelsis

Glory to God in the highest, and on earth peace to people of good will.
    We praise you.
    We bless you.
    We adore you.
    We glorify you.
We give thanks to you for your great glory.

The Small Verse

Behold, at that time I will deal with all your oppressors. And I will save the lame
    and gather the outcast, and I will change their shame into praise and renown in
    all the earth. At that time I will bring you home, at the time when I gather you
    together; yea, I will make you renowned and praised among all the peoples of
    the earth, when I restore your fortunes before your eyes, says the Lord.

Zephaniah 3:19–20

The Lord's Prayer

The Final Blessing

May the Lord bless us and keep us and cause His face to shine upon us from this
    day forth and forever more. *Amen.*

☙

Thursday, Month of September

The Office of Midnight

**Observed on the Hour or Half-Hour
Between 10:30 p.m.✠ and 1:30 a.m.**

The Call to Prayer

Bless the LORD, all you works of his, in all places of his dominion;* bless the
    LORD, O my soul.

Psalm 103:22

The Request for Presence

O LORD, let my prayer be set forth in your sight as incense,* the lifting up of my
    hands as the evening sacrifice.

Psalm 141:2, adapted

The Greeting

Our Father, forgive us our sins as we forgive those who have sinned against us.

325

The Canticle   *The Song of Mary*
                                                        Magnificat
My soul proclaims the greatness of the Lord, my spirit rejoices in God my Savior;*
    for he has looked with favor on his lowly servant.
From this day all generations will call me blessed:*
    the Almighty has done great things for me, and holy is his Name.
He has mercy on those who fear him*
    in every generation.
He has shown the strength of his arm,*
    he has scattered the proud in their conceit.
He has cast down the mighty from their thrones,*
    and has lifted up the lowly.
He has filled the hungry with good things,*
    and the rich he has sent away empty.
He has come to the help of his servant Israel,*
    for he has remembered his promise of mercy,
The promise he made to our fathers,*
    to Abraham and his children for ever.
Glory to the Father, and to the Son, and to the Holy Spirit:*
    as it was in the beginning, is now, and will be for ever. *Amen.*

                                                        Luke 1:46–55

The Psalm   *The LORD Is Their Help and Their Shield.*
O Israel, trust in the LORD;* he is their help and their shield.
O house of Aaron, trust in the LORD;* he is their help and their shield.
You who fear the LORD, trust in the LORD;* he is their help and their shield.
The LORD has been mindful of us, and he will bless us;* he will bless the house of
    Israel; he will bless the house of Aaron;
He will bless those who fear the LORD,* both small and great together.

                                                        Psalm 115:9–13

The Gloria

The Small Verse
I appeal to you therefore, brother, by the mercies of God, to present your bodies as
    a living sacrifice, holy and acceptable to God, which is your spiritual worship.

                                                        Romans 12:1

The Final Thanksgiving
I will greatly rejoice in the Lord, my soul shall exult in my God; for he has clothed
    me with the garments of salvation, he has covered me with the robe of
    righteousness, as a bridegroom decks himself with a garland, and as a bride
    adorns herself with her jewels.

                                                        Isaiah 61:10

326

The Petition
May the Lord God, father of all mercy, grant us who dwell here a peaceful night and a perfect end. *Amen.*

The Office of the Night Watch   Observed on the Hour or Half-Hour Between 1:30 and 4:30 a.m.

The Call to Prayer
Behold now, bless the Lord, all you servants of the Lord,* you that stand by night in the house of the Lord.
Lift up your hands in the holy place and bless the Lord;* the Lord who made heaven and earth bless you out of Zion.

Psalm 134

The Request for Presence
O God, come to my assistance.
O Lord, make haste to help me.

The Greeting
For you are the Lord, most high over all the earth;* you are exalted far above all gods.

Psalm 97:9

The Refrain for the Night Watch
Happy are they who have not walked in the counsel of the wicked,* nor lingered in the way of sinners, nor sat in the seats of the scornful!
Their delight is in the law of the Lord,* and they meditate on his law day and night.

Psalm 1:1–2

The Psalm   *Praise the Lord in the Heights*
Hallelujah! Praise the Lord from the heavens;* praise him in the heights.
Praise him, all you angels of his;* praise him, all his host.
Praise him, sun and moon;* praise him, all you shining stars.
Praise him, heaven of heavens,* and you waters above the heavens.
Let them praise the Name of the Lord;* for he commanded, and they were created.
He made them stand fast for ever and ever;* he gave them a law which shall not pass away.

Psalm 148:1–6

The Refrain
Happy are they who have not walked in the counsel of the wicked,* nor lingered in the way of sinners, nor sat in the seats of the scornful!
Their delight is in the law of the Lord,* and they meditate on his law day and night.

A Reading

Although it be good to think upon the kindness of God and to love Him and to
  praise Him for it, yet it is far better to think upon the naked being of Him and
  to love Him and Praise Him for Himself.

Anonymous (14th c.), The Cloud of Unknowing

The Refrain

Happy are they who have not walked in the counsel of the wicked,* nor lingered
  in the way of sinners, nor sat in the seats of the scornful!
Their delight is in the law of the LORD,* and they meditate on his law day and night.

The Litany

For the peace from above, for the loving-kindness of God, and for the salvation of
  my soul, I pray to the Lord.
  Lord, have mercy.
For the peace of the world, for the welfare of the Holy Church of God, and for the
  unity of all peoples, I pray to the Lord.
  Lord, have mercy.
For my city [town, village], for every city and community, and for those who live
  in them, I pray to the Lord.
  Lord, have mercy.
For seasonable weather, and for an abundance of the fruits of the earth, I pray to
  the Lord.
  Lord, have mercy.
For the good earth which God has given us, and for the wisdom and will to
  conserve it, I pray to the Lord.
  Lord, have mercy.
For deliverance from all danger, violence, oppression, and degradation, I pray to
  the Lord.
  Lord, have mercy.
For the absolution and remission of my sins and offenses, I pray to the Lord.
  Lord, have mercy.
Defend me, deliver me, and in your compassion protect me, O Lord, by your grace.
  Lord, have mercy.

The Thanksgiving

Lord, you now have set your servant free to go in peace as you have promised; for
  these eyes of mine have seen the Savior whom you have prepared for all the
  world to see: A Light to enlighten the nations, and the glory of your people
  Israel. *Amen.*

Nunc Dimittis

The Final Petition

Now guide me waking, O Lord, and guard me sleeping; that awake I may watch
  with Christ, and asleep, I may rest in peace. *Amen.*

The Office of Dawn   **Observed on the Hour or Half-Hour
                                              Between 4:30 and 7:30 a.m.**

The Call to Prayer

Worship the LORD, O Jerusalem;* praise your God, O Zion;
For he has strengthened the bars of your gates.

Psalm 147:13–14 a

The Request for Presence

My soul waits for the LORD, more than watchmen for the morning,* more than
   watchmen for the morning.

Psalm 130:5

The Greeting

Glory be to the Father, and the Son, and the Holy Spirit.
As it was in the beginning, it is now
And ever shall be, world without end. *Amen.*

Gloria Patri

The Hymn

'Tis so sweet to trust in Jesus,
and to take him at his word;
just to rest upon his promise,
and to know, "Thus saith the Lord."
Yes, 'tis sweet to trust in Jesus,
just from sin and self to cease;
just from Jesus simply taking
life and rest, and joy and peace.
Jesus, Jesus, how I trust him!
How I've proved him o'er and o'er!
Jesus, Jesus, precious Jesus!
O for grace to trust him more!

Louisa M. R. Stead

The Psalm   ***The LORD Has Pleasure in Those Who Fear Him***

He covers the heavens with clouds* and prepares rain for the earth;
He makes grass to grow upon the mountains* and green plants to serve mankind.
He provides food for flocks and herds* and for the young ravens when they cry.
He is not impressed by the might of a horse;* he has no pleasure in the strength of
   a man;
But the LORD has pleasure in those who fear him,* in those who await his gracious
   favor.

Psalm 147:8–12

329

The Gloria in Excelsis
Glory to God in the highest, and on earth peace to people of good will.
    We praise you.
    We bless you.
    We adore you.
    We glorify you.
We give thanks to you for your great glory.

The Small Verse
Therefore, since we are surrounded by so great a cloud of witnesses, let us also lay
    aside every weight, and sin which clings so closely, and let us run with
    perseverance the race that is set before us, looking to Jesus the pioneer and
    perfecter of our faith, who for the joy that was set before him endured the
    cross, despising the shame, and is seated at the right hand of the throne of God.
Hebrews 12:1–2

The Lord's Prayer

The Final Blessing
May the Lord bless us and keep us and cause His face to shine upon us from this
    day forth and forever more. *Amen.*

♣

Friday, Month of September

The Office of Midnight
                                   Observed on the Hour or Half-Hour
                                   Between 10:30 p.m.✠ and 1:30 a.m.

The Call to Prayer
Great is the LORD and greatly to be praised;* there is no end to his greatness.
Psalm 145:3

The Request for Presence
O LORD, let my prayer be set forth in your sight as incense,* the lifting up of my
    hands as the evening sacrifice.
Psalm 141:2, adapted

The Greeting
Our Father, lead us not into temptation, but deliver us from evil.

The Canticle   *A Song of Penitence*
Kyrie Pantokrator

O Lord and Ruler of the hosts of heaven,*
   God of Abraham, Isaac, and Jacob, and of all their righteous offspring:
You made the heavens and the earth,*
   with all their vast array.
All things quake with fear at your presence;*
   they tremble because of your power.
But your merciful promise is beyond all measure;*
   it surpasses all that our minds can fathom.
Lord, you are full of compassion,*
   long-suffering, and abounding in mercy.
You hold back your hand;*
   you do not punish as we deserve.
In your great goodness, Lord, you have promised forgiveness to sinners,*
   that they may repent of their sin and be saved.

Prayer of Manasseh 1–2, 4, 6–7

The Psalm   *For His Mercy Endures For Ever*

Give thanks to the LORD, for he is good,* for his mercy endures for ever.
Give thanks to the God of gods,* for his mercy endures for ever.
Give thanks to the Lord of lords,* for his mercy endures for ever.
Who only does great wonders,* for his mercy endures for ever;
Who by wisdom made the heavens,* for his mercy endures for ever;
Who spread out the earth upon the waters,* for his mercy endures for ever;
Who created great lights,* for his mercy endures for ever;
The sun to rule the day,* for his mercy endures for ever;
The moon and the stars to govern the night,* for his mercy endures for ever

Psalm 136:1–9

The Gloria

The Small Verse

Be sober, be watchful. Your adversary the devil prowls around like a roaring lion,
   seeking some one to devour. Resist him, firm in your faith, knowing that the
   same experience of suffering is required of your brotherhood throughout the
   world.

1 Peter 5:8–9

The Final Thanksgiving

I will greatly rejoice in the LORD, my soul shall exult in my God; for he has
   clothed me with the garments of salvation, he has covered me with the robe of
   righteousness, as a bridegroom decks himself with a garland, and as a bride
   adorns herself with her jewels.

Isaiah 61:10

331

The Petition
May the Lord GOD, father of all mercy, grant us who dwell here a peaceful night and a perfect end. *Amen.*

The Office of the Night Watch **Observed on the Hour or Half-Hour Between 1:30 and 4:30 a.m.**

The Call to Prayer
Behold now, bless the LORD, all you servants of the LORD,* you that stand by night in the house of the LORD.
Lift up your hands in the holy place and bless the LORD;* the LORD who made heaven and earth bless you out of Zion.

Psalm 134

The Request for Presence
O God, come to my assistance.
O Lord, make haste to help me.

The Greeting
For you are the LORD, most high over all the earth;* you are exalted far above all gods.

Psalm 97:9

The Refrain for the Night Watch
Happy are they who have not walked in the counsel of the wicked,* nor lingered in the way of sinners, nor sat in the seats of the scornful!
Their delight is in the law of the LORD,* and they meditate on his law day and night.

Psalm 1:1–2

The Psalm   *Praise Him in the Heights*
Hallelujah! Praise the LORD from the heavens;* praise him in the heights.
Praise him, all you angels of his;* praise him, all his host.
Praise him, sun and moon;* praise him, all you shining stars.
Praise him, heaven of heavens,* and you waters above the heavens.
Let them praise the Name of the LORD;* for he commanded, and they were created.
He made them stand fast for ever and ever;* he gave them a law which shall not pass away.

Psalm 148:1–6

The Refrain
Happy are they who have not walked in the counsel of the wicked,* nor lingered in the way of sinners, nor sat in the seats of the scornful!
Their delight is in the law of the LORD,* and they meditate on his law day and night.

A Reading

O thou whose divine tenderness ever outsoars the narrow loves and charities of
earth, grant me today a kind and gentle heart towards all things that live. Let me
not ruthlessly hurt any creature of thine. Let me take thought also for the welfare
of little children, and of those who are sick, and of the poor, remembering that
what I do unto the least of these his brethren, I do unto Jesus Christ my Lord.

John Baillie (1886–1960), Prayer

The Refrain

Happy are they who have not walked in the counsel of the wicked,* nor lingered
in the way of sinners, nor sat in the seats of the scornful!
Their delight is in the law of the LORD,* and they meditate on his law day and night.

The Litany

For the peace from above, for the loving-kindness of God, and for the salvation of
my soul, I pray to the Lord.
Lord, have mercy.

For the peace of the world, for the welfare of the Holy Church of God, and for the
unity of all peoples, I pray to the Lord.
Lord, have mercy.

For my city [town, village], for every city and community, and for those who live
in them, I pray to the Lord.
Lord, have mercy.

For seasonable weather, and for an abundance of the fruits of the earth, I pray to
the Lord.
Lord, have mercy.

For the good earth which God has given us, and for the wisdom and will to
conserve it, I pray to the Lord.
Lord, have mercy.

For deliverance from all danger, violence, oppression, and degradation, I pray to
the Lord.
Lord, have mercy.

For the absolution and remission of my sins and offenses, I pray to the Lord.
Lord, have mercy.

Defend me, deliver me, and in your compassion protect me, O Lord, by your
grace.
Lord, have mercy.

The Thanksgiving

Lord, you now have set your servant free to go in peace as you have promised; for
these eyes of mine have seen the Savior whom you have prepared for all the
world to see: A Light to enlighten the nations, and the glory of your people
Israel. *Amen.*

Nunc Dimittis

The Final Petition
Now guide me waking, O Lord, and guard me sleeping; that awake I may watch
with Christ, and asleep, I may rest in peace. *Amen.*

The Office of Dawn **Observed on the Hour or Half-Hour**
Between 4:30 and 7:30 a.m.

The Call to Prayer
Sing to the LORD with thanksgiving;* make music to our God upon the harp.

Psalm 147:7

The Request for Presence
My soul waits for the LORD, more than watchmen for the morning,* more than
watchmen for the morning.

Psalm 130:5

The Greeting
Glory be to the Father, and the Son, and the Holy Spirit.
As it was in the beginning, it is now
And ever shall be, world without end. *Amen.*

Gloria Patri

The Hymn
Standing on the promises of Christ my King,
through eternal ages let his praises ring;
glory in the highest, I will shout and sing,
standing on the promises of God.
Standing on the promises of Christ the Lord,
bound to him eternally by love's strong cord,
overcoming daily with the Spirit's sword,
standing on the promises of God.
Standing, standing, standing on the promises of Christ my Savior;
standing, standing, I'm standing on the promises of God.

R. Kelso Carter

The Psalm *Praise the LORD from the Earth*
Praise the LORD from the earth,* you sea-monsters and all deeps;
Fire and hail, snow and fog,* tempestuous wind, doing his will;
Mountains and all hills,* fruit trees and all cedars;
Wild beasts and all cattle,* creeping things and winged birds;
Kings of the earth and all peoples,* princes and all rulers of the world;
Young men and maidens,* old and young together.
Let them praise the Name of the Lord,*

Psalm 148:7–13a

334

The Gloria in Excelsis
Glory to God in the highest, and on earth peace to people of good will.
    We praise you.
    We bless you.
    We adore you.
    We glorify you.
We give thanks to you for your great glory.

The Small Verse
Now faith is the assurance of things hoped for, the conviction of things not seen.
    For by it the men of old received divine approval.

Hebrews 11:1–2

The Lord's Prayer

The Final Blessing
May the LORD bless us and keep us and cause His face to shine upon us from this
    day forth and forever more. *Amen.*

꒰ꓽ꒱

Saturday, Month of September

The Office of Midnight   **Observed on the Hour or Half-Hour**
                                     Between 10:30 p.m.✛ and 1:30 a.m.

The Call to Prayer
The LORD is gracious and full of compassion,* slow to anger and of great
    kindness.

Psalm 145:8

The Request for Presence
O LORD, let my prayer be set forth in your sight as incense,* the lifting up of my
    hands as the evening sacrifice.

Psalm 141:2, adapted

The Greeting
Our Father, Yours are the kingdom, the power, and the glory forever.

The Canticle   ***Glory to God***
                                                      Gloria in excelsis

Glory to God in the highest,
    and peace to his people on earth.
Lord God, heavenly King,
almighty God and Father,
    we worship you, we give you thanks,
    we praise you for your glory.
Lord Jesus Christ, only Son of the Father,
Lord God, Lamb of God,
you take away the sin of the world:
    have mercy on us;
you are seated at the right hand of the Father:
    receive our prayer.
For you alone are the Holy One,
you alone are the Lord,
you alone are the Most High,
    Jesus Christ, with the Holy Spirit,
    in the glory of God the Father. *Amen.*

The Psalm   ***How Manifold Are Your Works***
You appointed the moon to mark the seasons,* and the sun knows the time of its
    setting.
You make darkness that it may be night,* in which all the beasts of the forest prowl.
The lions roar after their prey* and seek their food from God.
The sun rises, and they slip away* and lay themselves down in their dens.
Man goes forth to his work* and to his labor until the evening.
O LORD, how manifold are your works!* in wisdom you have made them all; the
    earth is full of your creatures.
                                                      Psalm 104:20–25

The Gloria

The Small Verse
. . . God's love has been poured into our hearts through the Holy Spirit who has
    been given to us.
                                                      Romans 5:5b

The Final Thanksgiving
I will greatly rejoice in the LORD, my soul shall exult in my God; for he has
    clothed me with the garments of salvation, he has covered me with the robe of
    righteousness, as a bridegroom decks himself with a garland, and as a bride
    adorns herself with her jewels.
                                                      Isaiah 61:10

336

The Petition
May the Lord GOD, father of all mercy, grant us who dwell here a peaceful night and a perfect end. *Amen.*

The Office of the Night Watch   Observed on the Hour or Half-Hour Between 1:30 and 4:30 a.m.

The Call to Prayer
Behold now, bless the LORD, all you servants of the LORD,* you that stand by night in the house of the LORD.
Lift up your hands in the holy place and bless the LORD;* the LORD who made heaven and earth bless you out of Zion.

Psalm 134

The Request for Presence
O God, come to my assistance.
O Lord, make haste to help me.

The Greeting
Therefore my heart sings to you without ceasing;* O LORD my God, I will give you thanks for ever.

Psalm 30:13

The Refrain for the Night Watch
The heavens declare the glory of God,* and the firmament shows his handiwork.
One day tells its tale to another,* and one night imparts knowledge to another.

Psalm 19:1–2

The Psalm   Be Pleased, O God, to Deliver Me
Be pleased, O God, to deliver me;* O LORD, make haste to help me.
Let all who seek you rejoice and be glad in you;* let those who love your salvation say for ever, "Great is the LORD!"
But as for me, I am poor and needy;* come to me speedily, O God.
You are my helper and my deliverer;* O LORD, do not tarry.

Psalm 70:1, 4–6

The Refrain
The heavens declare the glory of God,* and the firmament shows his handiwork.
One day tells its tale to another,* and one night imparts knowledge to another.

A Reading

He who contends in the lists, although paired with his adversary on a just principle of arrangement, will nevertheless not necessarily prove the conqueror. Yet, unless the powers of the combatants are equal, the prize of the victor will not be justly won; nor will blame justly attach to the vanquished. . . . Thus He allows us to be tempted, but not "beyond what we are able"; for it is in proportion to our strength that we are tempted. And it is written that, in temptation, He will also make a way to escape so that we should be able to bear it. Yet it depends on us to use either the energy or feebleness of this power which He has given us . . . for to possess the power of conquering is not the same thing as being victorious.

Origen (ca. 185–254 CE), translated by Rufinus, De Principiis

The Refrain

The heavens declare the glory of God,* and the firmament shows his handiwork. One day tells its tale to another,* and one night imparts knowledge to another.

The Litany

O God the Father, Creator of heaven and earth,
> *Have mercy upon me.*

O God the Son, Redeemer of the world,
> *Have mercy upon me.*

O God the Holy Spirit, Sanctifier of the faithful,
> *Have mercy upon me.*

O holy, blessed, and glorious Trinity, one God,
> *Have mercy upon me.*

Remember not, Lord Christ, my offenses, nor the offenses of my forefathers; neither reward me according to my sins. Spare me, good Lord, spare your people, whom you have redeemed with your most precious blood, and by your mercy preserve us, for ever.
> *Spare us, good Lord.*

The Thanksgiving

Lord, you now have set your servant free to go in peace as you have promised; for these eyes of mine have seen the Savior whom you have prepared for all the world to see: A Light to enlighten the nations, and the glory of your people Israel. *Amen.*

Nunc Dimittis

The Final Petition

Now guide me waking, O Lord, and guard me sleeping; that awake I may watch with Christ, and asleep, I may rest in peace. *Amen.*

The Office of Dawn   **Observed on the Hour or Half-Hour
                                Between 4:30 and 7:30 a.m.**

The Call to Prayer
Worship the LORD, O Jerusalem;* praise your God, O Zion;
For he has strengthened the bars of your gates.

Psalm 147:13–14a

The Request for Presence
My soul waits for the LORD, more than watchmen for the morning,* more than
     watchmen for the morning.

Psalm 130:5

The Greeting
Glory be to the Father, and the Son, and the Holy Spirit.
As it was in the beginning, it is now
And ever shall be, world without end. *Amen.*

Gloria Patri

The Hymn
O Word of God incarnate,
O Wisdom from on high,
O Truth unchanged, unchanging,
O Light of our dark sky:
we praise you for the radiance
that from the hallowed page,
a lantern to our footsteps,
shines on from age to age.
O make your church, dear Savior,
a lamp of purest gold,
to bear before the nations
your true light as of old.
O teach your wandering pilgrims
by this their path to trace,
till, clouds and darkness ended,
they see you face to face.

William W. How

The Psalm   *Let Israel Rejoice in His Maker*
Let Israel rejoice in his Maker;* let the children of Zion be joyful in their King.
Let them praise his Name in the dance;* let them sing praise to him with timbrel
     and harp.
For the LORD takes pleasure in his people* and adorns the poor with victory.
Let the faithful rejoice in triumph;* let them be joyful on their beds.

Psalm 149:2–5

339

The Gloria in Excelsis
Glory to God in the highest, and on earth peace to people of good will.
> We praise you.
> We bless you.
> We adore you.
> We glorify you.
We give thanks to you for your great glory.

The Small Verse
In the beginning was the Word, and the Word was with God, and the Word was
> God. He was in the beginning with God; all things were made through him, and
> without him was not anything made that was made.

John 1:1–2

The Lord's Prayer

The Final Blessing
May the Lord bless us and keep us and cause His face to shine upon us from this
> day forth and forever more. *Amen.*

The Gloria
Glory be to God the Father, God the Son, and God the Holy Spirit. As it was in the beginning, so it is now and so it shall ever be, world without end. Alleluia. *Amen.*

The Lord's Prayer
Our Father, who art in heaven, hallowed be your Name.
May your kingdom come, and your will be done, on earth as in heaven.
Give us today our daily bread.
Forgive us our sins as we forgive those who sin against us.
Lead us not into temptation, but deliver us from evil;
for yours are the kingdom and the power and the glory
forever and ever. *Amen*

The following major holy days occur in October:
The Feast of St. Francis of Assisi: *October 4*
The Feast of St. Luke, the Evangelist: *October 18*
The Feast of St. James of Jerusalem: *October 23*
The Feast of St. Simon and St. Jude: *October 28*

Prayer for use in the observation of a holy day:
Almighty God, by your Holy Spirit you have made us one with your saints in heaven and on earth: Grant that in my earthly pilgrimage, I may always be supported by this fellowship of love and prayer, and know myself to be surrounded by their witness to your power and mercy. I ask this for the sake of Jesus Christ, in whom all my intercessions are acceptable through the Spirit, and who lives and reigns forever and ever. *Amen.*

✛ The Office of Midnight is always taken from the prayers for the day nearest to the hour of actual observation. Thus, if the office is to be observed at 10:30 p.m. on Sunday, the prayers will be taken from the Monday offices, and so forth.

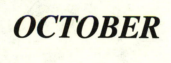

OCTOBER

Sunday, Month of October

The Office of Midnight   **Observed on the Hour or Half-Hour
                                  Between 10:30 p.m.✢ and 1:30 a.m.**

The Call to Prayer
O LORD, let my prayer be set forth in your sight as incense,* the lifting up of my
hands as the evening sacrifice.

Psalm 141:2, adapted

The Request for Presence
LORD, hear my prayer, and in your faithfulness heed my supplications;* answer me
in your righteousness.

Psalm 143:1

The Greeting
Our Father Who art in Heaven, hallowed be Your name forever.

The Canticle   *The Song of Moses*
                                              Cantemus Domino

I will sing to the Lord, for he is lofty and uplifted;*
    the horse and its rider has he hurled into the sea.
The Lord is my strength and my refuge;*
    the Lord has become my Savior.
This is my God and I will praise him,*
    the God of my people and I will exalt him.
The Lord is a mighty warrior;*
    Yahweh is his Name.
Who can be compared with you, O Lord, among the gods?*
    who is like you, glorious in holiness, awesome in renown, and worker of
    wonders?
With your constant love you led the people you redeemed;*
    with your might you brought them in safety to your holy dwelling.
You will bring them in and plant them*
    on the mount of your possession,
The resting-place you have made for yourself, O Lord,*
    the sanctuary, O Lord, that your hand has established.
The Lord shall reign*
    for ever and for ever.

Exodus: 15:1–6,11–13,17–18

The Psalm   *Happy Are the People Whose God Is the LORD!*
May our sons be like plants well nurtured from their youth,* and our daughters
    like sculptured corners of a palace.

344

May our barns be filled to overflowing with all manner of crops;* may the flocks in our pastures increase by thousands and tens of thousands; may our cattle be fat and sleek.

May there be no breaching of the walls, no going into exile,* no wailing in the public squares.

Happy are the people of whom this is so!* happy are the people whose God is the Lord!

Psalm 144:13–16

The Gloria

The Small Verse

Blessed be the God and Father of our Lord Jesus Christ, the Father of mercies and God of all comfort, who comforts us in all our affliction, so that we may be able to comfort those who are in any affliction with the same comfort with which we ourselves are comforted by God.

2 Corinthians 1:3–4

The Final Thanksgiving

I will greatly rejoice in the Lord, my soul shall exult in my God; for he has clothed me with the garments of salvation, he has covered me with the robe of righteousness, as a bridegroom decks himself with a garland, and as a bride adorns herself with her jewels.

Isaiah 61:10

The Petition

May the Lord God, father of grace and mercy, grant all who dwell here a peaceful night and a perfect end. *Amen.*

The Office of the Night Watch   Observed on the Hour or Half-Hour Between 1:30 and 4:30 a.m.

The Call to Prayer

Behold now, bless the Lord, all you servants of the Lord,* you that stand by night in the house of the Lord.

Lift up your hands in the holy place and bless the Lord;* the Lord who made heaven and earth bless you out of Zion.

Psalm 134

The Request for Presence

O God, come to my assistance.

O Lord, make haste to help me.

The Greeting

O Lord of hosts,* happy are they who put their trust in you!

Psalm 84:12

345

The Refrain for the Night Watch
Yours is the day, yours also the night;* you established the moon and the sun.

Psalm 74:15

The Psalm   The LORD God Is Both Sun and Shield
For the LORD God is both sun and shield;* he will give grace and glory;
No good thing will the LORD withhold* from those who walk with integrity.
O LORD of hosts,* happy are they who put their trust in you!

Psalm 84:10–12

The Refrain
Yours is the day, yours also the night;* you established the moon and the sun.

A Reading
Who can explain the kind of bodies in which the angels appeared to men, so that they were not only visible but tangible as well? And again, how do they, not by impact of physical stimulus but by spiritual force, bring certain visions, not to the physical eyes but to the spiritual eyes of the mind, or speak something, not to the ears, as from outside us, but actually from within the human soul, since they are present within it too? For, as it is written in the book of the Prophets: "And the angel that spoke in me, said to me. . . ." (Zech. 1:9) He does not say, "Spoke *to* me" but "Spoke *in* me." How do they appear to men in sleep, and communicate through dreams, as we read in the Gospel: "Behold, the angel of the Lord appeared to him in his sleep, saying. . . ." (Matt. 1:20) By these various modes of presentation, the angels seem to indicate that they do not have tangible bodies; yet this raises the very difficult question: How, then, did the patriarchs wash the angels' feet? (Gen. 18:4; 19:2) How also did Jacob wrestle with the angel in such a tangible form?
To ask such questions as these, and to guess at the answers as one can, is not a useless exercise in speculation, so long as the discussion is moderate and one avoids the mistake of those who think they know what they do not know.

St. Augustine (ca. 410 CE), Handbook on Faith, Hope, and Love

The Refrain
Yours is the day, yours also the night;* you established the moon and the sun.

The Litany
That it may please you to bless and keep all your people,
>   *I beseech you to hear me, good Lord.*
That it may please you to send laborers into your harvest and to draw all humankind into your kingdom,
>   *I beseech you to hear me, good Lord.*
That it may please you to give to all people increase of grace to hear and receive your Word, and to bring forth the fruits of the Spirit,
>   *I beseech you to hear me, good Lord.*

That it may please you to bring into the way of truth all such as have erred, and
are deceived,
 I beseech you to hear me, good Lord.
That it may please you to give me a heart to love and fear you, and diligently to
live after your commandments,
 I beseech you to hear me, good Lord.

The Thanksgiving
Lord, you now have set your servant free to go in peace as you have promised; for
these eyes of mine have seen the Savior whom you have prepared for all the world
to see: A Light to enlighten the nations, and the glory of your people Israel. *Amen.*

Nunc Dimittis

The Final Petition
Now guide me waking, O Lord, and guard me sleeping; that awake I may watch
with Christ, and asleep, I may rest in peace. *Amen.*

The Office of Dawn   **Observed on the Hour or Half-Hour**
                          Between 4:30 and 7:30 a.m.

The Call to Prayer
Let everything that has breath* praise the LORD! Hallelujah!

Psalm 150:6

The Request for Presence
My soul waits for the LORD, more than watchmen for the morning,* more than
watchmen for the morning.

Psalm 130:5

The Greeting
Glory be to the Father, and the Son, and the Holy Spirit.
As it was in the beginning, it is now
And ever shall be, world without end. *Amen.*

Gloria Patri

The Hymn
More love to thee, O Christ, more love to thee!
Hear now the prayer I make on bended knee.
This is my earnest plea: More love, O Christ, to thee;
more love to thee, more love to thee!
Once earthly joy I craved, sought peace and rest;
now you alone I seek, give what is best.
This all my prayer shall be: More love, O Christ, to thee;
more love to thee, more love to thee!

Elizabeth P. Prentiss

347

The Psalm   *Praise the LORD, Hallelujah*
Praise him for his mighty acts;* praise him for his excellent greatness.
Praise him with the blast of the ram's-horn;* praise him with lyre and harp.
Praise him with timbrel and dance;* praise him with strings and pipe.
Praise him with resounding cymbals;* praise him with loud-clanging cymbals.
Let everything that has breath* praise the LORD. Hallelujah!

Psalm 150:2–6

The Gloria in Excelsis
Glory to God in the highest, and on earth peace to people of good will.
    We praise you.
    We bless you.
    We adore you.
    We glorify you.
We give thanks to you for your great glory.

The Small Verse
Now when the LORD was about to take Elijah up to heaven by a whirlwind, Elijah
    and Elisha were on their way to Gilgal. And as they still went on and talked,
    behold, a chariot of fire and horses of fire separated the two of them. And
    Elijah went up by a whirlwind into heaven. And Elisha saw it and he cried,
    "My father, my father! The chariots of Israel and its horsemen!" And he saw
    him no more.

2 Kings 2:1, 11–12

The Lord's Prayer

The Final Blessing
May the Lord bless us and keep us and cause His face to shine upon us from this
    day forth and forever more. *Amen.*

ॐ

Monday, Month of October

The Office of Midnight   **Observed on the Hour or Half-Hour**
                                         Between 10:30 p.m.✠ and 1:30 a.m.

The Call to Prayer
Sing to the LORD a new song;* sing to the LORD, all the whole earth.

Psalm 96:1

348

The Request for Presence

O Lord, let my prayer be set forth in your sight as incense,* the lifting up of my
hands as the evening sacrifice.

Psalm 141:2, adapted

The Greeting

Our Father, may Your kingdom come on earth as in Heaven.

The Canticle   *A Song of Creation—Part One*
Benedicite, omnia opera Domini

Glorify the Lord, all you works of the Lord,*
    praise him and highly exalt him for ever.
In the firmament of his power, glorify the Lord,*
    praise him and highly exalt him for ever.
Glorify the Lord, you angels and all powers of the Lord,*
    O heavens and all waters above the heavens.
Sun and moon and stars of the sky, glorify the Lord,*
    praise him and highly exalt him for ever.
Glorify the Lord, every shower of rain and fall of dew,*
    all winds and fire and heat.
Winter and Summer, glorify the Lord,*
    praise him and highly exalt him for ever.
Glorify the Lord, O chill and cold,*
    drops of dew and flakes of snow.
Frost and cold, ice and sleet, glorify the Lord,*
    praise him and highly exalt him for ever.
Glorify the Lord, O nights and days,*
    O shining light and enfolding dark.
Storm clouds and thunderbolts, glorify the Lord,*
    praise him and highly exalt him for ever.

Song of the Three Young Men, 35–51

The Psalm   *Your Loving-Kindness Is Better Than Life Itself*

O God, you are my God; eagerly I seek you;* my soul thirsts for you, my flesh
    faints for you, as in a barren and dry land where there is no water.
Therefore I have gazed upon you in your holy place,* that I might behold your
    power and your glory.
For your loving-kindness is better than life itself;* my lips shall give you praise.
So will I bless you as long as I live* and lift up my hands in your Name.

Psalm 63:1–4

The Gloria

The Small Verse

Humble yourselves therefore under the mighty hand of God, that in due time he
    may exalt you.

1 Peter 5:6

The Final Thanksgiving

I will greatly rejoice in the LORD, my soul shall exult in my God; for he has
clothed me with the garments of salvation, he has covered me with the robe of
righteousness, as a bridegroom decks himself with a garland, and as a bride
adorns herself with her jewels.

Isaiah 61:10

The Petition

May the Lord God, father of grace and mercy, grant all who dwell here a peaceful
night and a perfect end. *Amen.*

The Office of the Night Watch   Observed on the Hour or Half-Hour
Between 1:30 and 4:30 a.m.

The Call to Prayer

Behold now, bless the LORD, all you servants of the LORD,* you that stand by night
in the house of the LORD.
Lift up your hands in the holy place and bless the LORD;* the LORD who made
heaven and earth bless you out of Zion.

Psalm 134

The Request for Presence

O God, come to my assistance.
O Lord, make haste to help me.

The Greeting

But as for me, O LORD, I cry to you for help;* in the morning my prayer comes
before you.

Psalm 88:14

The Refrain for the Night Watch

I commune with my heart in the night;* I ponder and search my mind.

Psalm 77:6

The Psalm   *O LORD, Your Enemies Shall Perish*

For lo, your enemies, O LORD, lo, your enemies shall perish,* and all the workers
of iniquity shall be scattered.
But my horn you have exalted like the horns of wild bulls;* I am anointed with
fresh oil.

Psalm 92:8–9

The Refrain

I commune with my heart in the night;* I ponder and search my mind.

A Reading

Cyprian to his brother Successus, greetings: The reason why I could not write to you immediately, dearest brother, was that all the clergy, being placed in the very heat of the contest, were unable in any way to depart hence, all of them being prepared in accordance with the devotion of their minds, for divine and heavenly glory. . . . Valerian has sent a rescript to the Senate to the effect that bishops and presbyters and deacons should immediately be punished; but that senators and men of importance and Roman knights should lose their dignity and moreover be deprived of their property; and if, when their means be taken away, they should persist in being Christian, then they should lose their heads as well. . . . But know as well that Xistus was martyred in the cemetery on the eighth day of the Ides of August, and with him four deacons. . . . I beg that these things be made known by your means to the rest of our colleagues, that everywhere, by their exhortation, the brotherhood may be strengthened and prepared for the spiritual conflict, and that every one of us may think less of death than of immortality; and dedicated to the Lord with full faith and entire courage, may rejoice rather than fear in this confession. . . . I bid you, dearest brother, ever heartily farewell in the Lord.

Cyprian, Bishop of Carthage (d. 258 CE), The Epistles of Cyprian, LXXXI

The Refrain

I commune with my heart in the night;* I ponder and search my mind.

The Litany

That it may please you to show your mercy to all prisoners and captives, the homeless and the hungry, and all who are desolate and oppressed,
> *I beseech you to hear me, good Lord.*

That it may please you to give and preserve to our use the bountiful fruits of the earth, so that in due time all may enjoy them,
> *I beseech you to hear me, good Lord.*

That it may please you to inspire all your people, in our several callings, to do the work which you gave us to do with singleness of heart as your servants, and for the common good,
> *I beseech you to hear me, good Lord.*

That it may please you to visit the lonely; to strengthen all who suffer in mind, body, and spirit; and to comfort with your presence those who are failing and infirm,
> *I beseech you to hear me, good Lord.*

That it may please you to strengthen such as do stand; to comfort and help the weak-hearted; to raise up those who fall; and finally to beat down Satan under our feet,
> *I beseech you to hear me, good Lord.*

That it may please you to grant to all the faithful departed eternal life and peace,
> *I beseech you to hear me, good Lord.*

351

That it may please you to grant that, in the fellowship of all your saints, I may
attain to your heavenly kingdom,
Son of God, I beseech you to hear me.
Son of God, I beseech you to hear me.

The Thanksgiving
Lord, you now have set your servant free to go in peace as you have promised; for
these eyes of mine have seen the Savior whom you have prepared for all the
world to see: A Light to enlighten the nations, and the glory of your people
Israel. *Amen.*

Nunc Dimittis

The Final Petition
Now guide me waking, O Lord, and guard me sleeping; that awake I may watch
with Christ, and asleep, I may rest in peace. *Amen.*

The Office of Dawn   Observed on the Hour or Half-Hour
Between 4:30 and 7:30 a.m.

The Call to Prayer
Hallelujah! How good it is to sing praises to our God!* how pleasant it is to honor
him with praise!

Psalm 147:1

The Request for Presence
My soul waits for the LORD, more than watchmen for the morning,* more than
watchmen for the morning.

Psalm 130:5

The Greeting
Glory be to the Father, and the Son, and the Holy Spirit.
As it was in the beginning, it is now
And ever shall be, world without end. *Amen.*

Gloria Patri

The Hymn
The King of love my shepherd is,
whose goodness fails me never.
I nothing lack if I am his,
and he is mine forever.
Where streams of living water flow,
my ransomed soul he leads;
and where the verdant pastures grow,
with food celestial feeds.
Perverse and foolish, oft I strayed,

but yet in love he sought me;
and on his shoulder gently laid,
and home, rejoicing, brought me.

Henry W. Baker

The Psalm   The LORD Sends Out His Command to the Earth

The LORD sends out his command to the earth,* and his word runs very swiftly.
He gives snow like wool;* he scatters hoarfrost like ashes.
He scatters his hail like bread crumbs;* who can stand against his cold?
He sends forth his word and melts them;* he blows with his wind, and the waters
  flow.

Psalm 147:16–19

The Gloria in Excelsis

Glory to God in the highest, and on earth peace to people of good will.
  We praise you.
  We bless you.
  We adore you.
  We glorify you.
We give thanks to you for your great glory.

The Small Verse

Let us know, let us press on to know the Lord; his going forth is sure as the dawn;
  he will come to us as the showers, as the spring rains that water the earth.

Hosea 6:3

The Lord's Prayer

The Final Blessing

May the Lord bless us and keep us and cause His face to shine upon us from this
  day forth and forever more. *Amen.*

ॐ

Tuesday, Month of October

The Office of Midnight   **Observed on the Hour or Half-Hour
                                        Between 10:30 p.m.✚ and 1:30 a.m.**

The Call to Prayer

For God alone my soul in silence waits;* from him comes my salvation.

Psalm 62:1

The Request for Presence

O LORD, let my prayer be set forth in your sight as incense,* the lifting up of my hands as the evening sacrifice.

Psalm 141:2

The Greeting

Our Father, may Your will be done, on earth as in Heaven.

The Canticle   The First Song of Isaiah

Ecce, Deus

Surely, it is God who saves me;*
    I will trust in him and not be afraid.
For the Lord is my stronghold and my sure defense,*
    and he will be my Savior.
Therefore you shall draw water with rejoicing*
    from the springs of salvation.
And on that day you shall say,*
    Give thanks to the Lord and call upon his Name;
Make his deeds known among the peoples;*
    see that they remember that his Name is exalted.
Sing praises of the Lord, for he has done great things,*
    and this is known in all the world.
Cry aloud, inhabitants of Zion, ring out your joy,*
    for the great one in the midst of you is the Holy One of Israel.

Isaiah 12:2–6

The Psalm   Happy Are They Who Trust in the LORD

I waited patiently upon the LORD;* he stooped to me and heard my cry.
He lifted me out of the desolate pit, out of the mire and clay;* he set my feet upon a high cliff and made my footing sure.
He put a new song in my mouth, a song of praise to our God;* many shall see, and stand in awe, and put their trust in the LORD.
Happy are they who trust in the LORD!* they do not resort to evil spirits or turn to false gods.
Great things are they that you have done, O LORD my God! how great your wonders and your plans for us!* there is none who can be compared with you.

Psalm 40:1–5

The Gloria

The Small Verse

Likewise the Spirit helps us in our weakness; for we do not know how to pray as we ought, but the Spirit himself intercedes for us with sighs too deep for words. And he who searches the hearts of men knows what is in the mind of the Spirit, because the Spirit intercedes for the saints according to the will of God.

Romans 8:26–27

The Final Thanksgiving

I will greatly rejoice in the LORD, my soul shall exult in my God; for he has clothed me with the garments of salvation, he has covered me with the robe of righteousness, as a bridegroom decks himself with a garland, and as a bride adorns herself with her jewels.

Isaiah 61:10

The Petition

May the Lord GOD, father of grace and mercy, grant all who dwell here a peaceful night and a perfect end. *Amen.*

The Office of the Night Watch   Observed on the Hour or Half-Hour Between 1:30 and 4:30 a.m.

The Call to Prayer

Behold now, bless the LORD, all you servants of the LORD,* you that stand by night in the house of the LORD.
Lift up your hands in the holy place and bless the LORD;* the LORD who made heaven and earth bless you out of Zion.

Psalm 134

The Request for Presence

O God, come to my assistance.
O Lord, make haste to help me.

The Greeting

"You are my God, and I will thank you;* you are my God, and I will exalt you."

Psalm 118:28

The Refrain for the Night Watch

You shall not be afraid of any terror by night,* nor of the arrow that flies by day;

Psalm 91:5

The Psalm   *Our Eyes Look to the LORD*

To you I lift up my eyes,* to you enthroned in the heavens.
As the eyes of servants look to the hand of their masters,* and the eyes of a maid to the hand of her mistress,
So our eyes look to the LORD our God,* until he show us his mercy.
Have mercy upon us, O LORD, have mercy,* for we have had more than enough of contempt,
Too much of the scorn of the indolent rich,* and of the derision of the proud.

Psalm 123

The Refrain

You shall not be afraid of any terror by night,* nor of the arrow that flies by day;

355

A Reading

Prayer is the guide to perfection and the sovereign good; it delivers us from every vice and obtains for us every virtue; for the one great means to become perfect is to walk in the presence of God: he Himself has said, "Walk in my presence and be ye perfect." (Gen. 17:1) It is by prayer alone that we are brought into this presence and maintained in it without interruption.

Madame Guyon (17th c. French mystic), A Short and Easy Method of Prayer

The Refrain

You shall not be afraid of any terror by night,* nor of the arrow that flies by day;

The Litany

For the peace from above, for the loving-kindness of God, and for the salvation of my soul, I pray to the Lord.
  Lord, have mercy.
For the peace of the world, for the welfare of the Holy Church of God, and for the unity of all peoples, I pray to the Lord.
  Lord, have mercy.
For the leaders of the nations and for all in authority, I pray to the Lord.
  Lord, have mercy.
For the aged and infirm, for the widowed and orphans, and for the sick and the suffering, I pray to the Lord.
  Lord, have mercy.
For the poor and the oppressed, for the unemployed and the destitute, for prisoners and captives, and for all who remember and care for them, I pray to the Lord.
  Lord, have mercy.
For all who have died in the hope of the resurrection, and for all the departed, I pray to the Lord.
  Lord, have mercy.

The Thanksgiving

Lord, you now have set your servant free to go in peace as you have promised; for these eyes of mine have seen the Savior whom you have prepared for all the world to see: A Light to enlighten the nations, and the glory of your people Israel. *Amen.*

Nunc Dimittis

The Final Petition

Now guide me waking, O Lord, and guard me sleeping; that awake I may watch with Christ, and asleep, I may rest in peace. *Amen.*

The Office of Dawn

**Observed on the Hour or Half-Hour
Between 4:30 and 7:30 a.m.**

The Call to Prayer
Hallelujah! Sing to the LORD a new song;* sing his praise in the congregation of
the faithful.

Psalm 149:1

The Request for Presence
My soul waits for the LORD, more than watchmen for the morning,* more than
watchmen for the morning.

Psalm 130:5

The Greeting
Glory be to the Father, and the Son, and the Holy Spirit.
As it was in the beginning, it is now
And ever shall be, world without end. *Amen.*

Gloria Patri

The Hymn
O Master, let me walk with thee
in lowly paths of service free;
tell me your secret; help me bear
the strain of toil, the fret of care.
Help me the slow of heart to move
by some clear, winning word of love;
teach me the wayward feet to stay,
and guide them in the homeward way.
Teach me your patience; still with thee
in closer, dearer company,
in work that keeps faith sweet and strong,
in trust that triumphs over wrong;
In hope that sends a shining ray
far down the future's broadening way,
in peace that only you can give,
with you, O Master, let me live.

Washington Gladden

The Psalm   *The LORD Shall Reign For Ever*
Happy are they who have the God of Jacob for their help!* whose hope is in the
LORD their God;
Who made heaven and earth, the seas, and all that is in them;* who keeps his
promise for ever;
Who gives justice to those who are oppressed,* and food to those who hunger.

357

The LORD loves the righteous; the LORD cares for the stranger;* he sustains the
orphan and widow, but frustrates the way of the wicked.
The LORD shall reign for ever,* your God, O Zion, throughout all generations.
Hallelujah!

Psalm 146:4–6, 8–9

The Gloria in Excelsis
Glory to God in the highest, and on earth peace to people of good will.
We praise you.
We bless you.
We adore you.
We glorify you.
We give thanks to you for your great glory.

The Small Verse
Trust in the Lord with all your heart, and do not rely on your own insight. In all
your ways acknowledge him, and he will make straight your paths.

Proverbs 3:5–6

The Lord's Prayer

The Final Blessing
May the Lord bless us and keep us and cause His face to shine upon us from this
day forth and forever more. *Amen.*

ॐ

Wednesday, Month of October

The Office of Midnight   **Observed on the Hour or Half-Hour
Between 10:30 p.m.✚ and 1:30 a.m.**

The Call to Prayer
Let all who seek you rejoice and be glad in you;* let those who love your
salvation say for ever, "Great is the LORD!"

Psalm 70:4

The Request for Presence
O LORD, let my prayer be set forth in your sight as incense,* the lifting up of my
hands as the evening sacrifice.

Psalm 141:2, adapted

The Greeting
Our Father, give us this day our daily bread.

The Canticle   *A Song of Creation—Part Two*
Benedicite, omnia opera Domini

Glorify the Lord, all you works of the Lord,*
    praise him and highly exalt him for ever.
In the firmament of his power, glorify the Lord,*
    praise him and highly exalt him for ever.
Let the earth glorify the Lord,*
    praise him and highly exalt him for ever.
Glorify the Lord, O mountains and hills, and all that grows upon the earth,*
    praise him and highly exalt him for ever.
Glorify the Lord, O springs of water, seas, and streams,*
    O whales and all that move in the waters.
All birds of the air, glorify the Lord,*
    praise him and highly exalt him for ever.
Glorify the Lord, O beasts of the wild,*
    and all you flocks and herds.
O men and women everywhere, glorify the Lord,*
    praise him and highly exalt him for ever.

Song of the Three Young Men, 52–61

The Psalm   *Be My Strong Rock*
In you, O LORD, have I taken refuge;* let me never be ashamed.
Be my strong rock, a castle to keep me safe;* you are my crag and my stronghold.
For you are my hope, O Lord GOD,* my confidence since I was young.
I have been sustained by you ever since I was born; from my mother's womb you
    have been my strength;* my praise shall be always of you.
Let my mouth be full of your praise* and your glory all the day long.

Psalm 71:1ff

The Gloria

The Small Verse
Therefore, if any one is in Christ, he is a new creation; the old has passed away,
    behold, the new has come. All this is from God, who through Christ reconciled
    us to himself.

2 Corinthians 5:17–18a

The Final Thanksgiving
I will greatly rejoice in the LORD, my soul shall exult in my God; for he has
    clothed me with the garments of salvation, he has covered me with the robe of
    righteousness, as a bridegroom decks himself with a garland, and as a bride
    adorns herself with her jewels.

Isaiah 61:10

The Petition
May the Lord GOD, father of grace and mercy, grant all who dwell here a peaceful night and a perfect end. *Amen.*

The Office of the Night Watch   Observed on the Hour or Half-Hour
Between 1:30 and 4:30 a.m.

The Call to Prayer
Behold now, bless the LORD, all you servants of the LORD,* you that stand by night in the house of the LORD.
Lift up your hands in the holy place and bless the LORD;* the LORD who made heaven and earth bless you out of Zion.

Psalm 134

The Request for Presence
O God, come to my assistance.
O Lord, make haste to help me.

The Greeting
Out of Zion, perfect in its beauty,* God reveals himself in glory.

Psalm 50:2

The Refrain for the Night Watch
It is a good thing to give thanks to the LORD,* and to sing praises to your Name, O Most High;
To tell of your loving-kindness early in the morning* and of your faithfulness in the night season.

Psalm 92:1–2

The Psalm   *Praise the LORD*
Hallelujah! Praise the Name of the LORD;* give praise, you servants of the LORD,
You who stand in the house of the LORD,* in the courts of the house of our God.
Praise the LORD, for the LORD is good;* sing praises to his Name, for it is lovely.

Psalm 135:1–3

The Refrain
It is a good thing to give thanks to the LORD,* and to sing praises to your Name, O Most High;
To tell of your loving-kindness early in the morning* and of your faithfulness in the night season.

A Reading
Neither ought anyone to have joy in himself, if you look at the matter clearly, because no one ought to love even himself for his own sake, but for the sake of

Him who is the true object of enjoyment. For a person is never in so good a state as when his whole life is a journey towards the unchangeable life, and his affections are entirely fixed upon that. If, however, he loves himself for his own sake, he does not look at himself in relation to God, but turns his mind in upon himself, and so is not occupied with anything that is unchangeable. And thus he does not enjoy himself at his best, because he is better when his mind is fully fixed upon, and his affections wrapped up in, the unchangeable good, than when he turns from that to enjoy himself.

St. Augustine (ca. 410 CE), On Christian Doctrine

The Refrain

It is a good thing to give thanks to the LORD,* and to sing praises to your Name, O Most High;

To tell of your loving-kindness early in the morning* and of your faithfulness in the night season.

The Litany

Father, I pray for your holy catholic Church;
That we all may be one.
Grant that every member of the Church may truly and humbly serve you;
That your Name may be glorified by all people.
I pray for all who govern and hold authority in the nations of the world;
That there may be justice and peace on the earth.
Have compassion on those who suffer from any grief or trouble;
That they may be delivered from their distress.
Give to the departed eternal rest.
Let light perpetual shine upon them.
I praise you for your saints who have entered into joy;
May I also come to share in your heavenly kingdom.

The Thanksgiving

Lord, you now have set your servant free to go in peace as you have promised; for these eyes of mine have seen the Savior whom you have prepared for all the world to see: A Light to enlighten the nations, and the glory of your people Israel. *Amen.*

Nunc Dimittis

The Final Petition

Now guide me waking, O Lord, and guard me sleeping; that awake I may watch with Christ, and asleep, I may rest in peace. *Amen.*

The Office of Dawn

Observed on the Hour or Half-Hour
Between 4:30 and 7:30 a.m.

The Call to Prayer
Hallelujah! Praise the LORD, O my soul!* I will praise the LORD, as long as I live; I
will sing praises to my God while I have my being.

Psalm 146:1

The Request for Presence
My soul waits for the LORD, more than watchmen for the morning,* more than
watchmen for the morning.

Psalm 130:5

The Greeting
Glory be to the Father, and the Son, and the Holy Spirit.
As it was in the beginning, it is now
And ever shall be, world without end. *Amen.*

Gloria Patri

The Hymn
Love divine, all loves excelling,
joy of heaven, to earth come down;
fix in us your humble dwelling;
all your faithful mercies crown!
Jesus, thou art all compassion,
pure, unbounded love thou art;
visit us with your salvation;
enter every trembling heart.
Come, Almighty to deliver,
let us all your life receive;
suddenly return and never,
nevermore your temples leave.
You we would be always blessing,
serve you as your hosts above,
pray and praise you without ceasing,
glory in your perfect love.

Charles Wesley

The Psalm   *Praise the Name of the LORD*
Praise the LORD, from the heavens;* praise him in the heights.
Praise him, all you angels of his;* praise him, all his host.
Praise him, sun and moon;* praise him, all you shining stars.
Praise him, heaven of heavens,* and you waters above the heavens.
Let them praise the Name of the LORD;* for he commanded, and they were
created.

He made them stand fast for ever and ever;* he gave them a law which shall not pass away.

Psalm 148: 1b–6

The Gloria in Excelsis

Glory to God in the highest, and on earth peace to people of good will.
> We praise you.
> We bless you.
> We adore you.

We glorify you.
We give thanks to you for your great glory.

The Small Verse

A voice cries: "In the wilderness prepare the way of the Lord, Make straight in the desert a highway for our God. Every valley shall be lifted up, and every mountain and hill be made low; the uneven ground shall become level, and the rough places a plain. And the glory of the Lord, shall be revealed, and all flesh shall see it together, for the mouth of the Lord has spoken."

Isaiah 40:3–5

The Lord's Prayer

The Final Blessing

May the Lord bless us and keep us and cause His face to shine upon us from this day forth and forever more. *Amen.*

⌘

Thursday, Month of October

| **The Office of Midnight** | **Observed on the Hour or Half-Hour Between 10:30 p.m.✛ and 1:30 a.m.** |

The Call to Prayer

Teach me your way, O Lord, and I will walk in your truth;* knit my heart to you that I may fear your Name

Psalm 86:11

The Request for Presence

O Lord, let my prayer be set forth in your sight as incense,* the lifting up of my hands as the evening sacrifice.

Psalm 141:2, adapted

363

The Greeting
Our Father, forgive us our sins as we forgive those who have sinned against us.

The Canticle   *A Song of Penitence*
                                                    Kyrie Pantokrator
And now, O Lord, I bend the knee of my heart,*
    And make my appeal, sure of your gracious goodness.
I have sinned, O Lord, I have sinned,*
    and I know my wickedness only too well.
Therefore I make this prayer to you:*
    Forgive me, Lord, forgive me.
Do not let me perish in my sin,*
    nor condemn me to the depths of the earth.
For you, O Lord, are the God of those who repent,*
    and in me you will show forth your goodness.
Unworthy as I am, you will save me, in accordance with your great mercy,*
    and I will praise you without ceasing all the days of my life.
For all the powers of heaven sing your praises,*
    and yours is the glory to ages of ages. *Amen.*

                                            Prayer of Manasseh 11–15

The Psalm   *The LORD Is King*
Tell it out among the nations: "The LORD is King!* he has made the world so firm
    that it cannot be moved; he will judge the peoples with equity."
Let the heavens rejoice, and let the earth be glad; let the sea thunder and all that is
    in it;* let the field be joyful and all that is therein.
Then shall all the trees of the wood shout for joy before the LORD when he
    comes,* when he comes to judge the earth.
He will judge the world with righteousness* and the peoples with his truth.

                                            Psalm 96:10–13

The Gloria

The Small Verse
Owe no one anything, except to love one another; for he who loves his neighbor
    has fulfilled the law.

                                            Romans 13:8

The Final Thanksgiving
I will greatly rejoice in the LORD, my soul shall exult in my God; for he has
    clothed me with the garments of salvation, he has covered me with the robe of
    righteousness, as a bridegroom decks himself with a garland, and as a bride
    adorns herself with her jewels.

                                            Isaiah 61:10

The Petition

May the Lord GOD, father of grace and mercy, grant all who dwell here a peaceful night and a perfect end. *Amen.*

The Office of the Night Watch Observed on the Hour or Half-Hour
Between 1:30 and 4:30 a.m.

The Call to Prayer

Behold now, bless the LORD, all you servants of the LORD,* you that stand by night in the house of the LORD.
Lift up your hands in the holy place and bless the LORD;* the LORD who made heaven and earth bless you out of Zion.

Psalm 134

The Request for Presence

O God, come to my assistance.
O Lord, make haste to help me.

The Greeting

Into your hands I commend my spirit,* for you have redeemed me, O LORD,
O God of truth.

Psalm 31:5

The Refrain for the Night Watch

Behold now, bless the LORD, all you servants of the LORD,* you that stand by night in the house of the LORD.

Psalm 134:1

The Psalm Help Me, O LORD

But you, O Lord my GOD, oh, deal with me according to your Name;* for your tender mercy's sake, deliver me.
For I am poor and needy,* and my heart is wounded within me.
I have faded away like a shadow when it lengthens;* I am shaken off like a locust.
My knees are weak through fasting,* and my flesh is wasted and gaunt.
I have become a reproach to them;* they see and shake their heads.
Help me, O LORD my God;* save me for your mercy's sake.

Psalm 109:20–25

The Refrain

Behold now, bless the LORD, all you servants of the LORD,* you that stand by night in the house of the LORD.

A Reading

For as the presidents of the public games do not allow the competitors to enter the lists indiscriminately or fortuitously, but after a careful examination, pairing in a most impartial consideration either of size or age, this individual with that. . . . so also must we understand the procedure of divine providence, which arranges on most impartial principles all who descend into the struggles of this human life, according to the nature of each individual's power, which is known only to Him who alone beholds the hearts of humanity; . . . so observe whether some such state of things be not indicated by the language of the apostle when he says: "God is faithful, who will not suffer you to be tempted above what you are able," that is, each one of us is tempted in proportion to the amount of our strength or power of resistance.

Origen (ca. 185–254 CE), translated by Rufinus, De Principiis

The Refrain

Behold now, bless the LORD, all you servants of the LORD,* you that stand by night in the house of the LORD.

The Litany

Grant, Almighty God, that all who confess your Name may be united in your truth, live together in your love, and reveal your glory in the world.
> *Lord, in your mercy, hear my prayer.*

Guide the people of this land, and of all the nations, in the ways of justice and peace; that we may honor one another and serve the common good.
> *Lord, in your mercy, hear my prayer.*

Give us all a reverence for the earth as your own creation, that we may use its resources rightly in the service of others and to your honor and glory.
> *Lord, in your mercy, hear my prayer.*

Bless all whose lives are closely linked with mine, and grant that I may serve Christ in them, and love even as he loves me.
> *Lord, in your mercy, hear my prayer.*

Comfort and heal all those who suffer in body, mind, or spirit; give them courage and hope in their troubles, and bring them the joy of your salvation.
> *Lord, in your mercy, hear my prayer.*

I commend to your mercy all who have died, that your will for them may be fulfilled; and I pray that I may share with all your saints in your eternal kingdom.
> *Lord, in your mercy, hear my prayer.*

The Thanksgiving

Lord, you now have set your servant free to go in peace as you have promised; for these eyes of mine have seen the Savior whom you have prepared for all the world to see: A Light to enlighten the nations, and the glory of your people Israel. *Amen.*

Nunc Dimittis

366

The Final Petition

Now guide me waking, O Lord, and guard me sleeping; that awake I may watch with Christ, and asleep, I may rest in peace. *Amen.*

The Office of Dawn

Observed on the Hour or Half-Hour Between 4:30 and 7:30 a.m.

The Call to Prayer

Hallelujah! How good it is to sing praises to our God!* how pleasant it is to honor him with praise!

Psalm 147:1

The Request for Presence

My soul waits for the LORD, more than watchmen for the morning,* more than watchmen for the morning.

Psalm 130:5

The Greeting

Glory be to the Father, and the Son, and the Holy Spirit.
As it was in the beginning, it is now
And ever shall be, world without end. *Amen.*

Gloria Patri

The Hymn

O splendor of God's glory bright,
O thou that brings the light from light;
O Light of light, light's living spring,
O day, all days illumining.
O Son, true Sun, on us your glance
let fall in royal radiance;
the Spirit's sanctifying beam
upon our earthly senses stream.
The Father, too, our prayers implore,
Father of glory evermore;
the Father of all grace and might,
to banish sin from our delight.

Robert S. Bridges

The Psalm   The LORD Has Pleasure in Those Who Fear Him

He covers the heavens with clouds* and prepares rain for the earth;
He makes grass to grow upon the mountains* and green plants to serve mankind.
He provides food for flocks and herds* and for the young ravens when they cry.
He is not impressed by the might of a horse;* he has no pleasure in the strength of a man;

But the LORD has pleasure in those who fear him,* in those who await his gracious favor.

Psalm 147:8–12

The Gloria in Excelsis

Glory to God in the highest, and on earth peace to people of good will.
We praise you.
We bless you.
We adore you.
We glorify you.
We give thanks to you for your great glory.

The Small Verse

When Abram was ninety-nine years old the LORD appeared to Abram and said to him, "I am God Almighty; walk before me, and be blameless. And I will make my covenant between me and you, and will multiply you exceedingly." Then Abram fell on his face; and God said to him, "Behold my covenant is with you, and you shall be the father of a multitude of nations. No longer shall your name be Abram, but your name shall be Abraham; for I have made you the father of a multitude of nations. . . . And I will establish my covenant between me and you and your descendants after you throughout the generations for an everlasting covenant to be God to you and your descendants after you."

Genesis 17:1–5, 7

The Lord's Prayer

The Final Blessing

May the Lord bless us and keep us and cause His face to shine upon us from this day forth and forever more. *Amen.*

Friday, Month of October

The Office of Midnight **Observed on the Hour or Half-Hour Between 10:30 p.m.✚ and 1:30 a.m.**

The Call to Prayer

I will confess my iniquity* and be sorry for my sin.

Psalm 38:18

The Request for Presence

O LORD, let my prayer be set forth in your sight as incense,* the lifting up of my
  hands as the evening sacrifice.

Psalm 141:2, adapted

The Greeting

Our Father, lead us not into temptation, but deliver us from evil.

The Canticle

A Song of Penitence
Kyrie Pantokrator

O Lord and Ruler of the hosts of heaven,*
  God of Abraham, Isaac, and Jacob, and of all their righteous offspring:
You made the heavens and the earth,*
  with all their vast array.
All things quake with fear at your presence;*
  they tremble because of your power.
But your merciful promise is beyond all measure;*
  it surpasses all that our minds can fathom.
O Lord, you are full of compassion,*
  long-suffering, and abounding in mercy.
You hold back your hand;*
  you do not punish as we deserve.
In your great goodness, Lord, you have promised forgiveness to sinners,*
  that they may repent of their sin and be saved.

Prayer of Manasseh 1–2, 4, 6–7

The Psalm

Give Ear to My Cry

Hear my prayer, O LORD, and give ear to my cry;* hold not your peace at my tears.
For I am but a sojourner with you,* a wayfarer, as all my forebears were.
Turn your gaze from me, that I may be glad again,* before I go my way and am no
  more.

Psalm 39:13–15

The Gloria

The Small Verse

Beloved, let us love one another; for love is of God, and he who loves is born of God
  and knows God. He who does not love does not know God; for God is love.

1 John 4:7–8

The Final Thanksgiving

I will greatly rejoice in the Lord, my soul shall exult in my God; for he has clothed
  me with the garments of salvation, he has covered me with the robe of
  righteousness, as a bridegroom decks himself with a garland, and as a bride
  adorns herself with her jewels.

Isaiah 61:10

369

The Petition
May the Lord GOD, father of grace and mercy, grant all who dwell here a peaceful
night and a perfect end. *Amen.*

The Office of the Night Watch   Observed on the Hour or Half-Hour
Between 1:30 and 4:30 a.m.

The Call to Prayer
Behold now, bless the LORD, all you servants of the LORD,* you that stand by night
in the house of the LORD.
Lift up your hands in the holy place and bless the LORD;* the LORD who made
heaven and earth bless you out of Zion.

Psalm 134

The Request for Presence
O God, come to my assistance.
O Lord, make haste to help me.

The Greeting
Your righteousness, O God, reaches to the heavens;* you have done great things;
who is like you, O God?

Psalm 71:19

The Refrain for the Night Watch
Darkness is not dark to you; the night is as bright as the day;* darkness and light
to you are both alike.

Psalm 139:11

The Psalm   *Your Way, O God, Is Holy*
I will meditate on all your acts* and ponder your mighty deeds.
Your way, O God, is holy;* who is so great a god as our God?
You are the God who works wonders* and have declared your power among the
peoples.
By your strength you have redeemed your people,* the children of Jacob and
Joseph.

Psalm 77:12–15

The Refrain
Darkness is not dark to you; the night is as bright as the day;* darkness and light
to you are both alike.

A Reading
But after we have learned by faith to know that whatever is necessary for us or
defective in us is supplied in God and in our Lord Jesus Christ, in whom it has

pleased the Father that all fullness should dwell, that we may thence draw as from an inexhaustible fountain, it remains for us to seek and in prayer implore of Him what we have learned to be in Him. . . . Hence the Apostle, to show that a faith unaccompanied with prayer to God can not be genuine, states this to be the order: As faith springs from the Gospel, so by faith our hearts are framed to call upon the name of God. (Rom. 10: 14) And this is the very thing which he had expressed some time before . . . i.e., *the Spirit of adoption*, which seals the testimony of the Gospels in our hearts, gives us courage to make our requests made known unto God, calls forth groanings which can not be uttered, and enables us to cry, Abba, Father!

John Calvin, Of Prayer

The Refrain
Darkness is not dark to you; the night is as bright as the day;* darkness and light to you are both alike.

The Litany
For the holy Church of God, that it may be filled with truth and love, and be found without fault at the day of your coming, I pray to you, O Lord.
Lord, in your mercy, hear my prayer
For all who fear God and believe in you, Lord Christ, that our divisions may cease, and that all may be one as you and the Father are one, I pray to you, O Lord.
Lord, in your mercy, hear my prayer.
For those who do not yet believe, and for those who have lost their faith, that they may receive the light of the Gospel, I pray to you, O Lord.
Lord, in your mercy, hear my prayer.
For my enemies and those who wish me harm, and for all whom I have injured or offended, I pray to you, O Lord.
Lord, in your mercy, hear my prayer.
For all who have commended themselves to my prayers; for my family, friends, and neighbors; that being freed from anxiety, they may live in joy, peace, and health, I pray to you, O Lord.
Lord, in your mercy, hear my prayer.
For myself; for the forgiveness of my sins, and for the grace of the Holy Spirit to amend my life, I pray to you, O Lord.
Lord, in your mercy, hear my prayer

The Thanksgiving
Lord, you now have set your servant free to go in peace as you have promised; for these eyes of mine have seen the Savior whom you have prepared for all the world to see: A Light to enlighten the nations, and the glory of your people Israel. *Amen.*

Nunc Dimittis

The Final Petition
Now guide me waking, O Lord, and guard me sleeping; that awake I may watch
with Christ, and asleep, I may rest in peace. *Amen.*

The Office of Dawn   **Observed on the Hour or Half-Hour**
Between 4:30 and 7:30 a.m.

The Call to Prayer
Worship the LORD O Jerusalem;* praise your God, O Zion;
For he has strengthened the bars of your gates.

Psalm 147:13–14a

The Request for Presence
My soul waits for the LORD, more than watchmen for the morning,* more than
watchmen for the morning.

Psalm 130:5

The Greeting
Glory be to the Father, and the Son, and the Holy Spirit.
As it was in the beginning, it is now
And ever shall be, world without end. *Amen.*

Gloria Patri

The Hymn
This is my Father's world,
and to my listening ears
all nature sings, and round me rings
the music of the spheres.
This is my Father's world:
I rest me in the thought
of rocks and trees, of skies and seas;
his hand the wonders wrought.
This is my Father's world,
the birds their carols raise,
the morning light, the lily white,
declare their maker's praise.
This is my Father's world:
he shines in all that's fair;
in the rustling grass I hear him pass;
he speaks to me everywhere.

Maltbie D. Babcock

The Psalm   *The Lord Takes Pleasure in His People*

Let Israel rejoice in his Maker;* let the children of Zion be joyful in their King.
Let them praise his Name in the dance;* let them sing praise to him with timbrel
 and harp.
For the Lord takes pleasure in his people* and adorns the poor with victory.
Let the faithful rejoice in triumph;* let them be joyful on their beds.

Psalm 149:2–5

The Gloria in Excelsis

Glory to God in the highest, and on earth peace to people of good will.
 We praise you.
 We bless you.
 We adore you.
 We glorify you.
We give thanks to you for your great glory.

The Small Verse

If I take the wings of the morning and dwell in the uttermost parts of the sea, even
 there your hand will lead me and your right hand hold me fast. If I say, "Surely
 the darkness will cover me, and the light around me turn to night," darkness is
 not dark to you; the night is as bright as the day; darkness and light to you are
 both alike.

Psalm 139:8–11

The Lord's Prayer

The Final Blessing

May the Lord bless us and keep us and cause His face to shine upon us from this
 day forth and forever more. *Amen.*

Saturday, Month of October

The Office of Midnight   Observed on the Hour or Half-Hour
Between 10:30 p.m.✝ and 1:30 a.m.

The Call to Prayer

Your love, O Lord, for ever will I sing;* from age to age my mouth will proclaim
 your faithfulness.

Psalm 89:1

The Request for Presence
O LORD, let my prayer be set forth in your sight as incense,* the lifting up of my
hands as the evening sacrifice.

Psalm 141:2, adapted

The Greeting
Our Father, Yours are the kingdom, the power, and the glory forever.

The Canticle   The Song of Zechariah
Benedictus Dominus Deus

Blessed be the Lord, the God of Israel;*
   he has come to his people and set them free.
He has raised up for us a mighty savior,*
   born of the house of his servant David
You, my child, shall be called the prophet of the Most High,*
   for you will go before the Lord to prepare his way,
To give his people knowledge of salvation*
   by the forgiveness of their sins.
In the tender compassion of our God*
   the dawn from on high shall break upon us,
To shine on those who dwell in darkness and the shadow of death,*
   and to guide our feet into the way of peace.
Glory to the Father, and to the Son, and to the Holy Spirit:*
   as it was in the beginning, is now, and will be for ever. *Amen.*

Luke 1:68–69, 76–79

The Psalm   To You, O LORD, I Lift Up My Soul
Be merciful to me, O LORD, for you are my God;* I call upon you all the day long.
Gladden the soul of your servant,* for to you, O LORD, I lift up my soul.
For you, O LORD, are good and forgiving,* and great is your love toward all who
   call upon you.
Give ear, O LORD, to my prayer,* and attend to the voice of my supplications.
In the time of my trouble I will call upon you,* for you will answer me.
Among the gods there is none like you, O LORD,* nor anything like your works.
All nations you have made will come and worship you, O LORD,* and glorify your
   Name.
For you are great; you do wondrous things;* and you alone are God.

Psalm 86:3–10

The Gloria

The Small Verse
Then Peter came up and said to him, "Lord, how often shall my brother sin against
   me, and I forgive him? As many as seven times?" Jesus said to him, "I do not
   say to you seven times, but seventy times seven."

Matthew 18:21–22

The Final Thanksgiving
I will greatly rejoice in the LORD, my soul shall exult in my God; for he has
  clothed me with the garments of salvation, he has covered me with the robe of
  righteousness, as a bridegroom decks himself with a garland, and as a bride
  adorns herself with her jewels.

Isaiah 61:10

The Petition
May the Lord GOD, father of grace and mercy, grant all who dwell here a peaceful
  night and a perfect end. *Amen.*

The Office of the Night Watch

**Observed on the Hour or Half-Hour
Between 1:30 and 4:30 a.m.**

The Call to Prayer
Behold now, bless the LORD, all you servants of the LORD,* you that stand by night
  in the house of the LORD.
Lift up your hands in the holy place and bless the LORD;* the LORD who made
  heaven and earth bless you out of Zion.

Psalm 134

The Request for Presence
O God, come to my assistance.
O Lord, make haste to help me.

The Greeting
I will give thanks to you, O LORD, with my whole heart;* I will tell of all your
  marvelous works.
I will be glad and rejoice in you;* I will sing to your Name, O Most High.

Psalm 9:1–2

The Refrain for the Night Watch
I will bless the LORD who gives me counsel;* my heart teaches me, night after
  night.

Psalm 16:7

The Psalm   *You, O God, Have Heard My Vows*
Hear my cry, O God,* and listen to my prayer.
I call upon you from the ends of the earth with heaviness in my heart;* set me
  upon the rock that is higher than I.
For you have been my refuge,* a strong tower against the enemy.
I will dwell in your house for ever;* I will take refuge under the cover of your
  wings.

375

For you, O God, have heard my vows;* you have granted me the heritage of those who fear your Name.

Psalm 61:1–5

The Refrain
I will bless the LORD who gives me counsel;* my heart teaches me, night after night.

A Reading
Paul, in the beginning of his epistle to Timothy, expresses himself as, "Paul, an Apostle of Jesus Christ by the commandment of God." He does not say here, "Paul called," but he says, "by commandment." He begins in this manner that Timothy may not feel any human infirmity from supposing that Paul addresses him on the same terms as his disciples. . . . And everywhere in his writings, Paul adds the name of "Apostle," to instruct his hearers not to consider the doctrines he delivered as proceeding from man. For an Apostle can say nothing of his own, and by calling himself as Apostle, he at once refers his hearers to Him who sent him. In all his epistles, therefore, he begins by assuming this title, thus giving authority to his words, as here he says, "Paul, an Apostle of Jesus Christ, according to the commandment of God our Savior."

St. John Chrysostom (ca. 347–407 CE), Archbishop of Constantinople,
On the Epistles of St. Paul the Apostle

The Refrain
I will bless the LORD who gives me counsel;* my heart teaches me, night after night.

The Litany
For the peace of the world, that a spirit of respect and forbearance may grow among nations and peoples, I pray to you, O Lord.
Lord, hear my prayer.
For those in positions of public trust, that they may serve justice, and promote the dignity and freedom of every person, I pray to you, O Lord.
Lord, hear my prayer.
For the poor, the persecuted, the sick, and all who suffer; for refugees, prisoners, and all who are in danger; that they may be relieved and protected, I pray to you, O Lord.
Lord, hear my prayer.
For the forgiveness of my sins, and for the grace of the Holy Spirit to amend my life, I pray to you, O Lord.
Lord, hear my prayer.
For all who have died in the communion of your Church, and those whose faith is known to you alone, that, with all the saints, they may have rest in that place where there is no pain or grief, but life eternal, I pray to you, O Lord.
Lord, hear my prayer

Rejoicing in the fellowship of the ever-blessed Virgin Mary and all the saints, I commend my self and all your faithful to Christ our God.
To you, O Lord our God.

The Thanksgiving

Lord, you now have set your servant free to go in peace as you have promised; for these eyes of mine have seen the Savior whom you have prepared for all the world to see: A Light to enlighten the nations, and the glory of your people Israel. *Amen.*

Nunc Dimittis

The Final Petition

Now guide me waking, O Lord, and guard me sleeping; that awake I may watch with Christ, and asleep, I may rest in peace. *Amen*

The Office of Dawn — Observed on the Hour or Half-Hour Between 4:30 and 7:30 a.m.

The Call to Prayer

Sing to the LORD with thanksgiving;* make music to our God upon the harp.

Psalm 147:7

The Request for Presence

My soul waits for the LORD, more than watchmen for the morning,* more than watchmen for the morning.

Psalm 130:5

The Greeting

Glory be to the Father, and the Son, and the Holy Spirit.
As it was in the beginning, it is now
And ever shall be, world without end. *Amen.*

Gloria Patri

The Hymn

Lead on, O King eternal, till sin's fierce war shall cease,
and holiness shall whisper the sweet amen of peace.
For not with swords loud clashing, nor roll of stirring drums;
with deeds of love and mercy the heavenly kingdom comes.
Lead on, O King eternal, we follow, not with fears,
for gladness breaks like morning where'er your face appears.
Your cross is lifted o'er us, we journey in its light;
the crown awaits the conquest; lead on, O God of might.

Ernest W. Shurtleff

377

The Psalm   *Sing to the Lord*

Sing to the Lord from the earth,* you sea-monsters and all deeps;
Fire and hail, snow and fog,* tempestuous wind, doing his will;
Mountains and all hills,* fruit trees and all cedars;
Wild beasts and all cattle,* creeping things and winged birds;
Kings of the earth and all peoples,* princes and all rulers of the world;
Young men and maidens,* old and young together.
Let them praise the Name of the Lord,*

Psalm 148:7–13a

The Gloria in Excelsis

Glory to God in the highest, and on earth peace to people of good will.
  We praise you.
  We bless you.
  We adore you.
  We glorify you.
We give thanks to you for your great glory.

The Small Verse

"For behold I create new heavens and a new earth; all the former things shall not
  be remembered or come into mind. But be glad and rejoice for ever in that
  which I create."

Isaiah 65:17–18a

The Lord's Prayer

The Final Blessing

May the Lord bless us and keep us and cause His face to shine upon us from this
  day forth and forever more. *Amen.*

The Gloria
Glory be to God the Father, God the Son, and God the Holy Spirit. As it was
in the beginning, so it is now and so it shall ever be, world without end.
Alleluia. *Amen.*

The Lord's Prayer
Our Father, who art in heaven, hallowed be your Name.
May your kingdom come, and your will be done, on earth as in heaven.
Give us today our daily bread.
Forgive us our sins as we forgive those who sin against us.
Lead us not into temptation, but deliver us from evil;
for yours are the kingdom and the power and the glory
forever and ever. *Amen*

The following major holy days occur in November:
The Feast of All Saints: *November 1*
The Feast of All Souls: *November 2*
The Feast of St. Andrew, the Apostle: *November 30*

Prayer for use in the observation of a holy day:
Almighty God, by your Holy Spirit you have made us one with your saints in
heaven and on earth: Grant that in my earthly pilgrimage, I may always be
supported by this fellowship of love and prayer, and know myself to be
surrounded by their witness to your power and mercy. I ask this for the sake of
Jesus Christ, in whom all my intercessions are acceptable through the
Spirit, and who lives and reigns forever and ever. *Amen.*

✣ The Office of Midnight is always taken from the prayers for the day nearest
to the hour of actual observation. Thus, if the office is to be observed at 10:30 p.m.
on Sunday, the prayers will be taken from the Monday offices, and so forth.

NOVEMBER

Sunday, Month of November

The Office of Midnight   **Observed on the Hour or Half-Hour Between 10:30 p.m.✢ and 1:30 a.m.**

The Call to Prayer
For God alone my soul in silence waits;* truly, my hope is in him.

Psalm 62:6

The Request for Presence
O LORD, let my prayer be set forth in your sight as incense,* the lifting up of my
hands as the evening sacrifice.

Psalm 141:2, adapted

The Greeting
Our Father Who art in Heaven, hallowed be Your name.

The Canticle   **You Are God**

Te Deum laudamus

You are God: we praise you;
You are the Lord; we acclaim you;
You are the eternal Father:
All creation worships you.
To you all angels, all the powers of heaven,
Cherubim and Seraphim, sing in endless praise:
     Holy, holy, holy Lord, God of power and might,
     heaven and earth are full of your glory.
The glorious company of apostles praise you.
The noble fellowship of prophets praise you.
The white-robed army of martyrs praise you.
Throughout the world the holy Church acclaims you;
     Father, of majesty unbounded,
     your true and only Son, worthy of all worship,
     and the Holy Spirit, advocate and guide.
You, Christ, are the king of glory,
the eternal Son of the Father.
When you became man to set us free
you did not shun the Virgin's womb.
You overcame the sting of death
and opened the kingdom of heaven to all believers.
You are seated at God's right hand in glory.
We believe that you will come and be our judge.
     Come then, Lord, and help your people,
     bought with the price of your own blood,

and bring us with your saints
to glory everlasting.

The Psalm   God Is Our Refuge and Strength
God is our refuge and strength,* a very present help in trouble.
Therefore we will not fear, though the earth be moved,* and though the mountains
   be toppled into the depths of the sea;
Though its waters rage and foam,* and though the mountains tremble at its tumult.
The LORD of hosts is with us;* the God of Jacob is our stronghold.

Psalm 46:1–4

The Gloria

The Small Verse
Blessed are the merciful, for they shall obtain mercy. Blessed are the pure in heart,
   for they shall see God. Blessed are the peacemakers, for they shall be called
   sons of God.

Matthew 5:7–9

The Final Thanksgiving
I will greatly rejoice in the Lord, my soul shall exult in my God; for he has clothed
   me with the garments of salvation, he has covered me with the robe of
   righteousness, as a bridegroom decks himself with a garland, and as a bride
   adorns herself with her jewels.

Isaiah 61:10

The Petition
May the Lord GOD, father of all mercy, grant us who dwell here a peaceful night
   and a perfect end. *Amen.*

The Office of the Night Watch   Observed on the Hour or Half-Hour
                                                 Between 1:30 and 4:30 a.m.

The Call to Prayer
Behold now, bless the LORD, all you servants of the LORD,* you that stand by night
   in the house of the LORD.
Lift up your hands in the holy place and bless the LORD;* the LORD who made
   heaven and earth bless you out of Zion.

Psalm 134

The Request for Presence
O God, come to my assistance.
O Lord, make haste to help me.

The Greeting

Lord, you have been our refuge* from one generation to another.
Before the mountains were brought forth, or the land and the earth were born,*
   from age to age you are God.

Psalm 90:1–2

The Refrain for the Night Watch

Happy are they who have not walked in the counsel of the wicked,* nor lingered
   in the way of sinners, nor sat in the seats of the scornful!
Their delight is in the law of the LORD,* and they meditate on his law day and night.

Psalm 1:1–2

The Psalm   *You Make the Dawn and the Dusk to Sing for Joy*

Happy are they whom you choose and draw to your courts to dwell there!* they
   will be satisfied by the beauty of your house, by the holiness of your temple.
Awesome things will you show us in your righteousness, O God of our salvation,*
   O Hope of all the ends of the earth and of the seas that are far away.
You make fast the mountains by your power;* they are girded about with might.
You still the roaring of the seas,* the roaring of their waves, and the clamor of the
   peoples.
Those who dwell at the ends of the earth will tremble at your marvelous signs;*
   you make the dawn and the dusk to sing for joy.

Psalm 65:4–8

The Refrain

Happy are they who have not walked in the counsel of the wicked,* nor lingered
   in the way of sinners, nor sat in the seats of the scornful!
Their delight is in the law of the LORD,* and they meditate on his law day and night.

A Reading

We pray in order that we may come unto the Darkness which is beyond light and,
   without seeing and without knowing, may see and know that which is above
   vision and knowledge, and this through the realization that by not-seeing and
   by unknowing we attain to true vision and knowledge; and thus praise,
   superessentially, It that is, even as those who, carving a statue out of marble,
   abstract or remove all the surrounding material that hinders the vision which
   the marble conceals and, by that abstraction, bring to light the hidden beauty.

Dionysius, the Areopagite, converted by St. Paul (Acts 17:34)
and first Bishop of Athens, Mystical Theology

The Refrain

Happy are they who have not walked in the counsel of the wicked,* nor lingered
   in the way of sinners, nor sat in the seats of the scornful!
Their delight is in the law of the LORD,* and they meditate on his law day and night.

The Litany

For all people in their daily life and work;
For my family, friends, and neighbors, and for those who are alone, I pray to you, Lord God.
For this community, the nation, and the world;
For all who work for justice, freedom, and peace, I pray to you, Lord God.
For the just and proper use of your creation;
For the victims of hunger, fear, injustice, and oppression, I pray to you, Lord God.
For all who are in danger, sorrow, or any kind of trouble;
For those who minister to the sick, the friendless, and the needy, I pray to you, Lord God.
For the peace and unity of the Church of God;
For all who proclaim the Gospel, and all who seek the Truth, I pray to you, Lord God.
Hear me, Lord;
For your mercy is great.

The Thanksgiving

Lord, you now have set your servant free to go in peace as you have promised; for these eyes of mine have seen the Savior whom you have prepared for all the world to see: A Light to enlighten the nations, and the glory of your people Israel. *Amen.*

Nunc Dimittis

The Final Petition

Now guide me waking, O Lord, and guard me sleeping; that awake I may watch with Christ, and asleep, I may rest in peace. *Amen.*

The Office of Dawn — Observed on the Hour or Half-Hour Between 4:30 and 7:30 a.m.

The Call to Prayer

Let everything that has breath* praise the LORD. Hallelujah!

Psalm 150:6

The Request for Presence

My soul waits for the LORD, more than watchmen for the morning,* more than watchmen for the morning.

Psalm 130:5

The Greeting

Glory be to the Father, and the Son, and the Holy Spirit.

As it was in the beginning, it is now
And ever shall be, world without end. *Amen.*

Gloria Patri

The Hymn

Now thank we all our God, with heart and hands and voices,
Who wondrous things hath done, in whom his world rejoices,
Who from our mothers' arm hath blessed us on our way
With countless gifts of love, and still is ours to-day.
O, may this bounteous God through all our life be near us,
With ever joyful hearts and blessèd peace to cheer us,
And keep us in his grace, and guide us when perplexed,
And free us from all ills in this world and the next.
All praise and thanks to God, the Father, now be given,
The Son, and him who reigns with them in highest heaven:
The One Eternal God, whom earth and heaven adore,
For thus it was, is now, and shall be evermore!

Martin Rinkart, translated by Catherine Winkworth

The Psalm   The LORD Loves the Righteous

Happy are they who have the God of Jacob for their help!* whose hope is in the
    Lord their God;
Who made heaven and earth, the seas, and all that is in them;* who keeps his
    promise for ever;
Who gives justice to those who are oppressed,* and food to those who hunger.
The LORD loves the righteous; the LORD cares for the stranger;* he sustains the
    orphan and widow, but frustrates the way of the wicked.
The LORD shall reign for ever,* your God, O Zion, throughout all generations.
    Hallelujah!

Psalm 146:4–6, 8–9

The Gloria in Excelsis

Glory to God in the highest, and on earth peace to people of good will.
    We praise you.
    We bless you.
    We adore you.
    We glorify you.
We give thanks to you for your great glory.

The Small Verse

"And the foreigners who join themselves to the LORD, to minister to him, to love
the name of the Lord, and to be his servants, every one who keeps the Sabbath,
and does not profane it, and holds fast my covenant—these I will bring to my
holy mountain, and make them joyful in my house of prayer; their burnt
offerings and their sacrifices will be accepted on my altar; for my house shall
be called a house of prayer for all peoples."

Isaiah 56:6–7

386

The Lord's Prayer

The Final Blessing
May the Lord bless us and keep us and cause His face to shine upon us from this
day forth and forever more. *Amen.*

⨪

Monday, Month of November

The Office of Midnight **Observed on the Hour or Half-Hour**
Between 10:30 p.m.✢ and 1:30 a.m.

The Call to Prayer
Oh, the majesty and magnificence of his presence!* Oh, the power and the
splendor of his sanctuary!

Psalm 96:6

The Request for Presence
O LORD, let my prayer be set forth in your sight as incense, the lifting up of my
hands as the evening sacrifice.

Psalm 141:2, adapted

The Greeting
Our Father, may Your kingdom come on earth as in Heaven.

The Canticle *A Song of Creation—Part Two*
Benedicite, omnia opera Domini

Glorify the Lord, all you works of the Lord,*
 praise him and highly exalt him for ever.
In the firmament of his power, glorify the Lord,*
 praise him and highly exalt him for ever.
Let the earth glorify the Lord,*
 praise him and highly exalt him for ever.
Glorify the Lord, O mountains and hills, and all that grows upon the earth,*
 praise him and highly exalt him for ever.
Glorify the Lord, O springs of water, seas, and streams,*
 O whales and all that move in the waters.
All birds of the air, glorify the Lord,*
 praise him and highly exalt him for ever.
Glorify the Lord, O beasts of the wild,*
 and all you flocks and herds.

men and women everywhere, glorify the Lord,*
praise him and highly exalt him for ever.

Song of the Three Young Men, 52–61

The Psalm   *Let Mount Zion Be Glad*

We have waited in silence on your loving-kindness, O God,* in the midst of your
temple.
Your praise, like your Name, O God, reaches to the world's end;* your right hand
is full of justice.
Let Mount Zion be glad and the cities of Judah rejoice,* because of your judgments.
Make the circuit of Zion; walk round about her;* count the number of her towers.
Consider well her bulwarks; examine her strongholds;* that you may tell those
who come after.
This God is our God for ever and ever;* he shall be our guide for evermore.

Psalm 48:8–13

The Gloria

The Small Verse

And Peter opened his mouth and said: "Truly I perceive that God shows no
partiality, but in every nation any one who fears him and does what is right is
acceptable to him."

Acts 10:34–35

The Final Thanksgiving

I will greatly rejoice in the LORD, my soul shall exult in my God; for he has
clothed me with the garments of salvation, he has covered me with the robe of
righteousness, as a bridegroom decks himself with a garland, and as a bride
adorns herself with her jewels.

Isaiah 61:10

The Petition

May the Lord GOD, father of all mercy, grant us who dwell here a peaceful night
and a perfect end. *Amen.*

The Office of the Night Watch   Observed on the Hour or Half-Hour
Between 1:30 and 4:30 a.m.

The Call to Prayer

Behold now, bless the LORD, all you servants of the LORD,* you that stand by night
in the house of the LORD.
Lift up your hands in the holy place and bless the LORD;* the LORD who made
heaven and earth bless you out of Zion.

Psalm 134

388

The Request for Presence
O God, come to my assistance.
O Lord, make haste to help me.

The Greeting
The LORD is in his holy temple;* the LORD'S throne is in heaven.

Psalm 11:4

The Refrain for the Night Watch
The heavens declare the glory of God,* and the firmament shows his handiwork.
One day tells its tale to another,* and one night imparts knowledge to another.

Psalm 19:1–2

The Psalm   *Show Us Your Mercy*
You have been gracious to your land, O LORD,* you have restored the good fortune
    of Jacob.
You have forgiven the iniquity of your people* and blotted out all their sins.
You have withdrawn all your fury* and turned yourself from your wrathful
    indignation.
Restore us then, O God our Savior;* let your anger depart from us.
Will you be displeased with us for ever?* will you prolong your anger from age to
    age?
Will you not give us life again,* that your people may rejoice in you?
Show us your mercy, O LORD,* and grant us your salvation.

Psalm 85:1–7

The Refrain
The heavens declare the glory of God,* and the firmament shows his handiwork.
One day tells its tale to another,* and one night imparts knowledge to another.

A Reading
He said that all consists in one hearty renunciation of everything which we are
    aware does not lead to God and that we should accustom ourselves to a
    continual conversation with Him; that we need only to recognize God as
    intimately present with us in order to address ourselves to Him every moment;
    . . . and that in this conversation with God, we are also to be employed in
    praising, adoring, and loving Him incessantly for His infinite goodness and
    perfection.

Brother Lawrence (ca. 1605–91 CE), The Practice of the Presence of God

The Refrain
The heavens declare the glory of God,* and the firmament shows his handiwork.
One day tells its tale to another,* and one night imparts knowledge to another.

The Litany
For the peace from above, for the loving-kindness of God, and for the salvation of my soul, I pray to the Lord.
Lord, have mercy.
For the peace of the world, for the welfare of the Holy Church of God, and for the unity of all peoples, I pray to the Lord.
Lord, have mercy.
For my city [town, village], for every city and community, and for those who live in them, I pray to the Lord.
Lord, have mercy.
For seasonable weather, and for an abundance of the fruits of the earth, I pray to the Lord.
Lord, have mercy.
For the good earth which God has given us, and for the wisdom and will to conserve it, I pray to the Lord.
Lord, have mercy.
For deliverance from all danger, violence, oppression, and degradation, I pray to the Lord.
Lord, have mercy.
For the absolution and remission of my sins and offenses, I pray to the Lord.
Lord, have mercy.
Defend me, deliver me, and in your compassion protect me, O Lord, by your grace.
Lord, have mercy.

The Thanksgiving
Lord, you now have set your servant free to go in peace as you have promised; for these eyes of mine have seen the Savior whom you have prepared for all the world to see: A Light to enlighten the nations, and the glory of your people Israel. *Amen.*

Nunc Dimittis

The Final Petition
Now guide me waking, O Lord, and guard me sleeping; that awake I may watch with Christ, and asleep, I may rest in peace. *Amen.*

The Office of Dawn   **Observed on the Hour or Half-Hour**
                                  Between 4:30 and 7:30 a.m.

The Call to Prayer
Worship the LORD, O Jerusalem;* praise your God, O Zion;
For he has strengthened the bars of your gates.

Psalm 147:13–14a

The Request for Presence
O God, come to my assistance.
O Lord, make haste to help me.

The Greeting
Glory be to the Father, and the Son, and the Holy Spirit.
As it was in the beginning, it is now
And ever shall be, world without end. *Amen.*

Gloria Patri

The Hymn
Jesus shall reign where'er the sun
does its successive journeys run;
his kingdom spread from shore to shore,
till moons shall wax and wane no more.
To Jesus endless prayer be made,
and endless praises crown his head;
his name like sweet perfume shall rise
with every morning sacrifice.
People and realms of every tongue
dwell on his love with sweetest song;
and infant voices shall proclaim
their early blessings on his name.
Let every creature rise and bring
honors peculiar to our King;
angels descend with songs again,
and earth repeat the loud amen!

Isaac Watts

The Psalm   *The LORD Sends Out His Command to the Earth*
The LORD sends out his command to the earth,* and his word runs very swiftly.
He gives snow like wool;* he scatters hoarfrost like ashes.
He scatters his hail like bread crumbs;* who can stand against his cold?
He sends forth his word and melts them;* he blows with his wind, and the waters
    flow.

Psalm 147:16–19

The Gloria in Excelsis
Glory to God in the highest, and on earth peace to people of good will.
    We praise you.
    We bless you.
    We adore you.
    We glorify you.
We give thanks to you for your great glory.

The Small Verse
Jesus taught saying: "My father gives you the true bread from heaven. For the
    bread of God is that which comes down from heaven, and gives life to the
    world." And they said him, "Lord, give us this bread always." Jesus said to
    them, "I am the bread of life; he who comes to me shall not hunger; and he
    who believes in me shall never thirst."

John 6:32b—35

The Lord's Prayer

The Final Blessing
May the Lord bless us and keep us and cause His face to shine upon us from this
    day forth and forever more. *Amen.*

⁓

Tuesday, Month of November

The Office of Midnight   **Observed on the Hour or Half-Hour**
                                         Between 10:30 p.m.✠ and 1:30 a.m.

The Call to Prayer
I will bless the LORD who gives me counsel;* my heart teaches me, night after night.

Psalm 16:7

The Request for Presence
O LORD, let my prayer be set forth in your sight as incense,* the lifting up of my
    hands as the evening sacrifice.

Psalm 141:2, adapted

The Greeting
Our Father, may Your will be done, on earth as in Heaven.

The Canticle   *The Second Song of Isaiah*
                                        Quaerite Dominum

Seek the Lord while he wills to be found;*
    call upon him when he draws near.
Let the wicked forsake their ways*
    and the evil ones their thoughts;
And let them turn to the Lord, and he will have compassion,*
    and to our God, for he will richly pardon.
For my thoughts are not your thoughts,*
    nor your ways my ways, says the Lord.

For as the heavens are higher than the earth,*
    so are my ways higher than your ways, and my thoughts than your thoughts.
For as rain and snow fall from the heavens*
    and return not again, but water the earth,
Bringing forth life and giving growth,*
    seed for sowing and bread for eating,
So is my word that goes forth from my mouth;*
    it will not return to me empty;
But it will accomplish that which I have purposed,*
    and prosper in that for which I sent it.

Isaiah 55:6–11

The Psalm   *Boast No More*

"I will appoint a time," says God;* "I will judge with equity.
Though the earth and all its inhabitants are quaking,* I will make its pillars fast.
I will say to the boasters, 'Boast no more,'* and to the wicked, 'Do not toss your
    horns;
Do not toss your horns so high,* nor speak with a proud neck.'"
For judgment is neither from the east nor from the west,* nor yet from the
    wilderness or the mountains.
It is God who judges;* he puts down one and lifts up another.
For in the LORD's hand there is a cup, full of spiced and foaming wine, which he
    pours out,* and all the wicked of the earth shall drink and drain the dregs.
But I will rejoice for ever;* I will sing praises to the God of Jacob.

Psalm 75:2–9

The Gloria

The Small Verse

Now Jesus did many other signs in the presence of the disciples, which are not
    written in this book; but these are written that you may believe that Jesus is the
    Christ, the Son of God, and that believing you may have life in his name.

John 20:30–31

The Final Thanksgiving

I will greatly rejoice in the LORD, my soul shall exult in my God; for he has
    clothed me with the garments of salvation, he has covered me with the robe of
    righteousness, as a bridegroom decks himself with a garland, and as a bride
    adorns herself with her jewels.

Isaiah 61:10

The Petition

May the Lord GOD, father of all mercy, grant us who dwell here a peaceful night
    and a perfect end. *Amen*

The Office of the Night Watch   **Observed on the Hour or Half-Hour**
Between 1:30 and 4:30 a.m.

The Call to Prayer
Behold now, bless the LORD, all you servants of the LORD,* you that stand by night
in the house of the LORD.
Lift up your hands in the holy place and bless the LORD;* the LORD who made
heaven and earth bless you out of Zion.

Psalm 134

The Request for Presence
O God, come to my assistance.
O Lord, make haste to help me.

The Greeting
Show me your ways, O LORD,* and teach me your paths.
Lead me in your truth and teach me,* for you are the God of my salvation; in you
have I trusted all the day long.

Psalm 25:3–4

The Refrain for the Night Watch
The LORD grants his loving-kindness in the daytime;* in the night season his song
is with me, a prayer to the God of my life.

Psalm 42:10

The Psalm   *Yours Are the Heavens*
Yours are the heavens; the earth also is yours;* you laid the foundations of the
world and all that is in it.
You have made the north and the south;* Tabor and Hermon rejoice in your Name.
You have a mighty arm;* strong is your hand and high is your right hand.
Righteousness and justice are the foundations of your throne;* love and truth go
before your face.
Happy are the people who know the festal shout!* they walk, O LORD, in the light
of your presence.

Psalm 89:11–15

The Refrain
The LORD grants his loving-kindness in the daytime;* in the night season his song
is with me, a prayer to the God of my life.

A Reading
Repentance effaces every sin when there is no delay in coming to it after the fall
of the soul, for thus the disease is not allowed to go on through a long interval.
Evil will not have the power to leave its mark in us, if it is drawn up at the
moment of its being set down like a plant newly planted.

Methodius, Bishop of Lycia, martyred ca. 311, Discourse Concerning the Martyrs

The Refrain

The LORD grants his loving-kindness in the daytime;* in the night season his song
is with me, a prayer to the God of my life.

The Litany

O God the Father, Creator of heaven and earth,
Have mercy upon me.
O God the Son, Redeemer of the world,
Have mercy upon me.
O God the Holy Spirit, Sanctifier of the faithful,
Have mercy upon me.
O holy, blessed, and glorious Trinity, one God,
Have mercy upon me.
Remember not, Lord Christ, my offenses, nor the offenses of my forefathers;
neither reward me according to my sins. Spare me, good Lord, spare your
people, whom you have redeemed with your most precious blood, and by your
mercy preserve us, for ever.
Spare us, good Lord.

The Thanksgiving

Lord, you now have set your servant free to go in peace as you have promised; for
these eyes of mine have seen the Savior whom you have prepared for all the
world to see: A Light to enlighten the nations, and the glory of your people
Israel. *Amen.*

Nunc Dimittis

The Final Petition

Now guide me waking, O Lord, and guard me sleeping; that awake I may watch
with Christ, and asleep, I may rest in peace. *Amen.*

The Office of Dawn
**Observed on the Hour or Half-Hour
Between 4:30 and 7:30 a.m.**

The Call to Prayer

Hallelujah! Praise the LORD from the heavens;* praise him in the heights.

Psalm 148:1

The Request for Presence

My soul waits for the LORD, more than watchmen for the morning,* more than
watchmen for the morning.

Psalm 130:5

The Greeting

Glory be to the Father, and the Son, and the Holy Spirit.
As it was in the beginning, it is now
And ever shall be, world without end. *Amen.*

Gloria Patri

The Hymn

Take my life, and let it be consecrated, Lord, to you.
Take my moments and my days; let them flow in ceaseless praise.
Take my hands, and let them move at the impulse of your love.
Take my feet, and let them be swift and beautiful for you.
Take my voice, and let me sing always, only, for my King.
Take my lips, and let them be filled with messages from you.
Take my silver and my gold; not a mite would I withhold.
Take my intellect, and use every power as you shall choose.
Take my will, and make it yours; it shall be no longer mine.
Take my heart, it is yours alone; it shall be your royal throne.
Take my love, my Lord, I pour at your feet its treasured store.
Take myself, and I will be, ever, always then with Thee.

Frances R. Havergal, adapted

The Psalm   *Praise the LORD from the Heavens*

Praise the LORD from the heavens;* praise him in the heights.
Praise him, all you angels of his;* praise him, all his host.
Praise him, sun and moon;* praise him, all you shining stars.
Praise him, heaven of heavens,* and you waters above the heavens.
Let them praise the Name of the LORD ;* for he commanded, and they were
    created.
He made them stand fast for ever and ever;* he gave them a law which shall not
    pass away.

Psalm 148:1b–6

The Gloria in Excelsis

Glory to God in the highest, and on earth peace to people of good will.
    We praise you.
    We bless you.
    We adore you.
    We glorify you.
We give thanks to you for your great glory.

The Small Verse

They shall come and sing aloud on the heights of Zion, and they shall be radiant
    over the goodness of the LORD, over the grain, the wine, and the oil, and over
    the young of the flock and the herd; their life shall be like a watered garden,
    and they shall languish no more. Then shall the maidens rejoice in the dance,
    and the young men and the old shall be merry. I will turn their mourning into
    joy, I will comfort them, and give them gladness for sorrow. I will feast the soul
    of the priests with abundance, and my people shall be satisfied with my
    goodness, says the LORD.

Jeremiah 31:12–14

The Lord's Prayer

The Final Blessing
May the Lord bless us and keep us and cause His face to shine upon us from this
day forth and forever more. *Amen.*

꒱

Wednesday, Month of November

The Office of Midnight   **Observed on the Hour or Half-Hour**
                                              Between 10:30 p.m.✚ and 1:30 a.m.

The Call to Prayer
Sing praises to God, sing praises;* sing praises to our King, sing praises.

Psalm 47:6

The Request for Presence
O LORD, let my prayer be set forth in your sight as incense,* the lifting up of my
hands as the evening sacrifice.

Psalm 141:2, adapted

The Greeting
Our Father, give us this day our daily bread.

The Canticle   **The Song of the Redeemed**
                                              Magna et mirabilia
O ruler of the universe, Lord God, great deeds are they that you have done,*
surpassing human understanding.
Your ways are ways of righteousness and truth,*
O King of all the ages.
Who can fail to do you homage, Lord, and sing the praises of your Name?*
for you only are the Holy One.
All nations will draw near and fall down before you,*
because your just and holy works have been revealed.
Glory to the Father, and to the Son, and to the Holy Spirit:*
as it was in the beginning, is now, and will be for ever. *Amen.*

Revelation 15:3–4

The Psalm   **Be Still and Know**
The LORD of hosts is with us;* the God of Jacob is our stronghold.
Come now and look upon the works of the LORD,* what awesome things he has
done on earth.

It is he who makes war to cease in all the world;* he breaks the bow, and shatters the spear, and burns the shields with fire.
"Be still, then, and know that I am God;* I will be exalted among the nations; I will be exalted in the earth."
The LORD of hosts is with us;* the God of Jacob is our stronghold.

Psalm 46:8–12

The Gloria

The Small Verse
Cast all your anxieties on him, for he cares about you.

1 Peter 5:7

The Final Thanksgiving
I will greatly rejoice in the LORD, my soul shall exult in my God; for he has clothed me with the garments of salvation, he has covered me with the robe of righteousness, as a bridegroom decks himself with a garland, and as a bride adorns herself with her jewels.

Isaiah 61:10

The Petition
May the Lord GOD, father of all mercy, grant us who dwell here a peaceful night and a perfect end. *Amen.*

The Office of the Night Watch   Observed on the Hour or Half-Hour Between 1:30 and 4:30 a.m.

The Call to Prayer
Behold now, bless the LORD, all you servants of the LORD,* you that stand by night in the house of the LORD.
Lift up your hands in the holy place and bless the LORD;* the LORD who made heaven and earth bless you out of Zion.

Psalm 134

The Request for Presence
O God, come to my assistance.
O Lord, make haste to help me.

The Greeting
O LORD, what are we that you should care for us?* mere mortals that you should think of us?
We are like a puff of wind;* our days are like a passing shadow.

Psalm 144:3–4

398

The Refrain for the Night Watch

Yours is the day, yours also the night;* you established the moon and the sun.

Psalm 74:15

The Psalm

Sing to the LORD

I will exalt you, O LORD, because you have lifted me up* and have not let my
  enemies triumph over me.

O LORD my God, I cried out to you,* and you restored me to health.

You brought me up, O LORD, from the dead;* you restored my life as I was going
  down to the grave.

Sing to the LORD, you servants of his;* give thanks for the remembrance of his
  holiness.

Psalm 30:1–4

The Refrain

Yours is the day, yours also the night;* you established the moon and the sun.

A Reading

The one peaceful and trustworthy tranquility, the one solid and firm and constant
  security, is this: for a man to withdraw from these eddies of a distracting world
  and, anchored on the ground of the harbor of salvation, to lift his eyes from
  earth to heaven . . . for when the soul, in its gaze into heaven, has recognized
  its Author, it rises higher than the sun and far transcends all earthly power and
  begins to be that which it believes itself to be.

Cyprian, Bishop of Carthage (d. 258 CE), The Epistles

The Refrain

Yours is the day, yours also the night;* you established the moon and the sun.

The Litany

From all evil and wickedness; from sin; from the crafts and assaults of the devil;
  and from everlasting damnation,
  Good Lord, deliver me.

From all blindness of heart; from pride, vainglory, and hypocrisy; from envy,
  hatred, and malice; and from all want of charity,
  Good Lord, deliver me.

From all inordinate and sinful affections; and from all the deceits of the world, the
  flesh, and the devil,
  Good Lord, deliver me.

From all false doctrine, heresy, and schism; from hardness of heart, and contempt
  of your Word and commandment,
  Good Lord, deliver me.

By the mystery of your holy Incarnation; by your holy Nativity and submission to
  the Law; by your Baptism, Fasting, and Temptation,
  Good Lord, deliver me.

399

In all time of tribulation; in all time of prosperity; in the hour of death, and in the
day of judgment,
> Good Lord, deliver me.

The Thanksgiving

Lord, you now have set your servant free to go in peace as you have promised; for
these eyes of mine have seen the Savior whom you have prepared for all the
world to see: A Light to enlighten the nations, and the glory of your people
Israel. *Amen.*

Nunc Dimittis

The Final Petition

Now guide me waking, O Lord, and guard me sleeping; that awake I may watch
with Christ, and asleep, I may rest in peace. *Amen.*

The Office of Dawn   Observed on the Hour or Half-Hour
Between 4:30 and 7:30 a.m.

The Call to Prayer

Hallelujah! Sing to the LORD a new song;* sing his praise in the congregation of
the faithful.

Psalm 149:1

The Request for Presence

My soul waits for the LORD, more than watchmen for the morning,* more than
watchmen for the morning.

Psalm 130:5

The Greeting

Glory be to the Father, and the Son, and the Holy Spirit.
As it was in the beginning, it is now
And ever shall be, world without end. *Amen.*

Gloria Patri

The Hymn   *Venite, exultemus*

Come, let us sing to the LORD;* let us shout for joy to the Rock of our salvation.
Let us come before his presence with thanksgiving* and raise a loud shout to him
with psalms.
For the LORD is a great God,* and a great King above all gods.
In his hand are the caverns of the earth,* and the heights of the hills are his also.
The sea is his, for he made it,* and his hands have molded the dry land.
Come, let us bow down, and bend the knee,* and kneel before the LORD our Maker.
For he is our God, and we are the people of his pasture and the sheep of his hand.*
Oh, that today you would hearken to his voice!

Psalm 95:1–7

The Psalm   *Praise the* LORD
Praise the LORD from the earth,* you sea-monsters and all deeps;
Fire and hail, snow and fog,* tempestuous wind, doing his will;
Mountains and all hills,* fruit trees and all cedars;
Wild beasts and all cattle,* creeping things and winged birds;
Kings of the earth and all peoples,* princes and all rulers of the world;
Young men and maidens,* old and young together.
Let them praise the Name of the LORD,*

Psalm 148:7–13a

The Gloria in Excelsis
Glory to God in the highest, and on earth peace to people of good will.
    We praise you.
    We bless you.
    We adore you.
    We glorify you.
We give thanks to you for your great glory.

The Small Verse
Rejoice in the Lord always; again I will say, Rejoice. Let all men know your
    forbearance. The Lord is at hand. Have no anxiety about anything, but in
    everything by prayer and supplication with thanksgiving let your requests be
    made known to God. And the peace of God which passes all understanding will
    keep your hearts and minds in Christ Jesus.

Philippians 4:4–7

The Lord's Prayer

The Final Blessing
May the Lord bless us and keep us and cause His face to shine upon us from this
    day forth and forever more. *Amen.*

༅

Thursday, Month of November

The Office of Midnight   **Observed on the Hour or Half-Hour**
                                              Between 10:30 p.m.✛ and 1:30 a.m.

The Call to Prayer
The LORD lives! Blessed is my Rock!* Exalted is the God of my salvation!

Psalm 18:46

The Request for Presence
O LORD, let my prayer be set forth in your sight as incense,* the lifting up of my
hands as the evening sacrifice.

Psalm 141:2, adapted

The Greeting
Our Father, forgive us our sins as we forgive those who have sinned against us..

The Canticle   *Song of Praise*
Benedictus es, Domine

Glory to you, Lord God of our fathers;*
    you are worthy of praise; glory to you.
Glory to you for the radiance of you holy Name;*
    we will praise you and highly exalt you for ever.
Glory to you in the splendor of you temple;*
    on the throne of your majesty, glory to you.
Glory to you, seated between the Cherubim;*
    we will praise you and highly exalt you for ever.
Glory to you, beholding the depths;*
    in the high vault of heaven, glory to you.
Glory to you, Father, Son, and Holy Spirit;*
    we will praise you and highly exalt you for ever.

Song of the Three Young Men, 29–34

The Psalm   *Tremble, O Earth, at the Presence of the Lord*
Hallelujah! When Israel came out of Egypt,* the house of Jacob from a people of
    strange speech,
Judah became God's sanctuary* and Israel his dominion.
The sea beheld it and fled;* Jordan turned and went back.
The mountains skipped like rams,* and the little hills like young sheep.
What ailed you, O sea, that you fled?* O Jordan, that you turned back?
You mountains, that you skipped like rams?* you little hills like young sheep?
Tremble, O earth, at the presence of the Lord,* at the presence of the God of Jacob,
Who turned the hard rock into a pool of water* and flint-stone into a flowing spring.

Psalm 114

The Gloria

The Small Verse
Love does no wrong to a neighbor; therefore love is the fulfilling of the law.

Romans 13:10

The Final Thanksgiving
I will greatly rejoice in the LORD, my soul shall exult in my God; for he has
    clothed me with the garments of salvation, he has covered me with the robe of

righteousness, as a bridegroom decks himself with a garland, and as a bride adorns herself with her jewels.

Isaiah 61:10

The Petition

May the Lord GOD, father of all mercy, grant us who dwell here a peaceful night and a perfect end. *Amen.*

The Office of the Night Watch   Observed on the Hour or Half-Hour Between 1:30 and 4:30 a.m.

The Call to Prayer

Behold now, bless the LORD, all you servants of the LORD,* you that stand by night in the house of the LORD.
Lift up your hands in the holy place and bless the LORD;* the LORD who made heaven and earth bless you out of Zion.

Psalm 134

The Request for Presence

O God, come to my assistance.
O Lord, make haste to help me.

The Greeting

More to be desired are your words than gold, more than much fine gold,* sweeter far than honey, than honey in the comb.

Psalm 19:10, adapted

The Refrain for the Night Watch

I commune with my heart in the night;* I ponder and search my mind.

Psalm 77:6

The Psalm   The Right Hand of the LORD Has Triumphed

The LORD is my strength and my song,* and he has become my salvation.
There is a sound of exultation and victory* in the tents of the righteous:
"The right hand of the LORD has triumphed!* the right hand of the LORD is exalted! the right hand of the LORD has triumphed!"
I shall not die, but live,* and declare the works of the LORD.

Psalm 118:14–17

The Refrain

I commune with my heart in the night;* I ponder and search my mind.

A Reading

Our Lord says, "I say unto you all, watch and pray." All of us, therefore, may, and all of us ought, to practice prayer. I grant that meditation is attainable, but by only a few; for few are capable of it. Therefore, my beloved brethren who are athirst for salvation, meditative prayer is not the prayer God requires of you, nor the one which I would recommend. . . . You must learn a species of prayer which can be exercised at all times, which does not obstruct outward employments, and which may be equally practiced by princes, kings, priests, soldiers, laborers, the sick, and children. It must not be a prayer of the head, but of the heart . . . for the prayer of the heart is not interrupted by the exercises of reason.

Madame Guyon (17th c. French mystic), A Short and Easy Method of Prayer

The Refrain
I commune with my heart in the night;* I ponder and search my mind.

Litany
That it may please you to bless and keep all your people,
> *I beseech you to hear me, good Lord.*
That it may please you to send laborers into your harvest and to draw all
humankind into your kingdom,
> *I beseech you to hear me, good Lord.*
That it may please you to give to all people increase of grace to hear and receive
your Word, and to bring forth the fruits of the Spirit,
> *I beseech you to hear me, good Lord.*
That it may please you to bring into the way of truth all such as have erred, and
are deceived,
> *I beseech you to hear me, good Lord.*
That it may please you to give me a heart to love and fear you, and diligently to
live after your commandments,
> *I beseech you to hear me, good Lord.*

The Thanksgiving
Lord, you now have set your servant free to go in peace as you have promised; for
these eyes of mine have seen the Savior whom you have prepared for all the
world to see: A Light to enlighten the nations, and the glory of your people
Israel. *Amen.*

Nunc Dimittis

The Final Petition
Now guide me waking, O Lord, and guard me sleeping; that awake I may watch
with Christ, and asleep, I may rest in peace. *Amen.*

The Office of Dawn   **Observed on the Hour or Half-Hour**
Between 4:30 and 7:30 a.m.

The Call to Prayer

Hallelujah! Praise the LORD, O my soul!* I will praise the LORD as long as I live; I
   will sing praises to my God while I have my being.

Psalm 146:1

The Request for Presence

My soul waits for the LORD, more than watchmen for the morning,* more than
   watchmen for the morning.

Psalm 130:5

The Greeting

Glory be to the Father, and the Son, and the Holy Spirit.
As it was in the beginning, it is now
And ever shall be, world without end. *Amen.*

Gloria Patri

The Hymn

Jesus, united by your grace
and each to each endeared,
with confidence we seek your face
and know our prayer is heard.
Help us to help each other, Lord,
each other's cross to bear;
let all, their friendly aid afford,
and feel each other's care.
To you, inseparably joined,
let all our spirits cleave;
O may we all the loving mind
that was first in you, now receive.

Charles Wesley, adapted

The Psalm   *He Covers the Heavens with Clouds*

He covers the heavens with clouds* and prepares rain for the earth;
He makes grass to grow upon the mountains* and green plants to serve mankind.
He provides food for flocks and herds* and for the young ravens when they cry.
He is not impressed by the might of a horse;* he has no pleasure in the strength of
   a man;
But the LORD has pleasure in those who fear him,* in those who await his gracious
   favor.

Psalm 147:8–12

The Gloria in Excelsis
Glory to God in the highest, and on earth peace to people of good will.
We praise you.
We bless you.
We adore you.
We glorify you.
We give thanks to you for your great glory.

The Small Verse
When you come into the land which the LORD your God gives you for an
inheritance, and have taken possession of it, and live in it, you shall take some
of the first of all the fruit of the ground, which you harvest from your land that
the LORD your God gives you, and you shall put it in a basket, and you shall go
to the place which the LORD your God will choose, to make his name dwell
there. . . . Then the priest shall take the basket from your hand, and set it down
before the altar of LORD your God.

Deuteronomy 26: 1ff

The Lord's Prayer

The Final Blessing
May the Lord bless us and keep us and cause His face to shine upon us from this
day forth and forever more. *Amen.*

⌘

Friday, Month of November

The Office of Midnight   **Observed on the Hour or Half-Hour
Between 10:30 p.m.✛ and 1:30 a.m.**

The Call to Prayer
Let all who seek you rejoice in you and be glad;* let those who love your
salvation continually say, "Great is the LORD!"

Psalm 40: 17

The Request for Presence
O LORD let my prayer be set forth in your sight as incense,* the lifting up of my
hands as the evening sacrifice.

Psalm 141: 2, adapted

406

The Greeting
Our Father, lead us not into temptation, but deliver us from evil.

The Canticle   *A Song of Penitence*
Kyrie Pantokrator

O Lord and Ruler of the hosts of heaven,*
    God of Abraham, Isaac, and Jacob, and of all their righteous offspring:
You made the heavens and the earth,*
    with all their vast array.
All things quake with fear at your presence;*
    they tremble because of your power.
But your merciful promise is beyond all measure;*
    it surpasses all that our minds can fathom.
O Lord, you are full of compassion,*
    long-suffering, and abounding in mercy.
You hold back your hand;*
    you do not punish as we deserve.
In your great goodness, Lord, you have promised forgiveness to sinners,*
    that they may repent of their sin and be saved.

Prayer of Manasseh 1–2, 4, 6–7

The Psalm   *You, O LORD, Are My Lamp*
With the faithful you show yourself faithful, O God;* with the forthright you show
    yourself forthright.
With the pure you show yourself pure,* but with the crooked you are wily.
You will save a lowly people,* but you will humble the haughty eyes.
You, O LORD, are my lamp;* my God, you make my darkness bright.

Psalm 18:26–29

The Gloria

The Small Verse
Never flag in zeal, be aglow with the Spirit, serve the Lord.

Romans 12:11

The Final Thanksgiving
I will greatly rejoice in the LORD, my soul shall exult in my God; for he has
    clothed me with the garments of salvation, he has covered me with the robe of
    righteousness, as a bridegroom decks himself with a garland, and as a bride
    adorns herself with her jewels.

Isaiah 61:10

The Petition
May the Lord GOD, father of all mercy, grant us who dwell here a peaceful night
    and a perfect end. *Amen.*

The Office of the Night Watch   **Observed on the Hour or Half-Hour**
Between 1:30 and 4:30 a.m.

The Call to Prayer
Behold now, bless the LORD, all you servants of the LORD,* you that stand by night
     in the house of the LORD.
Lift up your hands in the holy place and bless the LORD;* the LORD who made
     heaven and earth bless you out of Zion.

Psalm 134

The Request for Presence
O God, come to my assistance.
O Lord, make haste to help me.

The Greeting
When your word goes forth it gives light;* it gives understanding to the simple.

Psalm 119:130

The Refrain for the Night Watch
You shall not be afraid of any terror by night,* nor of the arrow that flies by day;

Psalm 91:5

The Psalm   *Deliver Me, O LORD*
Deliver me, O LORD, by your hand* from those whose portion in life is this world;
Whose bellies you fill with your treasure,* who are well supplied with children
     and leave their wealth to their little ones.
But at my vindication I shall see your face;* when I awake, I shall be satisfied,
     beholding your likeness.

Psalm 17:14–16

The Refrain
You shall not be afraid of any terror by night,* nor of the arrow that flies by day;

A Reading
Just as no one comes to wisdom except through grace, justice, and knowledge, so
     no one comes to contemplation except through intentioned thought, holy
     deportment, and devout prayer. Therefore, as grace is the foundation of the
     rectitude of the will and of the brightening of the reason, so at first we must
     pray. Then we live holily, then consider the wondrous evidences of truth and by
     understanding them, ascend gradually until we come at last to the exalted
     mountain where "there is seen the God of gods in Zion."

St. Bonaventure of Bagnoregio (13th c.), The Journey of the Mind into God

The Refrain
You shall not be afraid of any terror by night,* nor of the arrow that flies by day.

The Litany

That it may please you to show your mercy to all prisoners and captives, the homeless and the hungry, and all who are desolate and oppressed,
> *I beseech you to hear me, good Lord.*

That it may please you to give and preserve to our use the bountiful fruits of the earth, so that in due time all may enjoy them,
> *I beseech you to hear me, good Lord.*

That it may please you to inspire all your people, in our several callings, to do the work which you gave us to do with singleness of heart as your servants, and for the common good,
> *I beseech you to hear me, good Lord.*

That it may please you to visit the lonely; to strengthen all who suffer in mind, body, and spirit; and to comfort with your presence those who are failing and infirm,
> *I beseech you to hear me, good Lord.*

That it may please you to strengthen such as do stand; to comfort and help the weak-hearted; to raise up those who fall; and finally to beat down Satan under our feet,
> *I beseech you to hear me, good Lord.*

That it may please you to grant to all the faithful departed eternal life and peace,
> *I beseech you to hear me, good Lord.*

That it may please you to grant that, in the fellowship of all your saints, I may attain to your heavenly kingdom,
> *Son of God, I beseech you to hear me.*
> *Son of God, I beseech you to hear me.*

The Thanksgiving

Lord, you now have set your servant free to go in peace as you have promised; for these eyes of mine have seen the Savior whom you have prepared for all the world to see: A Light to enlighten the nations, and the glory of your people Israel. *Amen.*

Nunc Dimittis

The Final Petition

Now guide me waking, O Lord, and guard me sleeping; that awake I may watch with Christ, and asleep, I may rest in peace. *Amen.*

The Office of Dawn   **Observed on the Hour or Half-Hour Between 4:30 and 7:30 a.m.**

The Call to Prayer

Hallelujah! How good it is to sing praises to our God!* how pleasant it is to honor him with praise!

Psalm 147:1

409

The Request for Presence

My soul waits for the LORD, more than watchmen for the morning,* more than
watchmen for the morning.

Psalm 130:5

The Greeting

Glory be to the Father, and the Son, and the Holy Spirit.
As it was in the beginning, it is now
And ever shall be, world without end. *Amen.*

Gloria Patri

The Hymn

O food to pilgrims given,
O bread of life from heaven,
O manna from on high!
We hunger; Lord, supply us,
nor your delights deny us,
whose hearts to you draw nigh.
O Jesus, by you bidden,
we here adore you, hidden
in forms of bread and wine.
Grant when the veil is risen,
we may behold, in heaven,
your countenance divine.

15th c. German hymn, translated by John Athelstan and Laurie Riley

The Psalm   The LORD Takes Pleasure in His People

Let Israel rejoice in his Maker;* let the children of Zion be joyful in their King.
Let them praise his Name in the dance;* let them sing praise to him with timbrel
and harp.
For the LORD takes pleasure in his people* and adorns the poor with victory.
Let the faithful rejoice in triumph;* let them be joyful on their beds.

Psalm 149:2–5

The Gloria in Excelsis

Glory to God in the highest, and on earth peace to people of good will.
   We praise you.
   We bless you.
   We adore you.
   We glorify you.
We give thanks to you for your great glory.

The Small Verse

Do not be deceived, my beloved brethren. Every good endowment and every
   perfect gift is from above, coming down from the Father of lights with whom

410

there is no variation or shadow of change. Of his own will he brought us forth by the word of truth, that we should be a kind of first fruits of his creation.

James 1:16–18

The Lord's Prayer

The Final Blessing
May the Lord bless us and keep us and cause His face to shine upon us from this day forth and forever more. *Amen.*

꒕

Saturday, Month of November

The Office of Midnight   **Observed on the Hour or Half-Hour Between 10:30 p.m.✢ and 1:30 a.m.**

The Call to Prayer
Praise the LORD, you that fear him;* stand in awe of him, O offspring of Israel; all you of Jacob's line, give glory.

Psalm 22:22

The Request for Presence
O LORD, let my prayer be set forth in your sight as incense,* the lifting up of my hands as the evening sacrifice.

Psalm 141:2, adapted

The Greeting
Our Father, Yours are the kingdom, the power, and the glory forever.

The Canticle   **The First Song of Isaiah**
Ecce, Deus

Surely, it is God who saves me;*
    I will trust in him and not be afraid.
For the Lord is my stronghold and my sure defense,*
    and he will be my Savior.
Therefore you shall draw water with rejoicing*
    from the springs of salvation.
And on that day you shall say,*
    give thanks to the Lord and call upon his Name;
Make his deeds known among the peoples;*
    see that they remember that his Name is exalted.

411

Sing praises of the Lord, for he has done great things,*
and this is known in all the world.
Cry aloud, inhabitants of Zion, ring out your joy,*
for the great one in the midst of you is the Holy One of Israel.

Isaiah 12:2–6

The Psalm — Lift up Your Heads, O Gates

Such is the generation of those who seek him,* of those who seek your face,
O God of Jacob.
Lift up your heads, O gates; lift them high, O everlasting doors;* and the King of
glory shall come in.
"Who is this King of glory?"* "The Lord, strong and mighty, the Lord, mighty in
battle."
Lift up your heads, O gates; lift them high, O everlasting doors;* and the King of
glory shall come in.
"Who is he, this King of glory?"* "The Lord of hosts, he is the King of glory."

Psalm 24:6–10

The Gloria

The Small Verse

He looked up and saw the rich putting their gifts into the treasury; and he saw a
poor widow put in two copper coins. And he said, "Truly I tell you, this poor
widow has put in more than all of them; for they all contributed out of their
abundance, but she out of her poverty put in all the living she had."

Luke 21:1–4

The Final Thanksgiving

I will greatly rejoice in the Lord, my soul shall exult in my God; for he has
clothed me with the garments of salvation, he has covered me with the robe of
righteousness, as a bridegroom decks himself with a garland, and as a bride
adorns herself with her jewels.

Isaiah 61:10

The Petition

May the Lord God, father of all mercy, grant us who dwell here a peaceful night
and a perfect end. *Amen*

The Office of the Night Watch — Observed on the Hour or Half-Hour Between 1:30 and 4:30 a.m.

The Call to Prayer

Behold now, bless the Lord, all you servants of the Lord,* you that stand by night
in the house of the Lord.

Lift up your hands in the holy place and bless the LORD;* the LORD who made heaven and earth bless you out of Zion.

Psalm 134

The Request for Presence
O God, come to my assistance.
O Lord, make haste to help me.

The Greeting
As the deer longs for the water-brooks,* so longs my soul for you, O God.

Psalm 42:1

The Refrain for the Night Watch
It is a good thing to give thanks to the LORD,* and to sing praises to your Name, O Most High;
To tell of your loving-kindness early in the morning* and of your faithfulness in the night season.

Psalm 92:1–2

The Psalm   Incline Your Ear to Me
In you, O LORD, have I taken refuge; let me never be put to shame;* deliver me in your righteousness.
Incline your ear to me;* make haste to deliver me.
Be my strong rock, a castle to keep me safe, for you are my crag and my stronghold;* for the sake of your Name, lead me and guide me.

Psalm 31:1–3

The Refrain
It is a good thing to give thanks to the LORD,* and to sing praises to your Name, O Most High;
To tell of your loving-kindness early in the morning* and of your faithfulness in the night season.

A Reading
Virtue seeks and finds Him who is the Author and Giver of all good and who must in all things be glorified . . . for it is hard—nay, rather, it is impossible—for a person by and of his own strength alone or depending solely on the power of his own free-will truly to render all things unto God from whom they came. Rather, he will turn them to his own uses and to his own benefit, even as it is written, "The imagination of Man's heart is evil from his youth."

Bernard of Clairvaux (1091–1153 CE), On Loving God

The Refrain
It is a good thing to give thanks to the LORD,* and to sing praises to your Name, O Most High;

413

To tell of your loving-kindness early in the morning* and of your faithfulness in the night season.

The Litany

For the peace from above, for the loving-kindness of God, and for the salvation of my soul, I pray to the Lord.
Lord, have mercy.
For the peace of the world, for the welfare of the Holy Church of God, and for the unity of all peoples, I pray to the Lord.
Lord, have mercy.
For the leaders of the nations and for all in authority, I pray to the Lord.
Lord, have mercy.
For the aged and infirm, for the widowed and orphans, and for the sick and the suffering, I pray to the Lord.
Lord, have mercy.
For the poor and the oppressed, for the unemployed and the destitute, for prisoners and captives, and for all who remember and care for them, I pray to the Lord.
Lord, have mercy.
For all who have died in the hope of the resurrection, and for all the departed, I pray to the Lord.
Lord, have mercy.

The Thanksgiving

Lord, you now have set your servant free to go in peace as you have promised; for these eyes of mine have seen the Savior whom you have prepared for all the world to see: A Light to enlighten the nations, and the glory of your people Israel. *Amen.*

Nunc Dimittis

The Final Petition

Now guide me waking, O Lord, and guard me sleeping; that awake I may watch with Christ, and asleep, I may rest in peace. *Amen.*

The Office of Dawn   **Observed on the Hour or Half-Hour**
                                          Between 4:30 and 7:30 a.m.

The Call to Prayer

Let everything that has breath* praise the LORD. Hallelujah!

Psalm 150:6

The Request for Presence

My soul waits for the LORD, more than watchmen for the morning,* more than watchmen for the morning.

Psalm 130:5

414

The Greeting

Glory be to the Father, and the Son, and the Holy Spirit.
As it was in the beginning, it is now
And ever shall be, world without end. *Amen.*

Gloria Patri

The Hymn

Sing praise to God Who reigns above, the God of all creation,
The God of power, the God of love, the God of our salvation.
With healing balm my soul is filled and every faithless murmur stilled:
    To God all praise and glory.
What God's almighty power has made His gracious mercy keeps,
By morning glow or evening shade His watchful eye never sleeps;
Within the kingdom of His might, Lo! all is just and all is right:
    To God all praise and glory.
Thus, all my toilsome way along, I sing aloud Your praises,
That earth may hear the grateful song my voice unwearied raises.
Be joyful in the Lord, my heart, both soul and body bear your part:
    To God all praise and glory.

Johann J. Schutz, translated by Frances E. Cox

The Psalm   *Let Everything That Has Breath Praise the* LORD

Praise him for his mighty acts;* praise him for his excellent greatness.
Praise him with the blast of the ram's-horn;* praise him with lyre and harp.
Praise him with timbrel and dance;* praise him with strings and pipe.
Praise him with resounding cymbals;* praise him with loud-clanging cymbals.
Let everything that has breath* praise the LORD. Hallelujah!

Psalm 150:2–6

The Gloria in Excelsis

Glory to God in the highest, and on earth peace to people of good will.
    We praise you.
    We bless you.
    We adore you.
    We glorify you.
We give thanks to you for your great glory.

The Small Verse

And Jesus prayed, saying: "O righteous Father, the world has not known thee, but
    I have known thee; and these know that thou hast sent me. I made known to
    them thy name, and I will make it known, that the love with which thou hast
    loved me may be in them, and I in them."

John 17:25–26

415

The Lord's Prayer

The Final Blessing
May the Lord bless us and keep us and cause His face to shine upon us from this day forth and forever more. *Amen.*

The Gloria
Glory be to God the Father, God the Son, and God the Holy Spirit. As it was
in the beginning, so it is now and so it shall ever be, world without end.
Alleluia. *Amen.*

The Lord's Prayer
Our Father, who art in heaven, hallowed be your Name.
May your kingdom come, and your will be done, on earth as in heaven.
Give us today our daily bread.
Forgive us our sins as we forgive those who sin against us.
Lead us not into temptation, but deliver us from evil;
for yours are the kingdom and the power and the glory
forever and ever. *Amen*

The following major holy days occur in December:
The Eve of the Nativity of Our Lord: *December 24*
The Feast of the Nativity of Our Lord: *December 25*
The Feast of St. Stephen: *December 26*
The Feast of St. John: *December 27*
The Commemoration of the Holy Innocents: *December 28*
The Feast of the Holy Family: *December 30*
The Eve of the Feast of the Holy Name: *December 31*

Prayer for use in the observation of a holy day:
Almighty God, by your Holy Spirit you have made us one with your saints in
heaven and on earth: Grant that in my earthly pilgrimage, I may always be
supported by this fellowship of love and prayer, and know myself to be
surrounded by their witness to your power and mercy. I ask this for the sake of
Jesus Christ, in whom all my intercessions are acceptable through the
Spirit, and who lives and reigns forever and ever. *Amen.*

✤ The Office of Midnight is always taken from the prayers for the day nearest
to the hour of actual observation. Thus, if the office is to be observed at 10:30 p.m.
on Sunday, the prayers will be taken from the Monday offices, and so forth.

DECEMBER

Sunday, Month of December

The Office of Midnight   **Observed on the Hour or Half-Hour**
                                    Between 10:30 p.m.✛ and 1:30 a.m.

The Call to Prayer
Happy are the people who know the festal shout!* they walk, O LORD, in the light
of your presence.

Psalm 89:15

The Request for Presence
O LORD, let my prayer be set forth in your sight as incense,* the lifting up of my
hands as the evening sacrifice.

Psalm 141:2, adapted

The Greeting
Our Father Who art in Heaven, hallowed be Your name.

The Canticle   *The Song of Zechariah*
                                                  Benedictus Dominus Deus

Blessed be the Lord, the God of Israel;*
   he has come to his people and set them free.
He has raised up for us a mighty savior,*
   born of the house of his servant David.
Through his holy prophets he promised of old, that he would save us from our
   enemies,*
   from the hands of all who hate us.
He promised to show mercy to our fathers*
   and to remember his holy covenant.
This was the oath he swore to our father Abraham,*
   to set us free from the hands of our enemies,
Free to worship him without fear,*
   holy and righteous in his sight all the days of our life.

Luke 1:68–75

The Psalm   *The LORD Said Rule Over Your Enemies*
The LORD said to my Lord, "Sit at my right hand,* until I make your enemies your
   footstool."
The LORD will send the scepter of your power out of Zion,* saying, "Rule over
   your enemies round about you.
Princely state has been yours from the day of your birth;* in the beauty of holiness
   have I begotten you, like dew from the womb of the morning."

The LORD has sworn and he will not recant:* "You are a priest for ever after the order of Melchizedek."

Psalm 110:1–4

The Gloria

The Small Verse

In many and various ways God spoke of old to our fathers by the prophets; but in these last days he has spoken to us by a Son, whom he appointed heir of all things, through whom also he created the world.

Hebrews 1:1–2

The Final Thanksgiving

I will greatly rejoice in the Lord, my soul shall exult in my God; for he has clothed me with the garments of salvation, he has covered me with the robe of righteousness, as a bridegroom decks himself with a garland, and as a bride adorns herself with her jewels.

Isaiah 61:10

The Petition

May the Lord GOD, father of all mercy, grant us who dwell here a peaceful night and a perfect end. *Amen.*

The Office of the Night Watch   Observed on the Hour or Half-Hour Between 1:30 and 4:30 a.m.

The Call to Prayer

Behold now, bless the LORD, all you servants of the LORD,* you that stand by night in the house of the LORD.
Lift up your hands in the holy place and bless the LORD;* the LORD who made heaven and earth bless you out of Zion.

Psalm 134

The Request for Presence

O God, come to my assistance.
O Lord, make haste to help me.

The Greeting

Your way, O God, is holy;* who is so great a god as our God?

Psalm 77:13

The Refrain for the Night Watch

Behold now, bless the LORD, all you servants of the LORD,* you that stand by night in the house of the LORD.

Psalm 134:1

The Psalm   Submit to the LORD

Let me announce the decree of the LORD:* he said to me, "You are my Son; this day have I begotten you.

Ask of me, and I will give you the nations for your inheritance*and the ends of the earth for your possession.

You shall crush them with an iron rod* and shatter them like a piece of pottery."

And now, you kings, be wise;* be warned, you rulers of the earth.

Submit to the LORD with fear,* and with trembling bow before him;

Lest he be angry and you perish;* for his wrath is quickly kindled.

Happy are they all* who take refuge in him!

Psalm 2:7-13

The Refrain

Behold now, bless the LORD, all you servants of the LORD,* you that stand by night in the house of the LORD.

A Reading

Dearly beloved brethren: Unto us is born this day a Savior. Let us rejoice. . . . For the Son of God, when the fulness of time was come, took upon Himself the nature of humanity so that he might reconcile that nature to Him who made it; hence the devil, the inventor of death, is met and beaten in that very flesh which had been the field of his victory. . . . Learn, O Christian, how great one is who has been made partaker of the divine nature and fall not again by a corrupt manner of life. . . . Remember Whose body it is of which you are a member and Who is its Head.

Pope St. Leo (d. 855 CE), Sermons

The Refrain

Behold now, bless the LORD, all you servants of the LORD,* you that stand by night in the house of the LORD.

The Litany

Father, I pray for your holy catholic Church;
That we all may be one.

Grant that every member of the Church may truly and humbly serve you;
That your Name may be glorified by all people.

I pray for all who govern and hold authority in the nations of the world;
That there may be justice and peace on the earth.

Have compassion on those who suffer from any grief or trouble;
> *That they may be delivered from their distress.*

Give to the departed eternal rest.
> *Let light perpetual shine upon them.*

I praise you for your saints who have entered into joy;
> *May I also come to share in your heavenly kingdom.*

The Thanksgiving

Lord, you now have set your servant free to go in peace as you have promised; for these eyes of mine have seen the Savior whom you have prepared for all the world to see: A Light to enlighten the nations, and the glory of your people Israel. *Amen.*

> *Nunc Dimittis*

The Final Petition

Now guide me waking, O Lord, and guard me sleeping; that awake I may watch with Christ, and asleep, I may rest in peace. *Amen.*

The Office of Dawn — Observed on the Hour or Half-Hour Between 4:30 and 7:30 a.m.

The Call to Prayer

Hallelujah! Praise the LORD, O my soul* I will praise the LORD as long as I live; I will sing praises to my God while I have my being.

> *Psalm 146:1*

The Request for Presence

My soul waits for the LORD, more than watchmen for the morning,* more than watchmen for the morning.

> *Psalm 130:5*

The Greeting

Glory be to the Father, and to the Son, and to the Holy Spirit.
As it was in the beginning, it is now
And ever shall be, world without end. *Amen.*

> *Gloria Patri*

The Hymn

Hark! how all the welkin rings
Glory to the King of kings!
Peace on earth, and mercy mild,
God and sinners reconciled!
Joyful, all ye nations, rise,
Join the triumph of the skies;

Universal nature say,
Christ the Lord is born to-day!
Christ by highest Heaven adored,
Christ, the Everlasting Lord;
Late in time behold Him come,
Offspring of a Virgin's womb:
Veiled in flesh the Godhead see;
Hail th'Incarnate Deity,
Pleased as man with men to appear,
Jesus our Immanuel here!
Hail! the heavenly Prince of Peace!
Hail! the Sun of Righteousness!
Light and life to all He brings,
Risen with healing in His wings.
Mild He lays His glory by,
Born that man no more may die,
Born to raise the sons of earth, ·
Born to give them second birth.

Charles Wesley, adapted

The Psalm   Praise the Name of the LORD
Praise the LORD from the earth,* you sea-monsters and all deeps;
Fire and hail, snow and fog,* tempestuous wind, doing his will;
Mountains and all hills,* fruit trees and all cedars;
Wild beasts and all cattle,* creeping things and winged birds;
Kings of the earth and all peoples,* princes and all rulers of the world;
Young men and maidens,* old and young together.
Let them praise the Name of the LORD,*

Psalm 148:7–13a

The Gloria in Excelsis
Glory to God in the highest, and on earth peace to people of good will.
    We praise you.
    We bless you.
    We adore you.
    We glorify you.
We give thanks to you for your great glory.

The Small Verse
There shall come forth a shoot from the stump of Jesse, and a branch shall grow out
    of his roots. And the Spirit of the Lord shall rest upon him, and the spirit of
    wisdom and understanding, the spirit of counsel and might, the spirit of knowl-
    edge and the fear of the Lord. And his delight shall be in the fear of the Lord.

Isaiah 11:1–3

424

The Lord's Prayer

The Final Blessing
May the Lord bless us and keep us and cause His face to shine upon us from this
  day forth and forever more. *Amen.*

ॐ

Monday, Month of December

The Office of Midnight   **Observed on the Hour or Half-Hour**
                                    Between 10:30 p.m.✣ and 1:30 a.m.

The Call to Prayer
God is the LORD; he has shined upon us;* form a procession with branches up to
  the horns of the altar.
Psalm 118:27

The Request for Presence
O LORD, let my prayer be set forth in your sight as incense,* the lifting up of my
  hands as the evening sacrifice.
Psalm 141:2, adapted

The Greeting
Our Father, may Your kingdom come on earth as in Heaven.

The Canticle   *A Song of Creation—Part Three*
                                        Benedicite, omnia opera Domini

Glorify the Lord, all you works of the Lord,*
  praise him and highly exalt him for ever.
In the firmament of his power, glorify the Lord,*
  praise him and highly exalt him for ever.
Let the people of God glorify the Lord,*
  praise him and highly exalt him for ever.
Glorify the Lord, O priests and servants of the Lord,*
  praise him and highly exalt him for ever.
Glorify the Lord, O spirits and souls of the righteous,*
  praise him and highly exalt him for ever.
You that are holy and humble of heart, glorify the Lord,*
  praise him and highly exalt him for ever.
Song of the Three Young Men, 62–68

The Psalm   *He Shall Have Pity on the Lowly*

All kings shall bow down before him,* and all the nations do him service.

For he shall deliver the poor who cries out in distress,* and the oppressed who has no helper.

He shall have pity on the lowly and poor;* he shall preserve the lives of the needy.

He shall redeem their lives from oppression and violence,* and dear shall their blood be in his sight.

Long may he live! and may there be given to him gold from Arabia;* may prayer be made for him always, and may they bless him all the day long.

Psalm 72:11–15

The Gloria

The Small Verse

And many nations shall come, and say: "Come, let us go up to the mountain of the LORD, to the house of the God of Jacob; that he may teach us his ways and we may walk in his paths." For out of Zion shall go forth the law, and the word of the LORD from Jerusalem.

Micah 4:2

The Final Thanksgiving

I will greatly rejoice in the Lord, my soul shall exult in my God; for he has clothed me with the garments of salvation, he has covered me with the robe of righteousness, as a bridegroom decks himself with a garland, and as a bride adorns herself with her jewels.

Isaiah 61:10

The Office of the Night Watch   Observed on the Hour or Half-Hour
Between 1:30 and 4:30 a.m.

The Call to Prayer

Behold now, bless the LORD, all you servants of the LORD,* you that stand by night in the house of the LORD.

Lift up your hands in the holy place and bless the LORD;* the LORD who made heaven and earth bless you out of Zion.

Psalm 134

The Request for Presence

O God, come to my assistance.

O Lord, make haste to help me.

The Greeting

How glorious you are!* more splendid than the everlasting mountains!

Psalm 76:4

426

The Refrain for the Night Watch

Darkness is not dark to you; the night is as bright as the day;* darkness and light
to you are both alike.

Psalm 139:11

The Psalm   I Will Rejoice in the LORD

May the glory of the LORD endure for ever;* may the LORD rejoice in all his works.
He looks at the earth and it trembles;* he touches the mountains and they smoke.
I will sing to the LORD as long as I live;* I will praise my God while I have my
    being.
May these words of mine please him;* I will rejoice in the LORD.
Let sinners be consumed out of the earth,* and the wicked be no more.
Bless the LORD, O my soul.* Hallelujah!

Psalm 104:32–37

The Refrain

Darkness is not dark to you; the night is as bright as the day;* darkness and light
to you are both alike.

A Reading

For a possession which is not diminished by being shared with others—that is, if it
    is possessed and not shared—is not yet possessed as it ought to be possessed.
    The Lord says, "Whosoever has, to him shall be given." He will give, then, to
    those that have. That is to say, if they use freely and cheerfully what they have
    received, He will add to and perfect His gifts. The loaves in the miracle were
    only five and seven in number before the disciples began to divide them among
    other hungry people. But once they began to distribute them, though the wants
    of so many thousands were satisfied, they themselves still could fill baskets
    with the fragments.

St. Augustine (ca. 410 CE), On Christian Doctrine

The Refrain

Darkness is not dark to you; the night is as bright as the day;* darkness and light
to you are both alike.

The Litany

Grant, Almighty God, that all who confess your Name may be united in your truth,
    live together in your love, and reveal your glory in the world.
> *Lord, in your mercy, hear my prayer.*
Guide the people of this land, and of all the nations, in the ways of justice and
    peace; that we may honor one another and serve the common good.
> *Lord, in your mercy, hear my prayer.*
Give us all a reverence for the earth as your own creation, that we may use its
    resources rightly in the service of others and to your honor and glory.
> *Lord, in your mercy, hear my prayer.*

427

Bless all whose lives are closely linked with mine, and grant that I may serve
   Christ in them, and love even as he loves me.
   Lord, in your mercy, hear my prayer.
Comfort and heal all those who suffer in body, mind, or spirit; give them courage
   and hope in their troubles, and bring them the joy of your salvation.
   Lord, in your mercy, hear my prayer.
I commend to your mercy all who have died, that your will for them may be
   fulfilled; and I pray that I may share with all your saints in your eternal kingdom.
   Lord, in your mercy, hear my prayer.

The Thanksgiving
Lord, you now have set your servant free to go in peace as you have promised; for
   these eyes of mine have seen the Savior whom you have prepared for all the
   world to see: A Light to enlighten the nations, and the glory of your people
   Israel. *Amen.*

Nunc Dimittis

The Final Petition
Now guide me waking, O Lord, and guard me sleeping; that awake I may watch
   with Christ, and asleep, I may rest in peace. *Amen.*

The Office of Dawn   **Observed on the Hour or Half-Hour
Between 4:30 and 7:30 a.m.**

The Call to Prayer
Sing to the LORD with thanksgiving;* make music to our God upon the harp.

Psalm 147:7

The Request for Presence
My soul waits for the LORD, more than watchmen for the morning,* more than
   watchmen for the morning.

Psalm 130:5

The Greeting
Glory be to the Father, and the Son, and the Holy Spirit.
As it was in the beginning, it is now
And ever shall be, world without end. *Amen.*

Gloria Patri

The Hymn
From lands that see the sun arise,
To earth's remotest boundaries,
The virgin born today we sing,
The Son of Mary, Christ the King.

428

Blest Author of this earthly frame,
To take a servant's form He came,
That liberating flesh by flesh,
Whom He had made might live afresh.
The heavenly chorus filled the sky,
The angels sang to God on high,
What time to shepherds watching lone
They made creation's Shepherd known.
All honor, laud, and glory be,
O Jesu, virgin born, to Thee;
All glory, as is ever meet,
To the Father and to Paraclete.

Coelius Sedulius (ca. 450 CE), translated by J. M. Neale

The Psalm   The LORD Adorns the Poor with Victory

Let Israel rejoice in his Maker;* let the children of Zion be joyful in their King.
Let them praise his Name in the dance;* let them sing praise to him with timbrel
    and harp.
For the LORD takes pleasure in his people* and adorns the poor with victory.
Let the faithful rejoice in triumph;* let them be joyful on their beds.

Psalm 149: 2–5

The Gloria in Excelsis

Glory to God in the highest, and on earth peace to people of good will.
    We praise you.
    We bless you.
    We adore you.
    We glorify you.
We give thanks to you for your great glory.

The Small Verse

Consequently, when Christ came into the world, he said, "Sacrifices and offerings
    thou hast not desired, but a body hast thou prepared for me; in burnt offerings
    and sin offerings thou hast taken no pleasure. Then I said, 'Lo, I have come to
    do thy will, O God,' as it is written of me in the roll of the book."

Hebrews 10: 5–7

The Lord's Prayer

The Final Blessing

May the Lord bless us and keep us and cause His face to shine upon us from this
    day forth and forever more. *Amen.*

Tuesday, Month of December

The Office of Midnight   **Observed on the Hour or Half-Hour**
Between 10:30 p.m.✢ and 1:30 a.m.

The Call to Prayer
Sing to God, O kingdoms of the earth;* sing praises to the Lord.
He rides in the heavens, the ancient heavens;* he sends forth his voice, his mighty
   voice.

Psalm 68:33–34

The Request for Presence
O LORD, let my prayer be set forth in your sight as incense,* the lifting up of my
   hands as the evening sacrifice.

Psalm 141:2, adapted

The Greeting
Our Father, may Your will be done, on earth as in Heaven.

The Canticle   *The Third Song of Isaiah*

Surge, illuminare

Arise, shine, for your light has come,*
   and the glory of the Lord has dawned upon you.
For behold, darkness covers the land;*
   deep gloom enshrouds the peoples.
But over you the Lord will rise,*
   and his glory will appear upon you.
Nations will stream to your light,*
   and kings to the brightness of your dawning.
Your gates will always be open;*
   by day or night they will never be shut.
They will call you, The City of the Lord,*
   The Zion of the Holy One of Israel.
Violence will no more be heard in your land,*
   ruin or destruction within your borders.
You will call your walls, Salvation,*
   and all your portals, Praise.
The sun will no more be your light by day;*
   by night you will not need the brightness of the moon.
The Lord will be your everlasting light,*
   and your God will be your glory.

Isaiah 60:1–3, 11a, 14c, 18–19

The Psalm   *Blessed Be the Lord*

The chariots of God are twenty thousand, even thousands of thousands;* the Lord
   comes in holiness from Sinai.
You have gone up on high and led captivity captive; you have received gifts even
   from your enemies,* that the LORD God might dwell among them.
Blessed be the Lord day by day,* the God of our salvation, who bears our burdens.
He is our God, the God of our salvation;* God is the LORD, by whom we escape
   death.

Psalm 68:17–20

The Gloria

The Small Verse

Behold, I send my messenger to prepare the way before me; and the LORD whom
   you seek will suddenly come to his temple; the messenger of the covenant in
   whom you delight, behold, he is coming, says the LORD of hosts.

Malachi 3:1

The Final Thanksgiving

I will greatly rejoice in the LORD, my soul shall exult in my God; for he has
   clothed me with the garments of salvation, he has covered me with the robe of
   righteousness, as a bridegroom decks himself with a garland, and as a bride
   adorns herself with her jewels.

Isaiah 61:10

The Petition

May the Lord GOD, father of all mercy, grant us who dwell here a peaceful night
   and a perfect end. *Amen.*

The Office of the Night Watch   **Observed on the Hour or Half-Hour**
                                          Between 1:30 and 4:30 a.m.

The Call to Prayer

Behold now, bless the LORD, all you servants of the LORD,* you that stand by night
   in the house of the LORD.
Lift up your hands in the holy place and bless the LORD;* the LORD who made
   heaven and earth bless you out of Zion.

Psalm 134

The Request for Presence

O God, come to my assistance.
O Lord, make haste to help me.

The Greeting
You are my hiding-place; you preserve me from trouble;* you surround me with
shouts of deliverance.

Psalm 32:8

The Refrain for the Night Watch
I will bless the LORD who gives me counsel;* my heart teaches me, night after
night.

Psalm 16:7

The Psalm   Give Thanks to the LORD
Give thanks to the LORD, for he is good;* his mercy endures for ever.
Let Israel now proclaim,* "His mercy endures for ever."
Let the house of Aaron now proclaim,* "His mercy endures for ever."
Let those who fear the LORD now proclaim,* "His mercy endures for ever."

Psalm 118:1–4

The Refrain
I will bless the LORD who gives me counsel;* my heart teaches me, night after night.

A Reading
It is written: "When Jesus therefore perceived that they would come and take Him
by force to make Him a king, He departed again into the mountain Himself
alone" (John 6:15). Now who could so blamelessly have had principality over
men as He who could in fact have reigned over those whom He had Himself
created? But because He had come in the flesh to the end that He might not
only redeem us by His passion but also teach us by His conversation, offering
Himself as an example to His followers, He would not be made king but went
instead of His own accord to the gibbet of the cross.

Pope Gregory the Great (ca. 540–604), The Book of Pastoral Rule

The Refrain
I will bless the LORD who gives me counsel;* my heart teaches me, night after night.

The Litany
For the holy Church of God, that it may be filled with truth and love, and be found
without fault at the day of your coming, I pray to you, O Lord.
   Lord, in your mercy, hear my prayer
For all who fear God and believe in you, Lord Christ, that our divisions may cease,
and that all may be one as you and the Father are one, I pray to you, O Lord.
   Lord, in your mercy, hear my prayer.
For those who do not yet believe, and for those who have lost their faith, that they
may receive the light of the Gospel, I pray to you, O Lord.
   Lord, in your mercy, hear my prayer.

432

For my enemies and those who wish me harm, and for all whom I have injured or offended, I pray to you, O Lord.
Lord, in your mercy, hear my prayer.
For all who have commended themselves to my prayers; for my family, friends, and neighbors; that being freed from anxiety, they may live in joy, peace, and health, I pray to you, O Lord.
Lord, in your mercy, hear my prayer.
For myself; for the forgiveness of my sins, and for the grace of the Holy Spirit to amend my life, I pray to you, O Lord.
Lord, in your mercy, hear my prayer

The Thanksgiving

Lord, you now have set your servant free to go in peace as you have promised; for these eyes of mine have seen the Savior whom you have prepared for all the world to see: A Light to enlighten the nations, and the glory of your people Israel. *Amen.*

Nunc Dimittis

The Final Petition

Now guide me waking, O Lord, and guard me sleeping; that awake I may watch with Christ, and asleep, I may rest in peace. *Amen.*

The Office of Dawn

Observed on the Hour or Half-Hour Between 4:30 and 7:30 a.m.

The Call to Prayer

Worship the Lord, O Jerusalem;* praise your God, O Zion;
For he has strengthened the bars of your gates.

Psalm 147:13–14a

The Request for Presence

My soul waits for the LORD, more than watchmen for the morning,* more than watchmen for the morning.

Psalm 130:5

The Greeting

Glory be to the Father, and the Son, and the Holy Spirit.
As it was in the beginning, it is now
And ever shall be, world without end. *Amen.*

Gloria Patri

The Hymn

Come, thou long expected Jesus,
born to set your people free;
from our fears and sins release us,
let us find our rest in thee.

Israel's strength and consolation,
hope of all the earth thou art;
dear desire of every nation,
joy of every longing heart.
Born your people to deliver,
born a child and yet a King,
born to reign in us forever,
now your gracious kingdom bring.
By your own eternal spirit
rule in all our hearts alone;
by your all sufficient merit,
raise us to your glorious throne.

Charles Wesley

The Psalm   *The LORD Sends Out His Command to the Earth*
The LORD sends out his command to the earth,* and his word runs very swiftly.
He gives snow like wool;* he scatters hoarfrost like ashes.
He scatters his hail like bread crumbs;* who can stand against his cold?
He sends forth his word and melts them;* he blows with his wind, and the waters flow.

Psalm 147:13–19

The Gloria in Excelsis
Glory to God in the highest, and on earth peace to people of good will.
. We praise you.
We bless you.
We adore you.
We glorify you.
We give thanks to you for your great glory.

The Small Verse
. . . behold, an angel of the Lord appeared to Joseph in a dream, saying: "Joseph,
son of David, do not fear to take Mary as your wife, for that which is conceived
in her is of the Holy Spirit; she will bear a son, and you shall call his name
Jesus, for he will save his people from their sins." All this took place to fulfill
what the Lord had spoken by the prophet: "Behold, a virgin shall conceive and
bear a son, and his name shall be Emmanuel" (which means, God with us).

Matthew 1:20b–23

The Lord's Prayer

The Final Blessing
May the Lord bless us and keep us and cause His face to shine upon us from this
day forth and forever more. *Amen.*

434

Wednesday, Month of December

The Office of Midnight

Observed on the Hour or Half-Hour Between 10:30 p.m.✠ and 1:30 a.m.

The Call to Prayer
Some put their trust in chariots and some in horses,* but we will call upon the
Name of the LORD our God.

Psalm 20:7

The Request for Presence
O LORD, let my prayer be set forth in your sight as incense,* the lifting up of my
hands as the evening sacrifice.

Psalm 141:2, adapted

The Greeting
Our Father, give us this day our daily bread.

The Canticle
The Song of Simeon
Nunc Dimittis

Lord, you now have set your servant free*
   to go in peace as you have promised;
For these eyes of mine have seen the Savior,*
   whom you have prepared for all the world to see:
A Light to enlighten the nations,*
   and the glory of your people Israel.
Glory to the Father, and to the Son, and to the Holy Spirit:*
   as it was in the beginning, is now, and will be for ever. *Amen.*

Luke 2:29–32

The Psalm
God Reveals Himself in Glory

The LORD, the God of gods, has spoken;* he has called the earth from the rising of
the sun to its setting.
Out of Zion, perfect in its beauty,* God reveals himself in glory.
Our God will come and will not keep silence;* before him there is a consuming
flame, and round about him a raging storm.
He calls the heavens and the earth from above* to witness the judgment of his
people.
"Gather before me my loyal followers,* those who have made a covenant with me
and sealed it with sacrifice."

Psalm 50:1–5

The Gloria

The Small Verse

But you, O Bethlehem Ephrathah, who are little to be among the clans of Judah, from you shall come forth for me one who is to be ruler in Israel, whose origin is from of old, from ancient days.

Micah 5:2

The Final Thanksgiving

I will greatly rejoice in the LORD, my soul shall exult in my God; for he has clothed me with the garments of salvation, he has covered me with the robe of righteousness, as a bridegroom decks himself with a garland, and as a bride adorns herself with her jewels.

Isaiah 61:10

The Petition

May the Lord GOD, father of all mercy, grant us who dwell here a peaceful night and a perfect end. *Amen.*

The Office of the Night Watch   Observed on the Hour or Half-Hour Between 1:30 and 4:30 a.m.

The Call to Prayer

Behold now, bless the LORD, all you servants of the LORD,* you that stand by night in the house of the LORD.
Lift up your hands in the holy place and bless the LORD;* the LORD who made heaven and earth bless you out of Zion.

Psalm 134

The Request for Presence

O God, come to my assistance.
O Lord, make haste to help me.

The Greeting

I love you, O LORD my strength,* O LORD my stronghold, my crag, and my haven.

Psalm 18:1

The Refrain for the Night Watch

Happy are they who have not walked in the counsel of the wicked,* nor lingered in the way of sinners, nor sat in the seats of the scornful!
Their delight is in the law of the LORD,* and they meditate on his law day and night.

Psalm 1:1-2

The Psalm   *Sing to the LORD a New Song*

Hallelujah! Sing to the LORD a new song;* sing his praise in the congregation of the faithful.

436

Let Israel rejoice in his Maker;* let the children of Zion be joyful in their King.
Let them praise his Name in the dance;* let them sing praise to him with timbrel
    and harp.
For the LORD takes pleasure in his people* and adorns the poor with victory.
Let the faithful rejoice in triumph;* let them be joyful on their beds.

Psalm 149:1–5

The Refrain

Happy are they who have not walked in the counsel of the wicked,* nor lingered
    in the way of sinners, nor sat in the seats of the scornful!
Their delight is in the law of the LORD,* and they meditate on his law day and night.

A Reading

And when they returned, the Magi narrated to the men of that time those same
    things which were also written on the plates of gold (in Persia) and told them
    to this effect: When we came to Jerusalem, the sign together with our arrival,
    roused all the people. How is this, say they, that wise men of the Persians are
    here and that along with them there is this strange stellar phenomenon? . . .
    And we said: He whom you call Messiah is born. And they were confounded
    and dared not withstand us. But they said to us: By the justice of Heaven, tell
    us what you know of this matter. And we made answer to them. . . . Then the
    king of Judea sent for us and had some converse with us . . . but we left him
    without giving any greater heed to him than to a common person. And we came
    to the place where we were sent and saw the mother and child, and we said to
    the mother: What are you named, O renowned mother? And she says: Mary,
    Masters. . . . Then said we: Hast thou not a husband? And she answers: I was
    only betrothed . . . and while I was giving little concern to it, when a certain
    Sabbath dawned, and straightaway at the rising of the sun, an angel appeared to
    me, bringing me suddenly the glad tidings of a son. And in trouble I cried out,
    Be it not so to me, Lord, for I have not a husband. And he persuaded me to
    believe that by the will of God I should have this son. Then said we to her:
    Mother, mother, all the gods of the Persians have called thee blessed. Thy glory
    is great, for thou art exalted above all women of renown, and thou art shown to
    be more queenly than all queens.

Julius Africanus (ca. 180–ca. 250 CE), History of the World

The Refrain

Happy are they who have not walked in the counsel of the wicked,* nor lingered
    in the way of sinners, nor sat in the seats of the scornful!
Their delight is in the law of the LORD,* and they meditate on his law day and night.

The Litany

For the peace of the world, that a spirit of respect and forbearance may grow
    among nations and peoples, I pray to you, O Lord.
    Lord, hear my prayer.

For those in positions of public trust, that they may serve justice, and promote the dignity and freedom of every person, I pray to you, O Lord.

> *Lord, hear my prayer.*

For the poor, the persecuted, the sick, and all who suffer; for refugees, prisoners, and all who are in danger; that they may be relieved and protected, I pray to you, O Lord.

> *Lord, hear my prayer.*

For the forgiveness of my sins, and for the grace of the Holy Spirit to amend my life, I pray to you, O Lord.

> *Lord, hear my prayer.*

For all who have died in the communion of your Church, and those whose faith is known to you alone, that, with all the saints, they may have rest in that place where there is no pain or grief, but life eternal, I pray to you, O Lord.

> *Lord, hear my prayer*

Rejoicing in the fellowship of the ever-blessed Virgin Mary and all the saints, I commend my self and all your faithful to Christ our God.

> *To you, O Lord our God.*

The Thanksgiving

Lord, you now have set your servant free to go in peace as you have promised; for these eyes of mine have seen the Savior whom you have prepared for all the world to see: A Light to enlighten the nations, and the glory of your people Israel. *Amen.*

Nunc Dimittis

The Final Petition

Now guide me waking, O Lord, and guard me sleeping; that awake I may watch with Christ, and asleep, I may rest in peace. *Amen.*

The Office of Dawn   Observed on the Hour or Half-Hour Between 4:30 and 7:30 a.m.

The Call to Prayer

Hallelujah! Sing to the LORD a new song;* sing his praise in the congregation of the faithful.

Psalm 149:1

The Request for Presence

My soul waits for the LORD, more than watchmen for the morning,* more than watchmen for the morning.

Psalm 130:5

The Greeting

Glory be to the Father, and the Son, and the Holy Spirit.
As it was in the beginning, it is now
And ever shall be, world without end. *Amen.*

Gloria Patri

The Hymn

Lo, how a Rose e'er blooming
from tender stem hath sprung!
Of Jesse's lineage coming,
as those of old have sung.
It came, a floweret bright,
amid the cold of winter,
when half spent was the night.
Isaiah 'twas foretold it,
the Rose I have in mind;
with Mary we behold it,
the Virgin Mother kind.
To show God's love aright,
she bore to us a Savior,
when half spent was the night.

15th c. German, translated by Theodore Baker

The Psalm   Praise the LORD

Praise him for his mighty acts;* praise him for his excellent greatness.
Praise him with the blast of the ram's-horn;* praise him with lyre and harp.
Praise him with timbrel and dance;* praise him with strings and pipe.
Praise him with resounding cymbals;* praise him with loud-clanging cymbals.
Let everything that has breath* praise the LORD. Hallelujah!

Psalm 150:2–6

The Gloria in Excelsis

Glory to God in the highest, and on earth peace to people of good will.
    We praise you.
    We bless you.
    We adore you.
    We glorify you.
We give thanks to you for your great glory.

The Small Verse

And the Word became flesh and dwelt among us, full of grace and truth; we have
    beheld his glory, glory as of the only Son from the Father.

John 1:14

The Lord's Prayer

The Final Blessing
May the Lord bless us and keep us and cause His face to shine upon us from this
day forth and forever more. *Amen.*

✤

Thursday, Month of December

The Office of Midnight   **Observed on the Hour or Half-Hour**
                                             Between 10:30 p.m.✤ and 1:30 a.m.

The Call to Prayer
Sing to the LORD with the harp,* with the harp and the voice of song.
With trumpets and the sound of the horn* shout with joy before the King, the
    LORD.

Psalm 98:6–7

The Request for Presence
O LORD, let my prayer be set forth in your sight as incense,* the lifting up of my
    hands as the evening sacrifice.

Psalm 141:2, adapted

The Greeting
Our Father, forgive us our sins as we forgive those who have sinned against us.

The Canticle   *The Song of Mary*
                                                          Magnificat

My soul proclaims the greatness of the Lord, my spirit rejoices in God my
    Savior;*
    for he has looked with favor on his lowly servant.
From this day all generations will call me blessed:*
    the Almighty has done great things for me, and holy is his Name.
He has mercy on those who fear him*
    in every generation.
He has shown the strength of his arm,*
    he has scattered the proud in their conceit.
He has cast down the mighty from their thrones,*
    and has lifted up the lowly.

He has filled the hungry with good things,*
and the rich he has sent away empty.
He has come to the help of his servant Israel,*
for he has remembered his promise of mercy,
The promise he made to our fathers,*
to Abraham and his children for ever.
Glory to the Father, and to the Son, and to the Holy Spirit:*
as it was in the beginning, is now, and will be for ever. *Amen.*

Luke 1:46–55

The Psalm   *The Lord Has Girded Himself with Strength*
The Lord is King; he has put on splendid apparel;* the Lord has put on his
apparel and girded himself with strength.
He has made the whole world so sure* that it cannot be moved;
Ever since the world began, your throne has been established;* you are from
everlasting.
The waters have lifted up, O Lord, the waters have lifted up their voice;* the
waters have lifted up their pounding waves.
Mightier than the sound of many waters, mightier than the breakers of the sea,*
mightier is the Lord who dwells on high.
Your testimonies are very sure,* and holiness adorns your house, O Lord, for ever
and for evermore.

Psalm 93

The Gloria

The Small Verse
Behold, the days are coming, says the Lord, when I will raise up for David a
righteous Branch, and he will reign as king and deal wisely, and shall execute
justice and righteousness in the land. In his days Judah will be saved, and Israel
will dwell securely. And this is the name by which he will be called: "The Lord
is our righteousness."

Jeremiah 23: 5–6

The Final Thanksgiving
I will greatly rejoice in the Lord, my soul shall exult in my God; for he has
clothed me with the garments of salvation, he has covered me with the robe of
righteousness, as a bridegroom decks himself with a garland, and as a bride
adorns herself with her jewels.

Isaiah 61:10

The Petition
May the Lord God, father of all mercy, grant us who dwell here a peaceful night
and a perfect end. *Amen.*

The Office of the Night Watch **Observed on the Hour or Half-Hour**
Between 1:30 and 4:30 a.m.

The Call to Prayer
Behold now, bless the LORD, all you servants of the LORD,* you that stand by night
in the house of the LORD.
Lift up your hands in the holy place and bless the LORD;* the LORD who made
heaven and earth bless you out of Zion.

Psalm 134

The Request for Presence
O God, come to my assistance.
O Lord, make haste to help me.

The Greeting
Whom have I in heaven but you?* and having you I desire nothing upon earth.

Psalm 73:25

The Refrain for the Night Watch
The heavens declare the glory of God,* and the firmament shows his handiwork.
One day tells its tale to another,* and one night imparts knowledge to another.

Psalm 19:1–2

The Psalm *Bless Him All the Day Long*
Long may he live! and may there be given to him gold from Arabia;* may prayer
be made for him always, and may they bless him all the day long.
May there be abundance of grain on the earth, growing thick even on the hilltops;*
may its fruit flourish like Lebanon, and its grain like grass upon the earth.
May his Name remain for ever and be established as long as the sun endures;*
may all the nations bless themselves in him and call him blessed.
Blessed be the Lord GOD, the God of Israel,* who alone does wondrous deeds!
And blessed be his glorious Name for ever!* and may all the earth be filled with
his glory. Amen. Amen.

Psalm 72:15–19

The Refrain
The heavens declare the glory of God,* and the firmament shows his handiwork.
One day tells its tale to another,* and one night imparts knowledge to another.

A Reading
Now strive and sweat in all you can and may in order to get yourself a true
knowing and a true feeling of yourself as you are; and I trow that soon after
that you shall have a true knowing and feeling of God as He is. Not as He is in
Himself, for that may no human being do save God Himself; nor yet as you can

442

do in bliss with both body and soul together. But as it is possible, and as he vouchsafes to be known and felt of a meek soul living in this deadly body.

Anonymous (14th c.), The Cloud of Unknowing

The Refrain

The heavens declare the glory of God,* and the firmament shows his handiwork. One day tells its tale to another,* and one night imparts knowledge to another.

The Litany

For all people in their daily life and work;
For my family, friends, and neighbors, and for those who are alone, I pray to you, Lord God.
For this community, the nation, and the world;
For all who work for justice, freedom, and peace, I pray to you, Lord God.
For the just and proper use of your creation;
For the victims of hunger, fear, injustice, and oppression, I pray to you, Lord God.
For all who are in danger, sorrow, or any kind of trouble;
For those who minister to the sick, the friendless, and the needy, I pray to you, Lord God.
For the peace and unity of the Church of God;
For all who proclaim the Gospel, and all who seek the Truth, I pray to you, Lord God.
Hear me, Lord;
For your mercy is great.

The Thanksgiving

Lord, you now have set your servant free to go in peace as you have promised; for these eyes of mine have seen the Savior whom you have prepared for all the world to see: A Light to enlighten the nations, and the glory of your people Israel. *Amen.*

Nunc Dimittis

The Final Petition

Now guide me waking, O Lord, and guard me sleeping; that awake I may watch with Christ, and asleep, I may rest in peace. *Amen.*

The Office of Dawn **Observed on the Hour or Half-Hour Between 4:30 and 7:30 a.m.**

The Call to Prayer

Let everything that has breath* praise the LORD. Hallelujah!

Psalm 150:6

443

The Request for Presence
My soul waits for the LORD, more than watchmen for the morning,* more than
  watchmen for the morning.

Psalm 130:5

The Greeting
Glory be to the Father, and to the Son, and to the Holy Spirit.
As it was in the beginning, it is now
And ever shall be, world without end. *Amen.*

Gloria Patri

The Hymn
Hail to the Lord's Anointed, great David's greater Son!
Hail in the time appointed, his reign on earth begun!
He comes to break oppression, to set the captive free;
to take away transgression, and rule in equity.
To him shall prayer unceasing and daily vows ascend;
his kingdom still increasing, a kingdom without end.
The tide of time shall never his covenant remove;
his name shall stand forever; his name to us is love.

James Montgomery

The Psalm   Praise the LORD
Hallelujah! Praise the LORD from the heavens;* praise him in the heights.
Praise him, all you angels of his;* praise him, all his host.
Praise him, sun and moon;* praise him, all you shining stars.
Praise him, heaven of heavens,* and you waters above the heavens.
Let them praise the Name of the LORD;* for he commanded, and they were
  created.
He made them stand fast for ever and ever;* he gave them a law which shall not
  pass away.

Psalm 148: 1b–6

The Gloria in Excelsis
Glory to God in the highest, and on earth peace to people of good will.
  We praise you.
  We bless you.
  We adore you.
  We glorify you.
We give thanks to you for your great glory.

The Small Verse
Of John the Baptizer, Zechariah prophesied: And you, child, will be called the
  prophet of the Most High; for you will go before the Lord to prepare his ways,

444

to give knowledge of salvation to his people in the forgiveness of their sins, through the tender mercy of our God, when the day shall dawn upon us from on high to give light to those who sit in darkness and in the shadow of death, to guide our feet into the way of peace.

Luke 1:76–79

The Lord's Prayer

The Final Blessing
May the Lord bless us and keep us and cause His face to shine upon us from this day forth and forever more. *Amen.*

⤳

Friday, Month of December

The Office of Midnight **Observed on the Hour or Half-Hour Between 10:30 p.m.✢ and 1:30 a.m.**

The Call to Prayer
The LORD is King; let the earth rejoice;* let the multitude of the isles be glad.

Psalm 97:1

The Request for Presence
O LORD, let my prayer be set forth in your sight as incense,* the lifting up of my hands as the evening sacrifice.

Psalm 141:2, adapted

The Greeting
Our Father, lead us not into temptation, but deliver us from evil.

The Canticle *A Song of Penitence*
Kyrie Pantokrator

O Lord and Ruler of the hosts of heaven,*
    God of Abraham, Isaac, and Jacob, and of all their righteous offspring:
You made the heavens and the earth,*
    with all their vast array.
All things quake with fear at your presence;*
    they tremble because of your power.
But your merciful promise is beyond all measure;*
    it surpasses all that our minds can fathom.

445

O Lord, you are full of compassion,*
long-suffering, and abounding in mercy.
You hold back your hand;*
you do not punish as we deserve.
In your great goodness, Lord, you have promised forgiveness to sinners,*
that they may repent of their sin and be saved.

Prayer of Manasseh 1–2, 4, 6–7

The Psalm   *He Gives to His Beloved Sleep*
Unless the Lord builds the house,* their labor is in vain who build it.
Unless the Lord watches over the city,* in vain the watchman keeps his vigil.
It is in vain that you rise so early and go to bed so late;* vain, too, to eat the bread
of toil, for he gives to his beloved sleep.

Psalm 127:1–3

The Gloria

The Small Verse
But the hour is coming, and now is, when the true worshipers will worship the
Father in spirit and truth, for such the Father seeks to worship him. God is
spirit, and those who worship him must worship in spirit and truth.

John 4:23–24

The Final Thanksgiving
I will greatly rejoice in the Lord, my soul shall exult in my God; for he has
clothed me with the garments of salvation, he has covered me with the robe of
righteousness, as a bridegroom decks himself with a garland, and as a bride
adorns herself with her jewels.

Isaiah 61:10

The Petition
May the Lord God, father of all mercy, grant us who dwell here a peaceful night
and a perfect end. *Amen.*

The Office of the Night Watch   Observed on the Hour or Half-Hour
                                                Between 1:30 and 4:30 a.m.

The Call to Prayer
Behold now, bless the Lord, all you servants of the Lord,* you that stand by night
in the house of the Lord.
Lift up your hands in the holy place and bless the Lord;* the Lord who made
heaven and earth bless you out of Zion.

Psalm 134

The Request for Presence
O God, come to my assistance.
O Lord, make haste to help me.

The Greeting
I will confess you among the peoples, O LORD;* I will sing praises to you among
the nations.
For your loving-kindness is greater than the heavens,* and your faithfulness
reaches to the clouds.

Psalm 108:3–4

The Refrain for the Night Watch
The LORD grants his loving-kindness in the daytime;* in the night season his song
is with me, a prayer to the God of my life.

Psalm 42:10

The Psalm   *There Is a Future for the Peaceable*
I have seen the wicked in their arrogance,* flourishing like a tree in full leaf.
I went by, and behold, they were not there;* I searched for them, but they could
not be found.
Mark those who are honest; observe the upright;* for there is a future for the
peaceable.
Transgressors shall be destroyed, one and all;* the future of the wicked is cut off.
But the deliverance of the righteous comes from the LORD;* he is their stronghold
in time of trouble.
The LORD will help them and rescue them;* he will rescue them from the wicked
and deliver them, because they seek refuge in him.

Psalm 37:37–42

The Refrain
The LORD grants his loving-kindness in the daytime;* in the night season his song
is with me, a prayer to the God of my life.

A Reading
Don't be in a bigger hurry than God. Holiness is not achieved all at once. We need
to pray all of the time. And how can we pray all to him without being with
him? How can we be with him unless we think of him often? And how can we
often think of him unless by a holy habit of thought. You tell me I am always
saying the same thing. You are right. I say it because this is the best and easiest
method I know, and it is the only one I use.

Brother Lawrence (ca. 1605–1691 CE), The Practice of the Presence of God

The Refrain
The LORD grants his loving-kindness in the daytime;* in the night season his song
is with me, a prayer to the God of my life.

The Litany

For the peace from above, for the loving-kindness of God, and for the salvation of my soul, I pray to the Lord.
Lord, have mercy.

For the peace of the world, for the welfare of the Holy Church of God, and for the unity of all peoples, I pray to the Lord.
Lord, have mercy.

For my city [town, village], for every city and community, and for those who live in them, I pray to the Lord.
Lord, have mercy.

For seasonable weather, and for an abundance of the fruits of the earth, I pray to the Lord.
Lord, have mercy.

For the good earth which God has given us, and for the wisdom and will to conserve it, I pray to the Lord.
Lord, have mercy.

For deliverance from all danger, violence, oppression, and degradation, I pray to the Lord.
Lord, have mercy.

For the absolution and remission of my sins and offenses, I pray to the Lord.
Lord, have mercy.

Defend me, deliver me, and in your compassion protect me, O Lord, by your grace.
Lord, have mercy.

The Thanksgiving

Lord, you now have set your servant free to go in peace as you have promised; for these eyes of mine have seen the Savior whom you have prepared for all the world to see: A Light to enlighten the nations, and the glory of your people Israel. *Amen.*

Nunc Dimittis

The Final Petition

Now guide me waking, O Lord, and guard me sleeping; that awake I may watch with Christ, and asleep, I may rest in peace. *Amen.*

The Office of Dawn   **Observed on the Hour or Half-Hour Between 4:30 and 7:30 a.m.**

The Call to Prayer

Hallelujah! Praise the LORD from the heavens;* praise him in the heights.

Psalm 148:1

448

The Request for Presence

My soul waits for the LORD, more than watchmen for the morning,* more than
watchmen for the morning.

Psalm 130:5

The Greeting

Glory be to the Father, and the Son, and the Holy Spirit.
As it was in the beginning, it is now
And ever shall be, world without end. *Amen.*

Gloria Patri

The Hymn

O come, all ye faithful, joyful and triumphant,
O come ye, O come ye, to Bethlehem.
Come and behold Him, born the King of angels;
O come, let us adore Him,
O come, let us adore Him,
O come, let us adore Him,
Christ the Lord.
Sing, choirs of angels, sing in exultation;
O sing, all ye citizens of heaven above!
Glory to God, all glory in the highest;
O come, let us adore Him,
O come, let us adore Him,
O come, let us adore Him,
Christ the Lord.
Yea, Lord, we greet Thee, born this happy morning;
Jesus, to Thee be glory given;
Word of the Father, now in flesh appearing.
O come, let us adore Him,
O come, let us adore Him,
O come, let us adore Him,
Christ the Lord.

John F. Wade

The Psalm   *The LORD Has Pleasure in Those Who Fear Him*

He covers the heavens with clouds* and prepares rain for the earth;
He makes grass to grow upon the mountains* and green plants to serve mankind.
He provides food for flocks and herds* and for the young ravens when they cry.
He is not impressed by the might of a horse;* he has no pleasure in the strength of
a man;
But the LORD has pleasure in those who fear him,* in those who await his gracious
favor.

Psalm 147: 8–12

The Gloria in Excelsis
Glory to God in the highest, and on earth peace to people of good will.
    We praise you.
    We bless you.
    We adore you.
    We glorify you.
We give thanks to you for your great glory.

The Small Verse
The LORD said to my Lord, "Sit at my right hand,* until I make your enemies your
    footstool." The LORD will send the scepter of your power out of Zion,* saying,
    "Rule over your enemies round about you. Princely state has been yours from
    the day of your birth;* in the beauty of holiness have I begotten you, like dew
    from the womb of the morning." The LORD has sworn and he will not recant:*
    "You are a priest for ever after the order of Melchizedek."

                                                                    Psalm 110:1–4

The Lord's Prayer

The Final Blessing
May the Lord bless us and keep us and cause His face to shine upon us from this
    day forth and forever more. *Amen.*

ॐ

Saturday, Month of December

The Office of Midnight

**Observed on the Hour or Half-Hour
Between 10:30 p.m.✢ and 1:30 a.m.**

The Call to Prayer
Then shall all the trees of the wood shout for joy before the LORD when he comes.
                                                                    Psalm 96:12a

The Request for Presence
O LORD, let my prayer be set forth in your sight as incense,* the lifting up of my
    hands as the evening sacrifice.
                                                                    Psalm 141:2, adapted

The Greeting
Our Father, Yours are the kingdom, the power, and the glory forever.

450

The Canticle

Glory to God
Gloria in excelsis

Glory to God in the highest,
  and peace to his people on earth.
Lord God, heavenly King, almighty God and Father,
  we worship you, we give you thanks, we praise you for your glory.
Lord Jesus Christ, only Son of the Father, Lord God, Lamb of God,
you take away the sin of the world:
  have mercy on us;
you are seated at the right hand of the Father:
  receive our prayer.
For you alone are the Holy One, you alone are the Lord, you alone are the Most
  High,
  Jesus Christ, with the Holy Spirit, in the glory of God the Father. *Amen.*

The Psalm
He Shall Rescue the Poor and Crush the Oppressor

Give the King your justice, O God,* and your righteousness to the King's Son;
That he may rule your people righteously* and the poor with justice;
That the mountains may bring prosperity to the people,* and the little hills bring
  righteousness.
He shall defend the needy among the people;* he shall rescue the poor and crush
  the oppressor.
He shall live as long as the sun and moon endure,* from one generation to another.
He shall come down like rain upon the mown field,* like showers that water the
  earth.
In his time shall the righteous flourish;* there shall be abundance of peace till the
  moon shall be no more.
He shall rule from sea to sea,* and from the River to the ends of the earth.

Psalm 72:1–8

The Gloria

The Small Verse

Sing praises to the LORD, for he has done generously; let this be known in all the
  earth. Shout, and sing for joy, O inhabitants of Zion, for great in your midst is
  the Holy One of Israel.

Isaiah 12:5–6

The Final Thanksgiving

I will greatly rejoice in the LORD, my soul shall exult in my God; for he has
  clothed me with the garments of salvation, he has covered me with the robe of
  righteousness, as a bridegroom decks himself with a garland, and as a bride
  adorns herself with her jewels.

Isaiah 61:10

451

The Petition
May the Lord GOD, father of all mercy, grant us who dwell here a peaceful night and a perfect end. *Amen.*

The Office of the Night Watch   Observed on the Hour or Half-Hour Between 1:30 and 4:30 a.m.

The Call to Prayer
Behold now, bless the LORD, all you servants of the LORD,* you that stand by night in the house of the LORD.
Lift up your hands in the holy place and bless the LORD;* the LORD who made heaven and earth bless you out of Zion.

Psalm 134

The Request for Presence
O God, come to my assistance.
O Lord, make haste to help me.

The Greeting
Remember your word to your servant,* because you have given me hope.
This is my comfort in my trouble,* that your promise gives me life.

Psalm 119:49–50

The Refrain for the Night Watch
Yours is the day, yours also the night;* you established the moon and the sun.

Psalm 74:15

The Psalm   God Has Blessed You For Ever
My heart is stirring with a noble song; let me recite what I have fashioned for the king;* my tongue shall be the pen of a skilled writer.
You are the fairest of men;* grace flows from your lips, because God has blessed you for ever.
Strap your sword upon your thigh, O mighty warrior,* in your pride and in your majesty.
Ride out and conquer in the cause of truth* and for the sake of justice.
Your right hand will show you marvelous things;* your arrows are very sharp,
O mighty warrior.
The peoples are falling at your feet,* and the king's enemies are losing heart.
Your throne, O God, endures for ever and ever,* a scepter of righteousness is the scepter of your kingdom; you love righteousness and hate iniquity.

Psalm 45:1–7

The Refrain
Yours is the day, yours also the night;* you established the moon and the sun.

452

A Reading

I would warmly recommend it to all never to finish prayer without remaining some little time after in a respectful silence. It is also of the greatest importance for the soul to go to prayer with courage, and such a pure and disinterested love as seeks nothing from God but the ability to please Him and to do his will; for a servant who only proportions his diligence to his hope of reward renders himself unworthy of reward. Go then to prayer, not that you may enjoy spiritual delights, but that you may be either full or empty as it pleases God. This will preserve you in an evenness of spirit in desertion as well as in consolation.

Madame Guyon (17th c. French mystic), A Short and Easy Method of Prayer

The Refrain

Yours is the day, yours also the night;* you established the moon and the sun.

The Litany

O God the Father, Creator of heaven and earth,
  Have mercy upon me.
O God the Son, Redeemer of the world,
  Have mercy upon me.
O God the Holy Spirit, Sanctifier of the faithful,
  Have mercy upon me.
O holy, blessed, and glorious Trinity, one God,
  Have mercy upon me.
Remember not, Lord Christ, my offenses, nor the offenses of my forefathers; neither reward me according to my sins. Spare me, good Lord, spare your people, whom you have redeemed with your most precious blood, and by your mercy preserve us, for ever.
  Spare us, good Lord.

The Thanksgiving

Lord, you now have set your servant free to go in peace as you have promised; for these eyes of mine have seen the Savior whom you have prepared for all the world to see: A Light to enlighten the nations, and the glory of your people Israel. *Amen.*

Nunc Dimittis

The Final Petition

Now guide me waking, O Lord, and guard me sleeping; that awake I may watch with Christ, and asleep, I may rest in peace. *Amen.*

The Office of Dawn   **Observed on the Hour or Half-Hour**
                                          Between 4:30 and 7:30 a.m.

The Call to Prayer

Hallelujah! How good it is to sing praises to our God!* How pleasant it is to honor
   him with praise!

Psalm 147:1

The Request for Presence

My soul waits for the LORD, more than watchmen for the morning,* more than
   watchmen for the morning.

Psalm 130:5

The Greeting

Glory be to the Father, and to the Son, and to the Holy Spirit.
As it was in the beginning, it is now
And ever shall be, world without end. *Amen.*

Gloria Patri

The Hymn

O come, O come, Emmanuel,
And ransom captive Israel,
That mourns in lonely exile here
Until the Son of God appear.
Rejoice! Rejoice!
Emmanuel shall come to thee, O Israel.
O come, Thou Root of Jesse's tree,
An ensign of Thy people be;
Before Thee rulers silent fall;
All peoples on Thy mercy call.
Rejoice! Rejoice!
Emmanuel shall come to thee, O Israel.
O come, Desire of nations, bind
In one the hearts of all mankind;
Bid Thou our sad divisions cease,
And be Thyself our King of Peace.
Rejoice! Rejoice!
Emmanuel shall come to thee, O Israel.

12th c. Latin, translated by John M. Neale

The Psalm   *The LORD Loves the Righteous*

Happy are they who have the God of Jacob for their help!* whose hope is in the
   LORD their God;
Who made heaven and earth, the seas, and all that is in them;* who keeps his
   promise for ever;

454

Who gives justice to those who are oppressed,* and food to those who hunger.
The LORD loves the righteous; LORD cares for the stranger;* he sustains the orphan
  and widow, but frustrates the way of the wicked.
The LORD shall reign for ever,* your God, O Zion, throughout all generations.
  Hallelujah!

Psalm 146:4–6; 8–9

The Gloria in Excelsis

Glory to God in the highest, and on earth peace to people of good will.
  We praise you.
  We bless you.
  We adore you.
  We glorify you.
We give thanks to you for your great glory.

The Small Verse

And the angel said to them, "Be not afraid; for behold, I bring you good news of a
  great joy which will come to all the people; for to you is born this day in the
  city of David a Savior who is Christ the Lord. And this will be a sign for you:
  you will find a babe wrapped in swaddling clothes and lying in a manger." And
  suddenly there was with the angel a multitude of the heavenly host praising
  God and saying, "Glory to God in the highest, and on earth peace among men
  with whom he is pleased!"

Luke 2:10–14

The Lord's Prayer

The Final Blessing

May the Lord bless us and keep us and cause His face to shine upon us from this
  day forth and forever more. *Amen.*

Acknowledgments

Excerpts from *Eternal Wisdom from the Desert—Writings from the Desert Fathers,* edited by Henry Carrigan, Jr. ©2001 by Paraclete Press. Used by Permission.

Excerpts from *Incandescence: 365 Readings with Women Mystics,* translated by Carmen Acevedo Butcher. ©2005 by Paraclete Press. Used by Permission.

Excerpts from *Nearer to the Heart of God—Daily Readings with the Christian Mystics,* compiled and edited by Bernard Bangley. ©2005 by Paraclete Press. Used by Permission.

Excerpts from *The Oxford Book of Prayer,* edited by George Appleton. ©2002 by Oxford University Press. Used by Permission.

Excerpts from *Rooted in Faith—Meditations from the Reformers*, compiled and edited by Bernard Bangley. ©2003 by Paraclete Press. Used by Permission.

Excerpts from *The Royal Way of the Cross,* by François Fenelon, edited by Hal M. Helms. ©1995 by Paraclete Press. Used by Permission.

Excerpts from *A Short Breviary,* edited by the monks of St. John's Abbey. ©1949 by St. John's Abbey. Used by permission of the Liturgical Press.

Index